# The Sociology of Culture

# The Sociology of Culture

## Emerging Theoretical Perspectives

*Edited by*
*Diana Crane*

BLACKWELL
*Oxford UK & Cambridge USA*

Copyright © Basil Blackwell Ltd   1994

First published   1994

Blackwell Publishers
238 Main Street
Cambridge, Massachusetts 02142
USA

108 Cowley Road
Oxford   OX4 1JF
UK

*Library of Congress Cataloging-in-Publication Data*
The Sociology of Culture / Diana Crane [editor].
   p.    cm.
   Includes bibliographical references and index.
   ISBN 1-55786-462-4. — ISBN 1-55786-463-2 (pbk)
   1. Culture.   I. Crane, Diana, 1933-   .
HM101. S6939   1994
306—dc20                                 93-34717
                                              CIP

*British Library Cataloguing in Publication Data*
A CIP catalogue record for this book is available from the British Library.

Typeset in 10½ on 12½pt Palatino
by Graphicraft Typesetters Ltd., Hong Kong
Printed and Bound in Great Britain by
T. J. Press (Padstow) Ltd, Padstow, Cornwall
This book is printed on acid-free paper

# Contents

# List of figures

# Contributors

**Mabel Berezin** is Assistant Professor of Sociology at the University of Pennsylvania. She is completing a book entitled *Communities of Feeling: spectacle and politics in fascist Italy*.

**Anne Bowler** is Assistant Professor of Sociology at the University of Delaware. She has completed a dissertation entitled "Art and politics in the historical avant-garde: Italian futurism and Russian constructivism."

**David Brain** is Associate Professor of Sociology at New College at the University of South Florida. He has published a number of articles on cultural theory.

**Diana Crane** is Professor of Sociology at the University of Pennsylvania. She has served as Chair of the Sociology of Culture Section of the American Sociological Association. Her recent books are *The Transformation of the Avant-Garde: the New York art world, 1940–1985* (1987) and *The Production of Culture: media and the urban arts* (1992).

**Steve Derné** is Assistant Professor of Sociology at SUNY Genesco. He is preparing a book based on his research in India entitled *Culture in Action: ethnopsychology, family and gender in India*.

**Frank Dobbin** is Assistant Professor of Sociology at Princeton University. He has recently completed a book entitled *Forging Industrial Policy: France, Britain, and the United States in the railway age.* (1994).

**Ewa Morawska** is Professor of Sociology at the University of Pennsylvania. She is the author of *For Bread with Butter: the life* *worlds of East Central Europeans in Johnstown, Pennsylvania, 1890–1940* (1985) and the forthcoming *Insecure Prosperity: small-town Jews in industrial America, 1880–1940* (1994).

**Chandra Mukerji** is Professor of Communication at the University of California, San Diego. She is the author of *From Graven Images* (1983) and *A Fragile Power: scientists and the state* (1989).

**Richard Peterson** is Professor of Sociology at Vanderbilt University. A founder and former Chair of the Sociology of Culture Section of the American Sociological Association, he is the author of numerous articles on the production of culture, cultural policy, and popular music and editor of *The Production of Culture* (1976).

**Andrea Press** is Assistant Professor of Sociology at the University of Michigan. She is the author of *Women Watching Television: gender, class, and generation in the American television experience* (1991) and (with Liz Cole) *Imagining Our Lives: television, women's talk and the political culture of abortion* (forthcoming).

**Michael Schudson** is Professor of Communication at the University of California, San Diego. He is the author of several books, including *Advertising: the uneasy persuasion* (1984) and *Watergate in American Memory: how we remember, forget and reconstruct the past* (1992).

**Willfried Spohn** is Adjunct Professor of Sociology at the Free University of Berlin. He is completing a manuscript entitled "Religion and Working-Class Formation in Germany, 1840–1914".

# Preface

This volume is the first in a series of occasional volumes to be published by Blackwell Publishers on behalf of the Sociology of Culture Section of the American Sociological Association. During my term as Chair of the Section (1991–2), I was struck by the diversity of interests of members and the fragmentation of the field. The Section resembles a cluster of enclaves rather than a scientific community.

It seemed to me that we would all benefit from greater awareness of one another's theoretical perspectives and research. One way to accomplish this goal was to make it possible for Section Chairs to edit volumes reflecting their interests and their perspectives on the field. The first volume attempts to provide an overview of currently active areas of research. The chapters are not, however, intended to survey specific topics (although some of them do this as well) but to compare and contrast particular theoretical perspectives.

This volume does not attempt to provide a comprehensive overview of the sociology of culture. A number of areas have not been included, such as investigations of ethnic and minority cultures, religion, multiculturalism, and global culture. Future volumes in the series will presumably fill in these gaps.

For their assistance as "gatekeepers," I am very grateful to Craig Calhoun, Jeffrey Goldfarb, Magali Larson, Elizabeth Long, Michael Useem, and Vera Zolberg, as well as to the authors themselves as we struggled to find appropriate "frames" for these materials. My early thinking about this volume was aided by the comments of members of the Sociology of Culture's Publications Committee for 1991–2 (ably chaired by Sharon Zukin). I would also like to express my appreciation to Simon Prosser at Blackwell for his interest in and encouragement of this endeavor. Finally, I thank the University of Pennsylvania for providing funds for editorial assistance and Adrienne Hervé for completing the arduous task of typing the list of references.

Diana Crane
Paris, July, 1993

# 1

# Introduction: The Challenge of the Sociology of Culture to Sociology as a Discipline

## Diana Crane

Since the early 1970s, the sociology of culture has been virtually "reinvented" but, in the early nineties, the extent of its transformation is just beginning to be recognized by the rest of the discipline. The "new" sociology of culture is not a field *per se*; rather it consists of a number of distinct and independent subfields such as science, knowledge, religion, media, popular culture, and the arts as well as culturally oriented approaches to, for example, history, politics, organizations, stratification, and interpersonal behavior. Until very recently, these fields and approaches have been perceived as marginal rather than central to the concerns of the discipline of sociology as a whole (Wuthnow 1987: 27).

One reason culture has been perceived as peripheral to the concerns of American sociology is because of the way it has been positioned in the classical theories that have had the most impact on American sociology. Although Weber's historical studies of the impact of religious values on social and economic institutions were very influential in American sociology, their primary effect on the sociology of culture was to privilege the sociology of religion. For Durkheimians, as for Weberians, religion was a central component of culture, although, as Alexander (1988c) has pointed out, Durkheim's work on social structure was, until recently, more influential in American sociology than his work on culture. The sociology of religion was an active and prolific field, long before the emergence of fields dealing with other forms of culture.

While contemporary European versions of Marxism view control over the dissemination of culture as a form of power (the social structure is maintained by ideas as well as by force), American functionalism and Marxism have emphasized structural influences on cultural beliefs; American conflict theory has also tended to prioritize social structure. Only the symbolic interactionists assign cultural meanings a significant role in influencing human behavior, but ironically they have generally confined their attention to those "who occupy powerless positions in contemporary society" (Denzin 1992: 20) and have had little impact on those professing a "structuralist" or "macro" orientation.

Robertson (1988), a British sociologist, has described American sociology as a "culture-resistant discipline." Coleman's (1990) summation of contemporary sociological theory, *Foundations of Social Theory*, contains few references to any aspects of culture.[1] Rational choice theory, of which he is one of the leading proponents, exemplifies an impoverished view of culture (Münch 1992: 155–7). To American and some British structuralists, culture as a concept lacks a suitably rigorous definition. According to Archer (1988: 1), "the notion of culture remains inordinately vague ... In every way, 'culture' is the poor relation of 'structure' " (see also Wuthnow 1987: 5–6).

While the new "sociologies of culture" have been refining and defining the concept of culture in a myriad of contexts, much of mainstream sociology continues to view culture from the perspective of classical sociological theory and classical social anthropology. This position is exemplified in an introduction by Neil Smelser (1992) to a book entitled *Theory of Culture*. In order to assess the status of culture as a sociological concept, Smelser examines "selective formulations of culture during the past one hundred years," primarily from classical theory and anthropology.[2] The emphasis in these theories is upon culture conceived as the values, norms, beliefs and attitudes of the entire population or of subgroups within the population (subcultures, countercultures, civic cultures, etc.). Wuthnow and Witten (1988: 50–1) refer to this aspect of culture as "an implicit feature of social life ... constituting the underlying assumptions and expectations on which social interaction depends."

However, in contemporary societies, this emphasis on implicit culture is incomplete. Culture today is expressed and negotiated almost entirely through culture as explicit social constructions or products, in other words, through *recorded culture*, culture that is recorded in either print, film, artifacts or, most recently, electronic media. The new sociologies of culture deal largely with various types of recorded culture such as information, entertainment, science, technology, law, education and art.[3] Without analyzing the content and effects of recorded cultures as well as the factors that affect the content of recorded cultures, we cannot understand the role of culture in modern society.

Recorded culture is virtually absent from Smelser's discussion of culture and from other mainstream perspectives on culture. For example, Swidler's (1986) much-cited theory that views culture as a "tool-kit" defines culture as "symbolic vehicles of meaning, including beliefs, ritual practices, art forms and ceremonies" but, with the exception of art forms, the locus of these "symbolic vehicles" remains unspecified. Alexander (1990), in his review of theories of culture, discusses classical and contemporary theories but makes no mention of theories drawn from contemporary studies of recorded cultures. It appears that mainstream sociology tends to overlook the new sociologies of culture because of the low priority it accords to the study of recorded cultures. In spite of the fact that the enormous increase in the quantity and impact of recorded culture in this century is drastically changing the nature of modern societies, recorded cultures are not accorded major roles in mainstream sociological theories.

In most sociological theories, outside the sociology of culture, recorded cultures tend to be treated as exogenous variables. For example, science and technology just appear and, as a result, something else happens. Where science and technology come from, how they are socially constructed and by whom, is treated as irrelevant by the rest of the discipline (Cozzens 1993).

Defining culture as unrecorded rather than as unrecorded and recorded culture affects the types of hypotheses and theories that appear to be relevant. Smelser (1992: 10) discusses a single theoretical issue, the level of coherence and consistency in a nation's culture. In his view, this issue covers "a significant range of recent theorizing about culture." If culture consists of attitudes, values, and beliefs that are shared by all or most members of the population, questions of cultural integration and cultural consensus become major issues. However, as Smelser himself observes, these questions may be becoming less meaningful for large modern societies that are increasingly multicultural and that are notable for their lack of cultural coherence or "loose-boundedness" (Merelman 1984).[4]

Finally, this perspective in which culture is defined primarily as "a global unitary characteristic of the society or the group" (Smelser 1992: 22) leads Smelser to be highly critical of the concept and pessimistic concerning its future usefulness. For example, he claims that the concept of culture is vague because it can be interpreted in many different ways, and inclusive because it has been applied to such a wide range of phenomena. As a result, he concludes that it is difficult to explain culture or to use it as an explanatory variable (Smelser 1992: 21).

To summarize, classical sociological and anthropological theory emphasized a conception of culture as consistent and coherent that was more an ideal or an ideology than a reality. As such it reflected the modernist *zeitgeist* of the first half of the twentieth century. It is significant that mainstream sociological theory has not yet come to terms with the new postmodernist *zeitgeist* which emphasizes those aspects of culture that are inherently contradictory, inconsistent and incoherent.[5]

Ironically, contemporary anthropological theorists have subtly reformulated the notion of culture to include all social practices, not just norms, values, and beliefs – a view that is similar to conceptions of culture that have emerged from the study of science, technology and knowledge systems in general, as well as from some historical studies (see Morawska and Spohn chapter 3, this volume). From this point of view, culture is "embedded" in social structure, in the sense that all social structures convey cultural meanings, rather than being somehow a distinct and separate phenomenon (for a recent statement of this point of view, see Sewell 1992).

Perhaps because it is in itself a coherent, consistent, unitary theory, the classical sociological perspective on culture remains influential in the discipline in spite of its lack of empirical support or contemporary relevance while the impact of the new sociologies of culture has been more limited, precisely because they do not provide a unitary, global perspective.

## Sociology of Culture and the *Zeitgeist*

Nevertheless, the sociology of culture steadily expanded during the 1970s and 1980s, due to a change in worldview in which developments in several countries coalesced into a powerful movement favoring this type of research. New perspectives in the sociology of culture have been strongly influenced by other disciplines, such as anthropology (particularly the work of Clifford Geertz), history, political science, literary studies, cultural studies, feminist studies and ethnic studies and by perspectives from European sociological theory, such as poststructuralist theories in France, the British Cultural Studies group, and Science Studies in Britain.

For example, French theories, such as semiotics and poststructuralism, have inspired a greater interest in explicit or recorded culture. These theories are concerned with the ways in which texts can shape human behavior and can be used as a source of power by elites. Foucault (1972, 1977) is an obvious example. Bourdieu (1977, 1984) is another: he argues that knowledge of recorded culture is an important criterion for maintaining social status and social inequalities. Similar themes have been used in studies of science and technology. From these perspectives, science, technology, and knowledge generally cease to be viewed unproblematically as truth and become social constructions of particular social groups as well as instruments of power for those groups.

These theoretical perspectives have forced a reconsideration in sociological theory of what constitutes culture, the social impact of culture, and the necessity for new approaches to the study of culture. At the same time, earlier developments within American sociology, such as symbolic interactionism, ethnomethodology, Goffman's (1974) frame analysis, and the seminal work of Berger and Luckmann (1966) on the social construction of reality provided an intellectual environment in which these new influences could take root.

Finally, the change in worldview of which postmodernism is a symptom has increased the salience of cultural issues throughout the discipline. Specifically, the emphasis on predictability, coherence, and consistency which underlies the sociological method in most fields is being undermined by a new perspective which views culture as unpredictable, incoherent, and inconsistent.

This perspective is often identified with postmodernism but is actually broader than that particular movement.[6] However, postmodernism, in particular, challenges mainstream sociological theory because it gives more weight to culture than to social structure (Kellner 1990a: 269). As opposed to mainstream sociology's emphasis upon implicit or unrecorded culture, postmodernists stress the importance of what is defined here as recorded cultures, particularly the electronic media. At the same time, they view the overall impact of all forms of culture as fragmented and incoherent. Consequently, culture as depicted by this new paradigm is not easily assimilated into linear, cause–effect models of social science research,[7] while the emphasis on recorded cultures poses new problems in terms of interpretation and "meaning."

This change in worldview has forced a reconsideration of a perennial issue in sociological thought: how to conceptualize the relationship between structure and culture. Indicative of changes that are taking place in sociological theory is Sewell's (1992: 27) path-breaking essay in which he redefined the concept of structure to include the notion of "cultural schemas" that enable agents to mobilize "sets of resources that empower and constrain social action." His definition of structure differs from previous definitions because, as he says, he views structure as "a profoundly cultural phenomenon" (p. 27). However, the nature of the cultural schemas that underlie social structure remains vague in his discussion.

The effects of these changes can be seen in this volume in new interpretations of cultural integration (Schudson chapter 2), hegemony and political culture (Berezin chapter 4), organizational behavior (Dobbin chapter 5), and interpersonal behavior (Derné chapter 11), and in new approaches to problems of interpretation and meaning (Brain chapter 8, and Bowler chapter 10). It can also be seen in the emergence of new areas such as the sociology of reception (Press chapter 9), and new approaches to older fields, such as historical sociology (Morawska and Spohn chapter 3), and the sociology of science (Mukerji chapter 6).

## Culture and Social Structure: New Perspectives on Cultural Integration and Hegemony

Two major sites for the development of new conceptions of culture and social structure have been historical sociology and political culture. The two fields overlap because both have been concerned with political issues and with the formation and dissolution of nation states. Morawska and Spohn (chapter 3, this volume) find a wide range of coexisting positions in historical sociology on the question of the relation between structure and culture. While structure was undoubtedly preeminent in that field until the early 1980s, in the 1990s some historical sociologists see culture as more important than structure, while others attempt to give the two dimensions equal weight.

Those who perceive culture as being of equal or greater importance than structure define culture itself differently. Morawska and Spohn contrast two perceptions of culture among historical sociologists: culture as fixed and ordered or as indeterminate, flexible and contestable. As they show, both positions have been present in the sociological literature for decades but the latter is clearly winning more adherents among younger historical sociologists of the 1990s than was the case in the 1970s.

Culturally oriented historical sociologists are primarily interested in cultural change, in other words, how culture in conjunction with or independently from social structures has brought about changes in nation states, in relationships between or within social classes or ethnic groups, or in the conduct of everyday life. Again this orientation contrasts with earlier approaches to culture, which were concerned with identifying cultural values associated with different types of social structures or with engaging in so-called "thick description" à la Clifford Geertz, whose approach is beginning to be perceived as overly static and insufficiently sensitive to social and cultural dissensus and conflict (see Chartier 1989, cited by Morawska and Spohn, chapter 3, this volume).

A major theme in both historical sociology and the study of political culture is that of a dominant class imposing a coherent worldview on the population, either in the form of an ideology or as hegemony, when a worldview permeates all facets of everyday life to such an extent that it is accepted unquestioningly as common sense. While older approaches tended to stress the powerlessness of the dominated in the face of these types of cultural control, newer approaches examine the strategies of the dominated toward those who are attempting to impose ideological and hegemonic controls. For example, Morawska's studies (1985; 1994) of Slavic and Jewish immigrants in a small town in Western Pennsylvania trace their resistance to WASP hegemony. The Comaroffs' (1991) study examines the responses of a South African tribe to British colonialism.

In his review of recent literature on cultural integration, Michael Schudson (chapter 2, this volume) concludes that the notion of cultural integration in nation-states is problematic. Nation-states are increasingly fragile as a result of the pressures of subcultures and ethnic groups. Viewing culture as one among several types of integration at the macro level, he attempts to identify the "concrete mechanisms for its objectification, transmission, and distribution," such as language, education, the press, broadcasting, and even consumer goods. He argues that culture has both integrative and disintegrative effects: the notion of a dominant culture with predictable effects is becoming increasingly difficult to sustain as cultures both fractionate and globalize.

Other authors have depicted the dominant culture in a similar way. Kellner (1990b) has argued that "dominant ideological formations and discourses" should be seen as a site of struggle and conflict among different social groups. He sees hegemony as "a shifting, complex, and open phenomenon, always subject to contestation and upheaval." Studies by members of the British Cultural Studies group show that while the media generally present the views of the dominant class, they are not always successful in imposing hegemony. "Resistant subcultures" respond to the media and popular culture in unexpected ways. Finally, Wagner-Pacifici and Schwartz (1991) in their study of the Vietnam Veterans Memorial in Washington, DC show that while the purpose of the Memorial was to provide some sort of closure to the conflict that had surrounded the interpretation of the war and its aftermath, the public interpreted the Memorial in many different ways. The Memorial did not lead to consensus about the war but to the enactment of many different types of personal rituals; these rituals are intensely personal and do not create a sense of community in the Durkheimian sense.

The relationship between culture and social stratification has attracted considerable attention due in large part to the work of French theorist, Pierre Bourdieu (1984). Bourdieu assigns a major role to culture, especially recorded culture, in maintaining social inequality. Based on their social origins, individuals acquire capacities for interpreting and using cultural codes that affect their opportunities to maintain or change their social positions. This theory has produced a number of recent American studies that attempt to test, refine, and reformulate it (see Lamont and Fournier

1992; Peterson chapter 7, this volume; Press chapter 9, this volume).

## The Social Constructionist Approach

Perhaps the most profound change that the sociology of culture has brought about in the outlook of American sociologists is the idea that what they are studying is not necessarily an objective empirical reality but is instead a social construction. Social constructionism has revolutionized the study of the media, popular culture and science, spawned a new field of research, reception theory, and produced a new interpretation of the fundamental principles of organizational behavior.

The social constructionist approach argues that much of what we take for granted as objectively real or necessary in social life is actually "constructed" through social relationships and social behavior. This idea has been familiar to American sociologists since the publication of Berger and Luckmann's (1966) *Social Construction of Reality* but, in spite of the fact that the book was widely discussed, many American sociologists continued (and still continue) to accept the notion that "there is an empirical world out there that must be respected" (Denzin 1992: 120) in which definitive meanings could be established.[8]

Since the early 1970s developments both in the United States and Europe have provided the impetus for research based on a social constructionist perspective. In each field, the factors that initiated this type of research varied but they generally included some sort of cross-fertilization between American and European perspectives.

While Berger and Luckmann were primarily concerned with the social construction of implicit culture (social behavior), European theorists emphasized the social construction of explicit culture such as the media, knowledge, and science, as well as the ways in which these forms of recorded culture constructed social roles, such as class, gender and race.

By contrast, postwar studies of mass communication in the United States viewed media content as unidimensional and unambiguous. Individuals might use this content in different ways but this did not imply that meaning was negotiated or that it positioned different segments of the audience in different ways.[9] Later studies developed a conception of media content that was much more complex. For example, in the late 1970s, Tuchman (1978), influenced in part by Goffman (1974) showed how news was socially constructed by identifying frames that influenced how reporters perceived and collected information.

Building on studies by the British Cultural Studies group and theoretical perspectives from poststructuralists such as Lyotard and Baudrillard, more recent American studies of mass communication emphasize "struggles over meaning" in media discourses (Gamson et al. 1992: 382) and the ways in which various media discourses differ over the same or similar issues. For example, Gamson and Modigliani (1989) discuss the changes in media discourse concerning nuclear power in the postwar period.

New approaches to the audience's perceptions of the media that comprise the field of reception theory (see Press chapter 9, this volume) draw on theories from literary studies as well as work in the British Cultural Studies tradition. Central to this perspective is the notion that the meanings of texts are unstable and contestable (Fiske 1989). Texts may be interpreted and used in ways that are entirely opposed to the intentions of their creators or producers (see Press chapter 9, this volume). These studies raise questions concerning the nature of media and literary texts that make possible multiple readings by the audience and the ways in which class, ethnic, and gender groups within an audience accept or resist hegemonic messages.

As Mukerji (chapter 6, this volume) shows, the study of science changed course dramatically during the 1970s and early 1980s as a result of the impact of works by British sociologists that argued that science was no different from other types of knowledge, such as religion, philosophy, and so-called pseudo-science. These sociologists were influenced by scholars on both sides of the Atlantic: Thomas S. Kuhn (1970), an American historian of science, who developed the seminal notion of a paradigm to explain the social construction of scientific fields; Garfinkel's work on conversational analysis and ethnomethodology more generally; and poststructuralist versions of French semiotics.

Also in the late 1970s, some organizational theorists began to apply a social constructionist approach (influenced by Berger and Luckmann) to the analysis of rational principles of management in educational and later in economic organizations (see Dobbin, chapter 5, this volume). This research has shown that regulations and practices which had been considered the most efficient, rational, even scientific responses to market and other environmental pressures actually varied by type of setting and by time period, indicating the role of cultural factors in their adoption and evolution. In a sense, because it is "embedded" in social structure, the influence of culture is often "invisible" in realms of social life that are not depicted by the modern worldview as part of culture.

### Understanding Social Interaction: The Social Construction of Individual Behavior

During the 1970s and 1980s, sociologists began to reformulate models of individual behavior. The "classical" model of individual behavior viewed the individual as a passive recipient of cultural influences that defined their goals. A major reformulation of the "classical" model of individual behavior appeared in Swidler's (1986) model of culture as a "tool-kit." Swidler argued that culture offers the individual a wide range of choices. Instead of defining goals, culture provides tool-kits in the form of "symbols, stories, rituals, and world views" that people use to solve problems and to organize their activities over time. People are not passive "cultural dopes"; they are active, often skilled users of culture. Although people may share the same values, their behavior may be very different because their capacities to translate particular values into action vary. Not only do individuals use the same cultural components differently in formulating what Swidler calls "strategies of action," but culture itself is not a unified system that pushes action in a consistent direction. All real cultures contain diverse, often conflicting elements, a view of culture that is consistent with the postmodernist worldview discussed above.

In reformulating models of the relationship between culture and action, Swidler was influenced in part by French theorist, Pierre Bourdieu (1977)[10] and by anthropologists, such as Clifford Geertz, although her interpretation is less deterministic than theirs. Her view of culture was also consistent with those being developed at the same time by British and American theorists of the media concerning the "contested" and polysemic nature of media culture

and the audience's capacities to resist and redefine its messages
(see above).

Derné (chapter 11, this volume) develops a problematic aspect of
this perspective on culture: the ways in which culture constrains
rather than stimulates behavior. Drawing on social constructionist
and ethnomethodological theories from sociology as well as anthropological theory (Geertz 1973; Douglas 1982), Derné attempts to
reconcile "the idea of cultural constraint with the recognition that
individuals often contest cultural norms." Rather than asking how
reality is socially constructed, Derné looks at how socially constructed understandings of social behavior influence actual behavior.
He argues that individuals are motivated to conform when they
experience the social consequences of behavior that does not correspond to commonsense cultural understandings of social behavior,
but that the range of actual behavior is much broader than that
which is culturally indicated.

As we have seen, since the early 1970s sociological theories that
view human beings as passively submitting to cultural norms have
ceased to be compelling. Buchmann's (1989) research delineates
structural changes that have tended to increase the variability in
individuals' educational and occupational careers which may in
turn be associated with greater variability in conformity to cultural
norms. She argues that careers (broadly defined to include relationships between education, work and marriage) have become
much more diverse and much more irregular and this in turn has
affected cultural representations of life stages and appropriate
social behavior. In other words, as transitions from the educational
system to employment and marriage become more varied and less
predictable, leading to what she calls "the destandardization of
the life course," cultural imagery describing these trajectories has
also changed in the direction of increased flexibility. Like Swidler
and Derné, she argues that culture provides a general structure of
meaning which individuals use to figure out how to solve the
problems they face.

Because there is no longer a set of standard life patterns in which
individuals follow predictable paths from education to work and
marriage, individuals in the same demographic cohort experience
a wide diversity of life course patterns which tends to enhance
their belief that they are able to direct their own lives. It also

stimulates their concern with constructing multidimensional identities in which different elements are salient in different situations. Hence it is not surprising that the range of acceptable behaviors has greatly increased.

In view of recent work in the sociology of culture, it is all the more ironic that structurally oriented sociologists are turning to rational choice models of social behavior (Hechter 1989) that interpret behavior in terms of rewards and costs and do not adequately conceptualize possibilities for variations in behavior or for cultural contestation. These models ignore the lact that conceptions of rationality are influenced by cultural variables (see, for example, Dobbin chapter 5, this volume). As Münch (1992: 157) points out, rational choice theory is unable to reconstruct "cultural meaning-relationships" because its view of culture as "a variable in a deductive nomological explanation" is inadequate.

## "Creating Culture": Perspectives on the Production of Culture

One of the most active fields in the sociology of culture is the production of culture perspective which examines the relationship between the conditions surrounding the production of cultural symbols and the characteristics of the cultural symbols themselves. As Peterson's (chapter 7, this volume) comprehensive review indicates, the approach can be so broadly defined as to include studies dealing with many different aspects of culture. In fact, however, the term has generally been applied to studies of the arts, media and popular culture which have documented the effects of reward systems, market structures, and gatekeeping systems on the careers and activities of culture creators. Peterson shows how studies in other areas of culture, such as science and religion, can be interpreted within the same perspective and how these studies can broaden our understanding of this perspective.

As discussed by Tuchman (1988) and others, this perspective has been criticized on the grounds that it has tended to ignore questions of political economy and hegemonic control (but see, for example, Gitlin (1983) and, more recently, Turow (1992)) and to bypass the analysis of meaning. The reasons for this lie in the fact that, while the production of culture perspective applies to "personal interaction, relationships among organizations, and the workings of entire societies" (see Peterson chapter 7, this volume), most studies have dealt either with relationships among organizations or with effects of organizational structures and decisions on the activities of culture creators. As such, these studies provide an enormous archive of empirical information about how cultural institutions operate, but the use of the media or the arts to serve state, corporate, or elite goals has not been a central concern of this approach.[11]

The production of culture perspective has also been criticized for neglecting "meaning," in part because its practitioners do not study meaning using literary methods (which, as Peterson points out, risks "focusing on critical concerns and taking the 'sociology' out"). Instead, meaning may be examined using quantitative analyses, content analyses, or in terms of categories rather than critical interpretation. In other words, studies in the production of culture are likely to ask under what conditions one category of culture (such as avant-garde versus formulaic) will be produced rather than another, or who the creators are, what shapes their outlooks, and how much autonomy they have. While postmodernist ambiguity is rarely a theme of these studies, they do document the changing conditions under which culture is being created and which presumably contribute to the types of conditions that postmodernists describe.

Brain's (chapter 8, this volume) analysis of architecture presents a very different type of "production of culture" model, one which is designed to elucidate the implications of the social construction of cultural artifacts. Building on theories from Bourdieu and Foucault and from the sociology of technology, Brain argues that cultural "artifacts" ranging from art to technology embody "social relations, institutional practices, strategies of action, and possibilities for transformation." The cultural artifact is seen as a particular kind of cultural exemplar that requires and sustains certain types of social relationships and activities, in keeping with a growing tendency to view culture and social structure as intertwined rather than as separate entities. From this perspective, the cultural artifact is not the consequence of social-institutional arrangements but an integral part of these arrangements.

## Problems of Method and Meaning in the
## Sociology of Culture

As Berezin (chapter 4, this volume) points out, the sociology of
culture is a "fissured terrain," characterized by "epistemological
dissidence" between explanatory methods where the goal is to
explain social processes and interpretive methods where the objective is to interpret a wide range of materials in order to identify
what might be described as an underlying "gestalt."

Attitudes emerging in the field toward the question of explanation are increasingly likely to bring sociologists of culture into
opposition with scholars outside the field, particularly those who
are strongly committed to quantitative methodologies and who are
unfamiliar with historical research methods or skeptical of the value
of ethnography.[12]

Potentially disturbing to the methodological purist outside the
field is the way in which some recent work in the field questions
linear, cause–effect models. Brain in this volume (chapter 8) states
"The reflection of social structure in culture is not a correlation
between independent and dependent variables." Newer models of
cultural change either give more weight to culture as an explanatory variable or are non-deterministic. For example, Greenfeld (1992:
19–20) advocates a type of model where "the arrow of causality
may point both ways." In her model of nationalism, cultural conceptions of national identity are more important than social
structure.

When culture is perceived as being of equal or greater importance than social structure, as is the case for an important subset of
historical sociologists, then conventional notions of causality are
not applicable. As Morawska and Spohn (chapter 3, this volume)
show, the goal of sociological research ceases to be "a coherent
system of causal statements." Culture is perceived as "open-ended";
the number of possible outcomes is such that the future cannot be
predicted. These new sociological views of culture are consistent
with a postmodern worldview in spite of the fact that there is less
emphasis on incoherence and much less attention to the analysis of
texts *per se* than one finds in the works of leading postmodernists.

Brain argues that neither interpretation nor explanation are
satisfactory approaches on the grounds that the former leads to

reification of the cultural object and the latter to reductionism in which cultural artifacts are seen as the result of social conditions. He proposes an approach that recognizes the "duality of cultural production" in which "cultural or technical artifacts . . . stabilize the field of operations in which they are produced, the practices that produce them, and the social relations implied in both their production and use." In this approach, because the cultural object itself is conceptualized as a powerful embodiment of cultural meanings and practices, it is perceived as an influence on organizational and structural relationships rather than as merely the outcome of such relationships.

A related set of debates that are occurring in the field concern the question of "meaning" and how it should be approached both theoretically and methodologically. Some sociologists of culture bypass this issue by concentrating their attention on organizational and institutional influences on culture. Wuthnow (1987) argued that meaning is not an appropriate problem for sociological analysis, on the grounds that "meaning" is entirely subjective and therefore not susceptible to empirical analysis. Alternatively, Bowler (chapter 10, this volume) argues that meaning is intersubjective and, at least in the arts, requires analysis of meaning using methods that may not conform to traditional scientific standards. The field of reception theory is, of course, predicated on the notion that it is possible to assess people's subjective interpretations of meaning, but researchers in that field are also questioning the adequacy of ethnographic methods to capture "postmodernist notions of 'subjectivity' as fluid, destabilizing and shifting rather than the unified, coherent self which the ethnographic method was developed to investigate" (see Press chapter 9, this volume).

Finally, Denzin (1990) in his comment on Griswold's (1987a) study of critical reception in three countries to the work of a writer in the West Indies highlights one of the deepest "fissures" in both the sociology of culture and in the discipline as a whole: between those who believe that meaning is fixed and determinate and thereby subject to empirical analysis and those who believe that it is always indeterminate. He says (1990: 1,579): "[Meaning] is not an effect, a result, a product, or a static quality, or something that can be coded out of a review, or extracted from a passage in a novel . . . It cannot be translated, or moved, from one context to another." Griswold (1990: 1,582) responds with a call for "provincial positivism" in which, using "provincial, local terms," "predictions may be made, theories developed, regular relationships posited and tested that are likewise provincial."

As their conceptions of culture and of the meanings it embodies move farther away from the characteristics of variables as they were traditionally defined in sociological research, sociologists of culture will continue to wrestle with the question of how to conduct research and whether and how to redefine the criteria for what constitutes research.

## Conclusion

As we have seen, new perspectives in the sociology of culture cross-cut substantive issues. The same substantive area such as political culture or the sociology of science may be approached with different theoretical perspectives and methods. Throughout the field, sociologists of culture are reinterpreting perennial issues in sociological thought: (1) how to define and conceptualize culture in all its contemporary ramifications; (2) how to conceptualize the relationship between structure and culture; (3) how to conduct systematic studies of culture in its social contexts now that traditional notions of cause and effect no longer seem relevant.

As we have seen, many sociologists of culture view their subject matter as inconsistent, contradictory, complex, and unstable. Culture and social structure are seen as being tightly interconnected; "reflection" models are completely out of favor but there is an absence of consensus about how culture affects social structure and vice versa. Interpretive approaches coexist with explanatory approaches along with some voices that argue that neither are adequate for research on culture.

Finally, to a considerable extent, the sociology of culture has been concerned with demystifying and even debunking established cultures, such as, for example, science and so-called high culture, while at the same time it has often been able to show the unanticipated influences of minority cultures (ethnic, race, feminist) and their symbiotic relationships to established cultures. The "news" from the research frontier of the sociology of culture is more likely to challenge than to uphold established conceptions of American culture.

Because the sociology of culture has in some ways been an enclave (or more accurately a set of enclaves) in the discipline, it has fostered interpretations of culture and its relationship to social structure that are at odds with those in the rest of the discipline. Since the boundaries of the sociology of culture have proven to be exceptionally permeable and, as a result, the field has incorporated and assimilated theoretical perspectives from other countries and from other fields in the social sciences and the humanities, it is to be hoped that the sociology of culture will eventually serve as a channel for the revitalization of the rest of the discipline.

### Notes

I am grateful to Harold Bershady, Mabel Berezin, Frank Dobbin, Michèle Lamont, and Elizabeth Long for comments and suggestions.

1  See Brint (1992) for a discussion of the absence of culture in the work of another mainstream sociologist, Harrison White.

2  Almost two-thirds of the references cited in Smelser's chapter were published before 1970.

3  For recent reviews of research in some of these fields, see the following: Blau (1988); Tuchman (1988); Mukerji and Schudson (1991); Gamson et al. (1992); and Woolwine (1992).

4  Alexander and Smith (1993) revisit some of these issues. Although they redefine culture in terms of semiotic theory as sets of binary codes, they restrict the concept to "systems of symbolic codes which specify the good and the evil" (p. 196). In an analysis of the operations of these codes in American politics, they conclude that they are "internalized," provide a strong moral imperative, and endure over long periods of time.

5  That the necessity of doing so is beginning to be recognized is indicated by the publication of Seidman and Wagner (1993).

6  Feminist theory has also contributed to this change in worldview (see Collins, Patricia C. 1992) as well as chaos theory, although the impact of the latter in sociology has to date been minimal (see, for example, Hayles 1991).

7  For a recent statement concerning the centrality of causal models in mainstream sociology, see Lieberson (1992).

8  Denzin (1992) argues that symbolic interactionists who define their object of study as the negotiation of meanings in social interaction remain "outside the postmodern space" because of their commitment to a positivist view of scientific research.

9  For a review of the entire field of mass communication research that compares American and European perspectives, see Tuchman (1988).

10  Bourdieu's conception of the extent to which social behavior is determined

by structural variables varies from one book to another (see Sewell 1992; and in this volume, Brain chapter 8, and Morawska and Spohn chapter 3).

11  DiMaggio's (1982, 1992) work on cultural elites and the institutionalization of high culture combines a production of culture approach with a theoretical perspective based on the work of Bourdieu.

12  See Long (1993) for a discussion of resistance to and lack of comprehension of the sociology of culture perspective among her colleagues in other social sciences.

# 2

## Culture and the Integration of National Societies

### Michael Schudson

"The primary good that we distribute to one another is membership in some human community." So writes political theorist Michael Walzer (1981: 1). Edward Shils (1975: 7) writes that "membership in a political society is a necessity of man's nature." But which human community? Which political society? Today, when we hear more and more of transnational institutions, of border cultures, of the disintegration of states – the former Soviet Union, the former Yugoslavia, the former Czechoslovakia – of subcultures and subnationalisms, of multiculturalism and the creolization of the world, the complexity of the question is apparent. The difficulty of identifying the boundaries of a society should raise doubts about the customary practice in the social sciences of taking the nation-state as the basic unit of analysis. John Agnew (1989: 19) has criticized Marx, Durkheim, and Weber alike as "methodological nationalists," all of them accepting "state boundaries as coextensive with those of the 'societies' or 'economies' they were interested in studying."

The error of classical social theory, however, was not using the nation-state as the unit of analysis but failing to treat it as a problematic social and historical construction.[1] There is no mistake in recognizing the nation-state as the dominant human societal type in the world over the past 200 years. So the question I pose – what is the role of culture in establishing social membership? – is directed with special reference to the nation-state.

Human societies persist over time, held together by several mechanisms of integration. Territorial integration holds people together by their contiguity in space and by a shared attachment to place. Kinship is another chief means of integration. The incest taboo has sometimes been explained as an integrative mechanism:

by forcing sexual passions to seek satisfaction outside the family, people make sexual, marital, economic, political, and emotional links to other groups and so reduce the potential for conflict and warfare. In economic integration, people are bound together through exchange and markets.

In political integration, people who may be separated territorially or culturally are brought together under a central government. When a regime unifies people not only through a system of justice, an administrative apparatus for taxation, and a common center of political allegiance but also through recruitment of citizen armies, political integration may be especially powerful. Sharing a war experience may generate cultural memories and social institutions, like veterans' organizations, that are powerful integrative forces even during peacetime (Finer 1975; Mosse 1990). When a polity is organized along republican lines, accepting popular sovereignty at least in theory and establishing representative institutions, membership in the society is organized as citizenship. Citizenship raises expectations about and identification with the nation-state that contribute strongly to integration.

Finally, language, symbols, rituals, and stories – culture, in a word – bring individuals and families of varying circumstances and backgrounds together in a collectivity that people may strongly identify with, take primary meanings from, and find emotionally satisfying. Organized religions have often generated the most important and widely disseminated symbols and stories, sometimes offering a transcendent center for loyalty that threatens the sovereignty of the nation-state. Alternatively, the most powerful symbols may be part of a "civil religion," either in a mode of national self-worship (most extremely represented by Nazi Germany) or as a set of ethical principles that go beyond the state and hold it to account (Bellah 1970: 168).

Culture is paradoxically both the most visible and most problematic of forces for societal integration. It is most visible because the modern nation-state self-consciously uses language policy, formal education, collective rituals , and mass media to integrate citizens and ensure their loyalty. It has long been a tenet in social and political theory that societies can and should be integrated through common symbols, common culture, common education. State-building elites and officials have self-consciously used culture as an instrument of national integration. But a common culture is neither the sole condition nor a sufficient condition of integration. It may not even be a necessary condition, and in this regard its role in integration is problematic. Switzerland, for instance, its cantons deeply localist, its people split among four major language groups, persists even though "the Swiss have little emotional investment in the nation" (Bendix 1992: 784). Italy has been integrated by clientelist personal relations between the central government and local notables in the absence of a strong national myth or standard national culture (Tarrow 1977). When Italy became a united political nation in 1860, less than 3 percent of its population spoke Italian in everyday life (Hobsbawm 1990: 60–1). The character or quality of nationalist sentiment differs dramatically from society to society.

Most sociologists and historians do not take culture to be the central integrative mechanism for national societies. A scholar of modern China notes, for example, that since 1949 the folk culture of the villages has come under the influence of the high culture of the Communist Party, but that the greatest gains in cultural uniformity came "not in the ideological propaganda drenchings of Mao's later years, but during the first national land reform and early collectivization efforts of the 1950s" (Shue 1988: 65). Edward Shils (1975: 14) observes, likewise, that economic and political integration rather than cultural forces have borne the primary responsibility for the integration of the masses into modern states. "Culture," that is, a set of overarching symbols, beliefs, and modes of thought with a recognizable pattern, even if coherent and unified in its own terms, does not necessarily call forth integration at the level of societal action (Archer 1985).

There is no reason to privilege sociocultural integration over political order or social coordination as elements of societal integrity. It may be better to suggest not that there are several forces that help societies to cohere but that there are several different ways in which a society is integrated. Societies may be coherent *orders*, meaning that political control is effectively exercised. They may be coherently *coordinated*, meaning that people of different roles, interests, and values manage through various formal and informal mechanisms to interact peacefully. And they may be coherent *communities*, with shared allegiance to a common set of beliefs and values. All of these modes of integration rely on some level of common cultural understanding and some common means of communication, but political order relies notably on organization and force, social coordination on market, exchange, and face-to-face interaction, and sociocultural community on social relations oriented to common cultural practices, roles, and symbols.

All this acknowledged, it remains true that nation-states cannot be understood, or even defined, apart from their achievement of some degree of cultural identity. If we ask not what force integrates a society but what defines or identifies the boundaries of the society to which individuals are integrated, cultural features are essential. Nationalism, Akhil Gupta (1992: 71) writes, is a distinctively modern cultural form that "attempts to create a new kind of spatial and mythopoetic metanarrative," and it is characteristic that he, among many others, looks to literary or narrative theory to understand the meaning of nationalism and the nation-state.

All societies are fictive. Personal identification with any grouping of people beyond those one encounters face to face in daily life (and, perhaps, even there, too) depends on an imaginative leap. Cultural cues may lead people to identify themselves with coreligionists, or with coresidents of a territory, or with coworkers in an occupation, or with cocitizens of a national state, or with kin of an extended family group, or with brothers and sisters of a group defined ethnically. Each of these identifications is part of creating an "imagined community," as Benedict Anderson (1983) has put it. A sense of community is moored in *some* concrete, observable social features. But which? The contribution of the imagination is to deliver one or another (or sometimes several) of these possible groupings to the individual as the primary basis for personal identity and the establishment of extrafamilial allegiances.

## Theories of Culture and the Nation-State

Theorists differ in characterizing the link between culture and the identity of the nation-state. For Emile Durkheim (1915), the moral unity a society requires is rooted in the experience of its members coming together in a face-to-face relationship around common, sacred symbols of the group in moments of "collective effervescence." These moments energize the members at the time, and memories of those moments, preserved and reawakened through ritual objects and practices, contribute to social cohesion. The root of social solidarity lies in this moment of ecstatic submission to the higher authority of the group as a whole, and it is sustained in no small measure by the authority vested in cultural symbols and practices. In his early work, Durkheim (1933) saw this model fitting simple societies best. In modern societies, however, where people perform dissimilar tasks, and where integration may be a product of differentiation and interdependence rather than commonality, the moral and symbolic integration of society grows less vital. Later, Durkheim abandoned that position and came to argue that collective beliefs and rites and the shared moral and emotional tone they engender are essential in all societies (see Lukes 1985: 5).

Like Durkheim, Edward Shils emphasizes the consensual nature of cultural integration, but in his formulation there is a perpetual tension, and a perpetual ground for conflict, that is not present in Durkheim. For Shils, a society has a cultural center with powerful radiating influence, but the center implies also a periphery. The center is "the center of the order of symbols, of values and beliefs, which govern the society." It "partakes of the nature of the sacred"; it is equally a "structure of activities, of roles and persons" in which the beliefs are embodied (Shils 1975: 3). As soon as people are oriented to a "center," they are reminded just how far from it they live. Before the rise of the nation-state, most people lived "*outside* society," as Shils (1975: 13) writes, and only on their incorporation into society can they feel their remoteness from the center as "a perpetual injury to themselves." The center/periphery metaphor thus captures better than Durkheim the enduring cultural divisions in the nation-state that even ardent nationalism only temporarily overcomes.

Until recently, the concept of "integration" seemed somewhat old-fashioned. It tripped easily off the tongues of modernization theorists of the 1950s and 1960s, and it seemed to incorporate their general assumptions that we can speak of a single line of development all nations pass through, that we can speak of a single psychological, social, cultural, economic, and political entity called "modernity," and that we can put to the side ethnic loyalties as primordial ties that will be overcome as more modern and rational ways of thinking spread. As these assumptions went by the board in the 1970s and 1980s, so did the very language of "societal integration." The term, to the extent that it is recognizable at all in scholarship of the 1970s, came to have a negative connotation, as central national actors in a world economy incorporate peripheral nations into a world system while keeping them in a subordinate position or, with nation-states, as elites incorporate less developed regions or disfavored ethnic groups into integrated but subordinate positions. Notions of *conscience collective* or sacred centers give way to theories of hegemony or internal colonialism (see Hechter 1975).

In this light, the work of Antonio Gramsci (1971) has been especially influential. In Gramsci's view, the "center" is not so much a set of values commonly taken to have sacred significance but the home of a dominant class that promotes a worldview to the population at large that serves its own interests at the expense of others. This worldview comes to be accepted by subordinate groups as common sense, and so they conspire in their own subordination, accepting beliefs and values that justify the unequal distribution of power and rewards in society.

Benedict Anderson makes an argument not inconsistent with hegemony theory, but it is one that gives greater emphasis to the psychological primacy of the nation for its members. For Anderson (1983: 15–16), the nation is an "imagined community." It is "imagined" because its members never know or even hear of most other members, and yet they conceive of themselves as comembers of the same overridingly important unit. This imagined entity is "always conceived as a deep, horizontal comradeship" and this helps explain the willingness of many millions of people to die for this imagined object, the nation.

Frequently the claims made for national symbolic sharing, claims of ancient heritage, longstanding tradition, ethnic or family unity whose origins are lost in time, are inventions or even, it is not too much to say, forgeries. They may be, nonetheless, substantial psychological bases for a sense of membership. These inventions may arise out of central administrations seeking to solidify their rule, as Eric Hobsbawm has argued, or out of middle-class longings for power and meaning, as has been the case with romantic nationalist movements in Europe in the early nineteenth century or, for instance, Arabist nationalism in the twentieth century, or out of movements of resistance, especially in anti-colonial struggles (Hobsbawm 1983; Khoury 1991).

Culture, in relation to the nation-state, may urge either an overinclusive or underinclusive integration. (From the viewpoint of the nation-state, these may be understood as alternative avenues of disintegration.) Overinclusively, culture may be in the service not only of national societies but of imperial, global, and transnational entities. The Olympics, especially as televised, evoke participation in a global culture; the spread of Western-rooted natural science, Marx and Engels, and the Koran in national educational systems affirms allegiances beyond the national society; the spread of blue jeans, soccer, and rock music in consumer culture helps establish tastes and longings that throw national societies in question. Regional hegemonic powers spread their influence, too; it was not just the United States or European nations in their colonial or former colonial empires that did so. Egypt, especially in Nasser's day, exported its culture as well as its political influence over the Arab nations through radio and films (Hourani 1991: 392–3).

Mass media and other symbolic systems may also be underinclusive – that is, they may integrate across a group smaller than the national society. Traditions of regional music and art, or the languages and cultures and literatures of ethnic groups or religious groups within national societies may all prove disintegrative to the national society, as ethnic conflicts in the former Soviet Union or Yugoslavia or Sri Lanka, the persistent battles over language in Canada, or continuing strife among religious groups in Northern Ireland or India, make clear.

The capacity of states to overcome locality and of the idea of nationalism to endow states has been greatly aided by developments in transportation, communication, formal organization, and political ideology, especially the idea of the sovereignty of the people. The capacity of a national society to even approach cultural integration is made possible only through these facilities. To understand culture as a force for integration or a source of the definition of membership requires examining these concrete mechanisms for its objectification, transmission, and distribution.

## Language, Print, and Schooling

The medium of print has been closely associated with the integration of mass populations into national societies through political participation. Benedict Anderson (1983) has most strikingly made this point. For him, the nation-state is the product of "print capitalism" or, as he puts it more fully, the interaction of capitalism as a system of production, print as a technology of communication, and "the fatality of human linguistic diversity." Print capitalism consolidated the many and widely diverse spoken languages that existed in early modern Europe into a much smaller number of written languages distributed in the form of books and pamphlets through the market. This "laid the bases for national consciousness" by creating an assemblage of readers connected with one another through their common texts. (See Anderson 1983: 46–7.)

The assemblage of readers was a creation of the market as much as of the technology of print. Readership, of course, can be local as well as national, but since early newspapers were the media of political and economic elites, they both helped secure a sense of local identity in their place of publication and linked locals to larger worlds through news of markets and the affairs of state. Small town newspapers in nineteenth-century America helped to develop increased involvement in local public life and also connected townspeople to the nation by promoting the "highly prized ideal of citizen awareness – defined by the speed, accuracy, regularity, and currency of one's knowledge about the world" (Gilmore 1989: 112). The newspaper press, much more widely circulated in the United States than in Europe, along with representative government, helped make even rural citizens more actively oriented to the nation-state than their European counterparts.

The emergence of the newspaper in Europe did not quickly follow the development of printing. Regularly published sheets of news did not begin until the early seventeenth century, originating in The Netherlands and in England. In France and Germany, the newspaper developed more slowly and primarily as an attachment to government. But in the eighteenth century, as representative institutions began to play a larger role in the government of England and its American colonies, political communication became more oriented to the public. By the mid eighteenth century, pamphlets and newspapers in the American colonies were increasingly directed to all potential voters, not just to the legislature and elites, and might have a print run of several thousand copies, and were read aloud at the polls. The language of political writing began to change, too, eschewing the classical references that automatically restricted understanding to an educated elite and moving toward a more plain, "republican" style (for a summary, see Schudson 1989).

The development of newspapers in the United States and

Europe went hand in hand with the emergence of political parties and the drive for a wider franchise. The franchise, as it expanded, gave more people a stake in political life and reason to want to inform themselves about it. Newspapers grew up with (and often died with) specific parties and movements both in England and the United States. Parties, like the press itself, shifted in the nineteenth century from instruments of elite rule to mass-based organs of political communication, themselves (through interpersonal networks and organizing) as much media of communication and societal integration as the newspapers they sponsored. Parties mobilized citizens for political participation. In nineteenth-century United States, and in much of the rest of the world through World War II, newspapers existed primarily as the organs of political parties, and this was a vital part of their integrative force.

Intellectuals mediated the contribution of print capitalism to national identity. Scholars translated classical works into vernacular languages. In 1800, "Ukrainian" was regarded as a "language of yokels." But in 1804, with the founding of the University of Kharkov, intellectuals produced a boom in Ukrainian literature (Anderson 1983: 72). The first Ukrainian grammar was published in 1819 and by 1846 an intellectual established the first Ukrainian nationalist organization. Finnish nationalism emerged in the same era. The language of government in Finland had been Swedish in the eighteenth century. Except among peasants, it was the language of private life as well. But early nineteenth-century intellectuals, inspired by a romantic nationalism, pledged themselves to learn Finnish; folklorists rediscovered – and in part invented – national Finnish "epics," notably the Kalevala. By 1900, Finnish-language schools were well established, and Finnish-speaking secondary school students outnumbered those speaking Swedish. Serious scholars gave up the conviction that the Kalevala was authentically an ancient epic rather than a pastiche of folk stories assembled into an epic narration by folklorist Elias Lonnrot, but schools and the mass media continued well after World War II to promote the Kalevala as the sacred and genuine center of their ancient heritage (Wilson 1976).

The importance of language as an aspect of culture can scarcely be overestimated. Language is the fundamental human mass medium. It is the mass medium through which all other media speak. No other medium is so deeply rooted, so emotionally fraught, so insistently the basis for political aspirations, or so much an impediment to the efforts of states to use modern media for hegemonic control. A language is not a neutral medium for communication but a highly charged cultural object. "The use of a language not only permits acts of communion about particular objects, such as sacred objects or central objects," Edward Shils (1975: 76) writes, "it is also an act of communion in itself." Although there is not a one-to-one correspondence between national boundaries and the use of specific languages, nonetheless "the fatality of human linguistic diversity" has strongly guided the formation of nation-states.

Language evolves and a common language comes to be shared in a social group without explicit political directives. But in the modern age, the nation-state has increasingly played a central role in turning language to use for societal integration. The nation-state began using culture to promote national integration by providing – and by the end of the nineteenth century in most European states requiring – formal education. This has meant generally an emphasis on language instruction; language instruction to this day in elementary schools around the world, almost always in the national or official rather than local language, takes up about one-third of instructional hours (Benavot et al. 1991). The provision of nationally mandated and language-centered schooling is central to what we mean by a nation-state; in some respects it defines modern society. Ernest Gellner (1983: 34) writes, "The monopoly of legitimate education is now more important, more central than the monopoly of legitimate violence."

France provides an instance of what was happening in the nineteenth century all over Europe and would happen later all over the world. A law of 1833 required each commune to maintain an elementary school; by 1847 the number of schools in France had doubled. In 1881 elementary education was made free and in 1882 compulsory. In 1789, half of the French population spoke no French at all (Hobsbawm 1990: 60). In 1863, at least a fifth of the population of France did not speak what officials recognized as French; for many students, instruction in French was second-language learning. A report of 1880 in Brittany recommended "Frenchifying" the peninsula through schooling, which would "truly unify the peninsula with the rest of France and complete the historical annexation always ready to dissolve" (quoted in Weber 1976: 313).

The imposition of French in the schools came at the expense of local pride or self-esteem. Students who spoke Breton rather than French at school were punished or shamed, even though, as recent research suggests, there were local as well as national forces intent on Frenchification (McDonald 1989). Children were taught a new patriotism in the school. They learned that the "fatherland" was not where they or their fathers lived but "something vast and intangible called France" and their instruction in the language, as well as its history and geography, was part of the task of imagining the nation (Weber 1976: 332–3).

Third World states today, as Bruce Fuller and Richard Rubinson (1992: 4) argue, "hold the school institution as sacred; they regard it as being *the* organizational mechanism for delivering mass opportunity, economic growth, and national integration." Education, Francisco Ramirez and Richard Rubinson (1979: 79–80) have argued – in all nations – emphasizes the transmission of a national culture, national symbols, and a national language. It is therefore "an institutional agency for creating national uniformities among the heterogeneous status and class groupings in society." This is a matter not only of a certain propagandistic content in the curriculum but also of the perception of schooling as an egalitarian institutional mechanism that legitimates inegalitarian outcomes in economic and political positions. Through school systems in which socialization becomes highly purposive and self-conscious and focused on individuals as citizens, and through the mass media, where culture becomes purposive, self-conscious, and oriented to individuals as consumers, the very idea of a national society becomes graspable. Of course, empires and other societies before the nation-state had to resolve problems of integration, but they did so with bureaucratic and military means, integrating groups and notables, without needing to find participatory mechanisms for "individuals" as such. Universal membership of the people, or even all property-owning white males, was not taken to be a necessary basis for social cohesion.

Educational systems, then, do not so much integrate the people of a nation as they objectify the idea of the nation itself. Ernest Gellner argues that nationalism operates on a self-deception – that national feeling is an emotional attachment to primordial folk symbols and values when, in fact, the essence of nationalism is the imposition of a high culture from the center on the relatively isolated folk cultures of an area. The nation-state, in a sense, can be successfully Gramscian only when it presents itself as fully Durkheimian.

## World Consumer Culture and National Societies

The state is not the only agency of cultural forms of integration. The political party, as already briefly suggested, is another. The private business as a producer of symbolically significant consumer goods is yet another. The economy has a symbolic dimension in the meanings attributed to material goods. In modern society, many goods are mass produced and widely distributed, and these goods may become not only devices of practical import but symbolic structures that command attention and evoke devotion or allegiance for their own sake and from the fact that they have been shared. This view of consumer culture has been best developed by Mary Douglas and Baron Isherwood in *The World of Goods* (1979). Douglas and Isherwood argue that goods are elements in cultural classification schemes that people use to "construct an intelligible universe."

That intelligible universe has been increasingly a national one over the past two centuries. It includes, for instance, the emergence of both professional and organized amateur sports institutions organized within the boundaries of nation-states and developing rules and practices transcending local variations (Hobsbawm 1983: 301). In The Netherlands, for instance, all major sports (including soccer) have been imported from abroad, whereas indigenous ball games have practically vanished. Soccer teams are organized for nationwide competitions and have contributed to "directing public attention to the national scene" (Goudsblom 1967: 113–15).

As national markets linked people together in new ways, people have come to see and recognize their connections and distinctions from other people in the goods they consume. In the United States in 1800, most clothing for men and boys was made in the home; a century later, almost all of it was made outside the home. Many women still made their own clothes at home at that time, but increasingly according to patterns purchased from women's magazine companies. Fashion became a more extensive and exact signal system, placing people not only in social space in relation to other people but in social time: avant garde, au courant, or old-fashioned

(Schudson 1984: 156–7). Robert and Helen Lynd (Lynd and Lynd 1929) described the shift toward a world of mass produced and commonly recognizable consumer goods in "Middletown" in the 1920s. They suggested that changes in employment patterns, the increasing use of the automobile, and exposure to a world beyond Middletown through movies and other mass media, made mothers and grandmothers less often tutors of consumption than the women's magazines. The social order shifted, in their metaphor, from a set of plateaus to a single slope, and this provided a newly democratized field of vision and, along with it, what we might call a democratization of envy (Lynd and Lynd 1929: 83; Schudson 1984: 181–2).

Consumer goods may be the agents of a center colonizing the periphery. In highland Ecuador today leavened white bread, associated with the dominant metropolitan culture, has increasingly been substituted for barley gruel, the traditional staple of the early morning meal. M. J. Weismantel (1989), who studied the culinary practices of the town of Zumbagua, observes that the people "are constantly bombarded from within and without by images of their cultural practices as being backwards and wrong." The integration of the highland natives is easy to see "when the schoolchild is taught to salute the Ecuadorian flag," but it is equally present, Weismantel (1989: 88) writes, "when his mother hesitates over what foods to serve her family, fearful that there is something inadequate in a meal of homegrown foods unembellished by purchased foodstuffs or condiments."

The nationalization of consumer goods does not necessarily entail their standardization. In India, middle-class urban women since the 1970s, both as audiences and authors, have made English-language cookbooks of Indian cuisine a successful publishing venture. The new aspirations and tastes for foods in the middle-class home has paralleled other aspects of societal integration: new cuisine, both national and regional, has been learned at food stands in train stations and in railroad dining cars, army barracks (a standardized colonial Indian cuisine lived on in military culinary manuals and procedures even after independence), student hostels, and restaurants. The idea of a national Indian cuisine includes not only an effort to characterize Indian-wide principles of cookery but to celebrate regional variety in the national palate (Appadurai 1988).

In the Indian case, there is a dialectical interaction between regionalisms and nationalism. In the role of consumer goods in societal integration there is equally a complex interplay between nationalism and internationalism. The social status of consumer goods seems to be an international language, with Soviet teenagers wearing blue jeans and Japanese youths sporting jackets with American college insignia.

## The Persistence and Transformation of Durkheimian Collective Experience

A central medium for societal integration is the collective ritual, the repetitive, sacralized social activity whose fundamental function is the symbolic affirmation of key values. "Without rites and symbols," anthropologist David Kertzer (1988: 179) holds, "there are no nations."

Rituals, in contemporary society, may take a variety of forms. As with any collective medium, the ritual may be a force for integration or disintegration. The Chinese communists saw local and religious rituals as a serious barrier to their efforts at political integration and transformation. They criticized popular rituals as feudal superstitions that upheld the old order. In the first years after the 1949 revolution, the state confiscated ancestral halls and temples and turned them into schools, offices, and factories. Later, old trees that marked neighborhood shrines were sacrificed to backyard furnaces. In the Cultural Revolution, temples were destroyed; community involvement in burial, birth, wedding, funeral, and memorial rites to ancestors was ended, and these rituals, to the extent that they persisted, were confined to households. In rural China today, however, after the liberalization of state policy, even leading communist cadres restored their domestic altars, and funerals and weddings have returned to traditional ceremonies and extravagance (Siu 1989).

State-sponsored collective rituals, although important even in dynastic states for centuries, received a major boost as European states developed and sought to legitimate their colonial empires in the late nineteenth and early twentieth centuries. This was the heyday of the "invention of tradition," to use Eric Hobsbawm's phrase, a time in which the elaboration of ceremonies and festivals and the fabrication of historical origins took on worldwide significance (Hobsbawm and Ranger 1983).

In the twentieth century, the Bolshevik Revolution significantly accelerated the role of state ritual. During World War I, a newsprint shortage limited the possibilities for conventional propaganda and the Bolsheviks invented "agit-trains" and "agit-ships" to carry books, leaflets, posters, films, and trained agitators to the front to work among the soldiers. The new communist state instituted huge festivals on May Day and on the anniversary of the October revolution, erected statues and monuments, and encouraged a cult of Lenin (Tumarkin 1983). Fascism has also been self-conscious about inventing and appropriating collective rituals and a common patriotic culture. Hitler incorporated symbols (the swastika) and German folk traditions, invented patriotic holidays, and staged mass rallies and festivals in his effort to create fervent allegiance to the Third Reich (Mosse 1976).

The nation-state seems to require a history and to devote considerable resources to making one (Mosse 1976: 40). "No matter how culturally artificial or historically serendipitous the new national entity, it must be endowed with a sacred unity and made to seem a natural social unit," David Kertzer (1988: 179) writes. Indonesian political leaders, he goes on, speak of 350 years of Indonesia's suffering under colonial rule, despite the fact that "the whole notion of Indonesia is a twentieth-century invention" and much of what is now Indonesia came under colonial rule only at the end of the nineteenth century. This distortion is not peculiar to Indonesia. "Getting its history wrong is part of being a nation," Ernest Renan (cited in Hobsbawm 1990: 12) wrote.

Elections may be the single most central ritual in modern democracies. Whatever role they play in policy formation, they clearly legitimate state power and reaffirm the intimate connections of individuals to the society as a whole and to the state. It has even been suggested that this is the primary service elections perform (Ginsberg 1986). Certainly it is well established that elections have a ritualistic quality and can be analyzed with the tools anthropologists use to examine rituals in traditional societies (Baker 1983). The same may be said for other national political events, as Jeff Alexander (1988a) has shown for Watergate (see also Schudson 1992) and as can be seen in the commemorative activities even around such divisive events as the Vietnam war where there is no established social consensus (Wagner-Pacifici and Schwartz 1991).

## Broadcasting and Collective Identity

Broadcasting in most nations has emerged under the strict control or regulation of the state. Not surprisingly, legislation establishing broadcast systems has clearly identified national, integrative, and participatory goals for them. In Canada, for instance, broadcasting began as an effort to assert cultural autonomy against the hegemony of the United States. Yet it also was a decision to favor federal over regional control within Canada, in an effort to shore up national feeling (Raboy 1985). In seeking to renew its license in 1978, the Canadian Broadcasting Corporation suggested that "what the CBC is really all about" is "the creation of a national consciousness." The CBC claimed that its mission is to express the "Canadian identity" and that it had become "a living institution in Canada, a symbol of Canadian nationhood, a central constituent in the cement which binds this country together" (Ericson, Baranek, and Chan 1987: 28).

Just as broadcasting incorporates the medium of language – and to some extent alters it, nationalizing a standard or preferred version, so it has come to incorporate, and alter, collective rituals. It goes too far to declare, as some cultural critics have, that television is the church or altar of modern societies, much too far to suggest that people learn their values primarily from Big Brother television rather than parents or guardians at home. Television has not even necessarily done much to "deterritorialize" personal identity, although Joshua Meyrowitz (1985: 308) has elegantly articulated the position that "the traditionally interlocking components of 'place' have been split apart by electronic media." He contends that electronic media have undermined the tight bond between place and access to information (something that has been attributed also to writing and to print). For Meyrowitz, "electronic messages on television, telephone, and radio democratize and homogenize places by allowing people to experience and interact with others in spite of physical isolation." Electronic media "begin to override group identities based on 'co-presence,' and they create many new forms of access and 'association' that have little to do with physical location" (Meyrowitz 1985: 144).

It would be churlish to deny some truth in this claim, but it can be accepted only with qualifications. First, this view posits a decisive break with the electronic media that is not justified. Personal identification with vast assemblages of peoples one has never met, notably in identification with a nation-state, predates the electronic media. It is a mistake to see too radical a divide in the present day from a past of territorially dependent identity. As anthropologists Akhil Gupta and James Ferguson have written, we are now recognizing that the territorially distinct cultures anthropologists claimed they were studying were never as autonomous as they imagined; conventional anthropology allowed "the power of topography to conceal successfully the topography of power." Most of the tribal societies anthropologists examined were neither pristine nor autonomous, but were defined to a significant degree by their encounters with imperial powers and their agents. "People have undoubtedly always been more mobile and identities less fixed than the static and typologizing approaches of classical anthropology would suggest" (Gupta and Ferguson 1992).

Second, people are very well practiced at using new technologies and new cultural forms to reinforce old social habits. The telephone that theoretically freed people from dependence on locality is used overwhelmingly to call nearby friends and neighbors (Fischer 1992). The views of new worlds and broad horizons made possible by national and then international broadcasting are selectively perceived much of the time to reinforce preexisting attitudes and beliefs.

Still, broadcasting provides a novel form for the perpetuation and invention of collective rituals that can captivate audiences as wide as large-scale societies today. Daniel Dayan and Elihu Katz (1992) have studied the live broadcasting of "media events," including Kennedy's funeral, Sadat's visit to Jerusalem, the royal wedding of Charles and Diana, and transformative political events in Eastern Europe where, contrary to the incantation of the 1960s, the revolution actually was televised. In these cases, television news broadcasters depart from any pretense of objectivity to become cheerleaders for the nation. The event "swallows" the commentators and reporting becomes reverent or celebratory. This transformation affords the broadcasters and their organizations the opportunity of "repledging their allegiances to the central values of the commonwealth" (Dayan and Katz 1992: 108, 116, 193).

This is true for audiences as well as for broadcasters. An Indian student describes how her family prepared to view the Gandhi funeral: they washed and dressed "as if we were going to be physically present at the scene. My mother insisted that we wear long clothes and cover our heads as a mark of respect." People congregated together, crossing family and class boundaries as people watched together with their domestic servants (Dayan and Katz 1992: 123). Major media events in the United States, similarly, are often occasions for group viewings, either of a solemn and sacred or festive nature. The media event gives the audience an experience of *communitas*, a direct communion with the societal "center," as people engage in a ceremony together despite their dispersion (Dayan and Katz 1992: 146).

A ceremonial tone may be part of everyday television, too. Daniel Hallin (1986) argues that a "sphere of consensus" operates in contemporary American news reporting. When journalists report on a phenomenon where they take a societal consensus for granted, they display their values and abandon the strictures of "objective" reporting. When journalists took for granted that feminism was beyond the bounds, they presented feminist organizations and demonstrations in a jocular fashion, automatically trivializing and marginalizing them (Gitlin 1980; Tuchman 1978). When they cover a Fourth of July celebration or some other ceremony of national communion, they speak as if everyone shared the same values.

Broadcasting, like schooling, must accommodate itself to language and culture differences within states. In Zambia, for instance, where there are some 73 ethnic groups or "tribes" speaking about 15 to 20 major languages, radio, following the "tribal balancing" policy instituted by President Kenneth Kaunda upon Zambia's independence in 1964, has recognized a variety of languages. In 1967, broadcasting was in English, Bemba, and Nyanja. In the mid 1980s, Kaonde, Lozi, Lunda, Luvale, and Tonga also received broadcasting time allocations, but in 1988, all native Zambian languages were removed from the general radio service. As of 1990, Radio 2 and Radio 4 were broadcast in English only. On Radio 1, seven Zambian languages shared equal air time although the languages representing the largest groups of people received the best times of day for broadcasting. First among equals is English, the

national language, the language of government and higher education and the only language that is "ethnically neutral" because
native to none of the indigenous ethnic groups (Spitulnik 1992). To
resolve competition among linguistic groups, English becomes
the language of choice, reinforcing Zambia's incorporation into the
world political-economic system. In Tanzania, Swahili could become the national language in part because there were very few
native Swahili speakers and they did not represent a political threat
to more powerful ethnic groups (Mazrui and Tidy 1984).

Is it true, as Ellen Mickiewicz (1988), a scholar of the Soviet
Union's media, put it, that state broadcasting is a powerful homog-
enizing influence today? Before the Soviet Union disintegrated, she
described Soviet television as "a powerful force for integration"
and "a national medium attempting to forge a national consciousness and a national culture." Although she recognized ethnicity as
a potent centrifugal force in the Soviet state, she nonetheless argued
that the mass media were slowly overcoming it. In Azerbaijan, for
instance, Azeri and Russian language programs received equal time,
but the national programs had much superior production values
and provided content that made them better for language learning.
She judged the most popular Azeri language programs, ordinarily
featuring little besides ethnic music, ineffective at transmitting ethnic
culture. "In the Soviet Union, as everywhere else, differences and
traditions are slowly eroding as national television usurps the role
of keeper of the heritage" (Mickiewicz 1988: 207–8).

Obviously, subsequent events cast doubt on Mickiewicz's position. This is not to suggest that television has no nationalizing
power. Certainly Soviet television was among the media that
reinforced nationalization even if, as the center-periphery model
would remind us, it simultaneously may have nurtured resent-
ment among peoples at the periphery of the Russian-centred state.
In Eastern Europe the limited effectiveness of national media
systems was perhaps easier to recognize. In a 1977 collection of
essays, British experts on eastern Europe uniformly argued that
there was a great and growing gulf between the messages of national pride and unity in the official media and the public apathy
and cynicism with which these messages were regularly met (Gray
1977). National traditions and national understandings of politics
and history appeared unaffected by a full generation of elite
commitment to creating a new "socialist man."

Does broadcasting aid social integration by encouraging political participation? It is clearly the entree into political awareness for young children, at least in Western democracies. But young people who are politically engaged supplement it significantly with print by early adolescence. It appears that "reliance on TV alone may be associated with socialization away from politics" (Chaffee and Yang 1990: 138, 143). Daniel Dayan and Elihu Katz (1992: 59) argue that "television depoliticizes society, both because it keeps people at home and because it contributes to the false illusion of political involvement."

Nevertheless, television broadcasting has had notable institutional effects in electoral systems in many countries around the world as political parties have weakened. In the United States, television has grown as a central political mechanism at the expense of parties (Polsby 1983). Within parties, and within candidacies, public relations, polling, and advertising experts with no territorial constituency have prospered at the expense of party leaders or bosses with local followings. In Scandinavian countries, television is now the most important source of political information during campaigns. In the first television-centered elections, the political parties kept control of television time, but increasingly the broadcast media have become independent actors while the print media have moved from partisanship to neutrality. The result is that the news media have changed "from an effective campaign channel to an independent actor in election campaigns, having a strong influence on what issues actually are discussed" (Esaisson 1992: 13). National television can certainly push in the direction of nationalization, emphasizing more than any other medium that the nation is the appropriate context for political discussion.

### Resistance to hegemony and center

The mass media have often been seen as a powerful force for integration, both positively – assimilating different peoples to a common, civil culture – and negatively – stripping different peoples of their folk cultures and embracing them in an overbearing "hegemonic" culture produced by elites at the society's center. Either way, societies are said to grow more homogeneous and their people more docile as the mass media become more powerful and more pervasive. This assumption is widespread not only with reference to systems where the media are state-operated and governed by an ideology that advocates their use as propaganda, as in communist societies, but also in regard to liberal democracies where private ownership and profit-orientation produces strong tendencies to make news media into entertainment machines rather than engines of self-government. The work of Jürgen Habermas (1989), as well as earlier work in the Frankfurt school, emphasizes the "refeudalization" of media after an emancipatory moment of a "bourgeois public sphere" in the late eighteenth and early nineteenth centuries in Europe. But the assumption of a quiescent audience has been repeatedly challenged over the past decade as studies have documented that different audiences interpret the same cultural materials in conflicting ways (Liebes and Katz 1990; Radway 1984; Fiske 1987). Although many of these studies are based on small samples and focus on fairly limited cultural materials, their assertion that people retain significant control over how to interpret mass media messages is certainly reinforced in the wake of the evident integrative problems in the former Soviet Union, the former Yugoslavia, and the former Czechoslovakia, not to mention the troubled ethnic, linguistic, religious, and cultural divisions elsewhere around the world.

Even state-sponsored rituals with directly propagandistic aims and integrative functions may be subverted by dissident groups. This was well illustrated in the uprising of Chinese students in Tiananmen Square in 1989. A critical moment for the students was the funeral march of Hu Yaobang, when they turned this state-prescribed function into an occasion of protest. Funerals of politically important or wealthy Chinese figures have been occasions for public ritual for a long time, and funeral processions have been a forum for elites to symbolically display and reinforce the social order. But the very legitimacy of these forums provides dissidents an opportunity for public visibility (Esherick and Wasserstrom 1990: 840).

Historians Joseph Esherick and Jeffrey Wasserstrom make the interesting argument that these are cases of political theater rather than political ritual. Theater, they write, has "a critical power never possessed by ritual: it can expose the follies of tradition (or the follies of abandoning tradition), mock social elites, or reveal the pain and suffering of everyday life" (1990: 845). Where ritual invariably has a hegemonic role in confirming the political or social order, theater may often symbolically subvert it. In societies less repressive than China and with a more highly developed civil society, holidays and anniversary celebrations and the mass gatherings they occasioned have frequently provided an opportunity for theatrical protest, as in Poland and Hungary in the years before the velvet revolution of 1989.

One need not rhapsodize about the "weapons of the weak" and the powers of the disenfranchised to take politics into their own hands. The other lesson of Tiananmen Square, after all, is that resistance was repressed and state hegemony reasserted. This was an exercise in raw political and military power to integrate a nation where decades of cultural policy had failed to do so.

## Conclusion

The intertwinings of local, regional, national, and global cultures are now complex beyond reckoning. Cultures flow in, out, around, and through state borders; within states, centers radiate to peripheries but peripheries influence centers, too; in the world system the same phenomenon is repeated and culture flows in many directions (Hannerz 1987). The nation-state retains dominant influence but in a world reconstituting itself in new and surprising ways. Arab states confront pan-Arab and pan-Islamic ideologies. European states have had their national institutions of communication called into question by the "European community." The nation-state may lose out not only to supra-states like the European community but the transnational corporation.

Over the past two hundred years the nation-state has been the leading locus of political and societal membership. It has also been the leading advocate of the theory that a common culture is necessary for societal integration. In the present world framework, with transnational entities of such prominence and subnational entities of such renewed emotional power, there are good grounds not only to note the challenges to the nation-state but to question the validity of the theory of culture it has so long championed. Culture may be integrative, but it may also be disintegrative at the same time. It may ally acquiescent citizens under a common regime and common symbols, but it may also prove a focal point for division, contention, and conflict. In their cultural policy, nation-states provide less cultural unity than an authoritative statement of the terms in which union and division will be negotiated.

Sociology has too often and too easily relinquished control over its own province – the study of status, respect, and membership in human communities. Social phenomena have been explained, or explained away, by economic, political, or cultural features of the human landscape. Sociologists of culture and mass media have sometimes been among the guilty parties. As suggested through-out this chapter, the cultural sphere is neither overarching nor in any sense complete in itself. Social integration or disintegration is forged not in shared symbols but in shared lives, with economic, social, political, and cultural dimensions. If culture has any kind of priority in the question of integration, it is in providing common elements and clear boundaries to which meaning is attached and feeling invested. But this is a part of social life rather than the frame within which sociality is worked out. Just how to effect a reorientation to the social, and a renewed exploration of the role of meaning and membership as a constitutive feature of the social, is not clear. But the way the world looks in 1993, the forces encour-aging such a reorientation are everywhere.

## Note

1   Edward A. Tiryakian and Neil Nevitte (1985) have reviewed the intellec-tual history of the study of "nationalism" in sociology and find scattered through Weber's work some valuable commentary on the idea of the nation.

# 3

# "Cultural Pluralism" in Historical Sociology: Recent Theoretical Directions

## *Ewa Morawska and Willfried Spohn*

A spectacular resurgence of interest in culture – understood in this overview inclusively as the realm of symbolic forms (ideational, material, and institutional) that individual and collective actors invest with intersubjective meanings – has affected historical sociology no less strongly, if apparently in a less radical fashion, than some other subfields of the discipline (Alexander and Seidman 1990; Lamont and Wuthnow 1990).[1] A concurrent "cultural turn" in the closely affiliated specialization of social history (Hunt 1989a), and the emergence in the 1980s of historical anthropology, whose concerns move in an overlapping orbit (Comaroff and Comaroff 1992), have also pushed historical sociology toward this shift of attention. Particular conceptualizations and specific theoretical treatments of culture reflect at once different strands in the intellectual Great Tradition common to the entire discipline of sociology and influences from related areas of study as well as the agenda of the subfield itself and its ongoing debates.

Since its renaissance in the 1970s until quite recently, the dominant preoccupation of American historical sociology has been with macro-structural models of social change, or, at lower levels of social life, with the analysis of social-institutional settings as the producers and carriers of cultural meanings, identities, and activities, rather than of the latter themselves (see below). As a result, until recently, no serious attempts were made at a theoretical analysis of the position and operation of culture in the historical sociological perspective (for the latter, see, for example, Wuthnow 1989; Calhoun 1992b; also, in reference to specific subjects of their studies, see Mann 1986; Goldstone 1991; Skocpol 1992). In most case studies, these issues appear, if at all, implicit and unelaborated, and, when they are explicitly addressed, the concepts of culture and related matters are often inconsistently used. Alternatively, more general theoretical statements concerning the importance and impact of cultural phenomena in social life, placed usually in the introductions to studies, are not realized in the actual historical analysis. In addition, a number of studies recognized as historical sociological classics have been originally designed, conducted, and presented as deliberate polemics with the theoretical models the authors of the former considered as unsatisfactory. A polemical spirit driving research projects brings about, to be sure, welcome and creative results, but also, unless sagaciously monitored, distortions, usually by overstatements, of adversaries' as well as of one's own positions on the contested problems.

In order to assist us in interpreting particular historical-sociological studies we interviewed about two-thirds of the authors cited in this chapter in an informal way for interpretations of their own published work, and specifically their views concerning the place, operation, and effects of cultural phenomena in social life as well as for reflections as to how their thinking about these matters might have changed since the 1980s, particularly in a confrontation with postmodernist philosophies (see appendix 3.1 for a list of "survey" participants). Occasionally, we also asked our respondents to comment on another researcher's studies, especially when classifying a given work as representative of a theoretical approach seemed especially difficult.[2]

Particular works were selected for inclusion in this project on the following grounds:

- Identification by the author or by fellow historical sociologists as "historical sociology" (but we also included a few authors from the affiliated disciplines of social history and historical anthropology who have been widely read and influential among the former).
- Preference was given to scholars working in the United States.
- We considered as "recent," and therefore appropriate for consideration here, works published since about 1980, but excluded *a priori* studies authored by the "old guard" US historical sociologists (see below), even when they appeared during this time (for discussions thereof see Skocpol 1984; and Smith 1991); we included, however, some older works of European scholars if they were translated into English only recently and/or exerted a significant influence on the younger (post-1980) generation of American historical sociologists.

We examined selected historical-sociological studies (about 45 in total) with two questions in mind. First, we asked: How has "culture" been constructed (assuming, of course, that it was present in some tangible, i.e., identifiable, way)? For example, is culture viewed as interrelated with but distinct from society, or as simultaneously constituted by and constituting it through an ongoing process? How strong an influence is accorded to culture and how was it conceptualized: as derivative from the social structure, as (relatively) autonomous/causal, or as ubiquitous and all-pervasive? Is culture viewed as a structure of forms, codes, and rules (schemas) embedded in social institutions and/or social practice, or rather as intersubjective meanings, purposes, and identities embedded in social action and social institutions? Is culture represented as more (or mainly) fixed and ordered, or as more (or mainly) indeterminate, flexible and contestable?

Second, we asked: What kind of cultural analysis has been applied? (The mere presence of cultural material, and even commenting on culture's influence/causality, does not, as we discovered in the inspected studies, necessarily entail cultural analysis.) Are cultural phenomena the *explanandum* or "objects" to be explained, or rather the *explanans* or explanatory principles themselves, "capable of illuminating significant aspects of human existence" (Comaroff and Comaroff 1992: 49)?

Not surprisingly, considering what has been said earlier about "the data," the picture we have formed by the end of this exercise does not consist of distinct positions with clearly delineated boundaries, but, rather, of a diversity of overlapping viewpoints. We have nevertheless constructed a chart (see figure 3.1 in appendix 3.2) to provide a general orientation in which we tried to identify and relate to one another major theoretical approaches to culture in historical sociology.

The chart consists of the "lower" and the "elevated" plane: on the lower level, we have located approaches that construe culture as interrelated with but distinct from society, and on the elevated level, interpretation of culture and society as reciprocally constituted. We have positioned particular studies assigned to the lower plane in a field with two major coordinates. The horizontal axis represents the causal power attributed to culture, with positions ranging from a "social structure over culture" approach, assuming culture to be largely determined by the economic and political structures; to an interactive approach balancing social-structural and cultural influences; to a "culture over social structure" approach that construes culture as relatively autonomous and potent to transform itself as well as the economic and political structures. The vertical axis represents the conceptualization of culture, with positions ranging from a view of culture primarily as patterns, or a structure, of symbolic forms, codes, and rules (schemas); to approaches embedding in one another culture and social practices/ actions, emphasizing either the social or cultural side; to an understanding of culture as intersubjective meanings, value-orientations, and identities.

Works that present society and culture as an on-going reciprocal construction have been positioned in the upper or lower part of the elevated plane on the chart depending on whether they concentrate the analysis primarily on social actors pursuing their life purposes and thus transforming their social environment through the mediation of shared cultural meanings, or rather on the production and reproduction of sociocultural structures that are embodied in and acted out by interdependent people. Finally, regarding the remaining two question-dimensions of cultural analysis listed above: a conception of culture as fixed and ordered, or as indeterminate and flexible; and a treatment of cultural phenomena as the *explanandum* or as the *explanans*, works that lean toward the latter positions in each of these two issues are concentrated in the middle area of the chart on both levels, but especially on the elevated plane.

Without eliminating positions earlier held to be paradigmatic, current theory and research in historical sociology have been moving toward, most generally, the acknowledgment of the "reality of culture" as inherent in social life and social change in all their aspects. More specifically, this movement appears to occur in three intersecting directions:

- toward the conceptualization of culture and society, to use Anthony Giddens' (1976, 1984) coinage, as "the double structure," i.e., each structured by and structuring the other; or even toward the abrogation of these concepts altogether (as laden with conventional dualistic meanings)
- toward construing culture as indeterminate, flexible and contestable

- toward an increased, or even primary, interest in the "culture–power link," as it is sometimes called, or culture-mediated power relations.

Stated differently: in addition to, or instead of, investigating the origins, context, and transformations of cultural phenomena, there is a tendency to conceptualize them as historically particular epistemologies, and to analyze their capacity to define, rank-order, misrepresent, and exclude. (This latter capacity has also been referred to as culture's indirect, or imperceptible, power; the direct one meaning the capacity to impose one's will on others despite resistance.)[3]

In this chapter, different theoretical approaches to culture in historical-sociological studies are presented – first in a general outline, and then in selected illustrations[4] – following the direction of movement as sketched out above. A qualitative shift toward the analysis of culture conceived of as central to social life, but also flexible and contestable, and ubiquitous in exerting indirect power, tends to occur in a model that holds society and culture as reciprocally constituted, although some of the above emphases appear as well in an approach assuming the two as interrelated but distinct realms (see note 2 to figure 3.1).

We start with positions that assume culture and society as constituting interconnected but distinct spheres (the lower plane on the chart). In this group, we note first social-structuralist or reductionist approaches. Second, we discuss different combinations of social contexts and cultural forms or ideas, moving from conceptions of culture as subordinate to the social structure toward its representations as increasingly autonomous and "causal," or socially and politically transformative. Next, we consider another model that posits society and culture or (social) structure and action as "double" or reciprocal constructions (the elevated plane in figure 3.1), and present different versions of this approach. In conclusion, we briefly discuss the effects of the (new) "cultural turn" on historical sociologists as they perceive it themselves. Here we use information from our "interviews," research projects in progress or being considered, as well as recent, published and unpublished, debates on these matters. Different understandings of the historicism of culture are also noted (as we interpreted them) with the presentations of particular theoretical positions.

## Culture and Society as Interrelated but Distinct Spheres

### The macro-structuralists

The term "renaissance," to the extent it indicates resumption of a ceased activity, does not accurately describe the increased interest in historical analysis among some members of the younger generation of American sociologists in the 1970s, because this interest, although never a dominant stream in the discipline, has never disappeared (cf. renowned works by, for example, R. Bellah, S. N. Eisenstadt, S. M. Lipset, N. Smelser, B. Moore or R. Bendix). Instead, there was a radical overhauling of the theoretical models and main foci of research that had prevailed in post-World War II sociological studies of long-term social change, and that centered – like sociology as a whole – on cultural systems and personality structures attuned to them. Namely, representatives of the younger generation interested in large-scale social processes and transformations, having found the prevailing "culturalist" explanations historically incorrect, theoretically unsatisfactory, and ideologically suspect (a number of them had pro-Marxist and populist political orientations), shifted theoretical focus and research interests radically toward political and economic structures as the primary source of societal formations, power, and change.[5]

In the strongest, reductionist version, this approach assumes culture to be a residue of the macro-structures of political economy. Because of their epiphenomenal nature, cultural patterns are seen as being derived from the particular historical constellations of economic and political structures. Since matters of culture are interpreted as having no significant impact – either alone or even in interaction with the economy or political system – on the emergence and transformations of social formations in the historical process, the study of culture is as much epiphenomenal as its object itself. This position has been represented most fully in the historical sociology of the world-systems and global economies of Immanuel Wallerstein (1974, 1979, 1980).

More common, however, has been a less radical position: still strongly macro-structuralist, but not reductionist in the sense that, while according culture a decidedly lesser causal potency than that exerted by political-economic structures, particularly at the macroscopic level, it nevertheless acknowledges the former's existence and certain influence. But, beyond passing references, culture is absent in studies informed by this position, and is not an object of analysis either by itself or in a configuration with other, causally more potent factors. Two different illustrations of this approach can be found in works of two leading agenda-setting scholars in the US historical sociology in the 1980s: Charles Tilly's (1975, 1992); work on the historical process of state formation in Western Europe; and Theda Skocpol's (1979), comparative-historical study of states and social revolutions, treated here jointly with her rejoinder to William Sewell's (1985) polemic with this book.

In Tilly's case, a "bias" of omitting almost entirely cultural institutions, policies, ideologies, and civic/national identities in a study of the emergence of modern European states is explicitly admitted, but the effects of this omission are interpreted as making the study "incomplete," rather than in distorting the representation of the investigated process itself (Tilly 1975: 48–50). The reader is challenged, should she or he raise "the missing variable criticism," to show "that neglect of the variable causes a false reading of relationships among variables that *do* appear in the argument. The point is not to give a "complete" account (whatever that might be), but to get the main connections right" (Tilly 1992: 36).

The situation illustrated by the second case is more representative, we believe, of the orientations among American historical sociologists during the early 1980s. Neither an aversion to the functionalist/voluntarist model of society nor a preoccupation with puzzling out macro-structural configurations of the economy and politics provided incentives for a more profound theoretical reflection on culture and its relation to macrostructural contexts. But the same theoretical gap, as it were, made space for new ideas regarding the accommodation of culture into social-structural models.

One indication that this has occurred can be seen in a comparison of the severely structuralist treatment of social revolutions in Skocpol's 1979 study, in which she rejects the conventional voluntarist/intentionalist interpretations of the role played by ideology by discarding the "purposive image of the process by which revolutions develop" (Skocpol 1979: 15–16), with a position she takes in a 1985 reply to William Sewell's objections to her dismissal in *States and Revolutions* (1979) of the role of the ideology.

Ideology, according to Sewell, can be conceptualized not, as Skocpol has it, as ideas motivating particular actors, but, rather, as "an anonymous and collective, but transformable *structure*." Conceived in this way, ideology "plays a crucial role in revolutions, both as cause and as outcome" (Sewell 1985: 61, 84). In a discussion of this proposition, Skocpol, although still unapologetically macro-social-structuralist, acknowledges that she did less than she could have done to look at alternative conceptualizations of ideologies in her study of social revolutions, and, warming to the problem, aptly, if ironically given her reputation for structural determinism, criticizes Sewell for his overly structuralist, static treatment of the ideology. Skocpol then offers a narrower, more history-sensitive definition, and also introduces a notion of cultural idioms as shared background schemas about the world upon which "grow" more coherent systems of ideas (Skocpol 1985).[6]

## Macro-structural studies of ideological change

We now turn to positions that accord culture increased presence and causal potency, and more extensive analysis (as noted earlier, we found that these three did not necessarily go together), starting with the area on the left side of the (horizontal) social-structuralist-to-culturalist continuum, and in the lower part of the (vertical) axis stretching from structural to (inter)subjective understandings of culture in figure 3.1 in appendix 3.2. In this approach, analytical interest focuses on long-term macroscopic social change, while culture is construed as one among several structures of power and influence: economic, political, military. In the case of processes of state formation and disintegration, and social revolutions – the subjects of interest to the representatives of this perspective – culture refers primarily to ideologies defined as programmatically elaborated sets of ideas "carried" by organizations, and also to cultural frameworks or traditions underlying them defined as the "taken-for-granted," background symbolic codes and rules, and institutions representing them. What is distinctive about this approach is that the interpretation of a transformative power of culture (ideology) in the analyzed developments is historical, that is, contextualized, or time and place-specific and contingent on particular configurations of all structures and networks involved. Different variants of this approach are illustrated in two studies:

Michael Mann's (1986) *The Sources of Social Power*, and Jack Goldstone's (1991) *Revolution and Rebellion in the Early Modern World* (see also John A. Hall (1988) "States and societies: the miracle in comparative perspective").

Mann sees the task of historical sociology as explaining societies' structure and history in terms of the interrelations of what he calls the four sources of power: ideological, economic, and political, and military relationships. The "driving force" of these four kinds of power is engendered in their respective organizational capacity to achieve human goals, which in various times and places has enabled a particular form to attain prominence and "dictate for a time the form of societies at large." As the above indicates, Mann thinks in terms of direct power. But in his discussion of ideological power in its moments of historical apogee – the study is a narrative interpretation of a long-term history of different forms of power from the Neolithic Age to 1760 CE – Mann actually considers the indirect power of, for example, the ancient Greek concept of citizenship, or of Christianity as a normative system, to define, and include or exclude public issues and social groups. All this is done, however, in a conventional vocabulary of "leading role," "cause," and "primacy."

In the second illustration, Goldstone examines the causes of revolutions and major rebellions in the early modern world in order to develop a theory of revolutions. His study combines a demographic analysis with a model of state breakdown constructed on the premise that "social order is maintained on a *multiplicity* of levels. A theory of state breakdown must thus address how changes in economic, political, social, and cultural relations affect states *and* elites *and* different popular groups" (Goldstone 1991: xxiii, author's italics). The impact of particular forces on the state breakdown and the course of revolution depends on the phase of this process: while structural factors (economic, political, social) play leading roles in setting off these developments, the outcomes depend far more on ideology and cultural frameworks. The study ends with a set of general theoretical propositions concerning social change.

Goldstone's interpretation of the role of culture in this process as historically contingent converges with Mann's representation of the track-laying, transformative effects of the ideology surging at particular historical conjunctures, and then losing its thrust, or settling down, as it were, into social life. "The theories of culture," he states, "fail to appreciate temporal variation, that the role of culture may be quite different [dormant or active, and even at times transformative] in particular concrete historical settings" (Goldstone 1991: 457). But while culture is accorded a transformative, if momentary, potency, the manner in which these cultural patterns and ideologies "dominate" is not elaborated.

### *Structuralist*-culturalist perspective

Next to be considered is a group of approaches that we have located closer to the center of both axes in figure 3.1 in appendix 3.2: on the horizontal one, covering the area from the left side toward the middle of the structuralist-culturalist continuum, and on the vertical one around its center point, representing "action/social practice," that links structural and (inter)subjective understandings of culture. It may be jointly called a *social-structuralist*-culturalist perspective, with the emphasis on the first part of a diptych to indicate the distribution of explanatory weight, so to speak. One significant strand in this group emerged from a dissatisfaction with the reductionist, "unmediated" macro-structural model of the social world, combined with the influence of a "populist" social history popular since the 1970s and focused on the experiences of the lower classes, inspired by so-called cultural Marxism, especially the works of British historian E. P. Thompson and Raymond Williams. In other instances, a particular theoretical approach was taken as an attempt to redress the perceived imbalance in the conventional treatment of the subject that interested the author.

In this group of approaches, the analytic attention, and the location of immediate causality, so to speak, shift to the mezzo and micro-levels of social life. Macroscopic structures are present, and their significant impact acknowledged and elaborated, but rather than being the main focus of analysis, and the "cause" of the phenomena studied, they are treated as the background environment, or the constraining-and-enabling context. With this movement toward the micro-level, there also appear concrete historical actors (collective rather than individual) instead of the generic "state officials," "clergy," "peasantry," etc.

"Culture" is understood as a structure of symbolic forms, codes and schemas, or ideological systems, but also – the more so the more visible on the scene are human actors, besides social institutions – as shared meanings, identities, and purposes. It is also conceived of more dynamically, as "becoming" – whether in a longer or shorter period of time – through social practice in the social-institutional context (formal organizations or local communities). Construed in this way, culture also becomes more flexible and underdetermined. In most studies in this group, however, analytical attention focuses on the social mediators between society and culture, i.e., on the operation of more proximate social environments and the social practices constituting them, rather than on the cultural contents thereof and their effects on social surroundings. Consequently, neither cultural mediation of power nor culture's status as the episteme are generally of central analytical interest. At the same time, such social-contextual embedding of culture requires that its operation be conceptualized as historical, i.e., time-specific and place-specific, especially when the explanatory emphasis is placed on the social practice of historical actors.

As illustrations of this general perspective we selected a few different studies of collective action, namely Charles Tilly's *From Mobilization to Revolution* (1978), and *The Contentious French* (1986); Ronald Aminzade's *Class, Politics, and Early Industrial Capitalism* (1981); and Craig Calhoun's *The Question of Class Struggle* (1982).

Besides investigations of modern state formation and social revolution, the study of collective action of a contentious nature as pursued by the laboring classes, especially under modern capitalism in both its early and mature phases, has been the most popular research pursuit among US historical sociologists during the late 1970s and early to mid 1980s. Originated by Charles Tilly, the subject of collective action, and particularly the specific way of studying it by focusing on social-organizational resources rather than on states of mind and motivations, attracted a number of younger scholars, Tilly's own disciples as well as others. We will briefly consider three studies from this school, including the maestro's own work.

We labelled Tilly's approach as "plenty of culture without attention to it." His work on collective action has been perceived among historical sociologists as decidedly social-structuralist. The following evaluation in Craig Calhoun's recent paper on the origins and development of historical sociology in the US, was shared by practically everybody we talked to while preparing this essay: "In the work of Tilly, for example, collective action is the product of interests [. . .] and structure, but seldom of culture" (Calhoun 1993a).

In conversation, however, Tilly forcefully rejected our suggestion that there has been "no culture in his work on social protest." There has always been culture in this work, he insisted. Given his high stature in historical sociology, and his reputation of an a- (rather than anti-) culturalist, it may be of interest to quote here (more accurately, reproduce from our notes) some central statements relevant to the issue that he made during this conversation. Namely, Tilly understands culture as "shared understandings and their objectifications, such as representations and institutions" that are "embedded in social action, part of the means people employ"; for instance, "repertoires of contention are deeply cultural, derived from the past collective representations and schemas of actions." And to our question about a general significance of culture in social life, Tilly replied thus: "culture is crucial in two ways: as the accumulated historical experience [on which] build collective identities, and shared ways of confronting problems; [and] all social action is cultural in a sense that it is founded on schemas and worldviews, as action orientations."

We went back to Tilly's books about popular contention: unlike those on state-formation noted earlier in this chapter, they are full of people who share beliefs, worry, compose dreamy poems, celebrate traditions, have grievances, meet and talk in private as well as public places, decide to go out and protest – all these things are there. Each chapter, indeed, is "full of culture," but it is merely reported, and left uninterpreted and untheorized. Or, rather, culture is tacitly construed theoretically by the author as so deeply embedded in social practice, so inherent in it, that the analysis of culture is subsumed under, or taken over by the analysis of social action. It is the latter that absorbs Tilly the most, and it is – he explicitly states – mobilized primarily by interests and organizational resources. Our category "plenty of culture without attention to it," custom-made for Charles Tilly, is a compromise between what we have read and heard from the author (but more of Tilly is still to come).

In comparison, more cultural analysis – if mainly to argue culture's social embeddedness and its expression through collective action – appears in two other studies on popular contention. The emergence and evolution of working-class oppositional culture in mid nineteenth-century Toulouse in the context of macroscopic structural transformations, and specifically the growth of economic capitalism and the accompanying political developments, is the "object of analysis" (*explanandum* rather than *explanans*) of Aminzade's (1981) study. But the main theoretical argument guiding this investigation is the social origins of cultural developments. In a specific historical application, i.e., in early industrial capitalism in mid nineteenth-century France, it had been "changes which took place in working-class *associational forms, informal centers of sociability, collective actions, and political ideologies* [that] amounted to the creation of a new counter-hegemonic working-class culture [i.e., meanings, values, and identities]" (Aminzade 1981: 69, author's italics).

A similar approach to culture is found in Craig Calhoun's (1982) investigation of the radicalization of the English working class between Jacobinism and Chartism (1790s–1840s). The study is intended as a theoretical polemic with what the author perceives to be an extravagant "culturalism" of E. P. Thompson's (1967) classic reinterpretation of English workers' history in the eighteenth and nineteenth centuries, *The Making of the English Working Class*. " 'Consciousness,' Calhoun states critically, tends to great generality in Thompson, becoming nearly the equivalent of 'culture'" (Calhoun 1982: 32). Calhoun acknowledges the importance of English workers' popular culture in shaping their political attitudes and activities, and devotes a chapter to demonstrate how workers' traditional (preindustrial) values and identities served as a symbolic framework for their revolutionary struggles. The bulk of historical analysis, however, and, more importantly here, the main theoretical arguments are about the social foundations of collective action originating and played out in face-to-face interactions and personal relationships in workers' local communities – the condition he claims (and we disagree) that E. P. Thompson failed to incorporate into his cultural-Marxist interpretation of working-class history.

A few more studies from different fields of historical-sociological research are presented below as illustrations of other variants of a general social-structuralist-culturalist approach outlined above.

Previously Tilly's companion in a macro-social-structuralist approach that recognizes a certain lesser lower-level influence of culture on the course of social change, but is silent on this subject in historical analysis, Theda Skocpol accords a considerably greater potency and analytical attention to cultural phenomena (even though they remain dependent on the structural-institutional circumstances) in her book, *Protecting Soldiers and Mothers* (Skocpol 1992). Specifically "cultural" in this case are group identities and orientations, and the shared purposes of the actors, viz., middle-class American women as organized political activists who promoted special-purpose social policies between the 1870s and the 1920s.

In Skocpol's approach, effectiveness, or direct power, i.e., the capacity of women political activists to realize desired goals, is construed as contingent on the enabling historical conjuncture or "fit" between macroscopic social-structural conditions and the institutional setting. While the macro-structural conditions and the institutional context are accorded primacy (causality, if you wish) in creating the facilitating environment, it is through social practice in this environment of the actors sharing identity (gender), purposes (family, women, and child welfare), and resources (organized networks) that change (the implementation of social policies) occurs. While gender identities and relationships are unlikely to explain much by themselves, no matter how theorized, Skocpol nevertheless insists that "any approach to explaining the history of US social provision will certainly have to bring gender – as identity, agency, and relationships – fully into the analysis" (Skocpol 1992: 38).

While Skocpol's study is a theoretically grounded interpretation of a particular historical development, Robert Wuthnow's (1989) magisterial *Communities of Discourse* has a more explicit theoretical ambition. Namely, the construction of a long-term developmental model of the impact of macroscopic structural transformation, specifically the growth of European capitalism since the sixteenth century, and the accompanying development of political institutions, on the shaping of three ideologies central to "formal thinking about ourselves" in modern (western) society: the Reformation, the Enlightenment, and socialism.

Wuthnow rejects concepts of culture that represent it in subjective terms, i.e., distinguished from behavior and focused on beliefs, meanings, outlooks, and motivations, because they have no "readily available empirical referents," and are therefore "nearly impossible to reconstruct" (Wuthnow 1989: 528). Instead, he views culture as "a form of behavior itself and as the tangible results of that behavior" (p. 15). Since one of the major criticisms raised by reviewers of Wuthnow's study was the elimination of meanings from his concept of culture, we asked him whether indeed he thought meanings were unimportant. Of course they are important, he replied, but "meanings are embedded in cultural systems . . . so we have to look at the cultural field [to find them] rather than digging in individual consciousnesses" (citation from our notes). We went back to the book. Indeed, ideologies (a cultural field of concern) are referred to as "categories in which formal *thinking about ourselves*" takes place (p. 22, our italics). But this complete embedding of meanings in cultural structures is also responsible, we believe, for the fact that while Wuthnow's theoretical model, focused on cultural production, requires, as he emphasizes, producers engaged in action sequences, there is actually little human activity in his historical analysis. Wuthnow's study shares with Skocpol's book a theoretical and analytic concern with the significance of historical conjunctures between environmental (i.e., macro-structural) contexts, institutional settings, and "action sequences" (i.e., social practice), in bringing about social (political or cultural) change. In the subject matter Wuthnow investigates, the "fit" – he uses the same term – concerns the well-balanced articulation of an ideology and its social context in a particular historical time and place: if the articulation is not close enough or excessively so, an ideology is not likely to find wide and lasting social acceptance. Once it does, however, it disengages itself from, or, better, transcends its specific environment of origin. In comparison, Skocpol's theoretical model does not allow for an autonomous operation of culture at any "stage" of the historical process.[7]

Smaller in scope than Wuthnow's study, but sharing with it a conceptualization of culture as "becoming" in the articulation with its historical social-institutional context, is David Zaret's (1985) analysis of the ideological developments in Puritanism in pre-Revolutionary England, *The Heavenly Contract*. Zaret's purpose is to bridge two separate fields of inquiry, namely religious history focused on hermeneutic analysis of the evolution of scriptural texts and their interpretations, and social history interested in lay involvement in religious changes, by showing that "doctrinal developments of interest to specialists in religious history cannot be understood apart from organizational developments associated with new forms of intellectual independence and initiative in lay religious life" (p. 3). Accordingly, his concept of culture – here, a religious doctrine – combines intersubjective and structural understandings, embedding both in the social setting. Although

Zaret's historical analysis deals for the most part with the shaping influence of the institutional environment and social practices (lay activities) on Puritan religion rather than reciprocal effects thereof, he acknowledges "immanent tendencies" of systems of ideas that cannot be reduced to social (or economic) forms, and that exert a "relatively autonomous" influence on other spheres of social life.

## Society and culture as inseparable spheres
## (the center of the structuralist-culturalist continuum)

Around the center of the structuralist-culturalist continuum in figure 3.1 in appendix 3.2 we put a position that views society and culture as "inseparable" spheres, in the sense that they are so closely and continuously *inter*linked and *inter*acting that it is not possible to theorize or study historically (empirically) one without the other. These ongoing interactions turn the relationship of society and culture into a process and thus also historicize each of its sides. At the same time, however, each side of the social structure/culture relationship retains, at least potentially, a measure of "its own" variability and relative "dynamic autonomy." In this approach, culture is perceived as an intrinsic aspect of each and every side or "level" of social life (cognitive and emotional individual experience and human action, social relations, institutional structures). As such, it should be accorded "equal treatment": about as much investigative attention as its social-structural correlate. But while it is seen as inherent in human society, culture is not conceptualized or analyzed as the medium of power, although such an understanding of its operation is often, so to say, "clearly implicit" in concrete historical sociological studies displaying this general approach.

To illustrate this position, we selected three studies:

- William Sewell's (1980) *Work and Revolution in France: the language of labor from the old regime to 1848.*
- Willfried Spohn's (forthcoming) *Religion and Working-class Formation in Germany, 1840–1914* (see also Spohn 1991).
- Wendy Griswold's (1986) *Renaissance Revivals: city comedy and revenge tragedy in the London theatre 1576–1980.*

We will look first at the latter work, which we located at the center of the structuralist-culturalist continuum in figure 3.1, because the interactive model it proposes is theoretically most explicit, and also because it is applied most systematically, chapter by chapter, in actual historical analysis.

Griswold's (1986) book investigates the reconstructions of the meaning of Renaissance drama in the English theater over the period of four centuries. The analysis proceeds on three basic, and equivalent, premises. One of them demands a theoretical recognition of and analytical attention to the temporal dimension of cultural influences on both current practices and the results thereof. Just as a study of "the history of [theatrical] revivals helps us to understand the ongoing, mutually influential relationship between a society and its cultural products [theatrical plays] . . . the future meanings of [contemporary plays]," states Griswold, must be seen as "a function of both [past] cultural building material and the social contexts in which the constructions take place" (p. 2). Another, methodological, premise is what Griswold calls "the cultural diamond." At its apex there is a social context (e.g., Elizabethan England), at the base there is a cultural object or product (e.g., the genre city comedy); the left point of the diamond-shaped diagram stands for creators (artists; theater personnel), while the right point represents the recipients (the audience, or all those influenced by the cultural product, here a theatrical play). Griswold contends that "cultural analysis demands the investigation of the four points and six connecting lines of this diamond; studies that neglect some points or connections are incomplete" (pp. 7–8); her own study, we should add, in fact fulfills this requirement. The third and last fundamental premise informing the study assumes cultural practices and their products (here theatrical revivals of Elizabethan plays) to be invested with meanings, and demands that the latter's constructions, social receptions, and transformations over time be investigated as part and parcel of the cultural analysis outlined above.

The other two studies considered here as an illustration are thematically similar, as both investigate historical processes of working-class formation (although the respective locations and time periods are different); both authors, too, identify as their intellectual pedigree the "new" social history of the 1960s or "history from below," and cultural Marxism.[8] Instead of the diamond-shaped analytical model proposed by Griswold, Sewell and Spohn both use, as more fitting for the subject matter of their investigation, a collapsed version of it, namely, a triangular frame. It has the social/institutional context at one point (say, the top one), at another one (make it on the left side), social actors/workers (collapsed creators and audience or "those affected by a meaningful cultural object"), and at the third point (on the right side) there are symbolic meanings: workers' "language," i.e., the idiom and rituals, of individual-cum-collective rights in Sewell's study, and, in Spohn's, workers' religious beliefs, rituals, and identities. The studies investigate the changing configurations among three points of "the sociocultural triangle," and both, like Griswold's, demonstrate at the same time how past meanings and identities (here: pre-industrial "corporate" discourse in France, and religious worldviews in Germany) interact with social contexts in producing new, transformed symbolic codes and collective consciousness. Although all three studies consistently apply the interactive analytical model, the major difference between Sewell's and Spohn's investigations on the one hand, and Griswold's on the other that seems of relevance here (and probably reflecting for the most part quite different subjects of analysis) is that while in the former two cases the authors are most interested in the social agents as producers and implementers-into-action of these cultural meanings and identities, Griswold's attention focuses primarily on cultural objects (meaningful theater plays).

## Structuralist-*culturalist* perspectives

We now move to the other side of the center of the horizontal axis in our chart, shown in figure 3.1, viz., the area stretching in the direction of the culturalist end of the continuum. As in the previously discussed cases, on the "cultural" side, too, polemical studies are quite frequent – this time against what their authors perceive as the excessively social-structural emphasis of the dominant perspective in the "new" historical sociology (the latter emerged in protest against the overly culturalist approach prevailing in the 1950s and 1960s). But we have not identified in this group any representatives of an unqualified cultural determinism, in any case not a consistently defended one (such as, for example, Wallerstein's structuralism at the opposite extreme). While strong statements regarding *the* causality of culture in the social world can occasionally be found in particular studies, the more common tone of these analyses is corrective rather than combative.

What makes these approaches "culturalist" – more accurately, what made us decide to locate them in this category – is not primarily the placement of cultural phenomena at the center of analytical attention. Rather, first, it has been the explicit and consistent acknowledgment of culture as a continuously active and potent presence in social life, and, consequently, as an essential dimension of any sociological analysis. It should be noted, however, that while it is the main object of investigation, culture – whether understood as intersubjective meanings and identities, or as transpersonal structures of symbolic codes – is not generally conceptualized as the explanatory principle (although in some studies such understanding seems to be implied) and therefore its indirect power is not considered. In all the above respects, positions classified as "culturalist" do not differ significantly from those at the center of the continuum just presented. Where they do differ, and this is our second and distinctive reason for labeling them as "culturalist," is in the treatment of the social-structural contexts and processes.

A shared characteristic of approaches grouped in this category is the relatively limited influence, and, consequently, analytic attention, accorded social-structural factors: the latter are by and large considered mainly in the context of the origins of the investigated cultural phenomena and recede into the background or, as it were, into latency – "ontological" and analytical – once the cultural phenomena gain autonomy and causal prowess. To stress the shift in interpretative emphasis in comparison with approaches left-of-the-center on the continuum, we will call this group of positions social-structuralist-*culturalist*. (The center approach represented by the Griswold/Sewell/Spohn studies is then tagged *social-structuralist-culturalist.*)

Finally, the last characteristic shared by approaches grouped under this general label is a specific understanding of the historicism, or mutability of culture. While cultural change generated by refigurations in the social-structural "contexts of origin" is acknowledged, processes of reciprocal influences between cultural phenomena themselves, such as, for example, popular political culture and ideology, or ideology and national identity are of greater interest and analytically more elaborated.

As it happens, most studies in this group investigate the origins and development of nationalism and/or citizenship, and, in this context, nation and state building. We will begin with a study unrelated to this subject, which illustrates the use of a "culturalist" approach as outlined above, and will then discuss four historical-sociological studies of nationalism and related matters.

We begin with Viviana Zelizer's (1979, 1985, 1993, 1994) investigations of the ways in which culture informs different areas of economic life. Besides a broad subject matter, all Zelizer's studies express her criticism of narrow rational-choice models of economic behavior, and equally limited "economistic" conceptualizations of money and markets, used by social scientists that Zelizer views as fundamentally "unsociological." Her study of the changing social value of children in the United States over the last century, *Pricing the Priceless Child* (1985), as well as a more recent investigation of the transformation of the meanings and social handling of money in the United States between the 1870s and the 1930s, *The Social Meaning of Money* (1994), are undertaken as correctives to such reductionist, acultural conceptualizations of economic institutions and activities. Both studies are introduced as taking a resolutely culturalist position: the former, in a strong formulation, is announced as focusing on the "independent effects of cultural factors" on the market values of children (Zelizer 1985: 11); while the latter, in a more interactive mode presents an alternative model of money "as continually shaped and reshaped by different networks of social relations and varying systems of meanings" (Zelizer 1994). The actual cultural analyses of these historical transformations are placed within the respective broader social-structural "contexts of origin" (increasing societal differentiation in the first case, and a rapid growth of consumer economy in the second), but without the elaboration of specific links between the former and the investigated cultural phenomena.[9]

Two other illustrations of a culturalist approach as outlined above are, each in its genre, fundamentally a polemic with one of the master-models in the "new" historical sociology, namely that of nationalism and the formation of the modern western nation-state. The first case is represented by studies by Anthony Smith (1986, 1987, 1991), each of which is a somewhat differently elaborated argument against positing the state, and specifically state-making, "behind," so to speak, nation-building in the West, as the latter's long-term complex "cause." Smith formulates his position on this matter in two variants: one more, and the other less strongly culturalist, i.e., according phenomena from the cultural sphere – in this case, collective identities and shared "imagined communities" – more, or less, autonomously transformative potency. In a stronger formulation, rather than the outcome of state-building as proposed by social-structuralist interpretations (e.g., Tilly – see above), the development of ethnics-into-nations is seen as the foundation of effective statehood. In a weaker version, Smith appears to emphasize the process of the historical interplay between state-making and nation-building,[10] and points to a "third unit," as he calls it, namely, local community and solidarity, as the mediator between the former two. In both renditions, the inherent historicism of ethnic and national identities and shared symbolic meanings derives from their continuous reinvention and reinstitution.

The historical origins of nationalism in Europe and their relation to nation and state building are also the subject of Liah Greenfeld's (1992) comparative study of the above in England, France, Germany, Russia, and the United States. This project, too, has a polemical edge (sharper than Smith's, for that matter), similarly turned against interpretations making nationalism a byproduct of the modern nation-state rather than its source. Greenfeld opens her argument with the thesis that the "national idea" originating in early modern England and then spreading throughout the western world, has been essential in the emergence of nationalism(s) (understood inclusively as national identities and consciousness, and national collectivities).

Like Smith, Greenfeld is apparently hesitant about presenting a strong culturalist thesis. In her theoretical statement, she makes nationalism not only chronologically prior to state formation as well as other components of societal modernization, but also constitutive of these developments.[11] Her historical analysis of particular cases, however, is conducted within a more complex, multi-factorial frame, considering different configurations of social, political, and cultural elements that vary across five societies, and whose causal potency shifts over time. Nationalism, we are told in a summary of Greenfeld's extensive investigation in the conclusion of her study, "*both acknowledged and accomplished* the grand social transformation from the old order to modernity" (Greenfeld 1992: 487, our italics).

Less directly inspired by a disagreement with conventional

interpretations in the "new" historical sociology of nationhood, popular national cultures, and nation-state formation are other studies by Brubaker (1992) and Schwartz (1987).

Using comparative-historical analysis, Brubaker examines different forms of civic self-definition and patterns of civic incorporation, as well as differential political consequences thereof in two nation-states in Europe. "Tracing the genesis and development of the institution of citizenship in France and Germany," Brubaker's study shows "how differing definitions of citizenship have been shaped and sustained by distinctive and deeply-rooted understandings of nationhood" (Brubaker 1992: x–xi).[12] While he rejects an "instrumentalist" (i.e., according causal primacy to state or class interests) account of citizenship policies and practices, Brubaker does not subscribe to a purely culturalist explanatory perspective either. Rather, he shows "how particular cultural idioms – ways of thinking and talking about nationhood that have been state-centered and assimilationist in France, and more ethnocultural and differentialist in Germany – were reinforced and activated in specific historical and institutional settings; and how, once reinforced and activated, these cultural idioms framed and shaped judgements of what was politically imperative, and what was in the interest of the state" (Brubaker 1992: 16). Like Greenfeld's "nationalism" emerging in structural contradictions of the early modern estate societies, Brubaker's national idioms are perceived as "ultimately rooted" in historical and institutional settings (p. 16). Rather than acting as the originating force or the "first phase" of social development, however, the "ultimate" influence of the social-structural contexts on cultural formations is conceptualized by Brubaker in a dynamic way as an ongoing process, moving along with time (although, admittedly, the specific *hows* of this impact are not entirely clear to us).

As the last illustration of a culturalist approach as outlined earlier, we chose Barry Schwartz's historical-sociological study of the making of George Washington into an American national hero. Schwartz investigates the interplay – or, as he calls it, a process of "mutual reinforcement" – between the constitutive themes in the popular political culture, specifically "a way a society looked upon power," and the evolving civic and national consciousness of Colonial Americans, symbolized by "the heroization" of George Washington as the embodiment of the fundamental republican virtues. The focus of analysis throughout remains on *culture* which Schwartz considers, so to speak, as "autonomously active": in this case, these are intersubjectively shared ideas, meanings, and representations concerning American national character that are being bestowed upon Washington. "Culture contributes to its own change, or stability," Schwartz believes, although it occurs through the *mediation* of social institutions. And in fact, the study recognizes, although does not elaborate analytically, the influence of the social context such as the country's residential patterns, and political institutions upholding jointly a "dispersed" society, as well as ideological factors (English political thought and religious worldviews) as contributing to the formation of a political culture that would not accept as a national leader anyone visibly "authoritarian, power-hungry, or generally *out*standing among fellow citizens" (quotes from interview notes.)

## Society and Culture as Reciprocal Constructions

We move now to the second part of this presentation, i.e., onto the "elevated plane" in our chart in figure 3.1, where we have located approaches that fuse "culture" and "society," or even discard these two master concepts altogether, and, as a consequence, also abandon conventional explanatory discourse in terms of the relative autonomy and ultimate causality accorded particular levels of social life.

Thinking out this section was more difficult than the sections presented earlier: first, because about half of the approaches located in this group are just emerging, at least in the United States, as their basic ideas are becoming more widely known through translations into English of European works, specifically, from French of Pierre Bourdieu and his followers, and from German and Dutch of Norbert Elias and his school; and second, because the intellectual production of these scholars and of some others whom we have decided to place on the same plane in our chart in figure 3.1, (e.g., E. P. Thompson) has been subject to quite different, often sharply contradictory interpretations (much more so than any of the works cited in the previous section of this chapter).

In trying to clarify the theoretical positions of certain scholars whose works have been subject to quite different interpretations, we used substitute "informants" for scholars who were unreachable in the United States. That is, we turned for information (either verbal or written) to their disciples or expert intellectual followers, specifically: about E. P. Thompson to Willfried Spohn, about Bourdieu to Loïc Wacquant (1993 and personal conversations), and about Elias to Stephen Mennell (1989). From these and other interpretations, we chose those that could be fitted into a common conceptual framework that we eventually devised. Our joining of these theoretically polymorphous works in one category means that their approaches *can be* interpreted in a particular way, but by no means that they *must* be so represented.

Below are the results of our exegetic efforts. We first outline what we perceive as common theoretical features of a general approach on the plane, then point out some differences within this common perspective, and, finally, illustrate the above with some concrete historical-sociological studies.

As we see it, the common characteristics of the approach postulating the conceptualization of culture and society as "the double structure," i.e., each structured by and structuring the other, are the following (in order of importance):

- While this approach acknowledges the macroscopic, long-term, social-structural environment as an element of the context of origin or background of smaller-scale, shorter-term social life, with one exception (see below), it is the latter that is theoretically conceptualized in terms of "the double structure" and historically investigated as such.
- Social life, defined as mezzo/micro fields or (Eliasian) "figurations" of social relations both institutional and interpersonal, is conceptualized as a continuous and open-ended process.
- Culture, i.e., symbolic codes, meanings, and identities, is conceptualized as pervading all of social life, and the entire phenomenon as a ceaseless activity of shaping-and-reshaping through everyday social practices and thus conventional notions of "autonomy" and "causality" are inapplicable in social-cultural analysis.
- Consequently, this approach does not, and cannot, constitute a conventional, even fragmentary, theory in terms of a coherent system of causal statements linking particular levels or aspects of social life, but, rather, to use E. P. Thompson's (1978) phrase, it exemplifies "an empirical idiom of discourse".
- In this framework, the social ubiquity of culture "empowers" it in the indirect sense (or, conversely, power is construed as culture-mediated), through its capacity to define and evaluate experience, and to guide social action (both in the hegemonic and anti-hegemonic positions) in social-institutional and interpersonal relations. Investigation of the

process and social implications of the execution of culture's indirect power is considered an inherent part of structuration analysis, and an important, even central, task of any kind of sociological work.

The characteristics listed above are more or less common to the new cultural perspective in sociology at large, and not just to to its adherents among historical sociologists. What distinguishes the latter is not merely explicit acknowledgment of the historicity of the structuration process – namely, its embeddedness in time and space – but taking this attribute "seriously" by analyzing the implications of time and place contingency for different outcomes of this reciprocal construction. Within this shared perspective, there are of course differences. We note here only one, of direct relevance to the subject matter of this chapter, that also serves to organize studies used as the illustrations in two groups.

This differentiating feature concerns the conceptualization of agency, that is, human actors, in sociocultural life: whether as individuals from Latin "indivisible," and posited as distinct entities, or, rather, as Eliasian *homines aperti* ("open people"), inherently interdependent, social-relational beings. Related to this conceptualization of agency is the understanding of culture (since it is fused into society and infused by it at the same time, we should perhaps use quotation marks) as intersubjective meanings and identities, and as patterns of symbolic codes and discourses. Different scholars and works take positions that either concentrate the analysis primarily on socially embedded actors-individuals constructing their lives and thus social environment through the mediation of shared cultural meanings bestowed upon experience, or, rather, focus the analysis primarily on the production and reproduction of sociocultural structures that are embodied in and acted out by independent people. (We have located the former in the upper part, and the latter in the lower part of the elevated plane in figure 3.1.[13]) Below are some illustrations of these different approaches.

### Society and culture: the perspective of social actors

We begin in the upper part of the elevated plane, where (i) the mutual constitution, or the double-structure, of culture and society is construed as "becoming" through meaningful activities of social actors who in turn "make" their own lives through these meaningful activities; and (ii) the central task of sociological analysis is considered to be the interpretation of this actions-cum-meanings social process in its historical context. We placed in this group E. P. Thompson's (1967) classic *The Making of the English Working Class* (see also Thompson 1991); Ewa Morawska's (1985) *For Bread With Butter* and her (1994) sequel to this study, *Insecure Prosperity: Jews in small-town industrial America, 1880–1940* (see Morawska (1991) for a fragment of this book); and Jean and John Comaroff's (1991) *Of Revelation and Revolution.* A social historian, a historical sociologist, and a pair of historical anthropologists, each from a different intellectual lineage, share a similar theoretical perspective on the culture-agency-society package.[14]

E. P. Thompson's (1967) famous study of the formation of the English working class between 1792 and 1832 has been interpreted as both much too "cultural" (by fellow Marxists) and not "cultural" enough (by some cultural anthropologists); and most recently, as epistemologically faulty, because it imposes an ideological meta-narrative of "class" on workers' own cultural experiential narratives (Somers 1992a). We placed *The Making of the English Working Class* on the plane (see figure 3.1) because of, first, its explicit rejection of the mechanistic base/superstructure model; second, the equally explicit emphasis on social situations as at once shaping and being shaped by collective human experience invested with symbolic meanings that in turn change together with this experience itself; and, third and closely related to the above, the "empowerment" of culture – anti-hegemonic, in the case of English workers – that is, according shared values, traditions, and rituals the capacity to define and provide directions for actors' social experience.

These basic tenets of Thompson's approach are well summarized by himself. The idea of the reciprocity between structure and agency is captured in his view of class as a "historical category, describing people in relationship over time" in an active process of making. His book, as Thompson explains,

> "has a clumsy title, but it is one which meets its purpose: 'Making', because it is a study in an active process, which owes as much to agency as to conditioning. The working class did not rise like the sun at an appointed time. It was present at its own making." And again, "Class happens when some men, as a result of common experiences (inherited or shared), feel and articulate the identity of their interests as between

themselves, and as against other men whose interests are different from (and usually opposed to) theirs [. . .] Class-consciousness is the way in which these experiences are handled in cultural terms: embodied in traditions, value-systems, and institutional form." (Thompson 1967: 9f.)

Morawska's intellectual formation has been shaped in a large part by Florian Znaniecki's (1919, 1934, 1969, 1987) philosophy and social theory of culture. Another later influence on Morawska, after she came to the United States in 1980 and began working on immigrant histories, was the structuration theory of Anthony Giddens (1976, 1984; see also a recent refinement by Sewell 1992), cultural anthropology of ("middle phase") Clifford Geertz (1968, 1973), the cultural Marxism of Raymond Williams (1958, 1980) and E. P. Thompson and, in the last few years, the ("current phase") writings of Pierre Bourdieu (1992a, b).[15] The latter five are well known and do not need discussion here, but Znaniecki's theory of culture remains largely unfamiliar to American sociologists (although it was much more central in his scholarly work over a lifetime than his collaboration with W. I. Thomas on *The Polish Peasant in Europe and America* – Thomas and Znaniecki 1918–20). We briefly summarize Znaniecki's major points that correspond to characteristics outlined above as constitutive of a general approach "on the plane," and, specifically, those that inform Morawska's studies presented here.[16]

Znaniecki views the social world as "penetrated with culture throughout," as are its basic units, social actions. While social actions are founded on actors' definitions and evaluations of the situations they encounter, these meanings bestowed upon experience are themselves products of (earlier) social actions. However, this reciprocity does not, as Znaniecki strongly emphasized, entail mechanical reproduction: social actors are inherently creative, and originate (rather than merely respond to) social situations by undertaking new or modified actions founded on new or modified meanings. The entire social world has a Heraclitean nature: it is, as Znaniecki never tired of repeating, always and everywhere "pulsating with change," and therefore fundamentally historical. The task of a sociologist is to grasp and explain this process, but to do it with the famous "humanistic coefficient," i.e., by reconstructing chains of actions-meanings as they are understood and represented by their carriers, that is, social actors, located in time and place.

Last but not least, using the "humanistic coefficient" requires an inductive (rather than deductive) way of accumulating knowledge about the social world, while the continuous shifts in the latter preclude formulations of general sociological laws.

Morawska's two studies of the adaptation of East European immigrants and their children (Slavs first, then Jews) in a small town in Western Pennsylvania cover the period of mass migration at the turn of the century until World War II. Both studies investigate these peoples' efforts toward carving out for themselves, in the constraining socioeconomic and political context of a WASP-dominated company town, their own ethnic-communal space within which they strove to achieve a "good life" as defined by their changing group values and preferences. Considering the immigrants' subordinate (Slavs) or "insecurely marginal" (Jews) position vis-à-vis the dominant local society, their active use of group resources and cultural schemas toward the realization of preferred goals, can be viewed as instances of indirect anti-hegemonic power (although neither study explicitly refers to this concept). The basic argument is similar in both studies: were those immigrants in that place and time, to have adopted directly, without adjustment to their own situation (so-called "ethnicization"[17]), the values and achievement standards of the WASP middle class, they would have perceived themselves as failures. Instead, as they related their stories to the investigator, the lives they had made for themselves within their larger local environment – but also *against* its constraining walls – contained a sense of accomplishment.

The two studies differ in several aspects, mainly because the people are different, as are their experiences. Apart from this obvious distinction, however, while they are both conceptualized with the humanistic coefficient and in the structuration framework, the later "Jewish" study devotes considerably more space to actual cultural analysis. The latter occurred in part as a reflection of renewed interest in matters of culture evident in academic journals, at professional meetings, and in personal conversations among both sociologists and historians, but also, in part, because the author's own inner self resonated well during the fieldwork with nuances of meanings, contradictory cultural schemas, unresolved moral dilemmas, and other matters discussed with her respondents.[18]

Agency is also a central theme as the "mover" in social processes in the Comaroffs' (1991) study of the influence of early Christian missionaries, "footsoldiers of British colonialism," on the native culture of the Tswana people in southern Africa over the time span of a century, between 1820 and 1920. As the authors succinctly put it in their statement of a theoretical framework for their study, it is an investigation "of the colonization of consciousness and the consciousness of colonization in South Africa" (Comaroff and Comaroff 1991: xi). The main questions they are seeking to answer are: "How, precisely, is consciousness made and remade? And how is it mediated by such distinctions as class, gender, and ethnicity? How do some meanings and actions, old and new alike, become conventional . . . while others become objects of contest and resistance?" (pp. xi–xii).

In comparison with the previous studies in this group, the Comaroffs pay more explicit theoretical attention to the issue of power, which they define as central in their subject matter, and which they analyze both as hegemonic (the colonizers) as well as anti-hegemonic (the colonized). Theirs, state the authors, is the historical anthropology of ". . . culture and power . . . concerned at once with the colonizer *and* the colonized, with structure *and* agency" (p. 11, authors' italics).

In the middle-to-lower area of the elevated plane we located approaches focusing the analysis – and the task of sociology in general – on processes of production-and-reproduction of socio-cultural structures that are embodied in and acted out by inter-dependent people. We placed in this area historical sociologies influenced by the works of Elias and Bourdieu. These two schools, if they can be so called, resemble, as Loïc Wacquant aptly put it, orbiting spheres, now together, now separate; we placed them next to each other, but comment on them separately.[19] From Bourdieu's work we considered a recent study especially fitting the subject matter of this chapter, namely a historical-sociological investigation of the "making" of Flaubert in the French artistic field during the third quarter of the nineteenth century, *Les règles de l'art* Bourdieu (1992a; see also 1988a).[20] From a list of Bourdieu's followers pursuing historical-sociological research, we selected a study of Christophe Charle's (1990), *Naissance des "intellectuels," 1880–1900,* because it deals with matters similar to those in the Flaubert book, and also because it represents an example of a study that shows the influence of Bourdieu in a relatively "pure" manner, so that we can comment on the two jointly. We have to assume that readers are familiar with Bourdieu's basic concepts and propositions regarding the social world and its operation.[21] Below we note merely what is directly relevant to the present discussion, namely the assessment of the capacity of human actors conceptualized as social-relational beings in Bourdieu's model, and, more generally, the question of the latter's sociocultural-structural determinism.

Bourdieu's work, we believe, reflects considerable ambivalence regarding the above matters, so that the exact location of his position in the lower part of the "elevated plane" is impossible: it stretches, rather, between the conceptualizations of personality (subsumed under *habitus*) as more (bottom end) and less (middle) socioculturally determined.[22] (Elias is also ambivalent in this regard, but, as will be seen shortly, on different grounds.)

Bourdieu has made repeated, programmatic statements about the "intrinsically double" nature of social reality, whereby the sociocultural environment at once and inseparably shapes and is shaped by human experience. In other words, the participating actors can and have been interpreted (e.g., by Charle in *Naissance des "intellectuels"*) in the classical Durkheimian mode to the effect that actors – concretely, their habits, tastes, and goal-orientations – are viewed as embodiments of the surrounding social and cultural structures. Construed in this way, human minds and activities are thus wholly determined by social forces along with the cultural systems of their time and place. Bourdieu's definition of the *habitus* – the one most commonly cited, anyway – explicitly posits this kind of reproductive relationship: "As an acquired system of generative schemes objectively adjusted to particular conditions in which it is constituted, the *habitus* engenders all the thoughts, all the perceptions, and all the actions consistent with those conditions and no others" (Bourdieu 1977: 95; but see note 22 to this chapter). An image of human actors as fully represented by social structures and cultural codes particular to their historical situation is also conveyed by the language of Bourdieu's discourse, wherein the sociology of *culture* becomes a *political economy* of symbolic power (by constituting and reproducing the structures of domination in society), and the mediators between economic structures and cultural forms are *fields*, that is, social relations, of *[symbolic] production*.

There also exists, however, in Bourdieu's work another, less deterministic interpretation of the *habitus* (agency, human experience), whereby he conceives of its guiding influence on social practice not by way of mechanical reproduction, but, rather, as generative within definite constraints; in other words, *habitus* is accorded a limited ("relative") autonomy in shaping practices. This is an approach that we found prevailing in Bourdieu's recently published study of the genesis and impact of Flaubert-as-artist.[23]

In a scheme characteristic of Bourdieu's work, the investigation establishes, first, the changing relation of the literary field to the broader political field during the third quarter of the nineteenth century, and, second, the changing situation within the literary field itself. Within this "moving" context, the sociogenesis of Flaubert's innovative literary activities is analyzed. Bourdieu's historical-sociological investigation does not conform to Frederic Jameson's distinction between "old-fashioned interpretation which still asks the text what it *means*, and the newer kinds of analysis which ... ask how it *works*" (Jameson 1981: 108, author's italics). He does both, or, more precisely, the answer to *how it works* – his main consideration – is assumed to be equivalent with explaining *what it means*. This equivalence does not preclude individual creativity embedded in the opportunity structure of the field: at the foundation of Flaubert's genius (as a precursor of pure aestheticism in literature) was his ability to put himself, by the "exceptionally lucid consciousness" of his social situation, "in the position of pushing to their highest intensity all the questions [then] posed by and in the field" (Bourdieu 1988a: 558–9). In such an interpretation, *habitus* (here Flaubert's artistic talent) does not mechanically reproduce its original conditioning, but, rather, is accorded a transformative capacity, contingent on the social setting (a proposition uncannily resembling Skocpol's notion of a "fit" between social context, political circumstances, and actors' resources as agency-enabling).

And now for the "Eliasians." We considered, besides Elias' (1978–82) *The Civilizing Process*, two studies by his followers: Stephen Mennell's (1985) *All Manners of Food*, and Abram de Swaan's (1990) "Emotions in Their Social Matrix". Each of these studies closely corresponds to one of the major themes in Elias' *magnum opus*: a process of the emergence of more civilized, i.e., constrained and controlled, standards of conduct and everyday habits, investigated in interrelationship with social differentiation and interdependence as they increase over time (Mennell 1985), and, in a similar interaction, a concurrent process of the formation of a "self-steering" personality, i.e., of self-control in people's thinking and feeling (de Swaan 1990).

As with Bourdieu's model, we have to assume that readers are more or less familiar with Elias' main concepts and propositions regarding the workings of human society, and the basic ideas informing what he called an "empirical theory" of the civilizing process. As in the previous case, we note here only some points or problems that are directly relevant to our discussion. Unlike other approaches located on the plane that focus on structuration processes of short(-er) duration in mezzo-to-micro social life, Elias also constructs a grand "empirical theory" linking two long-term developmental models of socio- and psychogenesis: at the macro-level, the growing social-structural differentiation and interdependence of societal parts, and, at the micro-level, culture-mediated increasing self-control of the human actors. This "developmental" sociology, as he calls his approach, is not only "empirical," that is, based on a careful investigation of the minutiae of concrete peoples' mental states and behaviors, but also programmatically historical in the sense that the present is seen as inherently multipolar, and the future as open-ended. The patterns and routes of "development" are explainable only *ex post facto*, by looking backwards from the point of arrival. "Society is a process and it continues to change," writes de Swaan (1990: 5), "[But] these transformations do not have a single cause, nor a single direction; their course cannot be predicted." This ever-changing, processual nature of social life including its human participants as well as the figurations, or interdependencies, they form, is probably the most central premise of Eliasian historical sociology.

Like Bourdieu's, the Eliasian approach has often been identified on similar grounds as "social determinism," namely, because it views the individual as inseparable from, or, as it were, coextensive with, other people and the "figurations", viz., patterns of interrelations, they form, so that nothing can be "inside" that is not "outside." Again, there is support for this interpretation in the work of Elias and his followers. But there are also other statements that make possible a different interpretation. Namely, Elias, de Swaan, and Mennell have each repeatedly emphasized that the Heraclitean nature of social figurations and their participants (human beings are also construed as social processes), and their intertwining in continuous "becoming" precludes any kind of determinism. At the same time, they equally and explicitly reject any "separatist" conceptualizations positing distinct "worlds" (*pace* Popper), such as society and culture, structure and agency, objective and subjective – an approach that also precludes conventional social science discourse in terms of determinism and causality.[24]

Given Elias' and his followers' insistence on the elimination from historical-sociological thinking of the master-concept of the individual, the matter of agency requires further comment. As in Bourdieu's case, we were looking in Elias' pronouncements on this subject for ideas that would allow for a generative contribution in social life of human mind and activities. Elias formulates a quite unconventional argument.

Namely, he views human beings *qua* biological organisms as being equipped with an "instinct of exploration" unique among species:

> The uniqueness of man among other forms of life is shown by the fact that the meaning of the word "nature," when referring to mankind, differs in certain respects from its meanings in other contexts ... By nature – by the hereditary constitution of the human organism – human behavior is directed less by inborn drives and more by impulses shaped by individual experience and learning than is the behaviour of any other living creature. (Elias 1978: 109–11)

Although in the Eliasian approach these individual experiences and learning occur only within and through the social environment, the (underlying) biological nature of human beings contains an impulse for experimentation and innovation that in "games" with fellow species, in powerful figurations, may be effectively applied to transform the existing situations.

Like Bourdieu's concept of the field, Elias' notion of figurations is inextricably bound up with power. This power is of both kinds, direct and indirect (Bourdieu is more concerned with the latter), and it displays itself in all – micro, mezzo, and macro – social settings: e.g., parents versus children; king versus his officials; state versus state. The capacity to impose the terms of discourse by the more powerful might be called "hegemonic" (although this concept is not used). At the same time, however (an insight much less elaborated in Bourdieu's model), those relatively less dependent in the figurations at a time are nevertheless constrained by the same interdependencies they are part of. Therefore, rather than referring to power*ful* and power*less* (another rejected bipolarity), Elias and his followers talk about "power chances" and "power balances," emphasizing the reciprocally tempering and processual character of these relationships.

Before we complete this overview of positions on the elevated plane and move to the conclusion of this chapter, one more historical-sociological study – we situated it somewhere between Bourdieu and Elias – should be noted, namely, Philip Corrigan and Derek Sayer's (1985) *The Great Arch*. We find this book a particularly good illustration, first, of a recent "cultural conversion" observed in historical sociology, leading to the theoretical reformulation of concepts and propositions long regarded as taken for granted, and, consequently, to a redirection of research (we will shortly come back to this development in the conclusion of this chapter). Namely, *The Great Arch* is an innovative attempt[25] to reinterpret the process of state formation – a subject matter by and large "colonized" by historical sociologists of the social-structuralist persuasion (see earlier in this chapter) – in cultural terms, emphasizing, specifically, the role of state activities and rituals in "orchestrating" (not "causing") the constitution and regulation of citizens' social identities.

Second and specifically, both in its theoretical framework and actual historical work, Corrigan and Sayer's (1985) study exemplifies unusually well the abrogation of the social-structure/culture distinction: "What this book attempts is simultaneously to grasp state forms culturally and cultural forms as state-regulated" (p. 3). This programmatic statement from the introduction is subsequently elaborated theoretically and consistently applied in actual historical work.

The authors acknowledge the most significant contemporary intellectual influences on their work as cultural Marxism (especially E. P. Thompson's), French thought (Foucault[26] rather than Bourdieu, at least as mentioned by name), and Elias' historical sociology. There is here neither need nor space to identify these particular strands in Corrigan and Sayer's study; we only point out two major points of relevance to the preceding discussion. First is the authors' view of the centrality of power in the analysis of state formation (in both of the earlier specified understandings) as directly (by "external" enforcement) and indirectly (through internalized symbols and identities) exerted influence. This power, however, is conceptualized, Elias-like, not as hegemonic (i.e., complete) domination, but as shifting balances, built up and dissolved E. P. Thompson-like, "dialectically," in the course of oppositions, struggles, and readjustments.

The second point concerns the role assigned human agency, and, accordingly, the amount of analytical attention it receives. In this matter, Corrigan and Sayer do not follow in E. P. Thompson's steps, or, more accurately, follow only as far as rejecting the base/superstructure distinction, and making culture intrinsically present in, and shaping (as much as shaped by) political processes. Human agency is by and large absent in the book, and this absence is intended by the authors. Their study, as they state explicitly, is not "history from below" (i.e., about and by social actors) but, rather, a study of the state: its policies, routines and rituals – or "regulated forms of social relations" – and its moral and civic philosophy as expressed in legal texts and philosophical treatises. Indeed, while individuals are present in Corrigan and Sayer's (1985) study – the new moral/political order "orchestrated" by the state is at once externally regulative and internally constitutive – they appear mostly as objects of the state's penetrating influence. This approach, however, as the authors carefully note (p. 12), by no means implies a negation of the essential role of social actors in shaping their social world. Rather, it has been chosen – at the cost of leaving untold an important side of the story – for a particular purpose, namely to redress the overly social-structuralist or aculturalist emphases in accepted accounts of state formation, by elaborating the role of the state as a cultural producer.

## Conclusion

We noted at the beginning of this chapter, that historical sociologists, like their colleagues in the discipline at large, have in recent years developed increased "cultural consciousness." This statement needs to be specified. As we have seen, even though a macroscopic social-structural approach dominated in the "new" historical sociology after it established itself in the late 1970s in protest against the "cultural voluntarism" of postwar US social theory, a concern with culture and cultural analysis, inspired by cultural Marxism and a related commitment to "history from below," informed one strand in this subfield in the early 1980s. And an even smaller and dispersed minority of "culturalists" have persisted at the margins of historical sociology since this time. What has been happening in recent years, however, is that theoretical and research interests in the cultural dimension of social life seem to be moving to the center of attention of most practitioners of historical sociology, while cultural analysis, or, more accurately, a certain kind of cultural analysis (see below), appears to be increasingly perceived as one of the defining features of the subfield, together, and in fact in a close affinity, with a historical approach.

As conversations with our colleagues indicate, this current "cultural renaissance" in historical sociology, like its social-structuralist predecessor of the late 1970s, is taking place in several directions at once: in rethinking the concept of culture and the latter's place and role in social life, in epistemological and methodological critical reflection related to the above and a corresponding modification of research methods, and, resulting from the preceding two, in the initiation of new research projects. We will briefly summarize these developments by referring to "interviews" with our colleagues concerning their current thinking about matters of culture, and their ongoing or contemplated research projects, forthcoming publications, and discussions at professional meetings.

Besides expressions of an increased general interest in the problematic of culture, when asked about more specific perceptions of the place and role of culture in social life, many of our "survey" respondents tended to emphasize three points that correspond by and large to major characteristics of an approach "on the plane" discussed in the previous section. Namely, they stressed, first, the ubiquity of culture, rejecting by implication the conventional distinction between micro and macro-levels of social life. By the same token, they dismissed the conventional discourse about culture's influence in terms of its (relative) autonomy and causality. (Some colleagues, however, accepted the idea of culture's autonomy "for *analytical* purposes, but not ontologically," while others considered, in a Michael Mann-like approach, a sufficiency, or primacy, of a "cultural interpretive framework in particular moments of history.") Second, recurrent in our conversations was an idea of culture as an "epistemological tool," or the locus or medium of power; our respondents conceptualized this power, however, practically without exceptions, as ever-contestable or as fields of ongoing struggles.

Third, and related to the above two points, the majority of colleagues we talked to viewed culture as a process, and cultural meanings and identities as flexible, diversified, and multivalent – whether conceptualized primarily as embedded in and acted out by individuals, or as transpersonal symbolic codes, texts, and rituals.[27]

Once culture is conceptualized as inherently flexible, fluid and diverse, cultural analysis gains common ground with a historical approach that focuses, precisely, on specificity and difference, and emphasizes the intrinsically processual character of all aspects of social life. This affinity of culture and history was noted by some of our respondents. It has been more fully elaborated theoretically in Craig Calhoun's (1992b) essay, "Culture, history, and the problem of specificity in social theory," in which he argues for a "culturally sensitive and historically specific social theory" as both possible and desirable.

While most of them are, so to speak, embracing culture, and accepting cultural analysis as the *sine qua non* of historical-sociological work, our "survey" respondents reject a radical postmodernist, and specifically deconstructionist, textualism (an approach that seems to have gained more followers, for the time being anyway, among the affiliated disciplines of history and cultural anthropology). Rather, they are concerned about, as Charles Tilly put it, "the fragile philosophical foundations of our [the social sciences'] ontological realism," and applaud the polemical stands taken in recent years against a radical textualism and deconstructionism by fellow historical sociologists (see, e.g., Sewell 1990, 1993; Calhoun 1992b; Rose 1992a). Briefly stated, these protests are directed at an approach according epistemological precedence (or, in the most radical version, even exclusive ontological status) to concepts, meanings, and discourses over human experience, or, in other words, assuming the former to fundamentally or exhaustively structure the latter, and dismissing a reverse influence as irrelevant. Instead, the critics advocate what one of the polemicists, Sonya Rose (1992a: 7), calls "the 'double vision' of text and context," and what we have referred to here as the mutual constitution of society and culture.

While resolutely opting for a text-context approach to the study of the social world (i.e., for acknowledgment of the impact of the environment that exists *outside* of the discourse) historical sociologists nevertheless are developing increased epistemological self-awareness, or, better, collective and individual self-scrutiny. Such elevated epistemological consciousness results from the extension of an idea of culture as a particular episteme, and therefore subject to critical investigation, that also includes cognitive categories and conceptual frameworks constructed in a professional field (here, sociology) for the purpose of apprehending and explaining the social world.

What precisely might be the requirements for engaging in one's work with a relatively clean epistemological consciousness has not yet been sufficiently elaborated. Some general suggestions regarding social theory construction have been formulated by Calhoun (1992b: 258) who henceforth wants to see it "incumbent on social theorists ... both to situate themselves in their cultural context, and to open themselves to reformation by confrontation with other cultural contexts." More specific, and more radical, is Margaret Somers' (1992a, 1992b, 1993) proposal for a historical epistemology, based on what she calls "knowledge culture," which is "constituted by the specific range of thinking, reasoning, and institutional practices *possible in a given historical time and space*" (Somers 1993, author's italics).[28] Using this approach requires, as Somers envisions it, first, freeing our professional thinking and praxis from the conventional context of justification (in which we ask questions of validity, reliability, and verification), and placing it instead in the context of discovery (in which we define and select problems for investigation, and set up the conceptual vocabulary to formulate our research questions). Second and related, a study of a historical subject selected in the context of discovery requires a rejection of all conventional master-themes (concepts, theories, and, underlying them, presuppositions) found in a sociological "tool-kit," and using, instead, (i) "ontological narratives," or stories that social actors use – i.e., construct (not necessarily consciously) into what Somers calls sequences of "causal emplotments" embodied in time and place, and invested with meanings, to make sense of, and act in, their lives[29]; and (ii) "public/institutional narratives" or stories attached to ". . . intersubjective networks or institutions, however local or grand" (Somers 1992b: 15).

Somers' discussion has probably been the most theoretically elaborated treatment of narrative in historical sociology thus far; as a method (rather than a methodology), it has been already discussed, refined, and applied in historical research for quite some time. Preceding by a few years the current "cultural turn" in historical sociology, the interest in the narrative method arose, at first, from a concern with the intrinsic temporality of sociocultural life, beyond the reach of conventional statistical methods of analysis commonly used, for instance, by social history "from below" (on this issue, and the relevant advantages of the narrative method, see Ragin 1987; Abbott 1988, 1990; Isaac and Griffin 1989; Aminzade 1992; Sewell 1993). Most recently, however, as our conversations suggest, those who have made such a "cultural turn" (as outlined above), and who also embrace an idea of historical sociology as an intrinsically empirical-theoretical undertaking, appear interested in a larger project of "epistemologically responsible," (as one respondent put it) historical ethnography, of which time-and-culture sensitive narratives constitute an important part (on this matter, see, e.g., Chartier 1989;  Calhoun 1992b; Comaroff and Comaroff 1991; Steinmetz 1992).

And finally, so as to get a preview of the historical-sociological agenda in the coming years (say, until the year 2000), we asked our respondents about their work currently in progress and projects considered. Nearly all of them are studying, or intend to in the near future, explicitly culture-related or culture-centered problems (and culture being conceptualized more or less in a manner summarized above). The most common research topics pursued at present by our colleagues concern themes such as public and political cultures of different institutions and in different time periods, rhetorics of revolutions and social movements, power and class, gender, and ethnic identities.[30]

All these developments seem to bode well for cultural studies in historical sociology. We would like to hope that this "cultural renaissance" will neither turn into actorless and asocial hermeneutics nor prove only a passing excitement like so many other academic "fads".

**Appendix 3.1**

The following is a list of historical sociologist-respondents to our "survey":

Andrew Abbott
Ronald Aminzade
Rogers Brubaker
Craig Calhoun
Liah Greenfeld
Wendy Griswold
John R. Hall
Fred Kniss
Sonya Rose
Barry Schwartz
William Sewell
Theda Skocpol
Margaret Somers
Charles Tilly
Loïc Wacquant (for Pierre Bourdieu)
Robert Wuthnow
Viviana Zelizer
The authors also introspected, and "interviewed" each other.

---

Notes to figure 3.1
1 We have excluded from this representation historical-sociological studies, identified in the first section of this chapter as strongly social-structuralist, wherein culture is simply absent: Wallerstein (1974, 1979, 1980), Tilly (1975, 1992), Skocpol (1979).
2 We have calculated the combined average proportions of *positive* answers to the three questions concerning the treatment of culture (centrality, flexibility, *explanans*) and indicative of a general approach, in studies assigned to the social-structuralist, culturalist, and "elevated plane" areas in the scheme. They are, respectively, 32%, 53%, and 75%, suggesting a relative theoretical homogeneity within the above categories, especially the first and last.
3 The letter (n) marked by the name indicates that the author's work has been referred to only in a chapter note, not in the main text.
4 Dotted lines in the middle of the scheme by the names of W. Griswold, W. Sewell and W. Spohn, indicate that in their studies culture is understood both in terms of intersubjective meanings/identities and structural patterns.

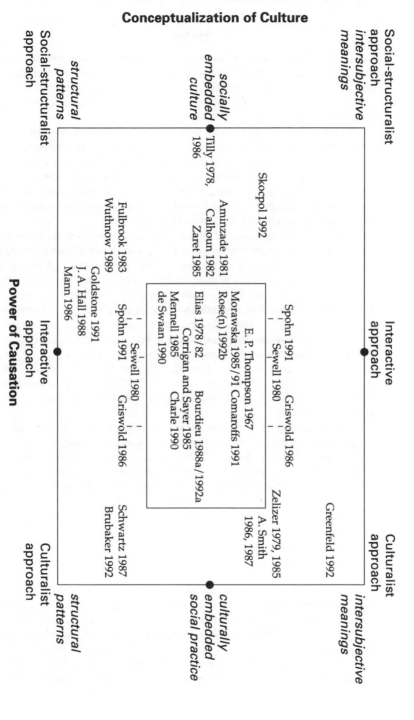

**Appendix 3.2**

**Conceptualization of Culture**

Social-structuralist approach
*intersubjective meanings*

Interactive approach

Culturalist approach
*intersubjective meanings*

Social-structuralist approach

*socially embedded culture*

*structural patterns*

Tilly 1978, 1986

Skocpol 1992

Aminzade 1981
Calhoun 1982
Zaret 1985

Fulbrook 1983
Wuthnow 1989

Goldstone 1991
J. A. Hall 1988
Mann 1986

Spohn 1991
Sewell 1980

Griswold 1986

E. P. Thompson 1967
Morawska 1985/91 Comaroffs 1991
Rose(n) 1992b

Elias 1978/82
Corrigan and Sayer 1985
Mennell 1985    Charle 1990
de Swaan 1990

Bourdieu 1988a/1992a

Sewell 1980
Spohn 1991
Griswold 1986

Greenfeld 1992

Zelizer 1979, 1985
A. Smith 1986, 1987

Schwartz 1987
Brubaker 1992

**Power of Causation**

Interactive approach

Culturalist approach

*structural patterns*

*culturally embedded social practice*

*intersubjective meanings*

**Figure 3.1**  Approaches to culture in historical sociology

## Notes

1 David Zaret (1991) argues, however, and we believe not without reason, that despite all the recent attention to the subject, cultural analysis still has marginal status within sociology. It can be captured "in a simple contrast: the sociology of culture is a specialty; the sociology of social structure is not" (p. 9).

2 With all this helpful assistance, which we heartily appreciate, the way in which this account of the various uses of culture in historical-sociological studies has been arranged, and the current developments (tentatively) interpreted, is, of course, ours, and, considering the difficulties mentioned above, by no means always accurate (whatever that means nowadays) or the only one possible. (For different treatments, see for example, John Hall 1990a; Calhoun 1992b; Griswold 1992a.)

3 Indirect power is understood in sociological literature in two, narrower and broader, meanings: the former refers to the power of dominant classes over their social subordinates, executed by the medium of hegemonic culture; the latter – which is used in this chapter – originates in cultural anthropology, and denotes the generic capacity to define the experienced world and guide action, regardless of social position (see Lamont 1989).

4 The editor requested that contributors do an *overview of theoretical approaches* to culture in their respective subfields, rather than a *review of literature* in the above. We tried to comply, but early on in this project decided to combine both; a "faceless" account would be much less informative, and in addition we found author-colleagues' comments on their work very helpful in constructing the interpretive framework for the whole discussion.

5 On the relationship between social biographies and theoretical and methodological preferences of the rebel-historical sociologists in the USA during the 1970s see Skocpol (1984), Smith (1991), Calhoun (1992). This reconfiguration inspired a number of historical sociological studies whereby culture became more or less absorbed in, or ultimately subordinated to macro-economic and macro-political structures.

6 In a conversation with Ewa Morawska about this change of disposition, Theda Skocpol mentioned that between 1980 and 1985 she read a study by Lynn Hunt, a leading cultural historian of the French Revolution (Hunt 1984), which influenced her thinking, and so did interests and ideas of her graduate students at Harvard.

7 Wuthnow's study, however, focuses on the process of production, selection, and institutionalization of each of the three major ideologies, rather than on their impact after "disengagement" from their historical context. Mary Fulbrook's (1983) interesting study, *Piety and Politics: religion and the rise of absolutism in England, Württemberg, and Prussia*, provides a follow-up on one of these "disengaged" ideologies, i.e., the Reformation, and specifically its impact on politics (the latter are understood as actions as

well as orientations). While the study accords considerable attention to culture that is, aims, ideals, and ethos of the Puritan and Pietist movements in the seventeenth and eighteenth centuries (without analyzing their indirect power, however), the main theoretical argument is that it is macrostructural and mezzo-institutional contexts that mediate between the religious doctrines and political outcomes.

8   A note from Willfried Spohn: I emphasize here those similarities between Sewell's and my approaches that are relevant to the subject matter of this chapter, namely those regarding the understanding of culture and its relationship to social structures and human actors, but our styles of work and their products of course differ from each other in other respects. One such difference between our studies considered here that may be worth noting concerns methodology, and reflects, it seems, additional intellectual influences on each of us that were not mentioned above: of cultural anthropology (Geertzian especially) on Bill Sewell, and of the structural-cultural approach of Barrington Moore, especially his studies of German working-class history, on myself.

And thus, Bill Sewell's investigation, carried out in a "thick" historical narrative, aims primarily at a close reconstruction of the changing socio-cultural relationship between workers and their environment in one particular location (France). In comparison, my project is larger in scope and uses a more analytical discourse aiming at, shall we say, broader comparative-historical generalizations. The investigation proceeds at three levels simultaneously – (German) workers' mentalities, their local communities and associations, and national movements and institutions – seeking to grasp social-cultural relationships both within and between each of these levels. In the next step of analysis, the German situation is compared with four other contemporary European cases.

9   Asked in conversation about these micro–macro connections, or, rather, absence thereof, in a manuscript version of her study of the social meanings of money that we inspected for this project (Zelizer 1994), Viviana Zelizer produced several interesting hypotheses that, as she told us, would be included in the final version of the manuscript.

10   "State" refers to a set of institutions and personnel possessing centralized political authority over a territorially demarcated area with a monopoly of authoritative binding rule-making (Mann 1988: 4). "Nation" refers to a national community sharing the same culture, i.e., common descent, history, ethnic background, language, religion, and high culture. "State" and "nation" may be divergent (for instance, "state-less nation") or congruent ("nation-state") (Gellner 1983: 1–7).

11   "In this belief," Greenfeld (1992: 18) states, "I reverse the order of precedence, and therefore of causality, which is usually, if sometimes tacitly, assumed to exist between national identity and nations, and nationalism and modernity . . . Rather than define nationalism by its modernity, I see modernity as defined by nationalism."

12    Brubaker's (1992) study does, in fact, seek to redress what he calls a "territorial bias" in the study of the state as conventionally practiced in political sociology, by emphasizing the fact that it is *also* an association of citizens. However, nowhere in the book can we find pronouncements denying the state's territoriality or representing it as exclusively or even mainly a membership organization. In a personal conversation about his book, Rogers Brubaker said he was "simply very interested in this particular problem," namely, the historically variant relationships between nationhood and citizenship, rather than fighting for or against this or another theory.

13    It should be stressed that, like approaches located on the structuralist-culturalist, horizontal axis presented earlier, particular positions in this group also overlap with each other, and therefore it is in a *part* of the field (upper or lower as marked on the elevated plane in the chart in figure 3.1), and not in well-defined *points* on it that we locate particular scholars and their works.

14    After this chapter was completed, we realized that a recent study by another historical sociologist, Sonya Rose, entitled *Limited Livelihoods: gender and class in 19th century England* (1992b), would also fit very well in this group; while it was to late to include it in the text as an illustration, we wish to mention this particular study especially because of its culturally and historically sensitive consideration of gender, or class-gender, rather, and more accurately yet, its actor-bearers (men and women workers in Lancashire textile industry) involved in a reciprocally structuring relationship with their social environment.

15    Rather ironically considering where (and when) Ewa Morawska came from, it is Giddens' structuration theory and cultural Marxism that have provided a solid social-structural grounding for her Znanieckian "culturalism" (he identified his approach by this term as oppositional to "sociologism," i.e., positivism à la Durkheim, whose lectures, by the way, he attended while in Paris and toward whom he later developed a love–hate orientation). So annoyed were we all in Poland in the 1970s with Soviet-style official Marxism that a culturalist approach, by a prewar Polish philosopher-sociologist at that, appeared fascinating, to the point of forgiving Znaniecki his lack of consideration for the macrostructural context.

16    This is not an appropriate place to discuss Znaniecki's social theory, but it should be noted that Znaniecki's thought reflected an enduring ambivalence concerning the antinaturalist/humanistic versus naturalist/positivistic model of sociology he wanted to pursue. The former approach strongly prevailed in his early works (and this, by the way, has influenced one of the authors of this chapter), while the latter influence predominated during Znaniecki's stay in the United States, first at Chicago and then at Columbia universities. His intellectual biographer, Piotr Sztompka (1986: 273), refers to this ambivalence in more constructive terms, by stating that

Znaniecki combined "humanism" and "positivism" (see also Szacki 1991). How successful he was in this respect is another matter.

17 The term "ethnicization" has been used in the immigration and ethnic studies to denote the process of blending of old-country traditions and the dominant (American) sociocultural patterns by the immigrants and subsequent generations as they adapt themselves to the host environment. On this concept, see Jonathan Sarna (1978); Olivier Zunz (1985); Kathleen Neils Conzen et al. (1992).

18 A note from Ewa Morawska: There is no need, and no space either, in this chapter to discuss epistemological problems involved in conducting this "Jewish" research, precisely because of my "resonating" so well with it, and, quite likely, inadvertently imposing my own "internal" agenda on my informants. I discuss these and related issues extensively in the introduction to *Insecure Prosperity* (Morawska 1994).

19 Apart from a few passing comments, we will not be able to compare these two scholars systematically – an undertaking worth someone's effort, because Bourdieu and Elias are increasingly common references in US sociological publications, often joined in cavalier fashion.

20 According to Loïc Wacquant, Bourdieu's collaborator, the latter views *Les régles de l'art* as his "first *complete* book," that is, most fully expressing the author's way of thinking and doing sociology (personal communication to Ewa Morawska).

21 In the pithiest summary, Bourdieu has expressed his theory in a formula: (*habitus*) × (capital) + field = practice (Bourdieu 1984).

22 This difference of emphases may also reflect changes in Bourdieu's thinking over time. In fact, Loïc Wacquant believes this is what has happened. Asked whether and how Bourdieu's thinking about these and related matters has changed since the late 1970s, Wacquant told us that there has occurred a shift toward more nuanced, "fluid," and dynamic, i.e., more historical representations; among other things, in his opinion, Bourdieu's recent work "accounts much better for the objectivist and subjectivist moments, [while] his previous book, *Distinction* [1984], was too [one-sidedly] objectivist" (personal communication to Ewa Morawska).

23 We have only read a much shortened version of Bourdieu's study, "Flaubert's Point of View" (Bourdieu 1988a), relying for more complete information and commentary on Loïc Wacquant. With the permission of the author, we also used Wacquant's letter to William Sewell, dated August 31, 1991, commenting on the latter's representation (Sewell 1992) – inadequate, in Wacquant's opinion – of Bourdieu's model as "mechanistic," and offering an extensive (seven single-space pages) discussion with illustrations of another, more "open" interpretation of the *habitus* (on Bourdieu's conceptualization of the "structure and agency" problem, see also Wacquant 1993).

24 In comparison, Bourdieu's advocacy of the dissolution of such false polarities has been, at least more recently (see note 22), equally vocal. As

for the Heraclitean representation of social relations (figurations, fields), in Bourdieu's model the "becoming" seems more easily, if only temporarily, immobilized by the theoretically central idea of class domination.

25 *The Great Arch* is not the first of its kind, however. For some other contemporary historical studies of state formation which articulate cultural themes, see, for example, Alessandro Pizzorno (1987), David Laitin and Ian Lustick (1989), or Pierre Bourdieu (1989); Michael Mann (1986), noted earlier in this paper, could be added to this list.

26 After some deliberation, we decided to omit Foucault from this overview, although he has been occasionally identified as a historical sociologist (he himself preferred, as is well known, to call his method "archeological"), and he was obviously and primarily interested in "cultural matters." We omitted him because he did not fit anywhere in our chart.

27 Characteristically, some of our respondents who in the 1980s considered themselves to be under the influence of Clifford Geertz, explicitly reject his approach today on the basis of its static, overstructured notion of culture as uncontested and free of symbolic power struggles; see Chartier (1989) for a critique of Geertz along these lines.

28 This understanding of "historical epistemology" offered by Somers strikes us as very similar to Bourdieu's concept of a "*field*," although neither this notion nor its author are referred to in the paper.

29 Although we find basically appealing the idea behind recent propositions of turning back to the actors and their point of view on the "story" we are researching, we still do not quite comprehend what exactly (besides – see below – the sharpened awareness of gendered character of the language) differentiates this supposedly new approach from, say, Bronislaw Malinowski's conception of the goal of ethnography as "grasp[ing] the native's point of view, his reaction to life, to realize his vision of his world" (Malinowski 1922: 25).

30 Interestingly, culture-oriented research projects are currently conducted or planned by the leading representatives of the social-structuralist approach in the "new" historical sociology of the early 1980s, e.g., Charles Tilly and Theda Skocpol. Tilly, who has been working for over a decade on a project concerning popular contention in Britain in the period 1758–1834, recently became interested, as he told us, in the influence of "the implicit causal and normative schemata" on the ways of thinking and acting of the participants in these activities, and intends to include this problem in the analysis. Skocpol, too, is presently working on two projects both of which directly involve the problem of culture: one is a collection of essays on revolutions where she intends to review and reformulate the long-standing debate on the role of cultural idioms and ideology; the other deals with the historical origins and formation of, as she put it, "the public culture of social security" in the United States.

# 4

# Fissured Terrain: Methodological Approaches and Research Styles in Culture and Politics

## Mabel Berezin

### Culture and Politics (1): Establishing Boundaries

As recently as the early 1980s, students of politics viewed culture as a somewhat murky variable that bore no relation to political outcome. Culture and politics evoked 1950s' modernization theories and political culture studies – theories and methods that were decidedly out of style in the 1970s and early 1980s.[1]

A virtual renaissance of interest in culture and politics has occurred in the social sciences since the early 1980s.[2] Various theoretical paradigms and academic disciplines vie for space in this analytic arena. Rational choice models (Cohen 1974) that view culture as a political resource compete with postmodern extremes that view politics as reducible to images.[3] The resurgence of interest within social science in culture, and the prevalence of the word "politics" in contemporary literary and aesthetic criticism, disciplines formerly beyond the purview of political analysis, suggest that it is useful to reflect upon where boundaries for the domain of politics and culture might lie.[4] The erecting of borders goes against the current academic grain of disciplinary melding. Scholars of all stripes invoke the terms "politics and culture" with a degree of imprecision that threatens to render both concepts meaningless.

This chapter lays out conceptual frames that suggest ways to delimit the sociological study of politics and culture. These parameters include: (1) analytic and empirical distinctions that facilitate the formulation of research questions; and (2) an elaboration of the epistemological underpinnings that govern current empirical studies. An *a priori* definition of politics and culture is not a particularly

useful entry to the field. Politics and culture, politics and economics, politics and whatever second term one might wish to propose
represents a relation and not a static category. Rather than offer a
definition of politics and culture, I propose an analytic question:
how would the study of politics differ if one chose to address it
from a cultural point of view? The union of cultural and political
analysis should enhance our understanding of the areas that students of politics typically study: nation-states, policy, organizations
including state bureaucracies and political parties, regime transitions, and collective action – ranging from voting behavior to full-
scale revolutions.

The empirical focus of politics would remain the same; the types
of analytic questions that we pose would change. In general, we
would ask how does meaning or culture – collectively held visions
of social order – influence first, public political actions from voting
to storming the Bastille and second, the institutional forms – nation-
states, bureaucracies, parties and laws – that structure political
action. This question would be nuanced depending upon the
particular empirical case under consideration.

For the purpose of studying political actions and institutions, it
is useful to invoke the anthropological view that considers culture
as the shared cognitive maps that pattern group visions of how the
world works. These maps are real to the extent that they are shared
and to the extent that they inform concrete political actions. An
analytic perspective that privileges collective meanings, actions and
institutions contains two presuppositions: first, that – borrowing
from Clifford Geertz (1973: 12) – culture and meaning are public
and hence discoverable; second, a concept of agency that is neither
completely voluntaristic nor completely structural.[5]

If we aim to explain how culture or meanings shape political
outcomes and processes, it is necessary to incorporate the vehicles
that disseminate or impose, explicitly or implicitly, meanings into
traditional political analyses. Broadly conceptualized, these vehicles
include cultural institutions, linguistic and symbolic practices, and
cultural actors. Religion, education and the organs of the public
sphere, such as mass media and voluntary associations, comprise
the institutional level.[6] The linguistic mode includes the presence
or absence of national modes of communication, a shared idiom in
which to articulate political ideas, as well as the discourses and
repertoires of ritual practices that emerge around political ideals.
Political communicators, intellectuals broadly defined to include

academics, writers and policy makers, are the agents of political persuasion and discourses about political values.

The operative analytic question delineated here is *how* does culture affect politics. Questions of what and why have been left aside. Formulating the question in this manner has the advantage of providing a focus that permits identification of existing scholarship across a range of academic disciplines that fits these criteria. This approach favors empirical studies of culture and politics that seek to account for political outcomes; it does exclude certain categories of study that other analytic frames might capture, such as purely theoretical works or works that offer normative judgments on the proper relation between culture and politics.

A literature review of all work in the social sciences that might conceivably fall within the bounds of politics and culture would cast an extremely wide net. A relatively short essay on a broad and loosely bounded field demands selectivity in the path that it charts through the disciplinary landscape and the scholarship that it discusses. The "American" centeredness of this article reflects diverse intellectual traditions and not ethnocentrism. Indeed, while the scholars discussed are, for the most part, American, they are hardly ethnocentric as their focus is Europe, Africa and Asia.

Continental Europe, particularly France and Germany, has generated an abundance of theory in the realm of politics and culture.[7] Recent studies that build upon Pierre Bourdieu's work document the pervasiveness of power in creating social boundaries (Lamont 1989; Lamont and Fournier 1992) and argue that status distinctions create and perpetuate the social inequalities that may or may not lead to political action. While this work is undeniably important, it is considered to fall within the area of social stratification and culture and outside the range of this essay. German theorizing has focused on legal theory and the distinctions between state and civil society. Empirical work on politics exists in European social science but tends to focus on social policy, political parties, labor unions, to name a few areas, and cultural variables, to date, have not figured in these analyses.[8]

## Culture and Politics (2): Epistemological Dissidence

Bringing cultural analysis to bear upon political analysis involves more than a simple shift in empirical focus. The wedding of culture

and politics raises the question of how political meaning, or
knowledge, is constituted and transforms the study of politics into
an epistemologically self-conscious enterprise. The emphasis upon
epistemological presuppositions places the study of politics and
culture at the center of current debates about the construction of
social knowledge and the constitution of the political subject that
the somewhat loose rubric of postmodernism subsumes.[9] If it were
not for the influence of Michel Foucault (for example 1977: 93–108,
1979) in anthropology (Ortner 1984) and history (Hunt 1989b; Joan
Wallach Scott 1988), much of this debate might have remained in
literature departments. While sociologists have not explicitly entered this particular academic fray, they have not entirely ignored
it either. The debate between Sewell (1985) and Skocpol (1985) on
the role of ideology and culture in political analysis, Charles Tilly's
(1991) comments on the problem of agency in his discussion of
James Scott's (1990) *Domination and the Arts of Resistance*, and the
essays by Calhoun (1992b) and Alexander (1992) on the problem of
knowledge, culture and theory in *Postmodernism and Social Theory*
(Seidman and Wagner 1992) suggest that the sociological troops
may be arriving at the barricades.

Epistemological dissidence characterizes the current approach
to politics and culture within the field delimited above. Broadly
conceptualized, the fissures lie between scholars who privilege the
possibility of explanation, and this does not necessarily imply a
notion of causality, and those who privilege exegesis or interpretation. One group seeks universality and generalizeability; and the
other seeks particularity. Whether political analysts address these
issues directly, their formulation of research questions, methodological choices and empirical data reflects how they position
themselves on the epistemological landscape.

Given the centrality ascribed here to epistemological concerns,
methodological approaches that represent four analytic styles have
been identified. Broadly categorized scholarship on politics and
culture tends toward explanation or interpretation. Scholars who
favor explanation tend to fall into two groups: those who pose
their questions in comparative historical terms and examine the
process of cultural and political interaction, and those who view
power, or hegemonic process, as primary. The interpretive disposition fractionates into macro and micro level studies that focus
upon, respectively, the "thick description" of various forms of public

politics and studies of political orientations, values and attitudes. Different academic disciplines are more or less inclined to explanation or interpretation although there is a good deal of overlap. Comparative historical sociologists and political scientists tend towards explanatory approaches; anthropologists, historians, and qualitative sociologists veer towards interpretation. In general, this chapter discusses, or cites, works that fit the conception of politics outlined above, engage epistemological questions, or define promising research agendas.

## Explanatory Approaches: Comparative Sociological Studies

In the 1970s, structuralism, driven by a generation of scholars who had rediscovered Karl Marx, was the dominant paradigm in political sociology. To the extent that "neo" terms have any meaning, many neo-Marxists were, or later became, neo-Weberians. Structuralist arguments limited the range of questions that scholars asked and defined the areas that they studied. Lynn Hunt's (1984) *Politics, Culture and Class in the French Revolution* broke with structural approaches to the study of revolution and made symbolic practices a legitimate part of the discourse of revolution.[10] Hunt's book was a flawed landmark. The first part of the book that dealt with "The poetics of power" only loosely articulated with the second half of the book, "The sociology of politics" that was an analysis of social class and political action. Hunt described the "unexpected invention of revolutionary politics" (p. 3) and argued that standard accounts to date had demonstrated a "programmatic disregard for revolutionary intentions" (p. 9). Hunt aimed to "uncover the rules of political behavior" (p. 10) and to examine political action through the prism of symbolic practices. She argued:

> In order to reconstruct the logic of revolutionary action and innovation, it is thus essential to examine both the politics of revolution and the people who practiced them. My contention is that there was a fit or affinity between them, not that one can be deduced from the other. The political culture of revolution was made up of symbolic practices, such as language, imagery, and gestures. These symbolic practices were embraced more enthusiastically in some places and by some groups than in other places and groups. (Hunt 1984: 13)

Hunt's theoretical weaponry was eclectic and wide ranging. She invoked Kenneth Burke, Northrup Frye and Jacques Derrida along with Michael Walzer and Clifford Geertz. While Hunt did not write in an explicitly Foucauldian mode, she did draw somewhat more heavily upon Foucault's ideas than is immediately apparent. Her definition of power is an instance of this borrowing: "Power ... was not a finite quantity possessed by one faction or another; it was rather a complex set of activities and relationships that created previously unsuspected resources. The surprising victories of the revolutionary armies were only the most dazzling consequence of this discovery of new social and political energy" (p. 72).[11] Comparing Foucault to Hunt, we find: "Power must be analyzed as something which circulates ... It is never localized here or there, never in anybody's hands ... Power is employed and exercised through a net-like organization. And not only do individuals circulate between its threads; they are always in the position of simultaneously undergoing and exercising this power" (Foucault 1977: 98). The diffuse conception of power or "political energy" that Hunt shares with Foucault renders explicit connection between the agents of symbolic practices and the audience for these practices unnecessary. The diffuse workings of power implicitly connect practices and audience. Paradoxically, Hunt's view of power by neutralizing its directedness vitiated it as a political concept.[12]

*Politics, Culture and Class in the French Revolution* (Hunt 1984) left a black box between symbolism and symbolic activity, social agents and political practice – what it purported to explain. Sociologists generally have greater affinity for filling black boxes than their colleagues in history and anthropology. Liah Greenfeld's (1992) *Nationalism* and Rogers Brubaker's (1992) *Citizenship and Nationhood in France and Germany* represent an explanatory approach to the study of culture and politics that emphasizes the role of cultural agents.[13] Both Greenfeld and Brubaker take a structural approach to the study of politics and culture, although their view of structure is not deterministic. Greenfeld (1992: 19) provides the most succinct description of the type of structuralism that they espouse. She criticizes "strict sociological structuralism" and "idealism" for their tendency to reify concepts and calls for a culturally sensitive view of structuralism where the "arrow of causality may point both ways" (p. 20). She states: "Neither 'structuralism' nor idealism recognizes the significance of the human agency, in which culture and structure are brought together, in which each of them is every day modified and recreated, and only by – not through – which both are moved and shaped, and given the ability to exert their influence" (p. 19).

In general, these sociologists seek to explain social processes. The contribution of states, institutions, elites, ideologies and traditions to cultural and political interaction provides their focus. Max Weber, and not Karl Marx, orients their conception of politics. Comparative history based upon primary sources is the method that characterizes their work. Brubaker asks the standard comparative question that seeks to explain different outcomes in view of similar social circumstances. Focusing upon citizenship law in France and Germany, he asks, "Why have citizenship policies not converged to reflect the underlying similarities in immigration processes, immigrant populations, and migration policies?" (p. 180). Greenfeld aims to explain the process by which a potent ideological movement, nationalism, became the *"constitutive element of modernity"* (p. 18) in Britain, France, Russia and the United States.

Greenfeld's arguments about the development of nationalism involve a view of ideology as produced. Greenfeld seeks to imbue a historical process with sociological meaning. Based on primary materials in four languages, *Nationalism* is a scholarly *tour de force*. Greenfeld has a clear, if somewhat idiosyncratic, conception of nationalism. In contrast to other theorists, who see nationalism as product of modernity, she views modernity as a product of nationalism. Nationalism is the Archimedian point from which all modern politics flows.

While it is difficult to do justice to the richness of Greenfeld's four hundred plus pages of text in a paragraph, her view of nationalism has three novel implications that are worth elaborating albeit in truncated form. First, national identity precedes state formation. Greenfeld documents this with a heuristic that she names the "zigzag pattern of semantic change" (p. 5). She argues that changes in the meaning of the word "nation" chart the diffusion of the consciousness of nationalism. This linguistic approach permits her to locate the origin of nationalism in Tudor England instead of early nineteenth-century continental Europe. Second, the linguistic approach allows her to argue that the form of nationalism associated with xenophobic extremism is only one type of possible nationalism and it results from a linguistic shift from the idea of a nation as a group of "sovereign people" to the idea of a nation as a collectivity of "unique people." From her linguistic analysis, she develops a typology of democratic and non-democratic nationalisms – non-democratic nationalisms are those that have inherently authoritarian tendencies. An individualistic-libertarian civic nationalism developed in England and later, the United States, and at the other extreme, a collectivistic-authoritarian ethnic nationalism developed in Russia and Germany. France stands in between both extremes with a collectivist-authoritarian civic nationalism. Third, she locates national identity, on the one hand, in the action and consciousness of elites when they experience social anomie, and on the other, in the social *ressentiment* of culturally disenfranchised groups.

Greenfeld's work has powerful implications for political development in post-1989 Europe. If her claim that the initial experience of nationalism determines the course of national political action is correct, we have only the worst to expect from the Europe that is emerging after 40 years of Communist rule. Greenfeld is aware of the implications of her argument. In the "Introduction," she states that she is demonstrating only "potentialities" for future political action. However, she concludes on a somewhat more pessimistic note. She argues that laws, institutions and cultural forms ensure that, "Forces shaped centuries ago continue to shape the destinies of mankind at the end of the twentieth century" (p. 491).

Brubaker picks up where Greenfeld leaves off and discusses issues of nationalism in terms of concepts of citizenship. His historical work contains implications for contemporary Europe – the other side of the post-1989 coin, the new Europe of 1992. Brubaker examines the political contexts and cultural idioms that shaped state policies towards citizenship in France and Germany and relates them to contemporary controversies over immigration to both countries. He begins with two theoretically novel propositions: first, that citizenship is a form of "social closure" – a way to exclude or include persons in participation in the nation-state; and that second, the nation-state is a "membership organization" as well as a territorial organization. Traditional theories of citizenship focus upon the rights and obligations of members of the polity and neglect criteria for membership. Exclusionary and inclusionary mechanisms are central to understanding the nature of citizenship and the specific forms that it acquires in different states.

Immigration policy in France and Germany suggests that

citizenship has become divorced from notions of rights and obligations. Immigrants, principally North Africans in France and Turks in Germany, enjoy social privileges. In some parts of Germany, the law permits them to vote in local elections. Citizenship, full membership in the polity, is more problematic. French citizenship, based upon the principle of *jus soli* is available for children of second generation immigrants born on French territory; German citizenship, based upon the principle of *jus sanguinis*, requires German ancestry. Germany's ethno-cultural notion of citizenship created the politically awkward situation where groups that have lived on the territory for over a generation do not have a legal right to citizenship. Conversely, it also means that groups that can demonstrate German ancestry automatically have a right to return to the territory.

Citizenship laws in France and Germany have not bowed to contemporary contingencies and have remained unchanged since the late nineteenth century. Ordinary French and German citizens are attached to the laws as they presently stand. Brubaker marshalls cultural and political variables to explain the differing legal outcomes in France and Germany. He argues that "deeply rooted understandings of nationhood" have led to a "state-centered assimilationist" view of citizenship in France and an "ethnocultural and 'differentialist' " view in Germany.

The contrast between Brubaker and Greenfeld is most striking when we compare their conception of the relation between state and nation. According to Brubaker, the idea of a nation developed in France in the post-revolutionary period to protect the bourgeois state. If the universalistic principles of the state, including the right to property (there is a fascinating discussion of inheritance law here (pp. 38–9)) were to be upheld, the French state had to be inclusionary. The idea to create "the French" came afterward. The reverse occurred in Germany where postulating a nation justified the state. The exclusion of those who were not true Germans became the cultural claim for the German state. Germany expended as much effort preserving communities of true Germans outside the territory as France spent turning peasants, or immigrants, into French men and women.

As immigration increases in Europe, citizenship becomes more salient as a political issue. If Europe is to develop a sensible and functional position on immigration, Brubaker argues that it will have to take into account a fundamental principle regarding citizenship law: "The politics of citizenship today is first and foremost a politics of nationhood. . . . it is a *politics of identity*, not a *politics of interest*. . . . The central question is not 'who *gets* what?' but rather 'who *is* what?'" (p. 182).[14]

## Explanatory Approaches: Models of Hegemony and Political Identity

Comparative sociology is effective at specifying the black box between cultural practices and political action; however, issues of power and domination remain implicit, rather than explicit, in its style of argumentation. Antonio Gramsci's concept of hegemony has captured the imagination of political scientists and anthropologists who wish to confront issues of power and domination in the cultural realm but who reject postmodern notions of the undirected pervasiveness of power.[15]

Hegemony was a frame that Gramsci used to construct a historical account of Italian political development. It is an attractive concept because it accounts for power relations in the hands of a dominant class as well as cultural forms without resorting to the economic or class determinism of traditional Marxist analysis. It permits the social analyst to incorporate culture into an analysis in a nonrelativist manner and allows for explanation.

The etiology of common sense is central to hegemony. The groups who have the power to construct the taken for granted aspect of society are the groups that possess hegemonic dominance. David Laitin's (1986) *Hegemony and Culture* and Jean and John Comaroff's (1991) *Of Revelation and Revolution* focus upon the commonsensical aspect of hegemony to debate theories of culture and politics.[16] Laitin, a political scientist, employs a combination of participant observation (he spent a year in Nigeria and regularly attended Christian and Muslim religious services), a small quantitative study, and historical documents to study the Yoruba tribe in Nigeria where he examined the effect of British colonialization on the formation of Yoruba political and cultural identity. The Yoruba were members of a tribe and a world religion. One segment of Yoruba were Christian and the others were Muslim. Religion is frequently a potent source of political conflict and mobilization. Yet, a high degree of religious toleration characterized the Yoruba who found their principal identities in their tribal affiliations.

In the Yoruba case, Laitin faces the difficult project of explaining why an expected outcome did not occur. He does this by addressing what he terms the two faces of culture. The first face of culture that he identifies with Max Weber and Clifford Geertz focuses upon symbols and ritual practices that provide collectively held meaning systems that pattern social actions. In the case of religion, this takes the form of doctrine and liturgical practices. The second face of culture that Laitin identifies with the work of Abner Cohen (1974) does not engage questions of meaning but rather views cultural practices as political resources that political actors strategically invoke to obtain desired political ends. According to Laitin, both notions are inadequate to explain the interaction of politics and culture in Yorubaland.

Laitin's reconceptualization of hegemony merges the first and second face of culture: "I [Laitin] define hegemony as the political forging – whether through coercion or elite bargaining – and institutionalization of a pattern of group activity in a state and the concurrent idealization of that schema into a dominant symbolic framework that reigns as common sense" (p. 19). Laitin argues that the Yoruba tribal identities were stronger than their religious identities due to the efforts of the British who, "... reinvested 'ancestral city' with political reality. The imposition of a system of stratification by a hegemon gave the resulting set of group identifications a sense of being real or obvious. ... The reification of the 'ancestral city' at the expense of 'religion' ... helps explain the long-term non-politicization of religion among the Yoruba" (p. 20).

British colonialism also engages the Comoroffs (1991) who focus upon the activities of Non-conformist Christian missionaries between the years 1820 and 1920 among Southern Tswana, a South African tribe. Their goal is to examine the "colonization of consciousness and the consciousness of colonization in South Africa" (p. xi) and to link this early missionary activity to the contemporary practice of apartheid. In contrast to Laitin who engaged standard social science theory, the Comoroffs, historical anthropologists, confront the "epistemological hypochondria" (p. xiii) that is afflicting their profession. While they readily acknowledge the limits of structuralism, they are not about to replace it with postmodern indeterminancy. They argue that "Human agency is practice invested with subjectivity, meaning, and to a greater or lesser extent power. It is, in short, motivated" (p. 10). They do find some value in the questions that postmodernism has raised about the instability of meaning, the polyvalence of symbolic practices and the diffuse nature of power. However, they argue that the proposition that meaning is inherently unstable flies in the face of empirical evidence, "How is it that ... if *all* meaning were potentially open to contest, *all* power potentially unfixed – history keeps generating hegemonies that, for long periods, seem able to impose a degree of order and stability on the world?" (p. 17).

To account for permanence and change, resistance and acquiescence in a manner that adequately accounts for power and culture, the Comoroffs develop a conceptualization of hegemony based upon a distinction between form and content. The Comoroffs parse hegemony to include culture, hegemony and ideology. Their definition of culture hinges on a conception of conscious human agency. Culture is the:

> ... space of signifying practice, the semantic ground on which human beings seek to construct and represent themselves and others ... it is not merely a pot of messages, a repertoire of signs to be flashed across a neutral mental screen. It has *form as well as content*; is born in action as well as thought; is a product of human creativity as well as mimesis; and, above all, is empowered. But it is not all empowered in the same way, or all of the time. (Comoroff and Comoroff 1991: 21–2, my emphasis)

Culture *unites* form and content; hegemony and ideology *separate* form and content. Hegemony is power embodied in the taken for granted "forms of everyday life"; it is the "non-agentive" face of power. Ideologies are the conscious texts or contents of power; it is "agentive." Ideology because it articulates a content is open to contestation, resistance and rebellion, whereas hegemony is subtle, pervasive and ultimately difficult to contest because it subsumes the forms that structure actions and beliefs. If ideology represents the conscious, hegemony represents the unconscious. Culture is the almost primordial desire to reconcile form and content – thus it is the terrain upon which resistance takes place but a resistance bounded by prevailing ideologies and hegemonies.[17]

"Conversion" and "conversation", the terms that the Comoroffs use to examine the dance of action and reaction on the part of the colonizer and the colonizee, occur in the liminal space between hegemony and ideology or in the cultural arena. The Tswana were not blank slates upon which the British missionaries could inscribe their views of the world. Rather, they were active participants in the process of colonization as they attempted to accommodate their traditional tribal practices to the new doctrines that the missionaries brought.

An apt example of this process is a dialogue between the village rainmaker and the British medical doctor that the Comoroffs recount (pp. 210–12). In this discussion, magic attempts to accommodate science, and science attempts to stamp out magic. The medical doctor argues that only God can make the rain and the rainmaker responds that he has medicines that make rain. The doctor insists that medicine is rational and no medicine exists that makes rain. After a bit of back and forth, the raindoctor points to the formal similarities between rainmaking and Western medical practice:

> I use my medicines and you employ yours; we are both doctors, and doctors are not deceivers. You give a patient medicine. Sometimes God is pleased to heal him by means of your medicine; sometimes not – he dies. When he is cured, you take the credit of what God does. I do the same. Sometimes God grants us rain, sometimes not. When he does, we take the credit of the charm. When a patient dies, you don't give up trust in your medicine, neither do I when the rain fails. If you wish me to leave off my medicines, why continue your own? (Comoroff and Comoroff 1991: 211)

The missionaries are not satisfied with imposing new ideologies that can easily be ignored or adapted; they wish to change the forms of social behavior – to impose a new hegemony.

### Macro-level Studies Using Interpretive Approaches: Historical Ethnography of Symbolic Political Practices

Human agency and its relation to political meanings and practices is a salient feature of the works thus far discussed. We will now turn to a mode of approaching politics and culture that is interpretive, rather than explanatory. Practitioners of this mode of analysis read meaning and power, and ultimately social structure, from political events and institutions. In prescient remarks, Clifford Geertz (1983) writing in the mid 1970s said, "Thrones may be out of fashion, and pageantry too; but political authority still requires a cultural frame in which to define itself and advance its claims" (p. 143).

Geertz's influence has ranged widely across sociology, history, political science and anthropology and to a certain extent, he defies facile categorization. His (1980) study of the *negara* state in nineteenth-century Bali provides a paradigmatic account of politics, power and ceremony. According to Geertz, *negara* was a "distinct variety of political order" (p. 9). The "theater state" distinguished itself through court ceremonies that enacted representations of the status order and the political order. In Bali, ceremony was the state and "power served pomp, not pomp power" (p. 13).

Geertz's methodological choices support his unusual view of the state. Standard methods of comparative history and ideal-type analysis are not adequate to understand the socio-cultural processes that created *negara*. Political meaning lies in an ethnographic analysis that permits Geertz to ". . . construct, both out of my own fieldwork and out of the literature, a circumstantial picture of state organization in nineteenth-century Bali and attempt to draw from that picture a set of broad but substantive guidelines for the ordering of pre- and protohistorical material in Indonesia (and beyond it) . . ." (p. 7). Ethnography as a method has certain unique features that facilitate understanding the Balinese case. The remnants of nineteenth-century Bali are available for ethnographic scrutiny because Bali did not undergo the transformation that Islamization and Dutch colonialism brought to other parts of Indonesia. Because Geertz aims to portray a political form rather than a historical state, ethnography frees him from the constraints of chronology.

The conception of power that Geertz offers at the end of *Negara* evokes Foucauldian notions of power and discipline. He challenges the definition of power that has reigned since the sixteenth century, which includes notions of coercion, violence and domination. While Geertz does not deny that such types of power exist, he argues that they are intrinsically incomplete. The prevailing view of power is tied to a particular "collective representation" and does not allow that other forms of "collective representation" exist (pp. 134–5). Geertz argues that the cultural forms of ". . . classical Bali comprised ... an alternative conception of what politics is about and what power comes to. A structure of action, now bloody, now ceremonious, the *negara* was also, and as such, a structure of thought. To describe it is to describe a constellation of enshrined ideas" (p. 135).

Political scientists have pursued some of the conceptual frames that *negara* suggests. Benedict Anderson's (1983) *Imagined Communities* pursues the notion of polity as idea. Timothy Mitchell (1991b) works out the Foucauldian implications of Geertz's view of power in *Colonising Egypt*. Anderson described the nation as an "imagined political community" where ". . . the members of even the smallest nation will never know most of their fellow-members, meet them, or even hear of them, yet in the minds of each lives the image of their communion . . . Communities are to be distinguished, not by their falsity/genuineness, but by the style in which they are imagined" (p. 6).

Anderson, who has become an obligatory reference in writings on nation-states, departed from standard conceptions of the nation by privileging its fraternal and emotional dimensions rather than its territorial boundaries. Anderson describes nations as "emotionally plausible" (p. 52) and state bureaucracy as "creating meanings" (p. 53). He asks how do persons become attached to the idea of the nation and become willing to die for it when they are in communication with only a limited number of the national community? Why would one die for France if one does not know all their fellow French? Anderson's answer ranges widely over cases and continents and hinges on linguistic consolidation. New modes of communication, including a developing national print media, fueled the diffusion of a national language and created the imagined community. Elite interests aided by expanding state structure harnessed capital and culture and were crucial to the nationalization process.

In contrast to Anderson who takes what we might loosely describe as a postmodern approach to politics, Mitchell (1990, 1991a, 1991b) casts his work on state formation and colonization in a definitively postmodern mold. *Colonising Egypt* (1991b) employs theories of Michel Foucault, Jacques Derrida and Pierre Bourdieu to provide an an historical exegesis of the "power to colonize" (p. ix). Beginning with a description of the Egyptian exhibition at the World Exhibition in Paris, Mitchell develops a concept of the "world

as exhibition." The exhibition is not the world; it is a representation of the world. Exhibiting is a mechanism of social "enframing"
that makes representation more real than action. Representation
is a mental phenomenon that derives its power from its ability to
disseminate images. The dissemination of images is primary because it makes British constructions of Egypt familiar to the general populace and creates a climate in which British colonization
appears natural and legitimate. The "inert objectness" of the "world
as exhibition" imbues it with the power to "order" which ". . .
makes there appear to exist apart from such 'external reality' a
transcendental entity called culture, a code or text or cognitive
map by whose mysterious existence 'the world' is lent its 'significance' " (p. 62).

The Western image of Egypt, nonrecognizable to the Egyptian
intellectuals who visit the exhibit, buttresses the British power to
"enframe" and hence colonize Egypt. "Enframing" is not merely a
mental category but a technique that allows for the "dividing" and
"containing" of social space and permits the colonizer to enforce
its vision of order. British institutional reform in Egypt such as
schools, housing and public health are the tangible frames of the
mental images that the "world as exhibition" conjures.

Mitchell's target is the Cartesian dualism that distinguishes between the mental and the physical. He argues:

> Disciplinary powers acquire their unprecedented hold upon the body
> by methods of distributing and dividing that create an order or struc-
> ture in which individuals are confined, isolated, combined together and
> kept under surveillance. This "order" is, in effect, a framework. . . . The
> framework, appearing as something pre-existent, non-material and non-
> spatial, seems to constitute a separate, metaphysical realm – the realm
> of the conceptual. (Mitchell 1991b: 176)

According to Mitchell, the Enlightenment's separation of mind and
body and its legitimation of mental and physical discipline made
colonization, as well as the other institutional forms of power such
as the modern state, legitimate.[18]

While one may disagree with Mitchell's epistemological assumptions, he has gathered a large and diverse array of primary
sources to support his claims. Mitchell is fluent in Arabic and
French and brings a specialist's knowledge to his analysis. It is

somewhat ironic to praise Mitchell on terms that his own theoretical assumptions would necessarily reject; however, his scholarship is powerful [sic] and rigorous. Scholars who either wish to take the postmodern turn in an empirical direction, or to empirically challenge it, will have to begin with Mitchell's work.

Sociologists have begun to develop accounts of ritual and symbolic politics (Alexander 1988b; Rothenbuhler 1988; Tiryakian 1988; Smith 1991). The difficulty that public ritual poses as an object of study has produced a scholarship on ritual that tends towards metaphor and detailed textual descriptions of single events (Kertzer 1988; Ozouf 1988). This methodological approach serves to underscore the official versions of ritual (Lukes 1975). It is, to borrow from James C. Scott (1990), effective at ascertaining the "public transcript" of events but less effective at explicating the "hidden transcript."

My work on public political ritual in Fascist Italy attempts to overcome the dilemmas of "thick description" by studying multiple events (Berezin 1994b). My previous writings on fascism and culture (Berezin 1991, 1994a) disprove the idea that the fascist regime politicized art. I now call into question the commonly held position that fascism aestheticized politics. Using previously unexploited historical materials, I analyze fascist rituals as arenas of cultural and political competition over diverse types of collective social identities – citizens, soldiers, mothers, Catholics. I use fascist regime calendars to establish the overall pattern of public ritual and personal and public narratives to examine the staging and imagery of selected events. My research yields a portrait of conflict over the meaning of time, space and memory that permits me to combine political explanation and cultural interpretation.

A discussion of a fascist holiday provides an example of my approach. In 1923, the Italian fascist regime began the process of commemorating its founding event – the March on Rome. The First Anniversary celebration was one of a series of celebrations that the regime institutionalized over the course of its 22 years in power. The fascist regime conceived and spoke of these events as *spettacolo* – performance. The proliferation of spectacle – a Fascist Party calendar from the the city of Verona lists 733 events in a 22-year period – in Fascist Italy suggests that the regime imbued public performance with the capacity to create political meaning and identity. To capture the "political meaning" of fascist spectacle, we must distinguish two levels of meaning as analytic categories that cannot always be held separate as empirical categories: first, the meaning of public spectacle to the regime; and second, the meaning of spectacle to the citizens – the audience for whom these events were aimed.

The first level of meaning involves questions of political intention; the second level includes issues of cultural resonance. The First Anniversary Celebrations established a repertoire of ritual actions around a group of core political ideas that the regime would continue to draw upon for the next 20 years. One such idea was the merging of the sacred and secular. The inclusion of the Catholic Church in fascist commemorative activity and the insertion of fascist ritual activity into Catholic liturgy was a fascist strategy to usurp a familiar Italian identity and ritual space. The merging of the secular and sacred became more problematic as a struggle over ritual turf emerged between the Church and the regime. The Church was a major competitor with the Italian state, fascist or otherwise, for holiday time and public display.

Public space is culturally resonant. Parades were the core action of the celebratory events. Italy as a social landscape combined the symbolic material of centuries with modern social spaces such as elaborately designed train stations. The salience of social space and the political possibilities that parading through it offered were not lost on the planners of fascist spectacle. The regime institutionalized the memory of the March in dramatic reenactments in public spaces. The fascist appropriation of public space was a particularly cogent communicative practice in a country that combined low literacy rates and a babble of regional dialects.

## Micro-level Studies Using Interpretive Approaches: Ethnographic Studies of Political Orientations, Attitudes and Beliefs

In contrast to scholars who focus upon historical exegesis of European cases, an emerging cohort of sociologists takes a cognitive approach to the study of contemporary American political culture. For these scholars the political meanings that lead to political actions are contained in the mental maps of meaning that political participants hold in their heads. Their principal method is ethnographic and sustained free-form interviewing that permits the voices of the social actors to explain themselves. To the extent that they reflect upon their methodological presuppositions, these scholars engage social science paradigms rather than epistemological theories. They discuss the representativeness of their samples rather than the possibility of theoretical knowledge.

Kristin Luker's (1984) *Abortion and the Politics of Motherhood* provides an example of this mode of analysis. In contrast to the other authors discussed here, Luker's data led her to a cultural conclusion. The book's placement in a series on "Social Choice and Political Economy" suggests the underlying questions that originally guided Luker's research. Luker wanted to know what motivated commitment to a social movement. Choosing one of the most volatile, the struggle over abortion in the United States, she interviewed 212 pro-choice and pro-life activists. Luker defined an activist as a person who spent over ten hours a week working on the movement in the case of the pro-life contingent and over five hours a week in the case of the pro-choice.

Luker discovered that the politics of value, and not the politics of rationality, governed movement commitment. Level of commitment to either movement was related to the differing values that activists placed on the ideal of motherhood. Material interests drove the affinity for motherhood. The pro-life women tended to be less educated and more dependent upon their husbands than the pro-choice women. They had an economic stake in the value of the family as an institution. An elaborate rhetoric about the "personhood" of the fetus and the value of human life articulated their economic dependence. Luker correctly predicted that debates about abortion in the United States were likely to become even more heated because they were about passionately felt values. In 1984, when resource mobilization theory was still a dominant paradigm in social movement theory, an approach that took the cognitive frames and values of social movement participants into account was novel.[19]

Jonathan Rieder's (1985) *Canarsie* and Rebecca Klatch's (1987) *Women of the New Right* pursue Luker's line of inquiry. Rieder and Klatch explore single cases that appear problematic if one does not take the intersection of meaning and political action into account. Both authors focus upon the emergence of nonliberal politics in the United States. Rieder viewed *Canarsie* as a crucible for the rest of the nation. Understanding the meaning of *Canarsie* permits us to understand why the word "liberalism" has negative, rather than positive, connotations for a large segment of the American population. Klatch wanted to understand the meaning of conservatism for women who were active in "new right" organizations and causes.

Rieder spent a year living in Canarsie, a lower-middle-class ethnic neighborhood in Brooklyn, New York that in the early 1970s was the scene of racial tension and social protest. Canarsie was the home of second generation Jewish and Italian immigrants who did not wish to share their neighborhood with African-Americans. The Italians were traditionally more conservative than the Jews on political issues. Yet, both groups were opposed to opening their neighborhood to outsiders. Rieder wanted to understand why the Jews who were traditionally liberal in their politics suddenly turned anti-liberal as they watched African-Americans move into their neighborhoods and schools.

The Italians and Jews of Canarsie were not highly educated and held jobs that gave them a tenuous grip on the labor market. Their social horizons were shrinking and buying a house in Canarsie was the principal form of upward mobility that many of its residents were likely to experience. While the contrasting ethnic experiences of the Italians and Jews gave them a different repertoire of cultural rhetorics with which to articulate their concerns, they shared the same hopes and fears. Canarsie was their "haven in a heartless world" and they sought to protect it.

By giving intolerance a human face, Rieder's ethnography permits us to see how values and culture translate into political action. Klatch takes a similar tack in her study of politically conservative women. Combining textual analysis of organization documents, participant observation and interviewing, Klatch presents a nuanced account of the conservative women's ethos. She finds that, contrary to popular liberal conceptions, conservatism is not a monolithic ideology. She identifies a group of "social" conservatives and "laissez-faire" conservatives. The social conservative women fit the standard image of conservatism – they were intensely religious and committed to traditional gender roles. The laissez-faire women were fiscally conservative but they espoused ideologies regarding gender roles that were not strikingly different from those of their feminist sisters. The voices of Klatch's subjects, like their counterparts in Canarsie, dramatize the link between cultural meanings and political actions.

Robert Bellah and his collaborators' (1985) *Habits of the Heart* and their (1991) follow-up study, *The Good Society*, take the interpretive mode of analysis in a new direction. *Habits of the Heart* opens with a moral question, "How ought we to live?" To answer that question, the authors explore how the private and public lives of Americans mesh and affect their visions of and actions in the broader society. According to Bellah et al., the cultural fact that an ideology of individualism lies at the core of American society lacks cogency, if we have no idea as to how individualism translates into political action.

*Habits of the Heart* aims to provide a cultural and political map of how ideas and values translate into action. The uniqueness of this book lies in its use of personal interviews to articulate broad themes about American society. *Habits of the Heart* – the phrase is taken from Tocqueville – employs the novel technique of introducing a cast of four "characters" in the first chapter whose social profiles suggest three broad cultural themes – success, freedom and justice – and four American social types – the independent citizen, the entrepreneur, the manager and the therapist. After establishing these benchmarks of American character and culture, the authors proceed to examine the values and institutions that define the private self. How is the family possible in a society that views love and marriage as a vehicle of personal fulfillment rather than social commitment? More voices are added to the opening quartet. How do Americans "find themselves" in a society that emphasizes the contradictory goals of individualism and connectedness?

After exploring the contradictory nature of American individualism on the private level, the authors turn to the institutions that structure public life – religion, citizenship, and local government. Therapists, volunteers, local political activists, clergy voice how Americans feel about themselves and the polity. The authors follow Tocqueville in that they see the revitalization of American life and culture coming from a new commitment to mediating institutions such as the family, the Church and local activism.

Bellah's group asks broad questions about the meaning of politics and weaves these questions into a general story of American character and culture. What differentiates this study from other treatments of its subject matter is the empirical cast that it brings

to the study of justice, equality and American liberalism. These areas
have more traditionally been the subject of political theorizing,
such as Michael Walzer's (1983) *Sphere of Justice*, rather than empirical analysis. *Habits of the Heart* also differs from normative and
synthetic discussions of American culture. Daniel Bell's (1976) *The
Cultural Contradictions of Capitalism*, although it ranges widely over
Europe and the United States, until quite recently was the only
sociological exemplar of this mode of analysis. In 1991, James
Davison Hunter's *Culture Wars* and Jeffrey C. Goldfarb's *The
Cynical Society* appeared. Both books provide extended arguments
about the current state of American culture and politics. Hunter
focuses on institutions such as family that concern the Bellah group.
Goldfarb whose concern is the emergence of cynicism in American
society and the threat that it poses to democracy is a direct heir to
the Daniel Bell tradition.

## Politics and Culture: Methods, Themes, Events

By way of conclusion are suggestions for some methodological
*caveats*, themes and events that could serve as the source of future
empirical work. In surveying the field as bounded here, several
features are striking: first, its multidisciplinarity – anthropologists,
political scientists, historians and sociologists have made important contributions; second, its tendency to focus on historical European cases; and third, the salience of nationalism and colonialism
as subject areas. The field tends to be multidisciplinary but not
interdisciplinary. A high degree of borrowing, or recognition of
each other's work does not exist among its practitioners. There are
certain theoretical constants. The comparative historical sociologists tend to look to Max Weber to formulate and theorize their
questions. Michel Foucault's influence is stronger in history and
anthropology than in political science or sociology. Clifford Geertz
is the one theoretical constant in all of this work and scholars across
a wide range of disciplines acknowledge his influence.

The sociological study of politics should include where appropriate discussions of meaning without abandoning its traditional
focus on social agents, institutions, and structures. The elucidation
of political meaning leads us to the vehicles of meaning – rhetorical
strategies and symbolic actions of political actors – whether they

be government leaders, clergy, artists, journalists or the "average" citizen, the iconography of political events from revolutions to elections, and exegesis of political documents that range from legal texts to pamphlets and posters.

Themes such as identity politics, ethics and political value, democracy and civil society that are newly capturing the sociological imagination are particularly amenable to empirical study that merges cultural and political analysis. Studies of identity politics and the symbolic actions that they frequently evoke cannot ignore their cultural dimensions. Social movements in the United States such as *Act Up* and *Operation Rescue* rely on symbolic actions. Contemporary neo-Nazi attacks in Europe that have targeted immigrants as undesirable others invoke symbols from the past. Studies that focus upon gender as a political category rather than as an exclusionary mechanism are laying the groundwork for forays into other types of identities. Recent work (Hunt 1992; Skocpol 1992) on the cultural meaning of the family and motherhood and its effect upon political outcomes points to new directions in the study of identity and political practice.

Political theory has frequently taken values as its subject (for example, Shklar 1984). An emerging interest in ethics has encouraged sociologists to frame political issues in terms of morality, and ultimately, culture. The Bellah studies were an early harbinger of this trend. The seminal questions that Alan Wolfe (1989) raises in *Whose Keeper?* and his "Morality and Society" series at the University of Chicago Press suggests that we can expect more work in this mode. For example, Jasper and Nelkin (1992) have cast their work on animal rights' activists in terms of moral issues.

In a recent *Public Culture* article aimed at drawing distinctions between the concepts of civil society and public sphere, Craig Calhoun (1993b: 267) argues that the phrase "civil society" now "finds its way into half the dissertations in political sociology." The revolutions in Eastern Europe have given the concept a new salience. In short, the phrase evokes an argument in democratic theory that emphasizes the institutions of shared public discourse such as mass media and voluntary associations. Current academic interest owes as much to Habermas (1989) as to Tocqueville. With rare exceptions such as Jeffrey C. Goldfarb's (1989, 1992) studies of Eastern Europe, Robert D. Putnam's (1993) analysis of Italian political culture and its effect upon the success of regional government and Victor M. Perez-Diaz's (1993) work on the Spanish transition to democracy, much of the discussion of civil society, as Calhoun's article suggests, has occurred within political theory (for example, Cohen and Arato 1992; Seligman 1992). The dissertations that Calhoun invokes probably will reverse the theoretical trend.

Political culture is a historically contingent area in sociology. It becomes salient in time of social upheaval. Its last renaissance was in the aftermath of World War II and the experience of Nazism and Stalinism. The fall of the Berlin wall in 1989, the re-resurgence of ethnic particularism in the new multicultural Europe of 1992, and the emergence of a new right in Europe and the United States provide grist for the empirical mill that fuels academic interests. Emerging political problems that standard notions of modernity and rationality cannot explain force a revival of interest in culture and provide an opportunity that sociologists should not forego.

## Notes

This article benefited from the thoughtful reading and critical comments of Diana Crane, Jeffrey C. Goldfarb, Krishan Kumar, Theda Skocpol and an anonymous reviewer.

1   Almond and Verba's (1989) paradigmatic study of political culture involved a quantitative analysis of values in different national societies. Inglehart's (1990) work on post-materialist values is a recent and prominent example that employs their methodology.

2   The influence of contemporary European social theory in American academic circles has undoubtedly fueled some of this interest. For a summary, see Lamont and Wuthnow (1990).

3   Friedlander's (1992) anthology on the representation of the Nazi Holocaust is an example of where the fascination with images might lead.

4   An example of the literary foray into politics is Susan Rubin Suleiman's *Authoritarian Fictions* (1992); Freedberg (1989) represents an art historian's view of power.

5   It is beyond the scope of this essay to offer a theory of politics and culture. Sewell's (1992) discussion of social structure and its relation to agency and transformation lays the groundwork for such a theory.

6   Mass media is a historically specific term. In eighteenth-century Europe, the mass media were limited to small local newspapers (Habermas 1989). In our late twentieth-century global world, mass media are technologically driven and include television, computers and cinema. As Michael Schudson's contribution to this anthology (chapter 2) discusses the media, I will not discuss studies of media and politics.

7    There is a British tradition of cultural analysis that departs from the Continental model. Early British studies were classically Marxist in orientation and focused upon the relationship between working-class culture and economic opportunity. Richard Hoggart's *The Uses of Literacy* (1992) is a prominent early example of this school. In the 1970s, Raymond Williams (1977) became interested in the Italian Marxist Antonio Gramsci's concept of hegemony and pushed the British school towards a more literary and media-oriented mode of analysis. In the United States, the British tradition has had its deepest influence in literature departments where "Cultural Studies" has flowered much to the consternation of conservative social critics.

8    There are "cultural" explanations for the European focus upon theory. European academics still tend to equate culture with civilization. Culture belongs to the realm of personal cultivation and politics belongs to the realm of rationality or theory. Europeans who study "culture," pursue literature or art history, not social science. This disposition may be in the process of changing, but old traditions die hard. Even European social scientists who study the "new social movements" – movements based upon identities and values and heavily dependent upon repertoires of symbolic practices – eschew the use of the word "culture" in their descriptions of these movements.

9    The literature on postmodernism is voluminous and growing. For useful summaries, see Giddens (1990); Hall (1990b); "Symposium on postmodernism", *Sociological Theory* (Volume 9, Fall 1991); Rosenau (1992). The briefest and most direct discussion of the problem of knowledge and culture, if not politics, is the debate between Denzin (1990) and Griswold (1990).

10   Skocpol (1979) provided the paradigmatic structural account. Goldstone (1991: 416–58), following Hunt and recent sociological debates about culture, attempts to theorize a role for culture in structural accounts of revolution.

11   Hunt cites *Discipline and Punish* (Foucault 1979) before she offers this definition.

12   For a critique of Foucault that takes a similar view of his notion of power, see Walzer (1988).

13   Earlier sociological studies of this type include Robert Wuthnow's (1989) *Communities of Discourse* and David Zaret's (1985) *The Heavenly Contract*.

14   This part of Brubaker's argument may soon be subject to revision. In late 1992, the German Parliament began to consider restrictions on the reincorporation of ethnic Germans into the state.

15   Because Gramsci defined this concept elliptically, it is somewhat difficult to adapt for theorizing. The classic collection of Gramsci in English is Hoare and Nowell Smith (1971). For a brief exegesis of the concept, see Adamson (1980: 169–201) and Williams (1977: 108–14). Laclau and Mouffe's (1985) *Hegemony and Socialist Strategy* (1985) a book that has been widely

influential in political theory provides a more detailed discussion of the
concept of hegemony and its effect upon political practice.

16 These studies are based upon single case analysis. Lustick (1993) has
   produced a comparative study of hegemonic process in French Algeria,
   British Ireland and the West Bank.

17 The Comoroffs' distinction between form and content articulates with my
   own work on the diffusion of political ideology in fascist Italy – where
   I argue that fascism affected the form and not the content of theatrical
   production (Berezin 1994a) – and Burns' (1992) study of the changing
   ideological practices of Catholic bishops.

18 Mitchell pursues both points in an article on power (1990) where he
   engages Geertz's conception of culture and an article where he challenges
   conceptions of the modern state (1991a).

19 Under the rubric of New Social Movements Theory (Cohen 1985; Melucci
   1985), Europeans were researching the peace, ecology and women's movements that focused upon the politics of value. In the United States, this
   trend has been late breaking.

# 5

# Cultural Models of Organization: The Social Construction of Rational Organizing Principles

## Frank R. Dobbin

Ever since the rise of modern organizational forms in the mid nineteenth century, social scientists have treated organizations and bureaucracies as instrumental social structures that are little affected by culture. Most organizations were thought to conform to general rules of efficiency rather than to local cultural dictates. This view resulted from a tendency to differentiate instrumental realms of social life, like science, economics, and management, that are oriented to objective "natural" laws from cultural realms of social life, like art, religion, and education, that are oriented to subjective "social" principles (i.e., values and norms). In organizational theory, this changed in the late 1970s when the "new institutionalists" described rational management theory and practice as myth and symbol, and began to explore the social construction of rationalized organizations.

## Weber and Parsons: Why Organizations are not "Culture"

One reason early organizational theorists did not think of organizations as "culture" is simply that the modern worldview presents instrumental institutions as nonsymbolic, on the principle that they reflect universal economic laws rather than local social customs. Another reason is that organizational theory has been a hybrid between a theoretical social science and an applied practical discipline; consequently practitioners pursue science-like laws and prescriptions. Nonetheless, it is difficult to understand why social scientists largely failed to see that rationalized organizational practices are essentially cultural, and are very much at the core of modern culture precisely because modern culture is organized around instrumental rationality. By neglecting rationality as a cultural construct we have acted the part of indigenous anthropologists who treat every aspect of social life as cultural *except* the elaborate, purposive customs designed to win the deity's help with the crop yield and fertility.

Max Weber's work illustrates the tension between the modern tendency to see rationality as acultural and the sociological tendency to see all practices and understandings as part of culture. Weber was caught between an Enlightenment vision of rationality as a unified canon with a singular progression of knowledge, and the methodological precepts of *verstehen* and value-freedom which suggested that all social practices are indeterminate and socially produced. The Enlightenment vision led Weber to interpret rationality in terms of a single ideal-type. He described rationalized bureaucracies as rule-governed, hierarchical, and specialized; offices as appointed, salaried, and situated in fixed career lines (Weber 1978, v. II: 956–63). These universal principles were taken to suggest that rational organization conforms to transcendental laws rather than emerging from idiosyncratic social practices. By contrast, Weber's more general exhortations about methods and social customs suggested that no universal social laws could possibly exist. In his works on religion, Weber linked the origins of instrumentally rational accumulative customs not to a set of universal economic laws that dictate the parameters of efficiency, but to the happenstance of Protestant religious evolution in the West. In his writings on sociological analysis, Weber (1978, v. I: 4) insisted that all social behavior is indeterminate and that social practices can be understood exclusively through interpretation: "In no case does [meaning] refer to an objectively "correct" meaning or one which is "true" in some metaphysical sense." Even rationalized social practices, such as those of modern bureaucracies, can only be interpreted subjectively. Rationally purposeful action is easily understood not because it is oriented to an objective standard of rationality, but because the actor "tries to achieve certain ends by choosing appropriate means on the basis of the facts of the situation, *as experience has accustomed us [scientific observers] to interpret them*" (Weber 1978, v. I: 5, emphasis added).

In extending Weber's work, Talcott Parsons (1951) explored these issues but ultimately constructed a theoretical framework that, rather than capitalizing on this contradiction between the seeming universality of rationalized precepts and the indeterminacy of social practices, divided the social world into rigid categories of instrumental action (adaptation and goal attainment) and cultural action (integration and latency). Parsons' theoretical contributions have been eclipsed, but this schema has had a lasting impact because the dividing line Parsons drew between the instrumental and the cultural reflected the modern worldview. One result has been the increasing balkanization of the social sciences, so that economists, and recently political scientists, organize their arguments about instrumentality around mathematical formulas that are thought to capture the asocial, acultural essence of universal economic laws, while anthropologists and sociologists organize their arguments about culture around empirical evidence that is thought to capture the non-rational, historical essence of localized social practices.

The effect of this analytic distinction on academic organizational theory was palpable. Early writers such as Frederick Taylor (1911) and Henri Fayol (1949), who were consultants or managers themselves, developed a body of theory that was decidedly instrumental in purpose. Then Parsons' disciples spun out rationalist abstract theories of organization, taking it as an article of faith that instrumental organizational practices were oriented to some higher-order set of universal principles. The task of managers, and organizational theorists, was to seek out and codify those principles just as the task of physicists was to seek out and codify the principles that governed the physical world. The presumption that the central characteristics of organizations were overdetermined by transcendental laws of rationality prevented analysts from exploring the cultural aspects of rationality within organizations. Analysts built on Weber's list of characteristics of rational bureaucracy, and sought to specify the conditional variables that increased the efficiency of formalization, hierarchy, and differentiation.

By the 1940s scholars were already challenging the undersocialized rationalist conception of organizations. However, their challenges took the form of internal critiques, in that they either suggested that the informal side of organizational life had been neglected, without undermining existing ideas about the formal, rational side, or explored what happens when the goals of rational actors who inhabit organizations do not jibe with the formal goals of the organizations themselves. Philip Selznick and his students challenged rationalists on both grounds by insisting that much important organizational activity is not scripted by formal rules, thus bringing to light the integration and latency side of rationalized organizations in Parsons' terms, and by showing in a series of empirical studies that explicit organizational goals are often subverted by managers in pursuit of their own goals (Selznick 1949; Clark 1960; Zald and Denton 1963). Natural-systems theorists treated organizations as organisms that were highly motivated to survive even after their goals had been achieved, and emphasized the nonrational elements of behavior (Blau 1956; Gouldner 1959). Early Human Relations theorists had similarly argued that formal goal-oriented organizational practices may produce dysfunctional individual-level behaviors if they do not take psychology into account. These insights spotlighted the informal and cultural in rationalized, formal organizations. However, these studies served as exceptions that proved the rule that modern organizations are ultimately oriented to transsituational tenets of efficiency. They failed to question the origins of broad notions of organizational rationality, or suggest that rationalized managerial precepts are social inventions. In the case of Selznick's work, this was true largely because he focused on the intra-organizational processes that create idiosyncratic patterns of action rather than on the construction of collective practices at the interorganizational level. In a similar vein, more recent works on "corporate culture" attend to the charismatic dimension of formal organizations, focusing on the organization-specific ethics that win employee compliance and enthusiasm (Deal and Kennedy 1982; Peters and Waterman 1982; Martin, Sitkin, and Boehm 1985). This chapter focuses on works that question traditional assumptions about the nature of rationality in organizations by exploring how models of organizing are constructed *among* organizations, and hence pays less attention to the "corporate culture" literature which focuses on models that emerge within individual organizations (Barley, Meyer, and Gash 1988; Kunda 1991; Martin 1992).

While the psychological "natural systems" (Scott 1987a) approaches to organizations that proliferated in the management literature of the 1960s and 1970s did nothing to undermine key ideas about the nature of rationality in organizations, except to suggest that rational managers should use Skinnerian or feel-good techniques to steer employees toward the organization's rational goals, neither did the new "open systems" approaches that paid greater attention to the organizational environment. Contingency theory (James D. Thompson 1967), transaction costs theory (Williamson 1975), population ecology theory (Hannan and Freeman 1977), resource dependence theory (Pfeffer and Salancik 1978) – each initially presumed that internal organizational structure was (rationally) responsive to environmental forces, and thereby took rationality to be unproblematic. Population ecology has since incorporated some of the insights of institutional theory (Hannan and Freeman 1989), but otherwise these approaches remain impervious to ideas about the role of culture.

## Organizations as Culture

The rationalist approach had generated a series of intellectual reactions among students of organizations. Early analysts such as Melville Dalton (1950) and Donald Roy (1952) highlighted contradictions between formal structure and workers' actual practices. Neo-Marxists argued that organizational practices were principally driven by labor control and surplus expropriation rather than by efficiency (Braverman 1974; Burawoy 1979; Edwards 1979), opening the door for further challenges to the abstract efficiency of common organizing principles. And a variety of scholars had made normative and intellectual challenges to organizational rationality, including those in the Human Relations school; Selznick and the early institutionalists; both Blau and Gouldner in their emphasis on the informal; and Douglas McGregor (1960) and Chris Argyris (1962) in their emphasis on psychology and self-esteem.

In 1977 two articles from what came to be called the neo-institutional perspective launched a more systematic, cultural critique of rationalist approaches to organizations. John Meyer and Brian Rowan's "Institutionalized organizations: formal structure as myth and ceremony" treated rationalized organizational principles as symbols of modernity and efficiency, rather than as acultural instruments of modernity and efficiency. Lynne Zucker's "The role of institutionalization in cultural persistence" explored the micro processes surrounding the construction of modern, rationalized, organizational practices. These pieces stressed the semiotic side of organizational practices, and hence the cultural dimension of the instrumental types of behavior that the Parsonian schema had dubbed "not culture." These formulations had little in common with the new institutionalism in economics and with either statist or "positive theory" variants of "new institutionalism" in political science (but see Scott 1992).

These works turned the prevailing rationalist approach to organizations on its head by arguing that supposedly universal precepts of organizational efficiency are simply abstractions from social practices that emerged for complex historical reasons. The project of rationalized, scientistic, social systems is to glean universal social laws from experience and apply those laws to the pursuit of collective goals. Neo-institutionalists insisted that understanding the social processes surrounding this project is the work of organizational sociologists.

The roots of this social constructionist approach are found in the social phenomenology of Alfred Schutz, and in Peter Berger and Thomas Luckmann's (1966) *The Social Construction of Reality*, which challenged realist approaches by arguing that rationalized social and economic laws are subjective social phenomena that are *derived from* experience rather than objective natural phenomena that are *revealed through* experience. At its core, this phenomenological view depends on a sociology of modernity that takes rationality not as the "end of history," but as one in a series of institutionalized worldviews. These works did not prescribe absolute cultural relativism or "deconstruction" as a means to transcend the limits of positivism, as humanist challengers of the precepts of modernity are wont to do. However, they did challenge the teleological nature of social-scientific approaches to modernity which presume that we are in the midst of a linear progression toward enlightenment about the true nature of the modern universe. By suggesting that instrumental rationality is just one in a series of constructed meaning systems, alongside mysticism, religion, and secular philosophy, the phenomenological approach to modernity problematizes foundations of rationality that most social scientists thought they did not have to explain. Not only rationality itself, but individualism, the nation-state, interests, science, economics, and the whole Durkheimian complex of modern institutions are seen in a different light if we take instrumental rationality to be problematic precisely because it was not the inevitable culmination of history. In other words, phenomenologists presume that instrumental rationality emerged for identifiable social and historical reasons that merit examination, rather than because, as a meaning system, it more accurately represents the nature of reality than mysticism, religion, or philosophy.

The new cultural approach to organizations, then, is embedded in a larger intellectual project spanning several disciplines that seeks to explain, sociologically, the emergence of a wide variety of modern institutions and the particular laws that are thought to govern those institutions. How did the modern system of nation-states emerge (Meyer and Hannan 1979; Thomas and Meyer 1984; Krasner 1993; Ruggie 1993), and how did nation-states' particular rationalized policy strategies arise (Dyson 1983; Hall 1993; Dobbin 1994)? How did individualism come to be so central to modernity, and how did citizenship arise as an institution to link individuals to nation-states (Anderson 1983; Ashcraft 1986; Watkins 1991; Soysal 1994)? How does labor become commodified (Hobsbawm 1968) and how does life itself come to be given particular economic value (Zelizer 1979, 1985)? How do economic laws become constructed and institutionalized over time (Veblen 1904; Commons 1934; White 1981; Granovetter 1985; Zelizer 1988)? How did science, and scientific methods, arise in their current form (Wuthnow 1980), and how are particular scientific precepts constructed (Bloor 1976; Knorr-Cetina 1981; Latour 1992)? How does knowledge in nonscientific academic realms become consecrated (Lamont 1987)? Finally, how did the formal organization come to eclipse all varieties of informal social organization (Perrow 1991a), and how did particular managerial precepts emerge? Neo-institutional approaches to organizations are part of a much wider intellectual endeavor that problematizes modernity, and questions the social origins of the whole constellation of institutions and at the same time seeks to grasp *not* the universal laws that generate social practices, but the social practices that generate universal laws and, in organizational theory, attendant management prescriptions.

History has produced an ideology and social order that creates three, embedded, levels of actors – the individual, the organization, and the society. Each is an abstraction and at the same time a reification, and the three are nested in ways that make them practically and conceptually inseparable (Friedland and Alford 1991: 242). One outcome of the historical construction of the society, or nation, as the highest-order collective actor is great uniformity among organizations at the national level; indeed great uniformity can be found among instantiations of any sort of instrumentality at the national level. This is not to say that regional organizational cultures are rare, but that modernity poses national-level "imagined communities" (Anderson 1983) as the proper level of intersubjective agreement about the nature of reality. Among organizations another key level is the "societal sector" (Scott and Meyer 1983) or organizational "field" (DiMaggio and Powell 1983; Scott 1994), consisting of the organizations in an industry and in adjacent positions (e.g., suppliers) or similar positions (e.g., kindred industries) that serve as a reference group – that organizations compare themselves to in assessing their own procedures and structures. Those fields have increasingly transcended international boundaries (Scott 1994) while at the same time the growing elaboration of universal rules of organizing tends to break them down so that sector and nation become irrelevant to managers (Meyer 1994).

Intersubjective agreement is key to the sustenance of cultural forms, for, "Social life is predictable and orderly because of shared role definitions and expectations, the authority of which rests in a shared conception of social reality" (Scott 1992: 19). The contention that intersubjective agreement is the foundation of local social practices is readily accepted by the students of societies and institutions that do not operate on strict principles of instrumental rationality, such as the pre-modern Balinese state (Geertz 1980) or even charismatic American sales organizations (Biggart 1989). In Durkheim's totemic societies, where natural symbols infuse all kinds of social practices and give meaning and order to social life, we readily recognize that different totems will be adopted by different groups, but that once adopted those totems will be represented in a wide range of social practices in each group. The circumcision mat inscribed with the totem is readily recognized by the ethnographer as both symbolic and instrumental. It is more difficult from within the frame of the modern, rationalized worldview to see our own rationalized totems, such as the organization chart, as simultaneously instrumental and symbolic.

## Four Themes in Cultural Approaches to Rational Organizations

The early empirical studies that provided evidence for this cultural approach to organizations were conducted on educational organizations. They shared several characteristics that made their arguments plausible even to the most die-hard rationalists. First, they were conducted on organizations that were designed to impart norms and values rather than on organizations that were strictly profit-oriented. It was quite plausible that myth and ceremony were central to the business of schools because in the Parsonian schema, as in the modern worldview, schools are part of the cultural realm of modern life. Second, they examined government-mandated organizational practices and treated government mandates as unproblematic. This allowed analysts to "black-box" the issue of how legitimating organizational practices are socially constructed; the source of these practices was self-evident. Third, they neglected the role of interested individual actors in institutionalization, which allowed them to bracket the problem of how power, interest, agency, and political processes contribute to the institutionalization of practices. Fourth, they focused on formal rules and structures that were decoupled from actual practice. That is, they showed that organizations formally adopted certain practices as window-dressing, and then failed to use those practices. In brief, by examining organizations

- that were self-consciously cultural in purpose
- that were subject to clear government mandates
- that adopted practices that had become institutionalized in the external environment by unspecified actors with unspecified interests
- that routinely adopted rules for the express purpose of achieving legitimacy without regard to implementation

neo-institutionalists were initially able to set aside a number of problematic issues in order to make a convincing, if minimalist, case for the role of culture in modern organizations. However, subsequent work has broadened this cultural approach by tackling all four of these limitations, and the remainder of this chapter charts those efforts. Each limitation is considered in turn.

## From culture qua norms to culture qua instrumental rationality

Early studies looked at schools, mental health providers, hospitals, and nonprofit organizations, in the belief that not-for-profit organizations subject to government regulation were most susceptible to pressures to achieve legitimacy by manipulating symbols of justice and efficiency. In their *Organizational Environments* (1983) John Meyer and W. Richard Scott made a distinction between organizations operating in the "institutional" sector (i.e., governmental and nonprofit organizations), where survival and success were largely dependent on legitimacy (i.e., the use of accepted rules and structures) and on public funding, and those operating in the "technical" sector (i.e., for profit organizations), where success depends more directly on the bottom line. Their point was interpreted by many in Parsonian terms to suggest that "instrumental" organizations in the "technical" sector are governed largely by rational, profit-oriented action and that organizations in the "institutional" sector are governed by cultural norms. Scott (1992: 16–17) has more clearly specified the distinction, arguing that most organizations depend simultaneously on *output controls* linked to technical considerations and *process controls* linked to institutional considerations, and as early as 1983 Paul DiMaggio and Walter Powell anticipated the need to specify the diverse processes by which organizations seize cultural models from the environment. Coercive isomorphism occurs when a powerful organization, such as the state, imposes rules and practices on organizations. Normative isomorphism occurs when organizations voluntarily adopt practices that afford legitimacy. Mimetic isomorphism occurs when organizations copy the cultural practices they see in the environment in order to achieve the outcomes they hope to achieve. This third form describes how profit-seeking organizations most often come to copy instrumental practices from one another. DiMaggio and Powell (1991: 32) have described the association of "institutional" characteristics with nonprofit sectors and "technical" characteristics with proprietary organizations as "no longer viable" as a result of a series of empirical studies that have underscored the role of "institutional" processes in the legitimation of "technical" practices in proprietary organizations. Powell (1991) argues that because all kinds of economic behavior are simultaneously cultural, the distinction has been a false one.

Acceptance of the insight that instrumental practices are at the same time cultural is particularly hard-won among American students of organizations, largely because neoclassical economic theory and rationalist organizational theories are based on generalizations from the American case. American organizational practices have been treated by theorists in these traditions as ideal-typical and pure, while the diverse organizational practices found in other countries were treated as adjustments to government meddling. This tendency was reinforced by the rhetoric of government nonintervention in America, the gist of which is that policies that enforce price competition among firms merely reinforce natural economic processes. Thus in America, active state intervention has been couched as "laissez faire" (nonintervention) and resulting organizational practices are thought to be outcomes of natural economic processes. The whole economic and organizational environment, then, came to be conceptualized as natural rather than human-made. While Karl Polanyi recognized the very same misconception in British thought as early as 1944, and showed that "laissez faire" was initially produced in Britain by a series of deliberate state actions rather than by governmental restraint, theorists have been reluctant to consider American regulatory policies as a form of intervention. The American belief in the naturalness of economic life was also bolstered by the huge size of the economy and the absence of proximate, developed neighbors with significantly different economic and organizational systems. Such a naturalized vision of the economy would be hard to sustain in France, for instance, where nearby countries operate successfully with dramatically different economic structures and organizational practices.

The empirical remedy to this natural-order conception of instrumental organizational forms came in studies that analyzed the social construction of key, rationalized, organizational practices. A series of studies challenged the premises of neoclassical economists and rationalist organizational theorists by seeking to show that as key organizations labelled new practices "efficient," organizations hungrily consumed them with little reflection about whether they were truly efficient and with little concern for whether those practices were suited to their own needs. Pamela Tolbert and Lynne Zucker (1983) studied the diffusion of municipal civil service reforms, designed to rationalize government employment, between 1880 and 1935 and found that while governments that had functional needs for improved authority adopted the reforms initially, once civil service reform became denoted as modern and rational, all kinds of municipalities with no particular need for reform jumped on the bandwagon. Neil Fligstein (1985, 1990) showed that changes in the focus of American corporate strategy, from manufacturing to marketing to finance, were driven not by some ineluctable evolutionary force as Alfred Chandler had argued but by the leadership of key corporations that promulgated new models of efficient organizing over time.

Fligstein and others highlighted the role of the federal government in the construction of particular organizing conventions as efficient, to the end of countering the notion of the neutrality of the American state while helping to specify the origins of certain conventions. These studies meanwhile undermined prevailing neoclassical and rational choice explanations of the same phenomena. Baron et al. (1986) showed that modern personnel systems were developed by networks of managers and federal officials during World War II, in response to new federal policies that regulated the movement of labor rather than in response to the imperatives of organizational size and union control as rationalists had suggested. Stephen Mezias (1990) found that federal regulatory agencies, early-adopting organizations, and accounting professionals participated in the diffusion of an important new accounting procedure among *Fortune 200* corporations, and that rational-actor approaches poorly explain diffusion. Dobbin et al. (1993) show that internal labor market practices, which labor economists link to the imperative of retaining firm-specific skills in select industries, diffused after 1964 in response to federal equal employment opportunity laws that led managers to focus attention on formalizing employee selection mechanisms. To show the cultural nature of instrumentality, each of these works examined the social construction of rationality from inside of organizations and organizational fields. They substituted an inductive and phenomenological approach to rationalized practices for the deductive and teleological approach typically adopted by organizational analysts.

Another approach has been to trace the diffusion of organizational practices that symbolize equity, such as affirmative action policies, grievance procedures, and due process mechanisms, across organizations in "instrumental" and "technical" sectors alike to show that even proprietary, profit-oriented organizations signify their commitment to norms of justice and equity (Dobbin et al. 1988; Edelman 1990, 1992; Sutton et al. 1994). These studies have found, for instance, that once due process mechanisms such as grievance procedures became socially constructed as necessary for protecting employees from arbitrary behavior on the part of managers, it became illicit for large, modern, organizations *not* to have them. Edelman and Petterson (1993) have taken this argument one step further by looking at the effects of affirmative action rules and departments: organizations install one type of affirmative action structure if they are most interested in symbolizing equity, and another type of structure if they are most interested in *achieving* equity. In turn, the first kind of structure has little effect on employment ratios while the second kind has significant effects. More generally, these studies have traced how the Western elaboration of the inherent rights and attributes of the individual leads to new social norms and conceptions of efficiency that may coincide in practice. By giving disadvantaged employees the right to be considered for promotion and to file grievances against the arbitrary actions of managers, for instance, organizations not only win external legitimacy but help to motivate those very employees to be more effective, or so managers argue (Dobbin et al. 1993).

## From "black-boxed" origins to historiography and ethnomethodology

Early studies bracketed the problem of the origins of new instrumentally rational organizational practices by focusing on practices promulgated by central authorities, or on the process DiMaggio and Powell (1983) term "coercive isomorphism." These studies tended to focus on forms that are constructed in response to the actions of governing units: professional bodies, legislatures, courts, regulatory bodies, certification and accreditation boards (Scott 1987b; Davis and Powell 1992: 355). The role of sponsoring institutions is certainly important in the creation of organizational practices, particularly because many "institutional sectors or fields contain environmental agents that are sufficiently powerful to impose forms and/or practices on subordinate organizational units" (Scott 1987b: 501). Yet a more interesting, and vexing, question concerns how organizations collectively come to agree on what is rational when state action is absent. Arthur Stinchcombe pointed out in 1965 that entire industries tend to take on the organizational structures common in the historical epochs in which they are born, so that new firms in established industries tend to adopt technical and managerial models that were popular when their older peers were founded. How, then, do particular historical models arise? Answering the question for an organizational rule, practice, or structure involves opening up the black box by chronicling debates among managers and charting the pattern of diffusion. Moreover initial causes are often difficult to tease out, because cultural norms, cognitions, and coercive arrangements often quickly come together:

> These dimensions of institutionalization presumably feed on each other, as when cultural prestige (e.g., a new organizational device is generally admired as more rational) leads to cognitive dominance (e.g., it is believed, by ordinary participants and by scientists, to work better, or indeed, to be the only model that really works) and coercive controls (e.g., managers who do not institutionalize it are deemed negligent). (Meyer 1994: 5)

Historical studies have explored the origins of a number of organizational practices by focusing on activity at the level of the interorganizational field, where managers actively champion solutions as efficient. They frequently find that practices that emerged for idiosyncratic conjunctural reasons unrelated to the problem to which they are eventually addressed are embraced as solutions simply because they are available. Baron et al. (1988) trace modern personnel theory and practice – often depicted as the result of an integrated, deductive, approach to human nature – to a hodge-podge of personnel practices that emerged, separately, in three different sectors of the American economy during the 1920s and 1930s. Calvin Morrill's (1991) analysis of the diffusion of the hostile takeover, and the elaborate executive culture that accompanies the takeover, charts the emergence of a new rationalized practice that arose among elite managers – without any apparent external sponsor in the form of a professional organization or government agency – and caught on like wildfire. A number of studies have shown that even when American legislation seems to be the direct cause of a new organizational practice, managers often actively negotiate with public officials and the courts over what will be deemed acceptable and tend to concoct compliance solutions out of spare parts from other organizational models. "Coercive isomorphism" is thus quite participatory in the United States because legislation typically provides only broad outcome-oriented mandates and then leaves it to managers and the courts to work out specific prescriptions for compliance (Edelman 1992; Dobbin et al. 1993; Abzug and Mezias 1993; Sutton et al. 1994). These studies have focused on interorganizational networks of managers who devise rational models of organizing, and the origins of the building blocks they work with.

Lynne Zucker's explicitly ethnomethodological approach represents an entirely different strategy for disassembling the black box. Her critique of the prevailing macroinstitutional approaches is, in essence, that they consider institutionalization to be a *state* rather than an active social *process*. As a result, macroinstitutional approaches to organizations frame problems at a level of analysis that precludes observation of the actual micro process of institutionalization. Zucker asks how the exteriority and objectivity that are central to the construction of regularized institutions are achieved at the interpersonal level. She has pushed this ethnomethodological solution to the problem of how regularized organizational practices emerge in a series of articles (Zucker 1977, 1983, 1987, 1991; Tolbert and Zucker 1983). Zucker's approach is in no way inconsistent with macroinstitutionalism, but it highlights the importance of local social processes in the creation and maintenance of meaning. Karl Weick (1979) has explored these very issues by examining the enactment of social structure in organizations. Organizational routines may be created at the interorganizational level, but they must be enacted locally to attain meaning and salience. Deirdre Boden's (1994) *The Business of Talk* employs the insights of conversation analysis to link micro behavior patterns to social structure, insisting that because social structure is made up of action, by treating social structure as independent of individual-level action, we reify it in a way that obscures its essential nature.

## From actor-less institutionalization to interest articulation

Charles Perrow (1987) and Paul DiMaggio (1988) have argued that early formulations of neo-institutional theory neglected agency, interests, and politics. Perrow implies that the perspective is inherently conservative in that it treats emergent rights for disadvantaged groups as social constructs, which he takes to suggest that disadvantage itself is a social fiction. In part, this perception results from the fact that early institutional studies focused on the symbolization of justice and equity, which consumers of organizational theory readily agree is normative, rather than on the symbolization of rationality, which they tend to see as "not symbolic." Recent treatments have restored agency, interests, and politics. For a number of institutionalists Ann Swidler's (1986) "Culture in Action" provided an opening for reintegrating agency, by defining culture as a "tool-kit" that gave substantial autonomy to actors while constraining the individual strategies they could conceive and carry out. Swidler offered a corrective to the oversocialized conception of actors that Mark Granovetter (1985) bemoaned in sociology by arguing that people can actively, and even self-consciously, use cultural symbols for their own ends. Of course, even this kind of deliberate use of culture is highly institutionalized in that the modern worldview posits a series of individuated self-interested actors who actively employ rationalized prescriptions for action, and who actively manipulate meaning and understanding, with the goal of utility maximization.

To incorporate interests most works have charted the role of interested groups in the construction of organizational practices and strategies, or have shown how public policy shifts mobilize particular groups to promote new practices and strategies. Fligstein's (1990) *The Transformation of Corporate Control* looks at competing managerial factions as self-interested groups that seek to promote their own expertise as the basis of organizational rationality. He charts the struggles among management factions to impose business strategies that privilege their own particular skills, such as skills in financial management. Mezias (1990) likewise charts the role of the accounting profession in constructing particular financial reporting practices as strategically rational among large corporations. Baron et al. (1986) and Edelman (1990) show how public policy shifts lead personnel professionals to promote employment practices under the guise of compliance with federal law, but with the aim of expanding the size, scope, and power of personnel departments. DiMaggio (1991b) charts the central, and self-interested, role of arts professionals in institutionalizing public art museums as we know them today, in the early decades of the twentieth century. Strang and Bradburn (1993) explore interest articulation in the creation of regulatory structures for health maintenance organizations, and show that state regulation is not truly exogenous to organizations but rather can be stimulated and shaped by the subjects of regulation themselves. Despite these correctives, most institutional/cultural studies continue to neglect interest articulation as it is traditionally envisioned – between classes. Even the growing body of literature on the effects of Equal Employment Opportunity legislation (Dobbin et al. 1988; Edelman 1990, 1992; Abzug and Mezias 1993. Dobbin et al. 1993; Edelman and Petterson 1993; Sutton et al. 1994; ) largely brackets the role of the Civil Rights movement in promoting key legal changes (but see Burstein 1985).

The most challenging theoretical insight that this perspective offers vis-à-vis interests is that interest groups themselves are historical social constructs rather than primordial units. The historical creation of the categories of labor and capital, line and staff, professional and nonprofessional, manager and worker, principal and agent, thus becomes a central focus of theory and research. At the societal level, this insight dates to Seymour Martin Lipset and Stein Rokkan's (1967) *Party Systems and Voter Alignments*, which traced how history produced interest groups based on class in some Western nations, and interest groups based on religion, race, region, ethnicity, or sector in others. More narrowly, Dobbin (1992) suggests that the "objective" material interests of labor and capital are socially constructed, showing that between the 1920s and the 1950s the perceived interests of business and labor groups on the question of social insurance versus employer-provided benefits were highly unstable and highly responsive to changing public policies and negotiated interpretations of interest.

Ronald Jepperson's (1991) elegant theoretical synthesis contains the important point that when Dahrendorf speaks of the "institutionalization of class conflict" he refers to a process, coincident with the institutionalization of class *categories*, whereby active struggle is replaced by a routinized form of struggle. In this process class conflict becomes scripted, ritualistic, and completely predictable as it becomes naturalized. More broadly, these analysts presume that the categories of actors, their patterns of action, and their underlying interests are all culturally constructed. They are, of course, in good sociological company (Berger and Luckmann 1966; Goffman 1974; Davis 1991; Lamont 1992). Yet for the most part, these theoretical insights about the institutional origins of key categories of actors, and of their interests, have remained untested by neo-institutionalists.

These treatments beg the more fundamental question: is self-interest itself as we now think of it somehow innate? Are humans biologically self-interested? Albert Hirschman's (1977) answer in *The Passions and the Interests* is that even this most taken-for-granted human characteristic is a product of history rather than biology. Lust for goods, power, and sex motivated action in the medieval world; *interest* and *advantage* came to govern behavior, cognitive structures, and identity formation only as moral, economic, and political philosophers transformed the passion of greed into a virtue that, properly harnessed by the state, could serve the project of modernization.

The whole field of organizations, of course, presupposes the historical construction of the organization (i.e., corporation) as a category of actor. James Coleman (1990) charts the legal evolution of the corporation as a legitimate social actor since the Middle Ages, and links it to the particular course that the differentiation of social activities took in the West: "The conception of the corporation as a legal person and the reorganization of society around impersonal corporate bodies made possible a radically different kind of social structure" (1990: 536). The nineteenth century saw legal changes that gave elaborate new rights and privileges to the corporation, such as limited liability, and reinforced its status as a primordial collective actor, alongside the nation-state and political party (Creighton 1990). Whether or not the corporation as a legal person was inevitable because it was functional, which Coleman and the institutionalists might disagree about, it is important to note that it is historically quite uncommon as a form – thus far only a flash in the long progress of human history. And those with their fingers on the pulse of contemporary business practices (Pfeffer and Baron 1988; Hirsch 1991; Davis-Blake and Uzzi 1993) have detected shifts away from stable organizational employment toward temporary employment and independent contracting: the information revolution might well lead away from the classic bureaucracy as Weber described it and toward a world made up of individuals engaged in contractual service agreements. The point of searching for the social origins of particular interest groups, of self-interest itself, and of organizational forms is that to think sociologically about these things, one must be able to think of the world as we know it as only one among many possible outcomes of history.

## From symbolic-because-decoupled to cultural-because-indeterminate

Early cultural studies of organizations demonstrated that particular formal rules and practices were fundamentally symbolic by showing that they were "decoupled" from *actual* practice. That is, they showed that organizations adopted elaborate sets of formal rules and practices to demonstrate compliance with, and attentiveness to, evolving conceptions of efficiency and justice within organizations, and then routinely ignored those formal rules and practices (e.g., Weick 1976; Meyer 1977, 1978; Meyer et al. 1978; Meyer et al. 1979). The result was that their policy and procedure manuals grew fat while their day-to-day operations changed little. "Yes, we have a policy covering that," administrators could say, while paying little attention to the policy. This approach provided compelling evidence that much of organizational practice was symbolic; however, it tended to reinforce the Parsonian distinction between the symbolic and the instrumental. The core practices that organizations *did* routinely perform appeared *not* to be symbolic or cultural.

The remedy came in the form of studies of organizational practices that are actively used. It is more difficult to show that practices that organizations *do* use routinely, and that organization members defend as efficacious and necessary to continued operation, are cultural phenomena. The analytic strategy most scholars have adopted is to demonstrate that rationality is highly indeterminate and variable over space or time. By showing that organizational rationality is not narrowly circumscribed by transcendental economic laws, but rather that economic laws permit a wide range of different organizational practices and strategies, analysts have sought to demonstrate that notions of what is rational are historically contingent and change dramatically over time and space, and thus are fundamentally cultural.

Marco Orrù, Nicole Woolsey Biggart, and Gary Hamilton's (1991) "Organizational isomorphism in East Asia" is a prime example of the strategy of demonstrating variability over space. In an analysis of Japan, Taiwan, and South Korea they seek to show that organizations and industries are structured similarly within nations, but that they take dramatically different forms across nations. They trace those differences not to unique disruptions of perfect market conditions across these countries, but to broader cultural patterns that have generated different approaches to economic organization (see also Hamilton and Biggart 1988). What is most compelling about their work, and about other comparative studies of the East Asian newly industrializing countries (see the papers in Deyo 1987), is that East Asia presents several very different models of economic organization that appear to be similarly successful in terms of promoting growth. No singular model emerges from the East Asian experience. Another approach to understanding cross-national differences is found in Robert E. Cole's (1989) *Strategies for Learning*, which examines the diffusion of a new organizational form, the small work group or quality circle, to show that national organizational and political structures promoted Japanese adoption, stalled US adoption, and had a mixed effect in Sweden. Similarly, in studying twelve matched firms in Germany and France, Maurice et al. (1984) find that the typical functional predictors of organizational employment structures – size, product, and technology – explain little of the variance but that national models of organizing explain much of it (see also Maurice et al. 1980). These studies suggest that broad institutional characteristics of nations, rather than universal economic laws, determine the sorts of organizational practices that become constructed as rational.

As Mark Granovetter (1985) has hinted, markets are highly variable in form and depend on intersubjective agreement about what is rational that frames expectations about the actions of others and produces prescriptions for the actions of ego. Such agreement emerges at the national level largely because the modern nation-state has become the locus of collective action and rationality. The pursuit of progress, via rationalized action and scientific knowledge, has been organized principally at the national level (Jepperson and Meyer 1991). Thus nations develop typifications of how rationalized social processes operate to produce growth, which frequently rely on naturalizing analogies (e.g., the functional parts of an organism or Darwinist natural selection) (Douglas 1986). It is also characteristic of modernity, however, that, as societies become increasingly organized around the secular nation-state, rather than around the primordial religious or ethnic group, all sorts of social structures diffuse across societies with increasing speed. Isomorphism increases and new structures will spread more quickly (Strang et al. 1992; Strang and Meyer 1993). One implication is that we may see greater convergence in organizational forms among nations, but not for the reasons cited by functionalist analysts. The functionalist/ economistic argument is that there is an optimal organizational form and that over time organizations throughout the world come to more closely approximate that form as they come to better understand it. In the phenomenological view described here, by contrast, managers believe wholeheartedly in the existence of an optimal form and engage in the quest for that form by actively searching the global environment for structures and practices that are marginally more efficient than those they already employ. Thus for phenomenologists the world's organizations are not converging toward some ideal-typical organizational form that is not yet fully understood, rather they are busy copying the latest fashions in organizing. The process is driven by widespread belief in the existence of law-like principles of social efficiency, to be sure; however, the history of management thought and practice suggests that consecrated organizational practices change with the regularity of womens' hemlines – following the pattern of fashion whims – rather than moving ineluctably and in a singular progression toward some ultimately efficient ideal.

A second approach to demonstrating the multiplicity and contingency of rationality has been to chart changes over time in notions of what is rational *within* a single country and industry. A number of the studies outlined above take this approach by charting the construction of new, rationalized, organizational strategies and structures over time. Amburgey and Lippert (1989) have charted the diffusion of managerial leveraged buyouts (LBOs) between 1980 and 1986, finding that news broadcasts about LBOs, and simple contagion, played important roles in popularizing this new organizational strategy. Tolbert and Stern (1989) found that bureaucratic structures for making decisions about attorney compensation have diffused among large, differentiated, geographically dispersed law firms. Such evidence of the emergence of new ideas about what is rational does not, in itself, undermine microeconomic or rational choice explanations. However, a number of these studies have found that managers imprint on successful organizations with the explicit aim of appearing up to date and precluding challenges to their own leadership. "We did it because IBM does it" seems to be the prevailing rationale for following the leader.

These approaches have been bolstered in the social sciences by a growing belief that history is not necessarily efficient (March and Olsen 1984; Krasner 1988; Scott 1992). While societies strive for purportedly optimal social arrangements, institutionalized practices place constraints on what is practicable and tend to shape what can be conceived in the first place. Thus even Douglass North, whose particular variant of institutional economics gives pride of place to rational action, has come to talk in terms of path dependence in the evolution of economic practice at the national level (North 1990).

## Conclusion

Prevailing rationalist approaches to organizations have been driven by a form of functionalist realism in which the central tenets of the modern worldview – that modern institutions are transparently purposive and that we are in the midst of an evolutionary progression toward more efficient forms – are taken at face value. The project of organizational analysts and management theorists , then, has been to glean the generalizable principles of rationality that can be found in modern organizations and to chart the evolution toward more efficient forms of organization. Elaborate teleological assumptions underlie this perspective. It is taken as an article of faith that existing organizational practices must serve a purpose, and must represent the world's best effort at creating efficiency. This precept is found both in structural-rationalist arguments (e.g., Blau and Schoenherr 1971) and in environmental-rationalist arguments (e.g., Williamson 1975). All of these models presume a social universe determined by a set of transcendental economic laws that define what is rational. The rationalist worldview suggests that transcendental economic laws exist, that existing organizational structures must be functional under the parameters of those laws, that the environment will eliminate organizations that adopt non-efficient solutions, and that individual-level utility maximization operates effectively to keep organizations efficient. A number of the prevailing organizational theories fail to question these assumptions.

New cultural approaches to organizations take none of this for granted, and as a result they begin with an entirely different set of questions. Like new cultural approaches to science, nation-states, public policy, and the whole gamut of modern rationalized institutions, cultural approaches to organizations question how our contemporary social categories and notions of rationality emerged. They presume that these categories and notions represent properly *social* phenomena, rather than transcendental rules of economic or political order. Charles Perrow (1991b) asks: Why is the modern world composed of organizations, and not simply contracts between individuals? Why are "capital" and "labor" key social categories, and why does capital hire labor rather than vice versa? Why are there stable jobs, and not simply skills? Stephen Krasner (1993) asks: Why do we have bounded nation-states rather than the Holy (or Rational?) Roman Empire? Why do we have public organizational bureaucracies that govern delimited territories rather than competing city-states? George Thomas and John Meyer (1984) ask: Why did the most farflung outskirts of "civilization" become part of the project of rationalization rather than continuing to operate under alternative worldviews? Charles Tilly (1984) asks: How did the fundamental social science categories we take to be natural emerge? As a cultural system, instrumental rationality has naturalized all kinds of social categories, relationships, and cause–effect designations under the theme that these institutions are shaped by natural laws of efficiency, rather than by the will of a transcendental deity. By taking the central ideas of rationalized cultural systems to be the objects of study, neo-institutionalists have reconceptualized the most fundamental components of modern organizations. Hence they have progressed from studying peripheral organizational practices to studying the core rationalized practices of modern organizations.

Underlying the idea that organizations are shaped by local, historical processes rather than by universal principles of rationality is the conviction that the evolution of organizational forms is haphazard, rather than a unilinear progression toward increasingly efficient practices. It goes without saying that the project of modernity is to achieve progress through scientific discovery and efficient social engineering; hence organizational practitioners claim increased efficiency as their primary goal. This idea is at the center of the post-Enlightenment rationalist *weltanschauung*. As a result, as organization men and women hone the definition of what is rational and develop increasingly complex theories and practices of rationality they believe they are part of a process of evolution from simpler, less efficient, social forms to more complex, and more efficient, forms.

This Darwinist imagery of societal evolution has been repeated in myriad realms of modern life. Charles Perrow (1991b) takes a new page from evolutionary theory (à la Stephen Jay Gould, 1989) to highlight the peculiarly asociological character of this approach. Gould uses fossils to show that biological evolution was a process of the decimation of diversity, and hence possibilities, through the decline in variety and heightening of particular biological traits. Randomness and happenstance, rather than the selection of better-adapted forms, characterized the process. Likewise, argues Perrow, institutionalization among organizations at any point in time involves a decline in variety and convergence toward particular forms, but not necessarily positive evolution toward some optimally rational form.

The great challenge of sociological subdisciplines that deal with rhetorically instrumental, and hence rhetorically acultural, realms of modern social life is to transcend naturalized categories, causal designations, and relationships among actors (collective and otherwise) in order to treat their social emergence as objects of study. In other words, it is necessary to treat *institutionalization* itself, or the "process by which a given set of units and a pattern of activities come to be normatively and cognitively held in place, and practically taken for granted as lawful" (Meyer et al. 1987: 13). By *not* treating these units and patterns as sociologically problematic, analysts run the risk of studying modernity with social categories and causal paradigms that are, themselves, endogenous to the object under study. The epistemological key to escaping this trap is to view all social categories and paradigms of causality as fictions. History indeed suggests we should take nothing for granted, because even today's most basic social unit – the individual – we know to be an historical social construct that was largely the product of the Enlightenment (Meyer et al. 1987; Ruggie 1993). Mayer Zald (1994) makes a parallel point: "Many of our major theories and theoretical schemas have in fact been conceptual abstractions from concrete historical and civilizational events and trends." As such, many of our theories have the same epistemological status as common sense, in that they take the form of laws gleaned from social experience, the meaning of which is socially constructed in the first place (Geertz 1983). By contrast, the cultural approach to the study of organizations described in this chapter suggests that the rationalized, universal, laws that purportedly constitute modern social practice are in fact *derived from* modern social practice.

## Note

My thanks to Diana Crane, Paul DiMaggio, Michèle Lamont, John Meyer, Calvin Morrill, Charles Perrow, W. Richard Scott, and Kathleen Thelen for helpful comments and suggestions.

# 6

# Toward a Sociology of Material Culture: Science Studies, Cultural Studies and the Meanings of Things

*Chandra Mukerji*

There is no question that science and technology have become central to modern industrialized (and post-industrial) cultures, and hence essential to any cultural analysis of contemporary social life. The authority of scientific knowledge may not be entirely unchallenged, but it remains by and large intact. Technological optimism may not be as high as it was in the nineteenth century, but today many people still seek technological solutions to the problems created by earlier regimes of science and technology without questioning the propriety of their activities. Reasons for the cultural primacy of science and technology abound in the social sciences. Science is revered because it epitomizes the rationality of modern life, because it is the legitimate voice of capitalist development, because it is a system for the rational exploitation of resources, because it has powerful advocates, because it is the knowledge system that most frequently "works" (whatever that means), because it is written in a language of measurement and precision that gives it authority, or because it is used by and is useful politically for the modern state (Hempel 1966; Habermas 1970: ch. 6, 1975, 1981; Leiss 1972; Bell 1973; Gouldner 1976; Laudan 1977).

Given this respect for the power of science (whether it be couched in laudatory or cautionary terms), there is obviously reason for sociologists of culture to pay attention to science and technology, but it is less than obvious how this should be done. There should be some lessons to be learned from the sociology of science, but it is not clear how the recent literature could enrich cultural analyses of contemporary societies, since the studies in it so rarely reach beyond the walls of scientific laboratories. As scholars from other disciplines engaged in contemporary cultural studies increasingly turn their attention to science and technology, sociologists of culture could make a contribution by drawing from the wealth of interesting insights that have been developed within the sociology of science. This chapter provides one starting point for doing this.

In the post-Foucauldian and post-Gramscian world of cultural studies, in which scholars strive for new ways to identify and characterize the social power of culture, much attention is given to the ways science as a knowledge system and technology as its instrument carry or concentrate power within the culture (Williams 1961; Foucault 1970, 1978; Hebdige 1979; Gitlin 1980; Ross 1989; Haraway 1991; Schudson 1992). As social analysts have considered the various ways systems of culture can help distribute and redistribute power within a society, what they have found interesting *within* culture are those arenas with particularly close ties to power (like science and technology).[1] The culture of science and technology, by most accounts, helps to reinforce and reproduce existing hierarchies, and, where possible, naturalizes them (Latour 1988a; Haraway 1989). The program for cultural studies is clear enough: follow the power of knowledge systems. Michel Foucault, Pierre Bourdieu, Jürgen Habermas, Antonio Gramsci, Donna Haraway and Bruno Latour are there to point out the terrain to explore (Foucault 1970, 1978, 1979; Habermas 1970, 1975, 1981; Bourdieu 1984; Latour 1987, 1988a; Haraway 1991).

But what if concentrating power or instituting hierarchies is not the only important purpose or power of culture? What if the power of science and technology is derived less from their status as knowledge systems than their role as systems of material practice, around which people form what Raymond Williams (1958) – among others – calls ways of life? How important to social process is material culture, not just in the processes of production, distribution and consumption but the design and uses of the objects themselves? We live in highly artificial environments with buildings, heating systems, sewers, sidewalks, chemically nurtured agricultural products, computerized weapons systems, air transport systems, and computer-based manufacturing and writing. Science and technology have been central means for building this world of things.

The physicality of objects can, as Foucault (1979) made clear, sometimes be central in shaping human relations. The Panopticon made manifest systems of classification that realized patterns of domination. As Langdon Winner (1986) more recently documented, if the bridges on a highway are designed explicitly to exclude buses and trucks, they limit the social contacts among those who live near that road; only those wealthy enough to own cars will be joined by such a system. More often than not, the material culture on which group life rides is not designed intentionally to limit social contacts, but is a byproduct of patterned, coordinated action. Still, they can act as constraints on some and facilitate other kinds of action. Bridges, canals, railroad lines, road systems, and even paths in the woods, precisely because they organize human movements, all contribute to the formation (or not) of social linkages. They may be built for economic and other practical purposes, but their consequences are not limited to pragmatic ones. They enter into a larger system of social construction: the production of an artificial environment for sustaining, organizing, and enhancing human life (unfortunately, usually just enhancing the life of some subgroup of the population). This constructed environment includes both what sociologists usually think of as the realm of social construction (a symbolic world of meanings embedded in language) and a meaningful *physical* setting for more or less coordinated social action. Importantly and surprisingly, the distinction between the physical and symbolic in the socially constructed environment often breaks down. The book, for example, lies as much in the world of goods as it does in some abstract realm of word-meanings, and its coordinating possibilities result in part from the symbols it carries and also in part from its physical reproducibility (Goody 1977; Eisenstein 1979; Latour 1990).

The physical features of our artificial environments help to forge social bonds that extend over time as well as social space. Buildings and language records, for example, can (like Latour's (1987) immutable mobiles) extend networks of actors beyond face-to-face interactions; they can even function as depots for social memories that help to define the cultural meaning of temporality and/or sustain residues of ways of life that are no longer favored by present systems of power. Where human constructs have a substantial physical presence, they can endure long after they have ceased to "make sense."[2]

To find a language to discuss how the material world is mobilized to construct ways of life, we can turn to that slightly dusty but hardly well-worn concept, material culture. The cultural artifacts located in the category are made out of natural resources and are brought into the social world to help direct human relations; these objects are part of the artificial world of human beings, located in the physical environment but dictated by human rather than natural order. Material culture is made up of the objects that people both derive and distinguish from the natural resources around them to make a visibly human environment in which to organize group life (Sahlins 1976; Douglas and Isherwood 1979; Csikszentmihalyi and Rochberg-Halton 1981; Mukerji 1983; Appadurai 1986b; Campbell 1987).

By most accounts, this material culture, this art, artifice, artifact, object world, since it is not natural, is removed from the realm of science, which is composed of natural objects. Science is about what lies beyond society, and material culture is the residue or achievement of patterns of social life. But contemporary sociologists of science and technology have helped to demonstrate that science itself is a product of material human practices and is a means by which the world is conscripted into culture through the production of new artifacts (specimens, computer read-outs, new bio-engineered life forms, etc.). Scientists and engineers have their own ways of life and material cultures that they use to increase their reach into the material world (Collins 1982; Hacking 1983; Rudwick 1985; Shapin and Schaffer 1985; Pickering 1992).

While the material productiveness of science and technology has become quite apparent to many sociologists considering scientific practice, sociologists have not yet provided rich accounts of the border crossings between science and nonscience inherent in science's material life and consequential for contemporary culture (except perhaps for Bell 1973). Scientists and engineers help to produce the material world we live in and gain power because of this. This chapter will first review previous approaches to the understanding of science and technology and then suggest how we can better understand the power of science and technology by tracing material practices.

## Perspectives From the Sociology of Science

It is not that sociologists of either science or culture have been sitting on their hands doing nothing. Both have been particularly valuable actors in the efforts to conceptualize the production of culture or scientific thought without recourse to stories of individual creativity.[3] Sociologists of science and technology have questioned the cultural assumption that what scientists know is true, and what others know is merely belief, and have asked what can be learned if that distinction is studied as a problem for scientists rather than assumed by social analysts. Simultaneously, students of culture have questioned the authority of art, including folk art, in relation to commercial or popular culture, asking what we can learn about human culture if we are not limited by the biases of the Great Tradition (Lowenthal 1950; Hirsch 1972; Denisoff 1975; Peterson 1976). Since there is no obvious universally accepted means for distinguishing the great from the mediocre in the arts or what will be a lasting "truth" rather than a provisional model in the sciences, making claims at this level makes little sense to many social scientists. And if we cannot make claims about the inherent superiority of these works, it is impossible to theorize about the genius (or lack of it) among the individuals doing the work.

In the sociology of both culture and science, eschewing "auteur" or "Great Man" theories of human creativity has been easier than trying to understand human thought and creativity in group rather than individual terms. How could more than one person think, inventing images for science or art (popular or esteemed)? One answer increasingly embraced by social analysts is language. Language is a shared cultural system that no one individual could create alone, for which human coordination is necessary, and with which individuals think and create. In fact, language is such a fundamental cultural system, seemingly essential to human life (since all humans apparently develop language, if they do not find one in their social environment), that it can be treated as the model or centerpiece of all culture (Lévi-Strauss 1966; Foucault 1970, 1978; Vygotsky 1978; Habermas 1981; Barthes 1983). Everything that humans make within their culture can be treated as essentially language-embedded or language-like, be it science, literature, or television shows.

This view has found a home in the sociologies of science and the arts with roots in symbolic interactionism or other microsociologies that treat talk as central to social life. If symbolic interaction, human communication, is reduced to language, then a whole subfield of sociology has to account for language in social action. If human activity can only become a sustainable part of group life when it is made symbolically meaningful through language, then language analysis is an essential tool of cultural inquiry for sociology. The sociologists reaching these conclusions have found themselves in recent years accompanying their colleagues in the humanities through a thicket of language studies.

## Language Analysis and Cultural Studies

There has been an enormous number of analytic positions asserted and abandoned within cultural studies since the early 1970s, all of which have been based on theories of language and culture: structuralisms of various sorts, semiotics, poststructuralisms, and most recently postmodernisms – again plural at each stage (see, as a start, Mukerji and Schudson 1986, 1991). In these incarnations of the analytic project, new aspects of language have been explored in ways that have underscored the communal properties of language and the collective life (conflictual as well as consensual) promoted through it.

Structuralism made the most radical break from the individual to the group. With that theory, language took on a life of its own, managed not by the perceptions and ambitions of individual speakers, but organized around principles of orderliness located in shared human capacities for language. Individual speakers only voiced the commonalities of a shared linguistic system. Some scholars thought this was because human beings were physically endowed with the mental structures for language-making and hence expressed those structures in their words; others claimed that it was because language was the highest group achievement and individuals could not be more than small contributors to and reproducers of the larger system. In either case, to be human meant to be involved in the group production of meaning through language. Human culture was essentially a system of formal orderliness or structured meaning, resulting not from social structuration but the structuration of language (Lévi-Strauss 1966; Douglas 1991).

Semiotics looked at how fundamental orderliness and language-like qualities appeared in areas of culture that were not easily reduced to forms of talk: films, wrestling matches, magazines and other parts of popular, and often material culture. Using linguistic models of analysis to approach these objects, semioticians located meaning-making of a linguistic sort in all culture. The point was not to reduce everything to language, but to take spoken language as the most elaborated and social of human enterprises – what we could do at our best. Other forms of cultural meaning-making were efforts in a similar direction, sites for the exercise of similar capacities; hence they had language-like properties. If films and clothing as systems of signs were imperfectly mapped by linguistic systems, it was because language was closer to the heart of the human enterprise and hence more perfect. It was the "form" against which the object worlds of semioticians would be held (Barthes 1983; Lurie 1983; Mukerji and Schudson 1991).

Poststructuralism moved away (not entirely but in direction) from claims about the essential qualities of language to questions of language use, the political intentionality of language systems and writing as an instrument of power. In this move, analysts had to consider the differences between writing and speaking. The connection to linguistics (as the study of speech) was attenuated when cultural analysis began to be focused on writing, a kind of language use with its own material practices. Language was no longer in the ether around groups or hardwired in human brains, but mobilized, materialized, and made to do work. Under poststructuralism, intentionality was restored to language, not by resurrecting the individual writer or speaker as the subject who makes meaning but by locating collective intentionality in the politics of language use and its embodiment in texts, mental hospitals, and the like. Semiotics, as the study of language-like culture in non-language forms, including material culture, was made continuous with poststructuralist analysis of language politics, particularly in the work of Foucault (1970, 1978). The orderliness of things and language found common cause in the politics of cultural life, the organization of domination through the intersection of language categories and the world of objects: in the order of things (Foucault 1970, 1979; Mukerji and Schudson 1991).

With postmodernism, politics remained in the analytic picture, but orderliness began to wither away. The possibilities of disorder and nonsense were explored, as analysts saw domination of the population less in the creation of false, politicized language-based realities than in the disintegration of meanings altogether – an end to the coordinating possibilities of language, a fruitlessness in speaking as a form of human action in the world, the possibilities for betrayal and (on the bright side) the escape from ideology that could occur when hegemonic language became misunderstood. Advertising might create a dream world of floating signs to which consumers might attach themselves, but the detachment of advertising images from reality made it more difficult for advertisers to shape the consciousness of consumers; TV viewers could as easily build new dreams of consumer passion from the swirl of images before them as they could stabilize and accept the ones presented to them on TV. Scholars now talked about signs and symbols dislodged from their moorings in ways of life, reused in new contexts where they did not make sense, where they could create a sense of cultural familiarity that could lull people into complacency. In the process, historical consciousness was erased and meaninglessness became the principle of domination. Group life was stabilized because individuals were immobilized in systems of culture that gave them no avenues for meaningful action – only pleasures that were located in the play of culture and language. The freedom in the system might open new possibilities of understanding and culture creation, but since the signs of a society were developed primarily for commercial purposes, they usually led people further toward meaningless play with objects (the pleasures of consumption) and farther from meaningful relations with others (Ross 1989; Lash 1990; Lipsitz 1990; Haraway 1991).

## Scientific Talk

Within science studies, the turn from the individual to the group took a different route, not without influence from cultural studies, but often uncoordinated with it. Kuhn (1970) was the first harbinger of change in his theory of scientific revolutions, when he argued that scientific "truths" were embedded in historical regimes of belief built by groups of researchers. The paradigms they upheld were based on assumptions shared by members of the group that limited and directed research agendas through their common understandings of what constituted good work. Scientists, he argued, have in different periods maintained paradigms that have addressed different aspects of the natural world. Each has had its own internal measures of quality that do not hold for work in other paradigms.

Paradigms change when anomalies arise in research that cannot be explained within an existing paradigm. Attempts to account for the anomalies can lead to the formation of a new paradigm and a revolution of scientific understanding. Kuhn argued that the engine behind science could not be individual scientific genius, since the most productive periods in the history of science occurred under stable paradigms, when most scientists were engaged in rather routine research. The powerful group life in science during these periods made scientific advances easiest to realize.

The sociology of science under Merton found much inspiration in Kuhn's approach because it put the group life of science so clearly in the center, but the content of science dropped from view, and with it, both the language and practice of science. Merton was interested in locating the distinctiveness of the scientific enterprise in the special values and institutions that had regulated the vocation/avocation of science, not so much in patterns of thought that resulted from it. Sociologists of science, under his guidance, tried to understand the community of scientists as well as its mores and norms, and to explain how this community affected the careers of individual scientists: when their work was cited or not, and how their institutional lives and informal social relations shaped their achievements (Hagstrom 1965; Crane 1972; Merton 1973).

During the anti-Mertonian revolution of the 1970s, language began to take on a larger role in defining the group life of scientists as sociologists made their analytic goal explanations of how scientists arrived at shared conceptions of the natural world. The new sociology of scientific knowledge (SSK) was derived from a range of microsociologies that used analysis of symbolic exchanges to explain how "reality" was socially constructed. SSK made particularly liberal use of conversational analysis, a technique from ethnomethodology that was itself meant to subvert and escape the scientism within sociology. The application of conversational analysis to science was spearheaded by Michael Lynch and Harold Garfinkel, and was absorbed in various ways in the work of Knorr-Cetina, Gilbert, Mulkay and others, all of whom looked at how scientific talk in and around laboratories was at the heart of scientific discovery and conceptual development (Garfinkel et al. 1981; Knorr-Cetina 1981; Gilbert and Mulkay 1984; Lynch 1985).

Latour and Woolgar (1982) took a similar stance at first, but included semiotics in their analytic strategy, allowing students of science to look at the artifactual life of language in laboratories, primarily in what they called inscription devices. Inscriptions could be pictures, numbers, or ordinary language. All were language-like, and all made the human coordination in science a multilayered activity. By drawing attention to writing and drawing, Latour and Woolgar not only brought ideas from poststructuralist versions of semiotics to science studies, but also pointed to aspects of language that conversational analysis could not touch (Latour and de Noblet 1985; Latour 1990). Following Goody (1977) and Eisenstein (1979), they argued that language (or pictures) in text had two important qualities that made it different from speech (or direct observation): it was immutable and mobile. Inscription devices gave ideas and observations a material existence that stabilized them, allowed their reproduction and distribution over time and space, and hence enhanced their power to organize scientific thought. To believe a finding, one need not have been in the presence of an experimental observation; there was no need to act as a witness in someone else's laboratory. One had only to read publications and review the charts and tables presented there. Virtual witnessing (Shapin and Schaffer 1985) no longer required copresence for a demonstration of authority; text could replace public experiments with much the same result. The embodiment of evidence in mobile images, ciphers and written words allowed scientists to extend networks of believers beyond the laboratory. Science gained power by joining the distant to the local through inscriptions.

For many sociologists of science, the trouble with Latour and Woolgar's approach was that it was devoid of political analysis at the societal or institutional level. Latour and Callon's collaboration (Callon 1986; Latour 1987; Callon and Latour 1992) yielded a kind of language study that seemed all the more removed from the institutional politics of science described by the Frankfurt School (Leiss 1972; Habermas 1984; Aronowitz 1988; Feenberg 1991). For British scholars rejecting Marxist analyses of science but still living in the proximity of the revival of British intellectual Marxism, this French cultural theory seemed to be either too ungrounded or too precious to swallow. While moving away from the macrostructural-ism of Marxism, many in SSK moved toward an interest model of scientific practice that, like Callon and Latour's (1992) theory, took laboratory life as the site of collective work, but that presumed scientists' ideas were swayed by their interests in larger institutional arrangements (Collins and Yearley 1992a, 1992b). Scientists fashioned their scientific beliefs, they argued, not just in local collectivities but in relation to nonlocal cultural and political circumstances that impinged on their lives. Scientific truths were built not just on reigning paradigms or regimes of talk but on institutional arrangements that gave practitioners shared (or opposing) interests. According to the interest model, scientists usually engaged in a group life that was filled with conflicts, where multiple groups competed for ascendancy. Because of science's cultural power, scientists' lives could never be completely disentangled from the larger social world (Bloor 1976; Barnes and Shapin 1979; Pickering 1984; Collins and Yearley 1992a, 1992b).

The attention to language in all the schools of SSK varied from one theoretical system to the next, but talk was a thread running through all their methodologies. Situated practices, local knowledge, networks, translations, and controversies were the objects of research pursued by all these groups with their tape recorders or archival records. All paid careful attention to the language recorded there. SSK researchers have stalked a scientific knowledge, lying in the words of scientists – spoken, published, or sketched on a board. Where words ended, pictures followed and were searched for their language-like qualities, the ways they helped to organize categories of the natural. By studying the communication systems in science, researchers in the sociology of science could maintain their focus on the constitution of knowledge, while considering the role of group process in that constitution. What they could not account for adequately this way was the material productiveness and intrusiveness of science and technology. To make sense of the mobilization of nature in laboratory work, they had to account for the material practices of researchers.

## Beyond Language Studies

While privileging language was useful in science studies to move accounts of scientific discoveries away from individualist explanations or organizational reductionism, it did not make SSK any more useful for cultural analysis of science than cultural studies itself. SSK became more conceptually innovative and distinctive as an area of sociological thought when it considered the material aspects

of local social practice. For researchers studying science using ethnographic techniques, it was hard not to notice and think about
how bits of the natural world entered into the labs: how specimens
were treated, how images of the skies were fixed, how microbes
were made materially as well as conceptually present to scientists.
Material analysis was not (as it was elsewhere in sociology) derived
from Marxist tenets, but rather anthropological ones: a way of
describing and accounting for how scientists acted in everyday life.
The material was not a realm of social life, but objects designed,
built and/or used in a local context.

Kuhn had argued that paradigm shifts were not just changes in
ideas about nature but also turning points in methodological
procedures, revolutions in material practice. The practice of science
became routinized during periods of normal science, allowing
researchers in different labs to compare their results. It is hard to
know if SSK derived its attention to practices from Kuhn or labs
themselves, but the pattern of interest is clear enough. Harry Collins
(1982), Steven Shapin (1989), even Bruno Latour (1987, 1988a) and
others (Henderson 1991) have pointed to a materiality in the life of
science that cannot be explained sufficiently as language games.
And in the philosophy of science, Ian Hacking (1983) has fed this
interest by providing new ways to think about experimentation as
material practice. He argues convincingly (against purely mentalist
accounts of science) that scientists learn about the world by participating in it, by acting in and with nature through experiments.
The special dialogue between sociologists and philosophers of
science has influenced the growth of SSK in many ways, including
the attention to practices and the material life of science.

## Science and Material Culture

Paying attention to the role of material culture in social life gives
us a new way to think about the power of science and to link
laboratory life in science to the broader culture. Science is a systematic means for acting in and with nature, creating new ways of
working with the material and hence finding means to make it
serve human (or inhuman) purposes. Nature is more than an ally
that can help scientists promote a conception of the natural world;
it is a source for the invention of new material culture. Critical

theorists from Horkheimer to Marcuse (and contemporary heirs to this tradition) recognized this; they argued that experimentation makes science powerful because in finding ways to ensure the physical domination of nature through experimentation, people also produce systems of social domination (Leiss 1972; Aronowitz 1988). Science is certainly important as a system for experimentation *in the world*, but its power does not just reside in the experimental exercise of engineered control. It also lies in the physically generative power of science and technology to alter the environment in which human groups act, adding to and redesigning the vast and elaborated system of material culture in which contemporary social life takes place. Where the material culture of the scientific laboratory moves beyond the buildings that house labs and enters into the material culture of the larger society, it engages with systems of power (Merton 1970; Layton 1974; Durbin and Mitcham 1978; Mukerji 1989).

It turns out that it is easy to follow the material life of science out of the laboratory and into the arena of state power, if you look at technology, particularly military weapon systems designed by scientists or developed and used according to scientific principles. It is hard to argue that military engineering has not been an important element in the history of state power.[4]

Not just in the last 400 years of Western history (McNeill 1982; Russel 1983; Brewer 1989) but elsewhere as well, weapons turn out to be among the most common objects that human beings make. Many microsocieties have them, and most large-scale ones only developed their size because of military strength. The desire for domination in larger societies is palpable in military museums all over the world that present in frightening abundance the fruits of years of human effort and ingenuity put in the service of the arts of war. Clearly in this case, experiments with metals, mechanics, and structural engineering have made a difference in violent political disputes.

To the extent that scientists and engineers engage in specific projects for designing and developing weapons or otherwise facilitate acts of war, they contribute (as Critical Theorists suggested) to the formation of a material culture designed for domination, destined to be used well beyond the walls of the laboratory, and affecting state power. The boundary between science and nonscience collapses and the cultural power of science grows as objects cross from science onto the battlefield or sites of strategic planning.[5] In this process, the world of science enters into the lives of ordinary people: the soldiers on the battlefields using these weapons, the suppliers who manufacture the new weapons of war, the groups whose political fate is tied to the outcome of the conflicts, and the families who will mourn the dead.

Many other forms of science and technology have less obvious roles as cultural actors and political forces. NASA is a good case in point. The space programs in the US and Russia have been touted as displays of the scientific and engineering prowess of the two countries. These have been quasi-military projects, weapons of the Cold War, demonstrating states' abilities to mobilize missiles in a technological game of "chicken." National scientists and engineers were called upon to manifestly assert the reach of the state into new realms of nature (space); they were recruited to make claims about future as well as present powers of the state through claims about science and technology. These political moves were not made so much with ideologically loaded language as with politically loaded material culture, necessarily symbolic and material at the same time (MacKenzie 1990; Tatarewicz 1990). They were, on one level, conspicuous displays in which the wealth, resources and technical capacity of the state were flaunted through dramatic acts of what, paraphrasing Veblen (1953), one might call "conspicuous waste." On the other hand, they were territorial gestures toward space, claiming a kind of dominion based on the capacity to get there. Science and technology were touted as the means to these glorious ends, and the material culture that went into space came out of laboratories (often military ones).

In oceanography, there is another interesting story to tell about how the world of military technology has entered the public realm. The Argo-Jason system, the research submersible with a remote sensing system (the robot Jason), was developed with Department of Defense money in part for military searches of the seafloor for lost military equipment, but also from the beginning the system was developed for research purposes, and was primarily used in early stages by scientists who wanted to study seafloor spreading (Mukerji 1989). Its military significance was not great, but the Jason did have important political value when this system was used for locating the *Titanic*. It was presented as a dramatic demonstration project, a materially embedded claim of US technological domination over the seafloor. Significantly, even though the discovery was made on a joint US–French cruise, the discovery was treated as a US victory because the Jason system was used.

The search for the *Titanic*, like much of the space program, is easy to characterize as a form of "conspicuous waste" with multiple meanings. It was (in all its complexity) a material experiment that straddled the boundary between science and nonscience, marrying new search equipment with an attempt to answer a popular historical puzzle about the fate of a ship that had become a symbol of the achievements and flaws of the technological optimism of the late nineteenth to early twentieth centuries. The video cameras on the Jason brought to the surface and into the public domain dramatic images of the elegant interiors of the great ship, left gathering sediment on the abyssal floor. The power of the images was not derived from the military origins of the Argo-Jason system or the comparable success of the Jason designers compared to those of the *Titanic*, but the way the search-surveillance system could speak to the culture's deep ambivalence toward technology, simultaneously pointing to past technological hubris, to the potential of new machinery, and to the ongoing commitment of the American government to make its military power at least in part contingent on technological experimentation.

This blurring of the boundaries between science and nonscience, this leakage of scientific material culture into other social realms beyond the control of scientists, may be most apparent near but does not just occur around the military. The power of science is easiest to point to there, but the movement of scientific material practices beyond the lab abounds elsewhere and contributes to the overall power of science and technology to the culture.

In medical research, too, crossovers from research routinely enter the everyday life of the population. Ways of manipulating chemicals, bodies, imaging technologies and the like are all material forms of scientific practice that move unquestioningly over these boundaries. MRI scanners and CAT scans are imaging technologies that have changed treatment practices in some areas of medicine – for example, cancer. Where there is evidence of illness in the soft tissues, these imaging systems are now routinely used in the US, and can help prolong the life of many patients. For people with cancer, these machines are terrors and wonders that enter their lives unexpectedly and abruptly from the world of experimental medicine through clinical practice. For clinicians, they are tools that they can use to enhance their success rates in treating patients, and hence their careers. The development of these technologies may not have been entirely distinct from image-enhancement work with roots in military surveillance, but more importantly, they have been part of a different domain of technological experimentation, providing a different conduit from scientific experimentation to broader cultural practices, where new technologies, bioengineered medicines, and the like meet clinical medicine.

Military and medical *technologies*, then, can carry scientific experimentation into the broader culture. However, if we take seriously what Marshall Sahlins (1976) says about material culture, we should see material culture as a much broader category than just technology, and science and technology should affect parts of material culture beyond the limits of technological innovation. For Sahlins, material culture includes all parts of nature that have been made meaningful within systems of cultural action. The material culture of science and technology, then, must include all the experimental objects that are fashioned in laboratories to represent nature inside experiments. It includes the parts of the deep ocean that are marked by sonar equipment to make them available for use; it is in the devastation that was caused at Hiroshima; it is embedded in the high-rise buildings that stand over cities; it is in the old bomb shelters that were built under US suburbs in the 1950s; it is in herb gardens that classify and mobilize nature for the kitchen; it is in the water systems of cities; it is in maps, drawings and photographs that give us cultural visions of space; it is in weather maps with the evening news; and it is in household appliances and the design of Central Park in New York City.

In seventeenth-century France, we can see one of the least obvious and most important sites where the resources of science and technology were mobilized to make nature serve systems of culture and power. While the modern state was being shaped late in the century through social innovations in bureaucracy, taxation, and monetary policy, it was also being constructed physically on the land. State formation was in many ways a kind of material practice accomplished through science and technology, resulting in the transformation of parts of nature into territories of political regimes. Making a state territory was not primarily an ideological development, the cultivation of ideas about French culture and the boundaries of France that was produced in words; it was more fundamentally a coordinated system of actions in the world. The boundaries of France were written in this period on maps and (more importantly) on the land itself in the string of fortress cities constructed by military engineers around its borders (Mukerji 1993). A new economic unit coinciding with the political unit was built not just with the monetarist theories for which the French were famous in this period (Appleby 1978), but also physically with canals that linked areas that previously had had little commerce with one another. The land itself in this period was restructured physically as it was covered with new kinds of plants and ways of growing them. Forests were tended to support the ship-building for Colbert's ill-fated navy and commercial crops were brought into the more successful domestic economic system. The list of material manipulations through the observatory, scientific academy, and other state institutions could go on and on. The point is that centralizing political power in the state was importantly an act of *material* manipulation, using the natural world to fashion a material culture of state power (Mukerji 1993). The result was that a new set of social relations could be built around this new material culture. The nation could be and would be eventually built inside of the territorial state.

In this case and others, material culture worked in fashioning human bonds and facilitating human life in ways that were interesting precisely because they were not the same as those of language. Pointing and manipulating, working hands, eyes, and things, material culture constitutes a kind of medium that is both essential to human beings, and a means for shaping relationships that is as central as language to human coordination.

The question for social scientists who look at science and the natural world need not just be how do people make nature cognitively meaningful, but how do people live in a material world that is not entirely human? How do people construct social meanings and group lives with hands as well as tongues? How does science fit with that project?

These questions lead us back to the material productiveness of science and technology. If some of the power of culture should be traced not to the realm of ideas but to the capacity of groups to act on and with material resources, then those sites in the culture in which people nurture their material skills constitute relatively hidden but important loci of power. Scientists and engineers who develop new materials for weapons systems end up both facilitating certain acts of war and filling the material environment with a new substance. If the new material is tried in other domains of engineering, it may result, say, in the design of a new kind of bridge. Scientists and engineers routinely find new ways to act on parts of nature and practice, getting predictable results from their actions. That is the heart of the experiment – and a source of material innovation.

Foucault (1979) argued that regimes of domination often have a material dimension that helps to distribute power through domains of life beyond the direct reach of explicitly political institutions. Social categories with their political force do not realize their power just in forms of speech, but in their manifestations in the built environment: the prison, mental hospitals and the school. Lefebvre (1974) contends that the exercise of power gains durability and hence some of its strength from embeddedness in physical markers of space that assume the categories of life generated by systems of material relations. Human life is lived in spaces that are simultaneously representational and constraining, framed by the needs of the economic system as both concepts and places. Haraway (1989) contends that categories of power are not just projected onto the mute elements of the natural world or the materials extracted from it. In the process of scientific research, nature (including animals) becomes physical demonstrations of social categories, naturalizing them. For example, primate families are used to provide us with lessons about "human nature." With this move, animals as well as nonliving materials from nature are conscripted into social processes through techniques of categorization. For all these theorists, in different ways, the actions of science and technology, in making the materials of nature available for cultural work, add to systems of power that are diffuse, dimly visible and definitive.

The limitation of all these theories is they assume that the material dimension gains its authority through its relationships to language categories. These writers help us understand how the power of language reaches beyond the range of the spoken word and how echoes of talk could resound within our built environments. Still, Lefebvre (1974), Foucault (1979) and Haraway (1989) see no separate existence in the forms of practice that can mobilize language categories this way: the role of handwork, crafts of material manipulation, traditions of working with materials, ways of designing objects, and using them to reach social goals.

Kuhn (1970) is the one theorist to give practice its due as a center of social coordination. Traditions of experimentation of the sort found in laboratories include not simply the application of scientific or technological theories to lab work, but the mobilization of routinized and improvised ways of working with and on the world with fingers, eyes, and ears that come from social groups and help to forge new ones. We can pay attention to the language categories being shaped through material manipulation, and learn a great deal, but we will not understand the exercise of power without making better sense of the social worlds of practice that are not mere translations from language. There we would find the material life of science and hints about its broader cultural consequences.

Bringing together sociologies of science and culture to understand the cultural power of science and technology may not be a straightforward project, but using material culture studies to begin the task at least provides some intriguing opportunities for rethinking the way we approach the cultural power of science and technology. It helps to relocate human beings outside of their minds, out of the prison house of language and inside the world – where (at least on the surface) we apparently all live.

## Notes

1   If, for example, as Bourdieu (1984) claims, culture is central to the reproduction of inequalities within a society, then what is interesting about culture is how it works in defining and locating distinctions, and abstract rationality (the kind cultivated in science and art) is the highest element of taste used for that purpose. Similarly, if Gramsci and his followers (Gramsci 1971; Gitlin 1980; Shafir 1980; Hallin 1986) are to be believed, culture is central to the stability of regimes by providing the ideological support for political arrangements. Since culture's ideological quality lies in its capacity to define reality, then, as Habermas (1975) noted some years ago, knowledge systems, like science and technology, are particularly powerful actors in establishing the legitimacy of state power.

2   Old roads, for example, that have become inefficient means of transportation for the larger economy may still keep towns in contact with each other and sustain some remnants of older trading patterns. Ancient water systems, household goods, and agricultural practices all are part of a culture of *longue durée* that can join past generations to present ones in a cultural line brought to our attention by Fernand Braudel (1976; see also Schudson 1992).

3   Before the 1970s, they began this process by looking at the organizational life of science and the arts (popular and elite) to explore the grounds on

which they could be viewed as fundamentally social realms. In the process, they made little effort to try to make sense of scientific theories, television plot lines, or the content of any other cultural form, using social analysis, with the exception of the Marxists who developed different, sophisticated, but often discredited reflection theories (Lowenthal 1950; Hauser 1951; Schiller 1969; Aronowitz 1973). In more recent decades, more sociologists have either joined or engaged in battles with colleagues in the humanities, trying to locate the group processes behind the content of human culture/knowledge. This move has necessitated fundamental questioning of the boundaries, on the one hand, between "real knowledge" and other ways of knowing, and, on the other hand, between "authentic culture" and other forms of human cultural construction, since the social forms mobilized in the production of "accepted" and "rejected" art or science seemed much the same. There has been little tolerance for *a priori* claims about the difference between the categories of science and superstition, the normal and paranormal, the beautiful and the ugly, scientific discoveries and other models of nature. These distinctions have been treated as fundamentally political, and therefore historical rather than essential.

4    John Brewer (1989) has shown that military spending and the modern state developed together in early modern Europe. The military clearly runs on its material strength; it has been said to run on its stomach, but it depends just as much if not more on its weapons and its fortifications; and these things cost money. The materiality of military life has also been enhanced by experiments in engineering. Robert Merton (1970) wrote in his dissertation that the autonomy of science from the state disappeared in warfare because science and technology could provide new power for politicians. More recently and significantly, William McNeill (1982) has shown how new cannon, fortification techniques, military drills, tactics, and muskets have changed the character of warfare in Europe, and with it, balances of power (see also Russel 1983; Brewer 1989).

5    Military planning as much as weapons development has had a technological history, tying scientific practices to the exercise of state power. While twentieth-century military planners worked with computers, developing scenarios to plan for future wars (Lehner 1989), their counterparts in seventeenth-century France used maps and models of towns to do much the same thing (Mukerji 1993). In these two periods and with these two material cultures, thinking about battle was as much embedded in material practices as the battle itself, and science and technology provided the means for rationalizing planning. On the other hand, neither the computer nor the map was wholly the child of the military. Both material systems were derived from efforts to develop new means and methods of measurement that had broad applicability. They were indeed used just as much outside the military as within it, but they were able to flourish as well as they did in part because of state sponsorship.

# 7

## Culture Studies Through the Production Perspective: Progress and Prospects

### Richard A. Peterson

The production perspective coalesced in the mid 1970s from numerous but widely dispersed research studies that reached the simple but powerful conclusion that the social arrangements used in making symbolic elements of culture affect the nature and content of the elements of culture that are produced. For example, in their study of the emergence of Impressionist art in nineteenth-century France, Harrison and Cynthia White (1965) found inadequate the prevalent theories of the time that changes in art are associated with changes in society or with the emergence of a few creative geniuses. Instead they found that the older academic art production system collapsed from inherent structural contradictions, and Impressionist painters came to the fore in the emerging art market developed by Parisian dealers and critics. Likewise, a set of studies begun in the mid 1970s showed that what is presented as "news" in contemporary America is neither an objective rendering of happenings nor a faithful reflection of media owners' beliefs, because "news" is unintentionally shaped[1] by the structure and functioning of reportorial and editorial routines in newspaper, news magazine, and television news departments (Molotch and Lester 1974; Barrett 1978; Schudson 1978; Tuchman 1978; Gans 1979).[2]

Work in the production perspective can be found in the study of art worlds, science laboratories, religious institutions, the legal system, popular culture, and similar sociocultural fields, or *realms* as we will call them here,[3] where cultural symbols are deliberately formulated within concrete situations bounded by explicit social, political, and economic environments (Crane 1992a). Practitioners of the perspective are not simply concerned with the *intended* content and meaning of cultural products such as works of art, scientific discoveries, church dogma, political ideology, or organizational propaganda. Rather, the methods which are used facilitate the uncovering of the so-called "unintended" consequences of purposive productive activity.[4] For this reason the perspective can be successfully applied to a range of quite different situations where the manipulation of symbols is a byproduct rather than the goal of the collective activity.

Two quite different examples may serve as cases in point. In the course of a study of English youth subcultures in Great Britain, Hebdige (1979) found that group modes of dress, talk, activity, and music served not only as a means of identification to the participants and outsiders, but came to form the constitutive statement of their resistance against the established society. While making a study of the patterns of industrial bureaucracy in an upstate New York firm, Gouldner (1954) witnessed a completely unpredicted wildcat strike. He found that the strike occurred because a newly hired manager violated the extra-bureaucratic organizational culture that had developed over the years.

## Establishing the Production Perspective

The production perspective emerged in the 1970s largely in response to the failure of the earlier dominant idea that culture and social structure mirror each other. This "mirror" or "reflection" view, had been developed by anthropologists such as Ruth Benedict (1934) who studied small preliterate groups where it seemed credible that a self-consistent set of social institutions would be reflected in a cognate coherent culture. A reflection view was held both by Marxists and by functionalists such as Talcott Parsons in the 1950s and 1960s. It proved to be of limited use, however, in understanding the relationship between social structure and culture in industrial societies and was also being widely questioned by anthropologists studying preliterate societies.[5] Breaking with the older mirror view that posited the existence of one integrated social system overarched by a single culture system, the production perspective (like all the other contemporary perspectives in culture studies, many of which are represented in this anthology) views both culture and social structure as emergent and the relationship between them as problematic (Peterson 1979).[6]

The publication of anthologies in 1976 and 1978 entitled *The Production of Culture*, edited by Peterson and Coser respectively, signaled the emergence of the production perspective as a coherent and self-conscious approach in culture studies claiming to be applicable across a wide range of specific fields and genres. Many of the early researchers in the perspective had been trained in the sociology of organizations, industry, and occupations and brought their skills in the analysis of material production to the fields of symbol production. Others came to the perspective with a love of or commitment to a particular form of cultural expression such as opera, rock, dance, television, or literature.

A number of developments since the 1970s show the progressive establishment in sociology of the production of culture perspective. First, as this essay attests, many scholars have found it a convenient way of framing their research concerns, and perhaps as many have found it a convenient foil against which to contrast their own distinctive interests (Wolff 1981; Aronowitz 1993). Second, a schematic has been developed to suggest the range of topics that go into a study within the production perspective (Peterson 1985, 1990).[7] Third, a textbook has appeared with the title *The Production of Culture* (Crane 1992a), and the perspective receives full chapters in recent texts in the sociology of art (Zolberg 1990) and in the sociology of culture (Hall and Neitz 1993). Fourth, numerous academic sessions have been devoted to work in the perspective, and a 1993 session of the Sociology of Culture Section of the American Sociological Association was devoted to a stock-taking of work in the perspective in the areas of law, science, religion, and art.[8]

Having introduced the perspective, it is useful to formally define it. The production of culture perspective focuses on how the content of culture is influenced by the milieux in which it is created, distributed, evaluated, taught, and preserved. In looking thus at "production" broadly conceived, practitioners of this perspective are most likely to focus on the fabrication of expressive-symbol elements of culture such as books, paintings, scientific research reports, religious celebrations, legal judgments, etc., which, in turn, embody, modify, and give concrete expression to the "norm," "value," and "belief" elements of culture. Research in the production perspective freely draws on the theories, methods, and concepts developed in other branches of sociology, as we will show in detail presently. It is, however, distinctive in focusing on the consequences of social activities for culture. Thus, for example, the "newsmaking" studies discussed above exemplify the production perspective because they were not simply satisfied to show the content of news or to trace organizational and occupational dynamics, but also highlighted the consequences of these for the formation and transformation of "news."

From the outset, the perspective promised not only a way to better understand the shape and form of any particular cultural expression but also to facilitate three kinds of comparisons: (a) comparisons across broad cultural production realms including art, popular culture, religion, science and law; (b) comparisons across the division between "high," "fine," or "scholastic," and "low," "cult," "common," or "mass" that tends to emerge in each realm; and (c) comparisons across societal, institutional or organizational, and micro levels of analysis (Peterson 1976). Progress toward achieving these goals has been uneven.

We will review progress and problems in working toward these three goals and point to several emerging lines of inquiry that link the production perspective to other approaches in cultural studies citing studies that *exemplify* the perspective even though the authors have not formulated their work in production terms. We begin by showing the utility of the perspective by reviewing a few specific lines of research. Because developments so far have been greatest in the broad realm encompassing the arts and entertainment, this analysis will focus there, briefly noting cognate work in the other realms as appropriate.

## Six Lines of Research in the Production Perspective

In the years since its inception, the production perspective has stimulated research on a wide variety of topics.[9] We have chosen six lines of inquiry to illustrate the diversity of problems attracting the attention of a substantial number of researchers.

### Comparative market structures

The structure of the market for cultural goods can involve billion-dollar multinational corporations, technologies unknown a decade ago, and star performers adulated by audiences numbering in the millions, as Turow (1992) shows for the case of television and the movies, or it can involve a few hundred creator-performers who play largely for each other and their students, as is the case of contemporary concert music composers (Gilmore 1988). One way of showing the influence of market structure in shaping the content of the symbols produced is to make parallel analyses of several similar but differently structured market systems. For example Rosenblum (1978) studied photographers working in three quite different markets, that of the daily newspaper, the fashion magazine, and the fine art world. For the first, the job involves the contacts, brashness, tenacity, and bravery to get "the story" on film; for the second, the job involves molding the model to "look right" on film; and for the third, the job involves doing what it takes to be enough like other art photographers to be considered an artist, and different enough to be hailed by the critics.

Gilmore (1987, 1988) focuses on three distinct classical music markets existing largely independent of each other on Manhattan Island. The midtown market revolves around Lincoln Center for the Performing Arts and consists of the large orchestras, well-known chamber groups, and star soloists who, for the most part, play music by dead composers. In this market the focus is on virtuosi performances and the quality of interpretation. The uptown "academic" market revolves around the Columbia School of Music and the established professors of composition, with audiences composed largely of their students. Here the focus is on innovative variations within the canon currently in vogue among academics. The downtown "avant garde" composers live and work in and around Greenwich Village. They reject both the other New York markets and, supporting themselves largely by day jobs, unemployment compensation, and occasional fellowships, create works for altered or newly constructed instruments. Here the accent is on music that will be recognized as novel.[10]

## Market structure over time

Following the early lead of White and White (1965) who analyzed the consequences of the transformation of the Parisian visual art market in the nineteenth century, a larger group of market structure studies focuses on the impacts on cultural production in a single market structure which changes significantly over time. Crane's (1987) analysis of the avant-garde visual art market centered in New York City over the 45-year period from 1940 to 1985 is an excellent case in point. She shows the changing roles that painter circles, dealers, critics, New York museums, regional museums, corporate patrons, the government, and auction houses have had on the flowering and market success of six successive schools of visual art work.[11]

In a more modest time frame, Peterson (1978) traces the "derustification" that took place in country music in the 1970s to the practices of many pop-rock disk jockeys who unwillingly became country music DJs when their pop-rock stations in large numbers were converting to the country music format. They brought with them the "top-40" strategy of programming current hits and accented sounds that were the least rustic and the most rock-like. In consequence many older artists like Ernest Tubb, and whole sub-genres including bluegrass and gospel, were eliminated, while the "outlaws" such as Willie Nelson and Waylon Jennings and a crop of younger artists and producers experienced in pop music, came to the fore forever changing country music.[12]

## Reward structure

Crane (1976) suggests that the elements of reward systems motivating specialists to be creative are the same in the realms of art, science and religion, and she identifies four distinct reward systems that historically have been found in each. Rosengren (1983) has shown that these four fall naturally along the diagonal of a Guttman scale, thus further suggesting their wide utility.

The first is the *independent* reward system in which cultural producers set their own standards of performance and allocate symbolic and material rewards. Thus the production system based on independent rewards has at its heart a self-perpetuating and self-evaluating group of peers. Their collective quest is an ostensibly universal goal such as salvation, knowledge, truth, or beauty, and their method of working toward this goal is stated in what are asserted to be universal terms, such as those used in science, the humanities, and theology. To be fully established, the organizational apparatus of an independent reward system, be it an arts academy, a network of laboratories, a court system, or the like, must be firmly sanctioned in law and financially supported by the state. In return it is expected to help maintain the legitimacy and further the goals of the state apparatus. The cultural products of an academic system are admired and highly valued, if not well understood, by laymen; the relative status of individuals, occupational groups, cities, and nations is based in part on the possession, appreciation, or access to the cultural capital created by these academic institutions.

Contemporary examples include basic science, and the legal system. Other examples include theology and the art world in the eighteenth century when the French Royal Academy effectively controlled who could be trained and work as an artist, the aesthetic standards of art works, and the flow of commissions for producing art works (Pevsner 1940; White and White 1965). The only clear-cut example in the arts in this century is to be found in the Soviet Union in the era of Stalin. Nonetheless, within academia there are attempts to establish independent reward systems as for example in the contemporary French world of higher learning (Bourdieu 1988b). Gilmore (1987, 1988) shows the tendencies toward an in-dependent reward system among university-based classical music composers, Coser et al. (1981) show that this sort of system operates for the more rarified academic presses, and Adler (1979) shows the bureaucratic constraints and habits of thought that lead arts schools to move in this direction, even when they espouse completely different reward systems.

The second reward system Crane (1976) calls *semi-autonomous*. Here the symbolic rewards are allocated by the creative producers, but consumers allocate material rewards. The contemporary field of visual arts provides an instructive example of this sort of sys-tem. In the latter half of the nineteenth century, Parisian dealers began to sell works by artists derisively labeled Impressionists and other contemporary artists. The dealers' success depended in large part on the artists' anti-establishment stance and the positive evaluations of their works by increasingly respected critics such as Emile Zola (White and White 1965). This market-based system for contemporary art has evolved to include others beside artists, dealers, and critics. The actions of auction houses, museums, govern-ment and corporate patrons, as well as celebrity-building mass media now also play roles in setting the value of works, artists, and schools of art.[13] In the process, claims of artistic genius that confront aesthetic standards have largely given way to claims of fashion and monetary value-potential. Now the values shockingly transgressed are more often moral than aesthetic (Dubin 1992). Martorella (1982) has shown the operation of a semi-autonomous reward system in the field of opera where prizes and awards are allocated within the creative community of opera, and yet economic survival depends on selling tickets to the general public. A similar mix of rewards occurs for authors of important general books in The Netherlands (Nooy 1991) and the United States (Powell 1978; Coser et al. 1981), architects (Blau 1984), fine art photographers (Rosenblum 1978) and nonprofit regional theaters (DiMaggio and Stenberg 1985).

The third reward system Crane (1976) identifies as *subcultural*. Here there is usually not a sharp distinction between producers and consumers, and rewards, which are largely symbolic, are allocated within the subculture. One model for subcommunity has been the enduring ethnic, racial, or religious group which sustains its own folk religion, science, and law while celebrating its own culture creators such as the New Orleans "Indian" Mardi Gras costume dancers or the Juju musicians of West Africa (Waterman 1990). The second model is of a group that coalesces around an activity such as little league baseball (Fine 1979), a newly formu-lated cult (Hall 1987) or expressive way of life. Hall and Jefferson's (1976) collection of studies of the flamboyant clothing, hairstyles, and music English working class youth-groups use to establish their identity is an excellent early case in point. Sato (1991) has studied the emergence of similar symbolic elaborations among the newly wealthy Japanese youth calling themselves "Yankees" and forming motorized gangs. Lachmann (1988) has studied the development of oppositional aesthetic standards among graffiti subway muralists or "bombers" as they call themselves in New York. Frith and Horne (1987) have traced the cliques of British visual arts school students including the likes of Mick Jagger and David Bowie that have evolved into rock bands, and Moorhouse (1991) has studied the evolution of the norms and aesthetics of hot-rod racers. Within each of these, and numerous other ethnographic studies of counter-cultural groups that could be mentioned, a tension develops between staying true to the goals and emerging aesthetic of the creative subgroup and compromising these for financial gain and acclaim in the much more materially rewarded world of mass-produced entertainment.

The fourth reward system identified by Crane (1976) she calls *heterocultural.* Here a few large corporations fashion symbolic products such as movies, TV programs, recorded music, and popular religion in the hopes of attracting large numbers of diverse customers (or parishioners) treated as if they were an undifferentiated mass. Finke and Stark (1992) show the development of consumer market-based religion in the United States over the past 200 years, but most of the research on heterocultural reward systems has focused on popular culture. In the early 1970s, Hirsch (1972) detailed the structure of reward systems that operate in the major popular culture industries, and a flood of more detailed studies have followed in the years since.[14] The most complete overall view of the consequences of heterocultural reward systems in shaping cultural products in the contemporary media markets that include many small specialty firms and independent producers that compete with and feed the surviving media conglomerates is provided by Turow (1992).

## Gatekeeping and decision chains

Art, as Becker (1982) has eloquently shown, is *collective* activity, and this is true of the work of a poet as much as that of a movie director, because even the appellation "loner genius" takes on meaning only when significant persons or organizations within an art world affirm its use by their actions. A number of researchers have focused on the ways in which such affirmations, reinterpretations, and rejections shape individual works and whole careers. The term *gatekeeping* (Powell 1978) has been applied when the focus is on judgments about admitting persons or works into a cultural field. When the focus is on the way that works are changed as they move from being ideas to being finished products, the term *decision chain* is appropriate (Ryan and Peterson 1982).

Greenfeld (1989) describes two different systems of production of the visual arts in Israel which have developed around distinct sets of gatekeepers. The gatekeepers of the system devoted to the production of *abstract* art are the public museum curators and the art critics for the leading intellectual publications. The curators select works to be shown on the basis of their fit with Israeli and international ideas of innovative art. In writing about these museum shows, the critics perfect the vocabularies through which the abstract works can be understood and appreciated by the relatively small class of academic and professional connoisseurs. These curators and critics play no great part in the other Israeli visual art world that is devoted to *figurative* art. Here the primary gatekeepers are art dealers who exhibit works in their own private galleries. The focus in this case is not on avant-gardism or on theories about art; rather the concern is with cultivating painters whose works will find favor with respected private art collectors, and thus with well-heeled tourists. Over the years dealers develop reputations for finding artists whose works will appreciate in value, so that selection by a leading dealer affords a painter access to willing buyers.[15]

There are other sorts of gates in art worlds besides those of aesthetic conformity and financial value. In periods when aesthetic standards become so tolerant of diversity that it is difficult for newcomers to produce works that are aesthetically provocative, they may try to gain notice by challenging political or moral sensibilities. While many artists in the 1930s confronted gatekeepers of political ideology, the contested issues today include gender, race, and personal expression which, as Dubin (1992) has graphically shown, are couched in moral terms.

Gatekeepers are also important when an artistic expression created in one art world is introduced into another. This has happened repeatedly to popular music as African-American expressions are appropriated into the mainstream. Not only is the work or its meaning changed in the process, but the art world of the appropriated community is changed as well. Drawing on an example from outside this society, Griswold (1992b) has shown the effect that English publishers, acting as gatekeepers for the work of Nigerian novelists, have had on the work that these novelists produce. She argues that the publishers have held an outmoded vision of tradition-versus-modernity, and in selecting novels that fit this model they have created a very influential genre of work which is at odds both with the reality of Nigerian life and with the intentions of most Nigerian authors.

In the arts, gatekeeping has to do with accepting or rejecting works or their creators and the consequences of these choices for subsequent works and creators. However, mass-production culture industries from book publishing to television regularly make decisions other than choose/reject. A work may be altered, or recontextualized and this can happen at each stage of a decision chain as it moves from being a germ of an idea to being offered to the public. Ryan and Peterson (1982) describe the consequences of three organizational systems in the music industry for the fate of songs as they pass (or fail to pass) down the decision chain. They note that at each decision point the question is not so much, "What have I got to say?" or even, "What does the music fan want to hear?" but rather, "What changes need to be made to get the song accepted by the next node in the decision chain?" So, for example, in the field of country music the question for the record producer in the early 1980s was how to shape a song so it would be played by the virtually all-male disk jockeys, even though the majority of country music record buyers were then women.

Like nineteenth-century books which appeared first in periodical installments, the basic character of television shows can be changed even *after* the series appears on the air (Cantor and Cantor 1992). In this vein Gitlin (1983: ch. 6) details the twisting fate of a plot idea developed and produced by Barney Rosenzweig. The basic premise of the series – a suburban white family plunked down in the middle of a multi-ethnic Chicago ghetto – went through a number of permutations before the pilot was aired as "American Dream," and changes were made even during the brief life of the series on the air. As Gitlin shows, the numerous changes in the show, from plot line and casting to locale and tone, were made to satisfy the needs and interests of people along the decision chain.

A number of studies of the fate of women as symbol producers have been put in gatekeeper or decision chain terms.[16] Tuchman (1989), for example, shows how nineteenth-century male editors and literary critics worked to elevate the aesthetic reputation of the novel form in part by denigrating the contributions of the numerous early female novelists. In the process these male gatekeepers changed the mix of themes expressed in novels. But critics are not the only gatekeepers who have disadvantaged women artists, as Lang and Lang (1990: 269–315) show in their comparative study of turn-of-the-century male and female etchers. The Langs show that many women etchers were critically acclaimed during their lifetimes and yet the reputations of most male etchers have survived far better than those of comparably acclaimed females. The primary reason they find is not critics but the different actions of the deceased etcher's spouse and family. The Langs show that the surviving wives of deceased male etchers often worked diligently to protect their husband's works and reputation; in contrast, surviving husbands and kin usually did not serve this function for deceased female etchers. Thus much of the work of the women has literally been lost to posterity.

Cantor (1987) notes that in the mass media most people have very little control over the work they do, and that women who wish to alter the formulaic perspective of the medium are censored when they try or simply are not hired. Cantor and Pingree (1983), however, document the roles that a few women have played in shaping and reshaping the soap-opera formula. Detailing the structural conditions that allowed women to become gatekeepers, Markert (1984) and Thurston (1987) showed that romance novels broke out of the tight "Harlequin sweet-girl formula" when female editors had gained enough success by making small changes in the formula to force the men who controlled the more powerful marketing departments to allow them to introduce both more sex-filled, and more religion-based, series of novels.

## Careers of creative workers

Some individuals involved in the production of culture view what they do as a job much like any other, but for many their craft is the major source of their sense of self-worth, so that self and work tend to become fused (Bensman and Lillienfeld 1991). This fusion can be seen in the study of the avant-garde visual art market that developed in the SoHo section of Manhattan made by Simpson (1981). He shows the impacts dealers, co-op galleries, critics, art buyers, and fellow artists have in shaping artists' careers, and, significantly, he also shows that the quality of the relationships with significant others tends to be quite different for successful and unsuccessful artists. Successful artists tend to have supportive partners, while the unsuccessful ones have partners that are supernurturent, overprotective, and smothering.

A number of studies in the production perspective mentioned in the sections just above might also be cited here to show that the ways in which careers are shaped in turn influences the cultural works that are produced.[17] Another line of production studies of careers, however, deserves special attention because it focuses at a more micro level and views the organization as the context of symbol production that imposes constraints. These studies focus on the norms and conventions of collaboration that allow art and craft workers to fabricate symbolic goods and to build careers in the process. In effect, as Fine (1992) notes, these works illuminate the culture of production. Focusing on restaurant cooks, Fine (1992), for example, shows the sets of occupational conventions, norms, and ideologies the creative workers, and by extension all workers (Bensman and Lilienfeld 1991), develop in order to build sufficient space to be able to create their own standards in their chosen field of activity. Likewise, Lachmann (1988) views the world of organizations and institutions as context and shows how the youthful graffiti muralists of New York developed their own conventions and aesthetic as a critical response to their environment. Finally, a number of studies of pop, punk, blues, heavy metal, rap, country, and rock music have underlined the self-defensive critical elements that develop in the culture of production among these stigmatized and marginalized groups of creators.[18]

### Structural conditions facilitating creativity

Some lines of research in the production perspective are focused around a single proposition. One example is the work that has examined the relationship between the level of competition among producers and the level of creativity in their productions. On the one hand, it has been argued that near-perfect competition forces all producers to make creations that are virtually identical, while oligopoly (the existence of only a few firms in a market), or the protection from competition by regular patronage, makes possible creative experimentation. On the other hand, it has been argued that competition heightens the incentive to be creative in order to survive, while oligopoly increases the incentive to create standard works in the hopes of offending few and increasing market share.

In 1975 Peterson and Berger published an article on changes over time in popular music showing that aesthetic innovation was associated with periods of high levels of competition among record companies, while homogeneity in the music was associated with periods of oligopoly in the industry.[19] Rothenbuhler and Dimmick (1982) replicated this research with similar results. Analogous findings, that oligopolistic markets make for homogeneity and competitive markets make for diversity and creativity, have been reported for book publishing, opera, television, and the movie industry.

Two subsequent, well-researched studies by Burnett (1992), Burnett and Weber (1989) and by Lopes (1992), however, suggest that innovation in popular music is now found in the contemporary conditions of oligopoly. This may be so, but there is reason to doubt their conclusions, based on the widespread problem in all culture studies of the stability of measures. While the methods of the two recent studies faithfully replicate those of the earlier studies, they do not consider the relevance of these measures in the contemporary popular music context, and it is quite possible that the measures no longer mean what they once did.[20] The high rate of turnover in hits on the "Hot 100" may no longer indicate rapid aesthetic innovation but rather *aesthetic exhaustion* as trivially different songs quickly reach the top of the charts and as quickly fade because they are so derivative.

Standing back from this specific set of studies, it is clear that there is something to the thesis that competition makes for creativity, and that curtailing competition tends to stifle it. Yet we know very little about the limits within which this relationship holds. Does it apply equally across the full range of the variables; does it hold for all kinds of competition; and does it apply to all realms of culture production? These questions are currently most hotly contested in studies of religion. The view of those who idealize the idea of a single "sacred canopy" and hold that religiosity in the United States is trivialized by an unseemly competition between denominations for souls and financial support, is being challenged by those who point to the lively competition in America as the *source* of its high rates of religious participation and committed belief (Blau et al. 1992; Finke and Stark 1992; Warner 1993). The cross-national comparisons of Iannaccone (1991) furnish an interesting perspective on the relationship between oligopoly and cultural innovation. He finds the highest rates of religious participation and beliefs in the United States, which has the most competition among religious organizations, and also in the most singularly Roman Catholic countries of Europe. He suggests that in these latter countries the Catholic church provides beneath its single organizational umbrella a wide range of cults, organizations, foci of worship, and levels of commitment. This, in turn, raises questions about the nature and consequences of competition among factions within large church organizations and between divisions of oligopolistic media corporations as well.

## The Promise of Comparative Analysis

As noted at the outset, one of the features of the production perspective is that it facilitates comparative analysis of three sorts: comparisons across symbol-producing realms, comparisons between elite and popular forms within each realm, and comparisons across societal, institutional and micro levels of analysis. The reason that the production perspective facilitates these comparisons is that it assumes a *nominalist* perspective in looking at all objects of inquiry and thus facilitates the use of the full range of social science and humanist tools of inquiry. While this may seem unexceptional on the threshold of the twenty-first century, symbols evoke emotions, and many people feel passionately about each of the forms under study. The production perspective underscores that, for the purposes of the inquiry at hand, there is nothing unique about any specific symbol system that prevents it being studied with standard social scientific and humanist methods, and there is, therefore, nothing sacrosanct about either nuclear physics or scientology, classical music or rap music, constitutional law or street-level law, or about established church doctrine or cult worship.

To date most studies in the production perspective have focused on particular fields, and progress toward fulfilling the promised benefits of comparison has been uneven, as we will show.

### Comparisons across symbol-producing realms

Mid twentieth century functionalists argued that cross-realm comparisons are fruitless because each has its own unique core value. Essentially Parsons (1961) argued that science deals in experimentally established fact, law deals in reason, art deals in aesthetics, and religion concerns faith in the supernatural. The nominalist stance of the production perspective, however, problematizes these differences making the assertion of uniqueness a residual to be asserted when no similarities can be established.

The expectation that the same range of processes is present in all realms of culture production, be they religion, art, science, law, etc., does not mean that new discoveries in physics are produced in the same way as new religious pronouncements. Rather it means that the differences can be explained, in large part, by the conditions of production in the two realms (Peterson 1976). For example, knowledge in physics today is largely controlled by a single subsidized and self-perpetuating worldwide "priesthood" that works to allocate resources and rewards in ways that perpetuate its views (Latour 1987); at the same time, religious doctrine varies greatly from country to country, and in the United States, as noted above, a wide range of religious specialists must compete with each other in an open market for the lay consumer's attention and for resources, loyalties, and rewards (Heirich 1976; Finke and Stark 1992; Warner 1993).

These differences, however, are not inherent in the nature of the subject matter of these two realms as can be seen by reference to earlier times when the production systems of science and religion were very nearly reversed. In the eighteenth century, English scientists supported themselves and their work by periodic shows of spectacular findings that induced laymen to give them further support, and in the seventeenth century religious scholars worked with the support and protection of an established church orthodoxy and defied it only in mortal peril of their lives (Kurtz 1983). Likewise, eighteenth-century French painters worked with the protection of an all-powerful Academy (Pevsner 1940), while today they work in conditions of near-perfect competition (Moulin 1987). In each of these instances, the movement from one sort of production system toward the other has had profound consequences for every aspect of the art world, including even what is considered to be art (White and White 1965; Becker 1982).[21]

As recent research on the roles of women in each of the symbol-producing realms has shown, much less dramatic changes in the nature of the production process may have major consequences for a particular class of producers.[22] Systematic comparison across realms will highlight the structural and symbolic underpinnings of such institutional discrimination.

Together these cross-discipline and over-time comparisons suggest how fruitful it could be to make more systematic comparisons across the major culture-producing realms. However, no one has yet proposed a general scheme for systematically making comparisons across culture-production realms, but the six lines of research in the production perspective discussed above provide a suggestive beginning. Also, DiMaggio (1987) has developed a propositional scheme for understanding classification in art, and this might, with the appropriate modifications, be extended to all culture-producing realms.

## Distinctions between high and low

An invidious distinction between high and low is found in each of the culture-producing realms, and this fact could furnish a great opportunity for comparisons both within and across production realms. To date, however, the distinction has done more to inhibit such comparisons because the truth-value vested in high (art, science, religion, law) symbols, and the status honor accorded to those in the fields where they are produced is often seen to render these fields incomparable with each other and also with the low counterparts in their own realms (Gans 1974).

Working from the nominalist stance of the production perspective, one can cut through these problems by asserting that any of the invidious high–low distinctions are not inherent in the cultural objects, but rather they involved a social, or better, a *cultural* construction of reality. At issue are the questions: who gets to make the designations, on what basis are they made, within what range are they accepted, and a host of other questions similar to those posed by DiMaggio (1987) in classifying art. There are a number of excellent case studies touching on these issues, but there has been very little thinking about the conditions supporting one system of evaluation or another across all the realms of cultural production. The most systematic efforts in this direction can be found in the works of Pierre Bourdieu and his colleagues.[23] In the paragraphs that follow, two issues are considered: the mobility between high/low categories, and the differentiation and de-differentiation of high and low.

### Cultural mobility

Are there general laws that can be adduced to explain the traffic between the aesthetic categories of what Moulin (1987) calls "junk" and "masterwork," between the moral categories of "art" and "obscenity" (Beisel 1992, 1993; Dubin 1992), between "orthodoxy" and "heresy" (Kurtz 1983), and in science between what Lynch (1985) calls "art" and "artifact"? In the arts, particular works and artists, and even entire genres experience aesthetic mobility over time (Becker 1982; Griswold 1986). Peterson (1972) details the sociopolitical and music industry conditions that caused the aesthetic mobility of jazz from folk to popular to fine art. And in the religious realm in the United States, there has historically been a cycle in which reformist church organizations become linked to civil authority, charismatic cults separate, the established church organization loses power, and then the surviving cults become ever-more established and church-like (Finke and Stark 1992). Still, there has been no progress toward explanations that apply across these realms.

### Differentiation–de-differentiation

As Levine (1988) has shown, the distinction between popular culture and high art that had become such a fixture of American society by the middle of the twentieth century (Gans 1974), only began to be clearly articulated a century earlier, and as DiMaggio (1982) showed in his detailed analysis of the development of the visual art and classical music worlds of Boston, the distinction was developed by a set of aesthetic entrepreneurs and served the class interests of the rising business elite of the city. Nonetheless, the promoters of the fine arts have not succeeded in establishing them as merit goods fully worthy of societal support (DiMaggio 1991a, 1992) so, as Lamont (1992) has shown, it is not now prudent to use arts appreciation as a measure of cultural capital in the United States.

Perhaps the high/low distinction in the arts has outlived its usefulness. In her discussion of high/low, Crane (1992b) suggests a classification of culture fields on the basis of their production organization, technology, distribution systems, and audiences. Specifically, she identifies "national core" which includes television, film and the major newspapers, "peripheral" which includes books, magazines, radio, and recorded music, and finally "urban" which includes the performing and fine arts, crafts, fairs, and parades. Since the differentiation of high/low was driven by the class interests of rising status groups, it may be that hierarchical distinctions are currently in the process of being reconstituted along new lines (Peterson 1992b).

## Micro, Institutional, and Societal Levels of Analysis

The production of culture model has been formulated at the level of personal interaction, relations among organizations, and the workings of entire societies. Ideally work at each of these levels complements work at the other two, and while this may happen in the best individual studies, the theoretical questions and research techniques employed at the three levels are different enough that research has tended to develop separately, and practitioners working at different levels of analysis do not learn all they might from each other.

The great strength of studies that explicitly take into account societal level conditions is their view of the culture industry as an expression and reinforcer of the sociopolitical system of the larger society and the attendant systems of domination and subordination, including social class, ethnicity, religion, and gender, and excellent studies can be cited.[24] The danger in looking from the societal level is that the workings of the production process may be seen to follow automatically from the society-level constraints.[25] This need not be the case as is shown in a number of empirical works which show the way in which societal values and beliefs are mediated by culture industries. Griswold's (1986) work on the successive reinterpretations over the centuries made by revivalists of two types of Elizabethan dramas documents the efforts to bring the values expressed in these works in line with the sociopolitical values of the day.[26]

Production studies that focus primarily on the organizational or institutional level take advantage of the decades of studies of particular organizations, occupations, industries, and the theoretical developments in these research specialties.[27] Because researchers want to remain value-neutral, they tend to bracket their own aesthetic and political views, and use uncritically the aesthetic judgments and ideological stances implicit in the symbolic field under study. A consequence, Bird (1979) and Wolff (1989) suggest, is that these researchers help to perpetuate the established categories of the systems they study.[28] At the same time, their reports expose to public review the workings of the systems which create and perpetuate self-serving classifications of a given field (cf. Lamont and Fournier 1992).

Production studies that focus primarily on the micro level of interaction between persons draw from the rich tradition of research in symbolic interactionism, as well as from the social-psychological elements of the sociologies of occupations and organizations. The most wide-ranging and influential work in this tradition is Howard

S. Becker's (1982) *Art Worlds*.[29] In their chapter titled "The Production of Culture," Hall and Neitz (1993: 163–90) focus primarily
at this interpersonal level of analysis.[30] They clearly show that by
bracketing the societal and institutional levels of analysis, one can
illustrate how groups of symbol producers create and are shaped
by the conventions of aesthetic judgment and collaboration in
culture production. In effect such micro-level studies focus less on
the production of culture and more on the culture of production.

Some micro-level studies can be criticized for unreflexively
(Bourdieu and Wacquant 1992) assuming the perspective of the
group or occupational category under study, and thus obtaining
an incomplete and misleading reading of the field under study.[31]
This "going native" as it were, is cognate to the problem of becoming
an unwitting apologist for the institution under study mentioned
just above, and the research strategy of comparison across subfields,
discussed in the section on Comparative Market Structures, is one
of the best ways of guarding against unreflexively adopting the
perspective of one of the groups in a production system.

The distinctions among levels of analysis just described roughly
follow the theoretical/methodological divisions between com-
parative/historical, institutional, and social-psychological levels
which have been institutionalized in sociology at large; thus it is
all the more difficult to compare across levels. The effort is richly
rewarding, however, as evidenced by Griswold's (1986) study of
the revivals of two classes of Elizabethan plays mentioned above,
Blau's (1984) study of the impact of changing macro-economic
conditions on the survival of architectural firms, and Simpson's
(1981) study of the interplay of organizational and interpersonal
factors in the making of artists' careers in the contemporary SoHo
art market in New York.

## Concluding Comments

The basic insight of the production perspective, that the way cultural
elements are produced affects their nature and content, can be helpful in formulating intellectual questions in a number of the other
areas of culture studies, problematizes the status of culture, and
returns us again to the question with which we began, the link

between culture and social structure. Each of these will be treated in these concluding comments.

### Reception and the autoproduction of culture

Reception by the reader, listener, viewer, or purchaser is a central concern in cultural studies (Press, chapter 9, this volume). "Reception" suggests the end of a communication process; nonetheless, it is an active process of selection, interpretation, and recombination of elements that can be seen as the "auto" production of a symbolic world which is meaningful for "consumers." The autoproductions of marginalized groups such as youth, ethnics, eccentrics, and the like,[32] have received much scholarly attention, but all individuals and collectivities create life-styles that display their patterning of cultural choices (Peterson 1983).

The systematic study of what is here called the autoproduction of culture is going forward rapidly along several fronts: (a) ethnographic studies of distinctive groups tease out the processes by which group members appropriate and incorporate cultural symbols for their own purposes;[33] (b) other studies show the reappropriation of autoproductions by mass media-disseminated pop culture producers;[34] and, (c) researchers are exploring the widening gap between social class (groups ranked by how they make money) and cultural class (groups ranked by how they spend money).[35] It is impossible to map the consequences of all such efforts, but, in linking production and reception theory, they hold promise of moving us toward an integrated theory of culture.

### Tradition, collective memory, and boundary formation

Early anthropologists, folklorists, and sociologists developed the idea of "tradition" as the repository of all that is ancient and virtually unchanging. In recent decades this view has been attacked on all sides as factually incorrect and self-serving (Hobsbawm 1983; Clifford 1988). The term "collective memory" is now often substituted for "tradition", acknowledging that the past is continually reinterpreted to fit the changing needs of the present (Halbwachs 1992).[36] Schwartz's (1991) study of the changing popular memory of George Washington is an excellent case in point.

Some studies point to specific individuals or groups of memory "doctors" who reshape collective memory to fit their own ends.[37] The transformation of the literary reputation of William Faulkner shows this clearly (Schwartz 1988). One of the most exciting applications of the idea of the mutability of collective memory has been in the study of the manipulation of memory in the service of making status distinctions along the lines of gender, race, ethnicity, class, etc. In one of the earliest works of this sort, Gusfield (1963) studied the role of status politics in the efforts of the (old-family Protestant) Women's Self-Temperance Leagues to stigmatize the alcohol-use norms of immigrant Catholics.[38]

## Keeping culture central in the production of culture

Some who focus on evaluating the products of cultural production including books, movies, legal decisions, religious beliefs, and the like argue that the production perspective in focusing on the mechanisms of production takes the "culture" out of the sociology of culture. Recognizing such criticism from those who take artists and art work to be the sole foci of the sociology of art, Howard Becker (1982), in the preface to *Art Worlds*, says, "it might be reasonable to say that what I have done here is not the sociology of art at all, but rather the sociology of occupations applied to artistic work" (p. xi).

It is quite legitimate to use art worlds, scientific laboratories, religious denominations, etc., as research sites for asking questions relating to the sociology of occupations or organizations, but that is not what Becker has done in *Art Worlds*. He makes a thorough study of several sorts of networks of cooperation and competition in which art is conceived, created, evaluated, and appreciated. What makes it an exemplary study in the sociology of culture, as here conceived, is that in each instance, he shows how the occupational, organizational, legal, and technological factors directly influence the nature of the art that is produced. Thus works in the production-of-culture perspective should clearly show how the production factors shape the culture that is produced. While this dictum is straightforward, it is easily overlooked as a sequence of studies takes on a life of its own.

If production studies run the risk of eliminating "culture" from the sociology of culture, researchers who focus on the content of cultural products run the risk of focusing on critical concerns and taking the "sociology" out. Griswold's (1986: 6–9) "cultural diamond" is a heuristic for guarding against a myopic focus on a narrow problem and for fairly taking into account all the primary elements of sociocultural interaction involved in the production of culture.

## No more culture versus society

An early formulation suggested that working within the production perspective should be seen as a necessary, if temporary, retreat from confronting the unanswerable questions about the causal links between society and culture (Peterson 1976). In the years since, the perspective has proved useful to so many, has developed in ways not contemplated in 1976, and continues to facilitate the formulation of questions many find interesting, that it still has utility in the pantheon of approaches to the study of culture. Not the least of the perspective's victories has been to show that in the production process, culture and social structure are so entwined that it is meaningless to ask whether society causes culture or vice versa.

### Notes

I greatly appreciate the comments and suggestions of a number of people including Judith Balfe, Judith Blau, Muriel Cantor, Gary Fine and the Sociology of Culture Study Group at the University of Georgia, Samuel Gilmore, Wendy Griswold, John Hall, Michael Hughes, Jennifer Joplin, Claire Peterson, Joseph Rhea, Karl Erik Rosengren, John Ryan, Janet Wolff, and Vera Zolberg who commented on an early and incomplete draft. Paul DiMaggio, Darren Sherkat and the anthology editor, Diana Crane, deserve special commendation for their continuing efforts to keep me on track. None of these will agree with all I have written, but I hope that it is stimulating enough to justify their considerable efforts. Thanks also to the generous support of the Mellon Foundation and the National Humanities Center in the early stages of this formulation.

1  The *intended* manipulation of symbols is also common and it has most often been studied as the formulation of "ideology" or "propaganda" (Altheide and Johnson 1980; Anderson 1983; Nimmo and Combs 1983; Parenti 1993).

2  These and later "news-making" studies also graphically illustrate the media's role in the cultural construction of political reality (Barrett 1978; Altheide and Johnson 1980; Nimmo and Combs 1983; Altheide and Snow 1991; Baughman 1992).

3 A number of terms have been used to denote all of the relevant actors and elements in a symbol production system. The word "realm" will be used to designate a major class of systems such as art/popular culture, science, religion, while the words "field" following Bourdieu (1984) and "world" following Becker (1982), "denomination", "discipline", "specialty", "genre" etc., as appropriate, will be used to designate specific arenas of culture production.

4 The distinction between *intended* and *unintended* productive activity is difficult to make and is, in practice, largely irrelevant because it is sometimes convenient to disguise intentions (Altheide and Johnson 1980). For example, in the 1990s large record companies have been vociferous champions of the freedom of speech in defending the distribution and sale of provocative rap and heavy metal recordings, but in the late 1950s they advocated suppressing the then-emerging rock music by every means possible. The key difference is that in the 1950s their financial interests were threatened by the new music, while by the 1980s they had learned how to profit from its popularity (Peterson 1990; Lopes 1992).

5 See especially Leach (1954); Geertz (1973); Bourdieu in Honneth et al. (1986) and Freilich (1989).

6 In their very useful collection of classic and contemporary articles, Alexander and Seidman (1990) show the numerous ways in which the structure and relationship between society and culture have become problematic, and this point has been underscored by Archer (1988) and by the postmodernist critique of modernism provocatively reviewed and extended by Stanley Aronowitz (1993).

7 Peterson (1985, 1990) focuses on six constraints on the production of any cultural phenomenon. By "constraint" is meant a "shaping force," which creates some opportunities while it cuts off others. This term is not ideal because it often connotes restraint, but other terms such as "force," "factor," "dimension," and the like, all carry their own unwanted connotative baggage. The first three constraints – *law, technology,* and *industry structure* – largely set the conditions within which the other three – *organization structure, occupational careers,* and *market* – operate, though, over time, each affects all of the others. No constraint is outside the dynamic system thus created. So, for example, law is not simply imposed from outside because many within the culture field devote a great deal of energy to shaping laws in ways congenial with their own interests (Scheppele 1988). Thus, a study must come to terms with each of the constraints and understand how collectively they operate in concert in shaping the content of culture.

8 The session was suggested by program chair, Paul DiMaggio and organized by Richard Peterson. The participants included Kim Scheppele (law), Karin Knorr-Cetina (science), Robert Wuthnow (religion), Judith Huggins Balfe (art), and Loïc Wacquant (comparative).

9 For a much more thorough review of studies in the production perspective see Crane (1992a), and for an alternative way of ordering research questions in the production perspective see Peterson (1985, 1990).

10 Crane (1992a) has generalized this model to apply to markets for urban culture in general. Numerous other comparative studies are worthy of attention. Just four receive mention here. DiMaggio and Stenberg (1985) focus on the structural sources of conformity and diversity in residential theaters in the United States. Zolberg (1980) shows that the market for contemporary art music is so different from that for the contemporary visual arts because patrons can purchase and speculate in art works but they have no chance to do so with compositions. Powell and Friedkin (1983), comparing public with commercial television, show that, ironic as it may seem, the programming content of public television is more dependent on the wishes of the few major corporations that "underwrite" programs than is commercial television, because commercial television depends on audience ratings in a more competitive market. And Greenfeld (1989) has made what is arguably the most extensive comparative market study to date. She focuses on the development in Israel of two alternative visual art market systems. One produces figurative art for the large (domestic and tourist) commercial market seeking representative works. The other produces abstract art that is exhibited in university galleries and evaluated in terms of the prevailing international standards of avant-garde art.

11 Studies that show changes in art market structures over time include among others: McCall (1977), Adler (1979), Becker (1982), Blau (1984), Moulin (1987), Wolff and Sneed (1988), Balfe (1993), and Peterson (1993).

12 Other studies that show changes in popular culture market structures over time include: Faulkner (1983), Gitlin (1983), Ryan (1985), Peterson (1990), Moorhouse (1991), Crane (1992a: 51–61), Goodwin (1992), Rothenbuhler and McCourt (1992), Turow (1992), and Ryan and Peterson (1993).

13 A number of researchers have contributed to understanding the contemporary visual art world now located primarily in New York City. See for example Simpson (1981), Moulin (1987), Becker (1982), Crane (1987), Blau (1988), Zolberg (1990, 1992a).

14 For a sampling of these reward-system related studies see: Peterson (1972, 1976, 1990), Peterson and Berger (1975), Powell (1978), Bennett (1980), Faulkner (1983), Gitlin (1983), Laing (1985), Ryan (1985), Neapolitan (1986), Burnett and Weber (1989), Burnett (1992), Frith (1992), Goodwin (1992), Grossberg (1992), Lopes (1992), Rothenbuhler and McCourt (1992), and Ryan and Peterson (1993).

15 The bifurcated art world that Greenfeld (1989) describes (see note 10) is clearly different from that of the contemporary New York (Simpson 1981; Crane 1987) and Paris (Moulin 1987) visual art worlds, where dealers, critics, galleries, and museums have all cooperated in building the avant-gardist art world. While the markets for figurative art in New York and Paris have received little research attention, it may well be that they operate in ways much as Greenfeld describes.

16 Randall Collins (1992) theorizes the gendered production of culture.

17 On this point see particularly Adler (1979), Kealy (1979), Balfe (1981),

Peterson (1982), Faulkner (1983), Blau (1984), Crane (1987), Bourdieu (1990a), and Cantor and Cantor (1992).

18  See in particular: Becker (1951), Keil (1966), Bennett (1980), Peterson and Ryan (1983), Laing (1985), Frith and Horne (1987), Lull (1987), George (1988), Weinstein (1991), and Ennis (1992).

19  The structural conditions fostering creativity in the music industry have been further explored by Peterson (1978, 1981, 1990, 1992c, 1993), Ryan (1985), Ryan and Peterson (1982, 1993), Peterson and Ryan (1983), George (1988), Goodwin (1992).

20  The 1976 study's measure of innovation was the number of records that reached the top ten of the weekly "Hot 100" chart. By the 1980s, however, popular music genres had become much more fractionated. There had been a great increase in the number of radio station music-formats and the proliferation of music television channels had added to the diversity. These changes were reflected in the rapid elaboration of popular music industry charts published by *Billboard* and other magazines. Thus the original *Billboard* "Hot 100" chart used in all these studies now reflects only a small fraction of the full range of popular music that is widely popular.

21  For cognate observations for the realm of religion, see Finke and Stark (1992) and for science, see Zuckerman (1988).

22  For studies of the impact of the production system on women writers, see Tuchman (1989); on women etchers, see Lang and Lang (1990); on women ministers, see Steward (1983) and Peterson (1986); on women scientists, see Zuckerman et al. (1991) and Long (1992); and on the view of women, rape, and sexual abuse in the law, see Scheppele (1993).

23  For example, see Bourdieu (1984, 1985, 1988b, 1990a) and Bourdieu and Wacquant (1992: 61–216).

24  Representative studies include Mills (1963), Wolff (1981), Garnham (1986), Giddens (1987), Bourdieu (1990a), and Tetzlaff (1992).

25  See especially Bell (1976) and Schiller (1992).

26  See also the work on consumer culture by Featherstone (1992) and Denzin (1991) on contemporary cinema, both of which take a postmodernist perspective.

27  Representative works include among many others Hirsch (1972), Peterson and Berger (1975), Zolberg (1980), Coser et al. (1981), Ryan (1985), Moulin (1987), Moorhouse (1991), Frith (1992), and Ryan and Peterson (1993).

28  Any social researcher may be co-opted by the system under study, and it has been suggested that researchers of law, science, religion, popular culture, and art among others, have become apologists for the groups that they study (Bourdieu and Wacquant 1992; Aronowitz 1993).

29  Other representative works include McCall (1977), Bennett (1980), Simpson (1981), Faulkner (1983), Neapolitan, (1986), and Lachmann (1988).

30  This follows, I think, from the sort of ethnographic definition of the term "culture" that they assume throughout their work (Peterson 1992a).

31  In my view Becker (1951) so completely identifies with the perspective of the dance musicians that he does not consider the legitimate expectations of others in the situation including club owners, critics, and audiences. In his study of music recording studios, Kealy (1979) takes the perspective of the recording engineers and reports as fact their exaggerated assessment of their own importance in the music recording process. Clignet (1985: 223–32) has been most outspoken in questioning what he calls the "theoretical, methodological, and ethical relativity" of work of this sort.

32  Studies of the cultural productions of English working-class youth provide early exemplars of studies in what is here called autoproduction. See for example Hall and Jefferson (1976), Hebdige (1979), and Frith (1983). Representative recent studies of marginalized groups include those on Swedish youth (Johansson and Miegel 1992), fantasy role-playing gamers (Fine 1983), working women in New York (Peiss 1986), graffiti writers (Lachmann 1988), affluent Japanese joyriders (Sato 1991), and hot-rod enthusiasts (Moorhouse 1991).

33  See, for example, Hall and Jefferson (1976), Fine (1979, 1983), Radway (1984), Peiss (1986), Hall (1987), Lachmann (1988), Liebes and Katz (1990), Press (1991), and Shively (1992).

34  Frith (1983), Laing (1985), Frith and Horne (1987), Lull (1987), Lachmann (1988), and Robinson et al. (1991) all show the reciprocal interchange between manufactured pop culture and autoproduced street culture.

35  See for example Hughes and Peterson (1983), Bourdieu (1984), Randall Collins (1992), Lamont (1992), Peterson (1992b), and Peterson and Simkus (1992).

36  See for example Geertz (1973), Griswold (1981, 1986), Anderson (1983), Peterson (1992d).

37  See, for example, Beisel (1992, 1993), and Peterson (1992c).

38  A wide array of applications of this sort of boundary formation can be found in Lamont and Fournier's (1992) anthology, *Cultivating Differences*.

# 8

# Cultural Production as "Society in the Making": Architecture as an Exemplar of the Social Construction of Cultural Artifacts

## David Brain

The sociology of culture has always been suspended uneasily between an interest in cultural forms as embodiments of symbolic meaning, and the generally reductionistic task of linking cultural forms to social structure. As a result, sociologists of culture have been pulled between interpretation and explanation; between reification and sociological reduction of historical categories of culture; between internal readings that refer to the formal qualities of cultural texts and external readings that refer to social and historical contexts. As the sociology of culture "has come to encompass a relatively diverse array of genres, approaches, and substantive topics" (Wuthnow and Witten 1988: 50), these dichotomies have been institutionalized as a menu of methodological choices that make it possible to circumscribe empirical problems but also to maneuver around fundamental theoretical questions rather than address them directly. The best results have depended on an *ad hoc* balance between the limiting extremes of interpreting a cultural form in its own terms, and dismissing its claims as a mask for the play of social interests or the reflex of some underlying social process. Ironically, at either end of the methodological spectrum, interpretive and structural approaches to the sociology of culture have tended (for different reasons) to reduce cultural artifacts to social conditions that are seen as determining their character or significance.

Since the late 1970s, a variety of work has indicated the need for new ways to think about the relationship between culture and social structure. Ethnographic studies of peer cultures have emphasized the active engagement of subjects in producing their own forms of accommodation to structurally determined circumstances, and their creative contribution to the reproduction of class (Willis 1977; Burawoy 1979; Hebdige 1979), gender (Holland and Eisenhart 1990; McRobbie 1991) or patterns of socialization (Corsaro 1985; Fine 1987). From this point of view, "cultural production" refers to the collective production of skills and practices which enable social actors to make sense of their lives, articulate an identity, and resist with creative energy the apparent dictates of structural conditions they nonetheless reproduce. However, emphasis on interpretive understanding of the active and local character of cultural practices has been difficult to reconcile with systematic explanation or concern for encompassing theoretical issues (Swidler 1986).

At a more general level, poststructuralist theorists have criticized the subjectivism of interpretive approaches and the reductionism of sociological accounts that reduce the form or content of cultural practices to the determining influence of social structures. A number of theorists have proposed ways to conceptualize cultural production at a level of analysis that encompasses both social and semiotic structures undergirding the production of discourse, the organization of social practices, and the meaning of artifacts (Foucault 1972; de Certeau 1984; Baudrillard 1988; Bourdieu 1990c). However, such dramatic epistemological reorientation has proven difficult to reconcile with the methodological choices that have traditionally characterized the sociology of recorded culture. In particular, empirically oriented sociologists of cultural production and theorists inspired by poststructuralist ideas have tended to talk past one another.

The main purpose of this chapter is to formulate new questions for a sociology of recorded culture that avoid the theoretical impasse created by the traditional dichotomy of culture and social structure, respond to the epistemological challenge of poststructuralist theory, yet offer the possibility for empirically grounded accounts of cultural phenomena. The first part of the essay develops a theoretical argument for conceptualizing the relationship between cultural artifacts and the social world in terms of practices that simultaneously constitute significant objects and particular forms of cultural agency. An analytical framework for specifying the practical modalities of cultural agency is proposed, including an empirical focus on the formation of particular disciplines of cultural production, the sociological conditions that sustain them, and, ultimately, the broader consequences of their particular interventions in the social world.

A general question is implied by Bourdieu's theory of practice (Bourdieu 1990c), and given a specific empirical twist by recent studies of the social construction of technology (Bijker and Pinch 1987; Latour 1988b): What social relations, institutional practices, strategies of action, and subjective possibilities are built into cultural artifacts? I suggest that the key to unravelling the sociology inscribed in artifacts is an analysis that captures the fundamental duality of cultural production. The social construction of artifacts is at the same time the materialization of a practice that enables particular kinds of agents to intervene productively in the world of things. Sociologists of technology have argued that the form and stability of artifacts entails the organization of heterogeneous elements (institutions, social actors, interests, other technical artifacts, texts, bits of nature, and so on) in an "actor network" (Callon 1987). As cultural or technical artifacts are stabilized, they stabilize the field of operations in which they are produced, the practices that produce them, and the social relations implied in both their production and use. Such actor networks constitute a field of operation for the authorship of cultural statements which can represent themselves as true, efficacious, or morally valid, and for the design of artifacts that can represent themselves as rational solutions to comprehensible problems.

Cultural production is, at two levels, "society in the making" (Callon 1987). The social construction of cultural artifacts entails the production of practices which, in turn, enact their own status in broader social contexts by inscribing both the boundaries of cultural domains and the social status of the author in qualities of the artifact. This duality of cultural production is reflected in two orienting questions: First, what is the practical logic imposed on techniques and strategies of cultural production by their implication in the reproduction of the relatively autonomous domains of culture in which they operate (e.g., science, art, etc.)? Second, in what ways are both the practical constitution and the sociological significance of particular cultural objects rooted in what will be referred to as the "art" of artifacts? In any artifact, there is an apparent arbitrariness of form that cannot be reduced to external conditions, the demands of representation, or subjective motives.

Typically, interpretive accounts refer these aspects of form to the distinctive vision of the creative subject or the influence of a common style or sensibility. I argue that formal qualities of artifacts constitute a practical rhetoric which, by referring to the status of the object and the presence of an author, give particular force and authority to the production and inscribe the capacities of subjects in the objective world. Aesthetic practices provide a dramatic instance of a tendency that is common – in different forms and degree – to a range of cultural products from technical artifacts to artistic expression.

The last part of the chapter looks at the case of modernism in American architecture to illustrate this analytical approach. Historical accounts of developments in architecture generally combine technological determinism with an interpretive history of ideas. 'Modernism' appears as both a reflex of technology and a general cultural sensibility that is given more or less powerful expression by creative individuals. In contrast, I argue that it represented a reconfiguration of "architecture" as a concrete set of practices for intervention in the built environment, as a technology addressed to needs construed in a particular way, and as an aesthetic object. Aesthetic judgment and technical rationality were woven together in a new way in order to reconstruct the authority of the architect and the capacity for authorship in the practice of design. The federal housing projects of the New Deal were a crucial site in which this complex reconfiguration was worked out.

## The Sociology of Artifacts

According to Bourdieu, our ability to enact our intentions in a way that both makes sense to us and reproduces the apparent regularities of the social world depends on the fact that all of our practices and representations refer to a common set of "generative schemes" of perception and action, and the system of "durable and transposable dispositions" that he calls the *habitus*. The *habitus* is the basis for an "art of inventing" which makes it possible to produce practices and representations that seem "objectively adapted to their outcomes without presupposed conscious aiming at the ends or an express mastery of the operations necessary in order to attain them" (Bourdieu 1990c: 53). It constitutes a "practical sense" which enables

agents "to partake of the history objectified in institutions, to appropriate them practically, and so to keep them in activity, continuously pulling them from the state of dead letters, reviving the sense
deposited in them, but at the same time imposing the revisions and
transformations that reactivation entails" (p. 141).

Action is structured by schemes of perception, cognition, and
motivation, that are produced according to the same principles as
those embodied in institutions, artifacts, rituals, the organization
of inhabited space, even typical postures of the body. A "logic of
practice," built in to the objective world at this level, enables social
actors to engage in improvisations that "tend to reproduce the
regularities immanent in the conditions in which their generative
principle was produced while adjusting to the demands inscribed
as objective potentialities in the situation as defined by the cognitive and motivating structures that constitute the *habitus*"
(Bourdieu 1990c: 52). Rather than simply reflect regularities in society, artifacts represent a practical enactment and objectification of
the principles that generate such regularities. These principles can
therefore be continually rediscovered, reinvented, and reenacted.
In our engagement in the world, we encounter problems that we
perceive in relation to the same principles that enable us to generate possible solutions – principles that are already implicit in the
world as it has been constructed historically, and built in to the
mutual structuring of the social world and the world of things.[1]

Crucial implications of Bourdieu's argument have generally been
overlooked, largely because the concept of the *habitus* is both too
encompassing and too limiting. Within the *habitus*, social practices,
cultural artifacts, schemes of perception, and systems of classification all boil down to a durable disposition to reproduce structures
of class and status. Like the night in which all cows are black, as
Hegel said, it makes finely drawn distinctions difficult. In addition,
the concept of *habitus* contains a built-in tendency to short-circuit
the theory of practice and encourage the sort of "objectivist" reduc-
tions to social structure that Bourdieu (1990c) explicitly criticizes.
Behind this concept, however, there is an important argument concerning the relationship between the social world and cultural
productions.[2]

Bourdieu (1984: 1) has argued that forms of cultural consumption provide "markers" of class distinction which play a crucial
function in reproducing and legitimating social inequality. However,

the distinctions of "taste" sustained by patterns of cultural consumption are not just a matter of associating oneself with objects
that fall within socially significant categories, but involve a capacity to exercise judgment in making distinctions between objects and,
in this way, to give practical substance to one's status (Bourdieu
1984: 25). Cultural products provide a site in which the substance
of status differences is elaborated and given objective status. The
relationship between cultural forms and social categories (including, but not limited to, classes) is acted out in practical judgments
that translate social distinctions into capacities of social subjects
constituted by their reflection in qualities that appear objectively
present in the world of things.

A central theoretical implication of Bourdieu's critique of "taste"
is that the capacities of socially situated subjects are anchored in
the perceptible qualities of artifacts. The practical sense embodied
in artifacts enables the social actor to act in a manner which positions both actor and action in a social context, and ensures that
sensible action will contribute (at least in some ways) to the
reproduction of the conditions that make that action possible. The
objective world is "made up of objects which are the product of
objectifying operations structured according to the same structures
that the *habitus* applies to them" (Bourdieu 1990c: 77). We recognize, interpret, and understand the practical significance of artifacts in terms of the same principles which govern the "objectifying
operations" that produce them. This argument has implications not
only for understanding the reproduction of class structure, but for
other socially constructed distinctions relevant to a more finely
grained analysis of an institutional order.

Latour's discussion of "inscription" offers a sharp formulation of
the way the social context is not only reflected but actively engaged
by the qualities of the artifact (Latour 1988b). He argues that
technical artifacts are intrinsically social in three senses: they are
made by human beings; they are "delegates" whose actions are
substituted for the actions of humans in particular contexts; and they
shape human action by imposing prescriptions back on the behavior
of humans engaged by the scenarios they define. He uses the
example of a hydraulic door closer as a simple machine – a
"nonhuman" – that is delegated responsibility for keeping the door
closed, standing in for either a citizenry responsible enough to close
the door after themselves, or a human porter assigned to the task.[3]

In substituting nonhuman for human actors, the mechanics who design a machine *transcribe* the scene as it might be played by humans into a scene that involves both humans and nonhumans. This transcription of social relations into machines *inscribes* certain kinds of actors in the scene (those who made the machine, those who use it, the machine itself) and *prescribes* qualities and behaviors to human as well as nonhuman actors. The door closer, for example, discriminates against those who are too small or weak to push the door open against the resistance of the hydraulic device, or too slow to get through before it pulls the door closed. Similarly, Renaissance paintings, traffic lights and navigational beacons are all designed to be viewed by humans positioned correctly in relation to them, each of whom is required to bring a certain competence to the scene as an agent capable of enacting possibilities implied in it. To a certain extent, we can refuse to subscribe to a position prescribed for us by any of these artifacts, but we are unlikely to do so as long as we are embedded in a series of interlocking scenes that cumulatively make up our social world (Latour 1988b: 307).

The empirical problem of unpacking the sociological content with which technological artifacts are infused has been addressed by recent "social constructivist" studies of technological innovation (Bijker and Pinch 1987). Where technology studies traditionally examined the social significance of technical success, the social constructivist program tries to account for the technical as well as the social success of a technological innovation in the same methodological move. The researcher begins by demonstrating the "interpretative flexibility" inherent in technological artifacts. Crucially, this interpretive flexibility affects not only the meanings associated with the artifact, but the way the artifact is designed (Bijker and Pinch 1987: 40). There are different ways in which any artifact might be designed, depending on how the salient dimensions of the problem are defined, how adequate solutions are constructed, and on the criteria for adequacy invoked by different agents. The analyst examines the concrete social and historical process by which the form of artifact was gradually stabilized, and by which relevant actors achieved a certain closure of debate over whether or not a particular artifact is an adequate approximation of some definition of success (Bijker and Pinch 1987: 24). The stabilization of an artifact does not imply that the problems are actually solved in a definitive and unquestionable way. Closure

can be achieved rhetorically, or by redefining the problem so that
some aspect of the artifact now appears as a solution. The key
point is that the social construction of a technological artifact is not
simply a matter of selecting new solutions to existing problems,
or new solutions to new problems, but a reconstruction of the
relationship between problems and solutions such that a particular
artifact, with recognized characteristics, is capable of representing
itself as a technical solution to a problem which it is empowered
to define.

The social nature of technological artifacts is sufficiently profound
to justify referring to the agents of technological innovation as
"engineer-sociologists," directly involved in the making of society
as well as the making of things (Callon 1987). The stability and form
of artifacts is seen as a function of the interaction of both human
and nonhuman components in a heterogeneous "actor-network."
For example, in the actor network that would have made the
electric car (VEL) possible in France in the early seventies, Callon
includes "the electrons that jump effortlessly between electrodes;
the consumers who reject the symbol of the motorcar and who are
ready to invest in public transport; the Ministry of the Quality of
Life, which imposes regulations about levels of acceptable noise
pollution; Renault, which accepts that it will be turned into a
manufacturer of car bodies; lead accumulators, whose performance
has been improved" (Callon 1987: 86). The construction of an
"actor-network" involves a simplification that defines such heterogeneous elements in terms of just those characteristics made salient
by the juxtapositions of the network. Not only does the artifact
depend on a particular array of actors in a network, but its engineer-
sociologists define both the characteristics of the artifact and the
"social universe" in which it is to function. To the extent that this
"heterogeneous engineering" is successful in holding the network
together, the simplifications (and social relations) involved are
stabilized and "built in" to the artifactual world (Law 1987: 113).

This empirical grasp of the stabilization of artifacts, along with
Bourdieu's conception of practice, adds up to an important
reconceptualization of the relationship between culture, action, and
social structure. Although the constructivist project tends to emphasize the process of arriving at closure, the analysis depends on
reopening the "black box" of technology, calling attention to the
mechanisms of closure and indicating that closure is always

provisional. The argument is not that technology comes to determine social life, but rather that artifacts represent a particular way of working on social relations and giving them a certain obduracy, at least for certain practical purposes. They also hold certain possibilities for destabilizing and even transforming those relations. One can specify the conditions under which closure is disrupted as well as achieved.

In cultural production, the stabilization of artifacts is not a matter of a singular achievement, but articulates a category of cultural object that is invested with significance, in part, as a result of its paradigmatic status. In this respect, it also entails a stabilization of interpretive practices, and of the principles that come to be at stake in the mutual configuration of problem and solution reflected in the artifact. In other words, it implies the stabilization of practices of design through which it is possible to give material form to artifacts such that they represent effective responses to explicitly defined problems. The referents of these problems may be social, political, technical, or cultural, but their translation into problems of form is a critical step often overlooked by sociologists of cultural production.

### The problem of agency

Bourdieu (1990c) is primarily interested in the way the schemes of perception and action of the *habitus* are "acquired through practice and implemented in the practical state without attaining explicit representation" (p. 95), and in the way these generative principles are manifested in a variety of cultural practices (rituals, marriage strategies, house plans, etc.). He gives less attention to the constitution of specific modes of self-conscious cultural production. In order to conceptualize the form of agency inscribed in an artifact, one needs to analyze the specific "objectifying operations" involved in the formulation of intentions, and the cultural work involved in the transcription of interests, social relations, institutional demands, and structural conditions into the material form of an artifact. Latour (1988b: 304) notes that the "enunciator" – the author of a text or the engineer who devises the machine – "is free to place or not a representation of himself or herself in the script." Actually, this inscription, in its various forms and with varying emphasis, is at the heart of the production of recorded culture. The agent's representation of his or her own agency is a crucial part of the constitution of a cultural object, and this mutual configuration of subject and object constitute distinctive practices of cultural production.

Foucault's "archeology" of discursive formations offers useful guidelines for specifying the form and conditions of cultural agency. Like Bourdieu, Foucault is interested in the way discursive knowledge is anchored in ostensibly insignificant features of the social world: the form of institutions, the arrangements of space, or movements of the body. He has focused, however, on the way the discourse that takes shape in heterogeneous fields of texts, institutional arrangements, social structures, and material conditions, constitutes specific "regimes of truth" and modes of technical intervention with which subjects are empowered (and to which they are subjected) at any historical moment. Interpretation treats discourse as "an element that ought to be transparent, but whose unfortunate opacity must often be pierced if one is to reach at last the depth of the essential in the place in which it is held in reserve" (Foucault 1972: 138–9). In contrast, Foucault proposes an analysis the aim of which "is not to neutralize discourse, to make it the sign of something else, and to pierce through its density in order to reach what remains silently anterior to it, but on the contrary to maintain it in its consistency, to make it emerge in its own complexity" (Foucault 1972: 47). He identifies regularities in discourse that cannot be reduced to an underlying meaning operating from within or to constraints imposed from without. These regularities characterize discourse itself as a practice which, on the one hand, constitutes subjective capacities, and, on the other hand, refers to contextual conditions as an organized set of resources and a terrain on which practical strategies operate, rather than as determinants of what is said.

An initial task is analysis of the various historical conditions that determine the way an object of discourse emerges as part of a "system of referentials": institutional arrangements, social and economic processes, norms, techniques, types of classification, modes of characterization, "principles of differentiation." These conditions are not what cause the object to exist in itself, but "what enabled it to appear, to juxtapose itself with other objects, to situate itself in relation to them, to define its difference, its irreducibility, and even perhaps its heterogeneity" (Foucault 1972: 45).

They are not determinants but resources that are actively and selectively taken up in a discourse that constructs its objects in particular ways.

The discursive practices that enable subjects to generate statements about these objects are organized by "enunciative modalities" that characterize the way a discourse identifies who is speaking, who is authorized to speak, how they come to be authorized, and the institutionalized position from which a discourse emerges. Statements always refer to a subject, not as the consciousness in which the statement originates as an intention, but as "a particular, vacant place that may in fact be filled by different individuals" (Foucault 1972: 95). The existence of a statement depends on the fact that the position of the subject can be assigned, and describing a statement consists "in determining what position can and must be occupied by any individual if he is to be the subject of it" (Foucault 1972: 95–6). Machines, buildings, visual objects like paintings, and actual texts are all cultural statements in that they entail "enunciative modalities" that locate them in a field of objects, and position an author in relation to an objective world in which a particular intervention is being made.[4]

A statement is always part of an "enunciative field" in which statements constitute "a domain of coexistence" for one another. In relation to an enunciative field, the statement assumes "a place and a status, which arranges for its possible relations with the past, and which opens up for it a possible future" (Foucault 1972: 99). Most crucially, a discourse is defined by the criteria according to which the truth of a statement can be assessed (the "domain of validity"), and the criteria according to which certain statements might be excluded as irrelevant to a particular domain of objects (a "domain of normativity"). In other words, the constitution of a discursive field can be described in terms of the way its boundaries are enacted in the practices of the discourse itself.

In the material character of statements, Foucault sees a particular conjuncture of the historical particularity of its object, the positioning of its subject, its placement in a field of related statements that it helps to constitute that situates it in a broader context. The materiality of statements includes not only the technology of inscription (ink on paper, modulated sound, etc.), but their relation to an institutional order that provides them with a status, defines the possibilities for their use and circulation, and determines "the mode according to which they become objects of appropriation, instruments for desire or interest, elements for a strategy" (Foucault 1972: 115). This materiality refers to what I have called the duality of cultural production. A cultural object, which represents itself as an objectification of subjective intention in material form, both relies on and helps to define a domain of related objects. A crucial part of its capacity for significance lies in its ability to position itself in relation to other objects, each of which calls attention to itself as an intentional product, and as part of a common field of related statements.[5]

The sociology of culture has commonly suffered from a tendency to look either at the special qualities of the world "inside" a domain of cultural practice (e.g., the laboratory, the artist's studio, the architect's office) or to look for political motives and interests that intervene from the outside. To put the question this way, however, is to accept the construction of inside and outside which ought, itself, to be explained. The analytical framework being developed here, by focusing on the historical specificity of a practice without assuming its identity from the start, highlights the articulation of the relationship between the specialized practices of cultural production and the broader social and institutional milieu as the crucial accomplishment at the heart of the production of a cultural form.

Latour (1983) pursued the methodological implications of a similar observation with regard to the social construction of scientific knowledge. The dichotomy of inside/outside assumes that one simply finds science in the lab, politics outside, and that the problem is figuring out how the latter affects the former. For Latour, the question is not what interests are served and/or obscured by scientific practices, but how the doing of science comes to be associated with any interests whatsoever outside the lab. In the case of Pasteur, for example, he examines the "dramatic short circuit" through which Pasteur's microbiology came to be the route to a solution to problems of hygiene, veterinary science, and French society (Latour 1983: 156). For this reason, we should focus "not on the laboratory itself but on the construction of the laboratory and its position in the societal milieu" (Latour 1983: 143). The problem is not linking actions inside with influences outside, but analyzing the way the "inside" positions itself as "inside" – the way it constructs a particular array of asymmetries that enable a position inside to provide leverage on things "outside."

The practices involved in the production of scientific knowledge – or any cultural artifact – imply the organization of their own context. The construction of an "inside" depends on a set of practices that position themselves in relation to an outside, that transcribe a distance between the producer and consumer of a cultural form in the artifacts themselves, that sustain specific asymmetries around which opportunities for agency are organized. Both science and art involve the formation of techniques for translation and inscription, for sustaining and crossing the permeable boundaries of the "inside" in order to assume a role of cultural agency in relation to the "outside." In this way, the content of practices is not separable from organization of the domains in which they are possible.

## The art of artifacts

One of the consequences of investigation of the social construction of technological artifacts is an awareness that artifacts are profoundly underdetermined by social processes or technical considerations. This underdetermined quality of artifacts has provided the grist for interpretation. Interpretive approaches begin, as Baxandall (1985: 14–15) notes, with the assumption that "[t]he maker of a picture or other historical artefact is a man addressing a problem of which his product is a finished and concrete solution." For any work, it is presumed, one should be able to sort out the ways in which it was historically determined, the frameworks of meaning it embodies, and the specific meanings invested in it by actors with a pragmatic stake in a particular context (Baxandall 1985; Griswold 1987b).

Paradoxically, such accounts often imply a kind of determinism insofar as they locate the sources of a specific project, and the specificity of its execution, in environmental contingencies, while at the same time they highlight the precise ways in which the project or product is underdetermined by its circumstances. Faced with objective constraints and operating within a framework of cultural presuppositions, the creative subject makes choices that reveal both a rational intent and a particular style of action. Against the background of imputed rational intent, an interpretive approach illuminates the agent of cultural production as a particular subjectivity. Interpretation traces the putative author's steps in producing a meaningful object, but takes for granted the skills and practices which enable the agent of cultural production to shape available material into a particular kind of response to the heterogeneous conditions of the brief – or, for that matter, to recognize a particular brief in a complex array of conditions which might support any number of cultural productions.[6]

In the world of artifacts, we are confronted with a play of qualities that present themselves as intentional (as the trace, expression, or purposeful act of a subjective capacity), and those that present themselves as natural or unintentional (as objective circumstance, as accident, or as noise). Bourdieu has referred to the "permanent teleological character" of things. Where interpretive approaches have sought to capture the teleology in "thick description," and structural approaches have sought to identify its determining conditions, my argument leads to the question of how this "teleological character" is registered. By what practices is the boundary between the intentional and the contingent marked in the material of the object itself, and what articulations of the social world are thereby implicated in the structuring of artifacts? The distinction between the subjectively intended and the objectively given is achieved, not found. It is an accomplishment that is far from automatic or natural, perhaps especially when it seems so.

The fit between form and function, or form and intention, or form and meaning, relies on a practical sense that underlies any intentional adjustment of an artifact or technology to the "objective" demands of a task, by determining the mutual configuration of task and technique. Form is given to function with what Bourdieu calls "the arbitrariness of culture," but in a manner that is rooted in the practical experience of a socially constructed world. The transcription of function or meaning into form involves a system of representation: even technical solutions to technical problems might be seen as not only solving the problem but representing themselves as solutions, in a particular interpretive context. Furthermore, the fitting of form to function is carried out with a rhetorical flourish that represents the intentional quality of the artifact, a practical rhetoric that utilizes what Foucault calls "enunciative modalities" to refer back to an agent. This practical rhetoric operates in the gap between rational intent and the thing itself, as a modulation of the residue of arbitrariness in any form, and establishes the status of the object, the status of the author, and, in this way, the character of the social world as a domain of practical action.

This, I argue, is the "art" of artifacts. What we recognize in both technical artifacts and works of art is a pattern of intention that refers to a domain of possible intentions, and our interpretive (as well as practical) grasp of this pattern depends on the way the artifact makes its intentional quality manifest. The "artful" quality of the object depends on the practical rhetoric with which the inscription of the author's status is effected. Bourdieu notes that artistic production "always contains something 'ineffable'" (Bourdieu 1990c: 34). I suggest that this "ineffable" quality is a fundamental aspect of the effect of signification. These aspects of the object cannot be interpreted directly as an expression of an intention because they are the condition for recognizing the object as intentional. In the inscription of patterns of intention in the world of things, in the qualities of artfulness that carry the rhetorical freight of this inscription, the authority of the subject is enacted and objectified. As technological artifacts are stabilized, they may come to look more and more like purely technical engineering, and, typically, to carry less and less representation of their authorship. The key difference between technical design and artistic production is that the latter involves particular rhetorical practices that represent distinct modes of intentionality.

In the arts, the specialization of aesthetic practices gives particular ritual emphasis to the inscribed author. In science, on the other hand, a great deal of energy is devoted to eliding the presence of an author in the finished product of scientific truth while allowing the author to remain useful as a point of reference for "science in action" (Latour 1987). The modalities of authorship inscribed in artifacts focus our interpretive attention, organize our capacities for self-conscious cultural creation, and embed our creations (as well as the act of creation) in a social world. They make it possible to recognize objective possibilities for subjective action in the world of artifacts. At the same time, they represent an inscription of a moral order, a configuration of relations between author and audience, and an authorization of an agent to undertake responsibility for a certain kind of representation.

Art offers a particularly clear and historically significant illustration of the social character of cultural production. Practical modalities in the work itself refer to the fact of an agent's involvement in the text, mark the work's status in an institutional field, and frame possibilities for interpretation. Abstracted from their original social settings, the interpretive practices associated with an "aesthetic disposition" have provided a paradigm for the embodiment of a theoretically informed practice in a specifically qualified and authorized agent. In this sense, an aesthetic disposition can be incorporated into a variety of practices, as a general strategy for translating the demands of a field of operation into capacities and dispositions of authorized subjects. Aside from its function as a means of social distinction, art is a ritualized and abstracted enactment of a form of agency that can be transposed to other practices – not just to those related to making social distinctions between the classes, but to the construction of other forms of cultural authority.

## The Practical Logic of Modernism

The analytical framework outlined above suggests an understanding of the transformative impact of "modernism" on architectural design in the USA that runs counter to the usual critical and historical accounts. Standard critical histories of architecture tend to focus on the evolution of paradigmatic architectural forms, a process reconstructed as cycles of creative innovation and stylistic elaboration. Social histories of architecture reveal the impact of social, economic, and political factors on the development of both ideas about architecture and architectural forms. My analysis attempts to fill the gap between a history of architectural ideas which focuses on their immanent logic, and a history of architectural developments which emphasizes their determination by broader social and historical forces. Architects have mediated between the external exigencies of social structures, economic constraints, political processes, and the organization of space and materials in the production of built form. As a discipline, architectural design is sustained by a specific structure of cultural agency that has been embedded in the social structure of the profession.

Since the historical argument is complex, this chapter focuses on only one aspect of it: the way architects responded to the task of translating the social problem of housing into an *architectural* problem in the context of the federally subsidized housing programs of the New Deal. In responding to the demands of these programs, architects accomplished two things at once. First, they enlisted government agencies, housing reformers, academics, planners, political constituencies, the prevailing winds, the angle of sunlight on building sites, construction techniques, and European formal paradigms in the actor network that enabled them to give form to these projects. At the same time, they institutionalized a new mode of design and redefined their own capacities as agents under new conditions: designing housing for an abstractly defined user group, in service to a bureaucratic agency within a democratic state, against the background of a market system in crisis. In this context, they were able not only to respond to the changing circumstances of the profession, but to reconstruct their own authority in a practice that could represent itself as rational and dictated by the demands of the task at hand.

As the discipline of design was first formed in the United States, the problem of professionalizing design was not simply the problem of monopolizing building technology, which architects have never been able to do, but of constructing a relatively autonomous domain of architectural judgment with a distinctive niche in the division of labor. The ability of an occupational group to translate an inchoate demand into a definite service depended on their active articulation of a distinctive form of work, and the ability, embodied in the work itself, to sustain a framework of interpretation which gave specific cultural content to professional design. The routine work of producing drawings provided techniques for visualizing and manipulating architectural forms, and the practical site on which a particular occupational group was able to isolate the composition of architectural statements as a distinct practice. Anchored in the craft of drawing, this practice derived its content and legitimacy from reference to elite cultural traditions, but emphasized the forms of judgment required to adapt historical models to modern needs – to produce an *artful* yet uniquely *appropriate* composition.

The abstraction of a formal aesthetic provided the basis for defining a disciplined practice across diverse building tasks. Over the course of the nineteenth century, architects elaborated a domain of judgments regarding the visual qualities of architectural form, abstracting a coherent and rationalized practice from a canon of traditional styles and anchoring it in professional institutions. A rhetoric of architectural form associated architectural design simultaneously with a structure of justification and the authoritative judgment of a specially equipped individual. The concrete practices of design linked the immediate reality of architectural work to the reproduction of the boundaries of a professional jurisdiction and a durable market for professional services.[7]

Even as the discipline of design was consolidated, however, it incorporated contradictions that it would finally confront in the first part of this century. Between 1890 and 1929, changes in the building industry, in the real estate market, and in the needs of an urban and commercial society, took a great deal of control over the physical form of buildings out of the architect's hands. The industrial production of new building materials and technological development in the area of mechanical services opened new architectural possibilities for which there were no governing precedents, while the economic demands of high-density urban land use called for structures which were taller and less functionally specific. The problem was made more pressing by the growing scale and complexity of urban building, and by the emergence of new building types: the office building, the department store, the apartment building. New urban building tasks strained the architects' ability to adapt historical styles to bigger and higher structures, and at many points severed the already strained logical connections between building purposes and varieties of stylistic expression. In the late nineteenth century, the elite core of professional architecture was dominated by Beaux-Arts design practices that reflected the duality in the architects' situation (Brain 1989). The discipline provided by the canon of historical styles, the rules of composition, and planning principles of Beaux-Arts design, enabled architects to produce disciplined and authoritative architectural statements, but had very little to do with the conditions to which the architect was increasingly expected to respond. Beaux-Arts design reflected with painful clarity the disjuncture between rational planning at the level of the building's function, and the persistent historicism at the level of architectural form.

In the first two decades of the twentieth century, the profession split into two distinct factions. From within Beaux-Arts orthodoxy, which maintained an emphasis on precedent, there was concern to articulate a relationship between modern building needs and the historical styles. The traditional architect argued for discipline, but it was a discipline rooted in traditions that remained vulnerable to the whims of client taste and fashion. Others sought to escape the historical styles altogether, as all too obviously inappropriate to modern needs, and called for the formation of a distinctively modern style. However, experimentation with "modern" styles only emphasized the arbitrariness of form, whereas the stripping of historical ornament raised doubts as to what would be left that was distinctively "architectural." At first, European modernism simply added to the eclecticism of the period (Benevolo 1977: 638). The link between form and function had no more apparent necessity than there had been with the historical styles. Throughout the 1920s, most of the profession seems to have given very little attention to contemporary European developments, except to note technical achievements or to disparage their architectural qualities.

Threats to the status and jurisdiction of professional architects posed by engineers, builders, and manufacturers in the 1920s were translated into the disciplinary problem of defining the relationship between aesthetic practice and technical rationality. What the discipline needed was a rhetoric of architectonic expression which could replace historical reference, representing both the fit between form and function, and their own agency. The achievement of an effectively modern mode of design was simultaneously a sociological and an architectural problem, since it would entail not only a new vocabulary of building forms, but the incorporation of new modalities of design into the institutional arrangements that sustained the coherence and status of a discipline, and the professional status of the architect. The public housing projects of the New Deal provided a context in which a new mode of design could be anchored in the practical realities of the profession.

In the first three decades of the twentieth century, the architecture of urban housing responded in direct and obvious ways to the economic demands of urban real estate. Moderate-cost housing presented a challenge to the architect, who had to work within tight budgets and respond to housing reformers' standards for the provision of space, light, air, and privacy. These limits were reflected in a simplification of ornament, a focus on site planning, and a kind of "gadgeteering" approach to design. As a design problem, the architectural quality of these projects resided in the way they translated economy into clever spatial arrangements and efficient architectural gestures (a few projecting brick courses, some terra-cotta pieces). However, these projects did not essentially challenge the status of the architects' discipline. They could include a nod toward the architectural sufficient to establish respectability, and the restriction of ornament could be read as an appropriate expression of middle-class thrift. The simplification of architectural elements was not a denial of their value, but a recognition of their differential appropriateness.

Whereas the problem of designing moderately priced housing for the middle classes had involved a moderation of architectural expression that could be intelligibly incorporated within a discipline that relied on the Beaux-Arts conception of a hierarchy of styles and building tasks, federally subsidized urban housing made it painfully clear that the distinctively architectural expertise of the Beaux-Arts architect was largely irrelevant. As the buildings were stripped to unornamented blocks whose forms were determined by various strategies for arranging basic apartment plans around a service core, the remnants of the Beaux-Arts aesthetic appeared only in the formal symmetry of apartment blocks arranged around central axes. The Beaux-Arts architect, operating at the level of scale demanded by the large housing project, could only treat the project as a kind of civic monument.

Public housing raised the fundamental question of the discipline with particular urgency: how to couple rationalized techniques with an aesthetic discipline that materialized the practical authority of the architect. In the late nineteenth century, architects had turned the distinction between architecture and "mere building" to their advantage. They responded to criticism and jurisdictional challenges by claiming to represent a distinctive sphere of cultural concerns (Wright 1980: 63). During the Depression, however, the significance of such a distinction shifted. Public housing could not be defined as an architectural problem, within the practical, ideological, and aesthetic framework of nineteenth-century design, with its dependence on historicism for its justification of form. If architecture were something more than mere building, then it seemed we could not afford it. Architectural statements were also inappropriate for political and ideological reasons. In publicly subsidized housing, there was no room for decorative elaboration, the imposition of a formal ideal, or traditional rhetorical flourishes. As a result, these projects constituted a serious threat to the theoretical core of the discipline and the practical status of the profession.

For this very reason, however, the public housing programs provided an ideal site for working out the practical terms of a new mode of translation of building function into architectural form.

First, these projects were an opportunity to design for an ideal rather than a real client, a user with abstract qualities and needs which could be expressed in quantifiable terms. Alfred Kastner called attention to this in 1938, in a discussion of the role of the architect in housing. In the past, the profession "revolved around the dominant thought that the juicy plums come from the rich" (Kastner 1938: 228). A necessary reorientation would have to shift the basic definition of architecture from a "Decorative Art" to a "Social Art." This would require a "methodical approach" rather than "the old line of eye-appealing facadism" (Kastner 1938: 229). "Houses can be designed, as they should be: from the inside out according to the physical and psychological needs of the tenants" (Kastner 1938: 234). These needs are basic and obvious – light, air, quiet, exercise – and, with the creative intelligence of the designer, require no extraordinary expense to fulfill. The modern architect designed not for the cultivated few, or for the cultural uplift of the masses, but for the human needs of the modern citizen, defined in terms of common rights and basic needs.[8]

This notion represented a dramatic shift in the representation of human needs in architectural form, a shift which also required abstraction from the traditional relationship of patronage. In the context of the federal housing program, with the state as the client and an abstractly defined "user," it was possible to associate architectural form with human needs and the public good, and for the architect to define both in abstract terms, rather than in accordance with the tastes and expressed desires of the client. In this setting, architects were able to reinvent the people for whom they designed (see Montgomery 1989) and to give new significance to their authority as technical experts.

Second, the scale of the projects made it possible to relocate the aesthetic object inscribed in built form. This relocation is indicated by the way aesthetic questions – traditionally tied to questions of taste – were displaced from the center in the discussions of housing design. Catherine Bauer, a well-known housing reformer, noted that elements of modern housing are defined by a set of minimum standards for the provision of basic needs: decency, health, amenity, and comfort and convenience. New building forms "grow, on the one hand, out of the new standards and materials and methods and functions, and are related just as clearly on the other to that quickening and renewal of aesthetic sensibility which we call 'modern' in the best twentieth-century painting and sculpture and photography" (Bauer 1934: 148). The key task, however, is to link a form which is organic (unfolding from within) to a visible order which is legible from without.

One point where the new synthesis of functional form and visual order emerges is in a changing conception of standardization. Against those who resisted public housing programs on the grounds that they impose an unwanted standardization on American living, Bauer argued that we have always had standardization – standard lots, standard plans, but "in an excessively wasteful and ugly and unproductive form." In contrast, "functional" standardization would open up important new opportunities for design:

> For the first time, it is possible to build up groups and balanced masses and rhythms merely out of the varied forms required for specific functions. Standardized parts, instead of creating dull uniformity, become a positive force in creating a unified whole. Meaningless surface ornament, once applied to distract the eye from the unbearable bleakness and monotony underneath, becomes not only unnecessary but ridiculous. Good materials, simple lines, and geometric forms become, when combined with carefully designed and planted open spaces, all the elements necessary to an authentic modern architecture. (Bauer 1934: 164)

This statement of what can be recognized as a modernist orientation extols the virtues of standardization as the starting point rather than the unfortunate lack of design, replacing reliance on "meaningless surface ornament" with an aesthetic that draws its force from the apparent fit of formal arrangements to the logic of functions. The crucial change lies not in the new formal images imported from Europe, but in their new practical significance. Strikingly, the discussions of housing design by Bauer and others used forms associated with European modernism with little or no comment. Aesthetic qualities appear both directly in the discussion, and implicitly in the illustrating images, as *indicators* of the functional quality of good design, rather than as its central intention or crucial accomplishment. In this respect, American architects and housing reformers took advantage of the "symbolic objectivity" of European modernism when they invoked its images (Jordy 1963).[9]

Third, association with a federal program anchored the emergent design practices in bureaucratic as well as technical rationality.

The historical peculiarity of the modernist association of certain formal images with functional principles was effectively "black boxed" by its institutional incorporation into the practical guidelines of the Public Works Administration (PWA), and the bureaucratic standardization later imposed by the Federal Housing Authority. This incorporation is evident in the design guidelines published by the PWA in 1935 (published both as a pamphlet, and as a major part of one issue of *Architectural Record* (March 1935)). These guidelines were presented as suggestions to architects submitting proposals to the PWA, and as labor-saving devices that would allow the local architect to submit preliminary plans without extensive research or excessive design time. The architect was provided with guidelines for neighborhood location, orientation, density, site planning, and a repertoire of unit plans for solving a variety of spatial puzzles. Particular emphasis, however, was put on the site plan as an orderly arrangement of buildings responsive to the need for an economy of land use, the functional arrangement of buildings and open spaces, and an appropriate orientation to the sun and prevailing winds.[10]

There was considerable variation in the quality and character of the projects as some architects adapted more easily to the new modality than others. The point is not that these projects had an effect because of their consistently modern style, or their paradigmatic quality as monumental buildings. Public housing provided a practical site in which modernist design could make relevant and persuasive claims. Over the course of a decade, these projects helped to effect a dramatic inversion of the discipline of design. Whereas multiple family urban housing represented the lower limit of the architectural for the nineteenth-century architect, public housing could now represent the epitome of architecture as technology, as a means for accomplishing a socially significant task. In the context of PWA housing projects, the technical gadgetry of late nineteenth-century and early twentieth-century apartment design was reworked into architecture.

Whereas the framework of justification of historicist design had imposed formal ideals that penetrated building from the top down, modernist design reversed this relationship. In the former case, architecture dwindled into mere building as one moved down the hierarchy of building functions from public monument to utility shed, from Newport mansions to the working class house.

Modernist design made it possible to recognize the domain of the architectural the moment a lintel is set across two posts, enabling Architecture (as cultural object and as practical intervention) to permeate "mere building" in a way that it could not have done before. Even the apparent failures of many of the designs (as architecture or as housing) were understood as an indication of the need to perfect modernist practices rather than question modernist assumptions.

Beaux-Arts design was a rationalization of historicist design, but its rationalism was at the level of functional planning while the formal constraints of the historical styles prevented a detailed articulation of aesthetic form and functional intent. In modernist design, the rhetorical aspects of design were located in construction techniques, in a set of strategies for solving spatial problems posed by a particular conception of a social problem, and in formal arrangements that operated at a particular level of scale: the level at which standardization and repetition could be modulated for effect. The aesthetic quality of these designs was located in the use of repetitive elements, and the modulations of forms within a system of regular, standardized parts. It was at this level that the "modern" architect established the logical relations that enabled the design to represent the fitting of form to function, and it was at this level that the architect represented the formal ideals of the discipline. In this way, it became possible to produce buildings that not only looked modern, but were, as the modernists liked to claim, "authentically" modern/and authoritatively designed.

It has often been pointed out that American architects took up the forms of European modernism without the spirit, or the left-wing utopian ideology, with which it had been associated. The modernism that took root in American architectural practice was pragmatically rather than ideologically motivated. The images and forms associated with European modernism were selectively incorporated into the discipline as a particular response by the profession to the practical and disciplinary problems of professional design in the United States. These problems came to a head during the Depression, although they have a long history. In the first decades of the twentieth century, architects recognized the need for an architecture that could register both its authority and its appropriateness to modern conditions. European modernism offered forms that were aggressively modern, but its integration of form and function was initially regarded as either anti-architectural or unconvincing for most American architects. The practical incorporation of certain modernist forms and images into both critical discourse and bureaucratic practices surrounding the problem of subsidized housing, created a field in which these forms came to appear as self-evidently motivated. The public housing programs of the thirties provided a context of public authority and limitations without which modernist design could not have been construed as a coherent mode of representation or incorporated into the institutional framework of the profession. In these federal programs, it was possible to locate architectural judgment at a level where the formal rhetoric of European modernism could operate. The constriction of the market by broader economic conditions gave them a particular urgency and enabled publicly subsidized projects to occupy a dominant place in the profession. After this insertion of European modernist design into the heart of socially progressive American architecture, it could represent modern conditions and rational purposes with an effective rhetorical force. In the following decades, the aesthetic possibilities of modernist modes of design were elaborated, refined, and qualified, but they remained anchored in the articulation with technical rationality achieved during the thirties.

## Conclusion

This brief sketch of the practical logic of "modernism" in American architecture was intended to illustrate the way the stabilization of a particular kind of artifact can imply the construction of a particular form of cultural agency. The peculiar dilemma of a modern architecture was to reconstruct design as technical response to factual problems, while at the same time keeping the gap open between form and function necessary for the construction of architectural modalities that sustain authorship. Although architects sought some recognition as technical experts, they could not reduce architecture to mere technology without undermining the social and historical foundations of the discipline of architectural design. In the course of translating the social problem of public housing into an "architectural" problem to which they could provide a solution, architects reconstituted their own authority as agents, reconstructed the practice of design in a manner that both addressed contemporary conditions and incorporated new modalities of authorship, and relocated the object of their discipline (architecture) in the social technology of building. This account of modernism builds on an interpretive construction of the intentions of modernist design and the significance of modernist forms, but differs in a crucial way from a straight interpretive account: the "objective intentions" apparent in modernist architecture are indicators of a practical logic that governs the mutual configuration of the object and agent of architectural production.[11] This discussion was also intended to suggest three questions that might be pursued in a more extensive investigation:

1  How have the social structures and institutional arrangements entailed in the historical formation of the profession imposed a particular logic on the practice of design? Ultimately, it is at that level that the relationship between cultural production and social structure can be understood without reduction.[12]

2  These new practices of design have to be understood not only as responses to changing historical conditions, but as a disciplinary reconstruction that depended on the "heterogeneous engineering" carried out by key actors in the profession, under specific historical conditions. What were the actual components of the actor network on which the form and stability of public housing design depended? How were they actually assembled in the course of producing federally subsidized public housing? What, exactly, were the conditions and mechanisms of stabilization?

3  As a result of this process, what kinds of practical expertise and theoretical discourses have been inscribed in public housing as a particular social technology? More broadly, what were the consequences of the modernist reconstruction of design for the social production of urban space, and the way the social world is inscribed in the built environment? This points back to the question raised at the beginning of the chapter: What social relations, institutional practices, strategies of action, and possibilities for transformation are built into cultural artifacts? In the case of architecture, we can examine not only the forms of buildings, but the form-giving practices that account for particular buildings and, in their constitution, reveal crucial features of the whole field of discourse, theoretical knowledge, and practical action related to the production of the built environment, a field of which architectural design is only one, well-illuminated, part.

More generally, the sociology of culture has worked its way into a theoretical impasse as a result of a fundamentally dichotomous view of culture and social structure. Instead of regarding cultural objects as evidence of common subjective sensibilities, or an indication of common determinants of cultural products, it is possible to see them as the empirical traces of practices that mark off the accidental from the significant, the necessary from the desirable, nature from culture. An implication of Bourdieu's theory of practice is that we understand the artifactual world, and engage it in practice, in terms of "objectifying operations" that are already implied in it. A crucial part of the capacity to engage the artifactual world is the capacity to recognize the distinction between that which can be referred back to an intentional actor and that which is mutely objective.

I propose a sociology of culture that looks at the practical construction of socially positioned agency, and at the way particular forms of agency are objectified in domains of artifacts. The modalities of objects refer to procedures and practices that inscribe agency in artifacts, give objective status to agents, and enact the boundaries of the domains in which they are empowered to act, in which the available technologies of production operate. It makes no sense to regard facts and artifacts as determined by the social world, since they are the social world, and represent the practices and historical processes responsible for the coproduction of "nature" and society.[13]

This orientation involves a focus on the process of creating possibilities for transcription: the historical formation of material technologies and the fields of operation in which they operate; the articulation of modalities of authorship at the heart of these technologies; and the practical logic that governs the operation of these technologies insofar as they reproduce the institutional conditions that support them. Methodologically, an historical approach is useful for reopening the questions that have been closed in the stabilization of artifacts or the institutionalization of practices, and for investigating social processes and specific institutional arrangements involved in stabilization.

Giddens (1987: 214) has noted that a theory of cultural production has to involve an adequate theory of "the nature of human agents." The reverse might also be true: a theory of cultural production is necessary for an adequate theory of agency. He argues that an explication of human agency has to involve two elements: "practical consciousness" and "the contextuality of action." Practical consciousness is the level at which "human beings reflexively monitor what they do as an intrinsic part of what it is that they do" (p. 215). If, as suggested above, practical consciousness is constituted by a certain correspondence between the social world and a particularly constituted artifactual world, then the reflexive monitoring of action that Giddens associates with practice is structured in ways that are socially constructed and historically specific. Its specificity may then be the object of sociological analysis, and its inscription in an artifactual world renders it empirically accessible.

The contextuality of action is a matter of the way the settings of action "are integral to the structured form which both social life and language possess" (Giddens 1987: 215). The social world is not just the context that imposes constraining conditions on cultural production, but a terrain with features that are selectively and actively incorporated into practices whose construction is both historically contingent and characterized by a distinctive logic. The reflection of social structure in culture is not a correlation between independent and dependent variables, but an articulation achieved in and through historically formed practices. Such correspondence is a practical accomplishment that refers to (and thereby constitutes our immediate experience of) the range of possible action.

In the process of cultural production, aspects of the social world are transcribed into systems of "practical operators" that enable its regularities to be reenacted, transformed, and, as Bourdieu points out, misrecognized. Things are not just reflections of the social world, nor simply instruments of social interests, but sites where the social world is given an objective (and relatively obdurate) quality. Historical analysis of the construction of categories of cultural artifacts can reveal the practical logic of cultural production, and the way artifacts establish (to borrow a phrase from Marx) social relations between objects and material relations between people. In this way, the production of cultural objects can be more closely tied to the conditions of possibility for social action in general – not only at the level of meaning, but at the level of the capacity to conceive and enact strategic action. Such a sociology of cultural production illuminates the making of the social world that goes on in the practices through which culture producers inscribe intentions in artifacts, and social actors, generally, make sense *with* things. From this angle, the sociology of culture might make an integral contribution to a sociological theory of agency, rather than remain a special case of the sociology of organizations or an adjunct to cultural history.

## Notes

1 Particular cultural objects cannot be reduced to structural conditions or actors' intentions, since they result from "the necessary yet unpredictable confrontation between the *habitus* and an event that can exercise a pertinent incitement on the *habitus* only if the latter snatches it from the contingency of the accidental and constitutes it as a problem by applying to it the very principles of its solution" (Bourdieu 1990c: 55).

2 In responding to a symposium in *Contemporary Sociology* (Zolberg 1992b), Bourdieu himself has noted a common tendency (especially among American sociologists) to misread his theoretical position by not attending to his emphasis on the need to construct a theory of practice *as* practice, that is, as an activity based on cognitive operations involving a form of knowledge which is not that of theory, logic, and concept. As a result, he feels his commentators have been able to reduce the empirical foundation and theoretical refinements of his analyses to a few simple or simplistic propositions (Bourdieu 1992b: 160).

3 Callon and Latour (1992) note that, in Britain, a speed bump is referred to as "a sleeping policeman," but that it is not the same as an actual policeman, a sign that tells drivers to slow down, or a spirit of caution ingrained in drivers. "What is interesting, though, is that campus managers decided to shift the program of action 'slow down cars on campus' from a culturally learned action to a mere piece of behavior – the physical shock of concrete bumps on the suspension of cars. The program of action 'Slow down please for the sake of your fellow humans' has been translated into another one: 'protect your own suspension for your own benefit'" (Callon and Latour 1992: 361). Although they are not arguing for naive determinism, they want to make the point that this translation from one program to another makes a difference; otherwise engineers would not bother.

4 De Certeau (1984: 19) makes a related point when he refers to the resemblance between the (enunciative) procedures which articulate actions in both the field of language and the network of social practices.

5 This conception of practice reflects what Giddens has called the "duality of structure": the fact that "the structured properties of social systems are simultaneously the medium and the outcome of social acts" (Giddens 1983: 19).

6 Swidler (1986: 273) has made the important point that interpretive accounts imply (and rely on) a model of social action in which culture affects action only by its effects on the interests and/or values of individuals. She notes that culture shapes action also by providing individuals with specific capacities for the construction of strategies of action. Strategies of action are a matter of skills, habits, and styles that result in persistent ways of ordering action through time. They are transindividual and not reducible to the interests they may serve, the purposes to which they are put, or the functions they might fulfill in any particular interest.

7   This argument has been developed in greater detail elsewhere (see Brain 1991).

8   Le Corbusier's modulor, developed somewhat later, is the perfect emblem of this citizen: a system of architectural proportion supposedly based on the human figure, but actually referring to a typical man defined abstractly in terms of a set of mathematically defined proportions. See Le Corbusier (1980).

9   Jordy (1963) argues that although European modernists claimed to produce forms that were objective translations of building problems in terms of modern construction technology, the forms they created were more symbolic references to modern technology than actual embodiments of new building methods. I am suggesting that American architects both borrowed this symbolism and gave it a particular credibility.

10  For example, the architect was encouraged to experiment with scale models consisting of small wooden blocks cut to represent the masses formed by assembling standard apartment units into buildings. The wooden blocks could then be arranged and rearranged in order to work out the geometries of the site plan, and could serve as a device for presenting the solution to the relevant authorities when approval was sought for the plan. As a design technique, this put an obvious emphasis on aesthetic qualities that could be expressed in modulations of form apparent only at the scale of a project as a whole, not at the level of individual buildings, or at the level likely to be apparent to people walking amidst them.

11  This conception of objective intentions has been developed by Baxandall (1985).

12  I have pursued this question elsewhere (see, for example, Brain 1989, 1991).

13  Callon and Latour (1992) have addressed the problem of a similar dichotomy plaguing the sociology of scientific knowledge, which has alternated between nature and society in its effort to explain the construction of scientific facts. Callon and Latour (1992: 350) suggest a reversal of this frame: the activity of scientists and engineers and of all their human and nonhuman allies is the cause, of which various states of nature and societies are the consequences.

# 9

# The Sociology of Cultural Reception: Notes Toward an Emerging Paradigm

## Andrea L. Press

### Introduction: Origins of the Field

The sociological study of cultural reception is interdisciplinary in origin; it can be traced to two main theoretical traditions. In the American university, its origins lie in the field of literary theory and in the tradition of American Cultural Studies to which literary studies of reception have given rise. In Britain (and through cross-over in the US beginning in the 1970s) reception study was located in the field of British Cultural Studies, a tradition based in the explicitly political Marxist theory characterizing radical British politics at the time. This chapter considers these traditions in turn, focusing on how each has contributed to framing the problem of reception and inspired specific reception studies.

Cultural studies in the American university has had a complex evolution. Beginning in literature departments as a critique of an orthodox canon which highlighted certain classical texts on the basis of aesthetic criteria, those first identified with cultural studies in the US urged the counter-orthodox examination of popular texts, deemed important because they appealed to the greatest number of readers, and had long been ignored in most relevant disciplines. Highlighting the popular was the first innovation; the second was what Allen (1987: 74) calls the development of "reader-oriented criticism," an approach to literary analysis which takes the experience and interpretation of readers into account (see also Crane 1992a). This emerging broader emphasis in the experience of readers led to an interest in sociological and anthropological investigations of the experience of readers and consumers of other types of popular cultural products; such studies began to be viewed as integral to the full understanding of texts and their meanings.[1]

Reader-oriented approaches led to many works which have been central in reception study. In particular, Janice Radway's (1984) and Elizabeth Long's (1986, 1987) studies of books and their readers have emerged in part from this tradition. Lichterman's (1992) innovative study of self-help books and their readers emerges in dialogue with this tradition, in particular with its central concept of "interpretive community." These works will be discussed in more detail in the section on the reception of popular and middlebrow culture below.

British cultural researchers seconded this interest in ethnographic studies of the experiences of those consuming popular culture. The British tradition stressed ongoing struggle occurring through culture, between different subcultural, marginal groups, and those in power – what were sometimes referred to as members of the "dominant" culture (Hall et al. 1978; Williams 1978).[2] British Cultural Studies emphasized an explicitly political context and set of questions for its work, in contrast to the customarily American tendency to skirt overtly political questions.

The British Cultural Studies tradition has inspired a great many studies of reception by American social scientists. Seiter et al. (1989), Cruz (1994), Rose (1989), Morley (1980, 1986), and my own work (Press 1991, Press and Cole 1994, forthcoming) all bear the influence of this extremely rich theoretical tradition. In addition, the tradition has been so influential that it dominates the context in which much reception work is read, even that by researchers not directly influenced by it, as Radway notes about her work in the introduction to the 1991 revised edition of *Reading the Romance*.

Of course, reception study itself predates the interpretive turn exemplified by these two traditions. Current work must be read in dialogue with earlier traditions in sociology and mass communication as well. Primary among these are the Chicago School of sociology, exemplified in now classic works such as the Lynds' (1929) *Middletown*, Whyte's (1943) *Street Corner Society*, and Becker's (1963) *The Outsiders*. In this tradition researchers used ethnographic methods to uncover practices and meanings among subcultures – either dominant or marginal – in industrial societies. In important ways, sociologists and others investigating cultural reception today continually draw on the insights of this rich tradition. Consequently, in many works the investigation of the reception of specific cultural products, in which "reception" is narrowly defined, intersects with a definition of reception which is defined in more broadly cultural terms. One can see this dialectical interplay of the notion of culture, and the related notion of reception, in the work of Radway and Long, for example, and in many others in the field.

Reception researchers also enter into dialogue with mainstream mass communication research, both directly and indirectly.[3] Often dismissed outright as reductive in its conceptualization of culture and of the active nature of reception, as in Gitlin's sweeping critique of the "dominant paradigm" in mass communication research in 1978, or in Morley's (1989) or Lewis's (1991) more current discussions, "reception" studies which take as their focus one particular cultural (or in particular, media) product nevertheless owe a great deal to mass communication researchers who established the media and its reception as an interesting, and important, area of study. In many ways the interdisciplinary study of reception is haunted by a dialogue with the earlier mass communication tradition, which current researchers are continually attempting to prove wrong, misguided, or insufficiently critical in their theoretical inception.

It is a difficult task to characterize the field of reception study, interdisciplinary in its roots and practices, as a whole. Nevertheless, I hope that by teasing out the multiple theoretical influences which are continual dialogical (though more or less invisible) presences in this field of study, we can begin to see some of its unifying threads, and begin to unravel some of its more dense, and at times opaque, concepts. To this end, the remainder of this chapter looks further at the specific substantive and methodological issues preoccupying the field at present. It concludes with a discussion of what the contours of this emergent interdisciplinary field might look like, and what future work is needed for its continued theoretical development.

## Substantive Issues in the Study of Reception

### The reception of high culture: class and cultural authority

The work of the French sociologist, Pierre Bourdieu (1977, 1984, 1990b), has been crucial for the framing of the issue of the relationship between class and cultural authority. Particularly influential has been his pathbreaking work *Distinction* (1984). In this work Bourdieu investigates and analyzes the cultural tastes and preferences of different occupational sectors of the French population, arguing that these cultural styles contribute to the reproduction of social inequalities.[4]

Many scholars have been interested in exploring the implications of Bourdieu's theories for American society. Halle (1989, 1991a, 1991b, 1992, 1994), for example, influenced by the work of Bourdieu and British Cultural Studies, has undertaken an ambitious project in which he looks at a wide range of cultural artifacts in the modern home (1991b: 217, 1994). Motivated by a desire to incorporate what he calls a "materialist" perspective into the sociological analysis of art reception in the modern context (1991a: 241–2), Halle describes modes of arrangement and display of landscape paintings (1989, 1991a), of family photographs (1991b) in modern homes, and of the display and appreciation of abstract art (1992), and reports on interviews with the residents of these homes about these artifacts. Halle's subject group is drawn from communities of three social class levels: upper-class urban, upper-middle-class suburban, and lower-middle-class suburban. As was evident in his earlier project (1984), Halle operates with a general notion of the "culture" of differently situated social class groups, as well as, in this project, a more specific notion of culture focused on the existence of cultural artifacts and products.

In particular, Halle is interested in investigating the applicability of some of Bourdieu's insights into the function of taste and of the placement and meaning of cultural objects vis-à-vis social stratification. With this in mind, Halle compares differences between the discourse of his three class groups about the landscape paintings, the family photographs, and the abstract art in their homes. Here he uncovers interesting material, such as the fact that the upper-class and to some extent upper-middle-class residents are more likely to be able to name the artists of their paintings, and concomitantly to speak about their value. Landscapes in upper-class and upper-middle-class homes are much more likely than those in lower-middle-class households to represent the landscapes of Japan, France, or England, or to be historically set. For the upper-class and upper-middle-class, these works do seem to function in part as a manifestation of their owners' status, power, and social mobility. Interestingly, he finds fewer differences between class groups vis-à-vis their display of family photographs (1991b).

Regarding the display and interpretation of abstract, or modern, art, Halle (1992) also finds fewer differences between social class groups than Bourdieu's theory might lead us to expect. While slightly more upper-class households display abstract art, when owners are asked about the reasons for their preferences, they respond that they like its decorative value, and often visualize landscapes in their configuration of shapes and colors. For Halle, this belies the notion that a preference for abstract art is related to the development of any particular critical, or creative, faculties, which members of the working-class groups might not possess.

Halle finds that he is unable to trace the clear link between preferences in art and culture, and the preconditions for entry into, and continued membership in, dominant classes in the USA (1989: 400), which Bourdieu posits for French society. In the complexity of his findings concerning the relationship between facility with "high" art and membership in the dominant classes, then, Halle finds that reception becomes a complicated process involving not only the existence of powerful cultural authority but a complex and sometimes oppositional reaction to it as well. Ultimately, in an important departure from Bourdieu, Halle concludes that in order to understand culture in modern Western societies, we must make reference to considerations other than the relationship between culture and power. Culture and power are simply not neatly consonant in the American context.

As further evidence of this finding, Halle cites an important new work by the American cultural sociologist, Michèle Lamont (1992). In a comparative study of upper-middle-class managers in France and the USA, Lamont describes at length the anti-intellectualism, and consequent lack of involvement with high art forms, of Americans vis-à-vis the French. Confirming earlier work on the American corporation by Kanter (1979), Lamont describes how too much involvement with high culture in the American organization can be a distinct liability, labelling the individual an egghead or an outsider (1992: 127). In the American context, people are more likely to use their knowledge of baseball or other popular cultural forms to gain status and make valuable contacts and alliances.

Lamont's study was also inspired in part by the work of Pierre Bourdieu. While Bourdieu focused on the role and use of cultural styles in maintaining social inequalities, Lamont argues that in focusing primarily on French (and in particular, Parisian) attitudes, Bourdieu exaggerates the importance of cultural boundaries (1992a: 181). In her own study, a comparison of French and American upper-middle-class men living in both culturally central and peripheral geographic locations, Lamont finds variations in the degree to which cultural preferences function as markers of inequality. Other preferences, such as moral and ethical judgments, act as important markers of differentiation as well, particularly in the USA, and particularly for those residing in peripheral rather than central cities. Lamont's study both builds on and challenges Bourdieu's theoretical apparatus, and sheds light on some of the aspects of his theories which are peculiar to French culture, and to large, central, urban locations.

In another set of important reception studies, Wendy Griswold (1986, 1987a, 1992b, 1993), sets the stage for a cross-national study of reception which spans Western and third-world cultures. In one study she investigates the participation of cultural elites in defining the meaning of popular novels, comparing the critical reception of the work of the Barbadian novelist George Lamming by reviewers writing in the British, American, and West Indian press (Griswold 1987a). Griswold questions the notion that a cultural object has a stable set of meanings, and in the study investigates one portion of the process through which the meanings of these novels are formed, comparing this process as it takes place in three quite different national contexts which, though nominally distinct, are linked by the context of colonialism. Griswold's study is pioneering in that it moves beyond the one-nation framework, and comparative frameworks confined to the West, and in raising questions concerning the export of meaning beyond national borders and the transformations in meaning which occur through this process. Particularly interesting is her treatment of the meaning of race, both race as treated in the novels and with respect to the race of the author himself (he is Barbadian). Race is highlighted in American reviews of Lamming's novels, yet virtually ignored in British discussions, which focus instead on the novels' language and literary qualities. In contrast to both, West Indian reviewers concentrate on questions of personal and national identity. With this study, Griswold offers another example of the focus on elite participation in the construction of cultural meanings.

Griswold's latest work focuses on the interpenetration of Western narrative ideas and forms into the content of Nigerian novels. These enter through the control Western publishing companies exert over the production of almost all Nigerian novels. With this study, Griswold again considers the colonial context of elite control of cultural production. Investigating the image of the village in Nigerian novels published between 1952 and 1992 either in Nigeria or in the UK, she finds that novels set in traditional villages rather than urban settings, and featuring a particular, romanticized image of traditional village life, while overall a minority of novels authored by Nigerians, are more likely to be published in the UK, and therefore distributed in Britain and the USA – Achebe's *Things Fall Apart*, the most widely read Nigerian novel worldwide, being the most prominent example (Griswold 1992b: 718). The popularity of these "village novels" has in turn influenced Nigerian writers to continue to imagine village communities in systematically misleading ways. She concludes that this romanticized image of the traditional village, reinforced by the selective publishing strategy favored in the West, colors the image of African life in both Western and African imaginations. Griswold demonstrates that a publishing industry formed in the context of colonialist relationships between nations continues to influence our predominant cultural images of life in non-Western societies.

### From text to context, reception of popular and middlebrow texts: texts, cultural authority, and resistant subcultures

While Bourdieu's work emphasized the importance of elite preferences for high culture in establishing and consolidating their position of social dominance, researchers in the American context have investigated the interpenetration of these "middlebrow," more popular preferences in the cultural tastes and judgments of the middle-class majority. Researchers such as Radway (1984), Long (1986, 1987), and Lichterman (1992), influenced initially by developments in American literary studies that led to a new interest in popular texts and their critical appropriation by marginal or oppressed groups, investigated the reception of both high cultural but also more popular – and so-called "middlebrow" – texts.

Radway's personal academic development since the publication of her classic work *Reading the Romance* in 1984, eloquently recapitulated in the new introduction to the second edition of the book in 1991, illustrates the changing scholarly discourse about reception characterizing the interdisciplinary field of American cultural and literary studies throughout the 1970s and 1980s, and is somewhat emblematic for this group of researchers. *Reading the Romance* was actually inspired by a series of debates about the status and importance of popular texts in the study of American culture and literature (Radway 1991: 4–5). This led to work which converged propitiously with the similar attention being paid to popular texts and their critical appropriation by researchers working in the Birmingham School tradition. As she mentions, although Radway herself was totally unaware of work done in the British Cultural Studies tradition while writing *Reading the Romance*, this tradition (also known as the Birmingham School of Cultural Studies) "now dominates the context within which *Reading the Romance* is read" (1991: 2). Without conscious design, then, Radway's work effortlessly pioneered the shift in American cultural studies from a focus on the importance of, and interpretation of, texts, to an emphasis on questions regarding the role of the audience in determining textual meaning, and in resisting culturally dominant meanings.

By her own account, Radway began research for *Reading the Romance* with the notion that it was the interpretation of the texts themselves which was what was interesting and important about the reception of romance novels. In the context of American cultural studies Radway's approach challenged the orthodoxy of focus on the "high cultural" texts, traditionally deemed important by the ostensibly objective aesthetic judgments of critics. While Radway was unaware at the time of the British stress on the context of reception, and of the many factors which might determine the interpretation of cultural products by their consumers, Radway nevertheless concluded that contextual factors were pertinent to understanding the meaning of romance reading for women readers. Radway's informants themselves directed her attention to the importance of context in their cultural lives, and to its political implications (Radway 1991: 8–9). In her finished product Radway discusses the uses of romance reading as an activity along with the range of interpretations and preferences her interviewees exhibited. The *act* of reading itself had meaning, Radway argued, in the context of the patriarchal family within which her informants lived; it served women as a means of declaring, both spatially and temporally, their separateness and independence from the demands of their families. In addition, she discusses particular feminist meanings women readers gave to romance heroines and plots. In looking back upon and reevaluating her own work, then, Radway was forced to take cognizance of the focus on the political uses of ethnography nurtured by the British tradition, and to acknowledge her own role in introducing ethnographic investigation into the tradition of American literary studies.[5]

A similar trajectory of project choice characterizes the work of another important reception researcher, Ien Ang, working in Europe. Ang's early work, in particular her book *Watching Dallas* (first published in 1982; English translation published in 1985) was influenced by literary theory, and was also directly inspired by British Cultural Studies' emphasis on the creative, resistant subject as cultural receiver. In this book, Ang collected letters from the television show *Dallas'* fans in The Netherlands who responded to an advertisement she placed in a newspaper calling for viewers' responses to and comments on the television show. She proceeded to analyze these letters interpretively, using concepts inspired by the Birmingham School.[6] Consequently, Ang emphasized the polysemic nature of the television text; in particular, she emphasized the plethora of reasons viewers offered to explain their pleasure in watching *Dallas*. Ang also raised the interesting possibility that soap opera was indeed pleasurable to many female viewers, partly because of its escapist qualities, but also because some viewers were able to offer explicitly feminist interpretations of the show. Her work, while focusing on television rather than books – a not insignificant distinction – bore remarkable resemblance to Radway's initial reception study. Not only did Ang focus on television, but on soap opera television, identified with the female audience and consequently as low in status within the arena of television as Radway's romances were within the world of publishing.

## Reading groups and cultural authority

Long's (1986, 1987) work is an excellent example of the new theoretical model for studying reception emerging within cultural sociology. She constructed an extremely sophisticated model of reception as a site of struggle between cultural industries, critics, and receivers, a model which attempts to account for both sides of this equation. This model emphasizes both the importance of cultural judgments of authority, and the responses of groups with differential power in relation to these judgments. Incorporating insights developed by earlier researchers into the importance of cultural authority in determining the structure of the reception process, Long used ethnographic and interviewing methods to study reading groups. Her choice of reading groups, and consequent focus on books, is not a random one. By focusing on books rather than, for example, television or some other more clearly popular cultural form, Long was able to engage discourses about high culture, the literature about reading and interpretive communities, and Bourdieu's notions of cultural authority.

Long described cultural reception as an extremely complicated process. Readers do not simply choose books in a cultural vacuum, nor interpret them as such; notions of cultural authority, and of the judgments cultural authorities have already made about the books they read, are an intrinsic part of the selection and reception process for readers. Through a complicated process of the silences, teasing, and structured proposals which characterize group discussions about book selection, such notions directly influence those books which are put on the agenda.

Long argued that book group members' interpretations of the books they read, however, are less structured by their notions of cultural authority than is their actual selection of books. In this she keeps alive the focus on resistance to cultural authority so salient in the Birmingham School tradition. Long found that readers' interpretations of books were partly determined by cultural authority, and partly resistant to it. Of particular interest to the cultural sociologist preoccupied with postmodernist notions of the subject, more often than not group members' remarks overtly criticized the postmodernist notions of the fragmentation of the subject which dominates critical literature about books.[7] More traditional criteria such as the believability of characters and situations, characters' morally uplifting qualities, and the ability of members to identify with particular characters, standards of evaluation reminiscent of a pre-postmodern era, dominate member evaluations of the literature they discuss. In general, abstract, or formalist criteria – e.g., those that are more likely to be seen cited in book reviews published in erudite journals as the basis for praise or censure of serious literature – were often belittled and rejected outright as illegitimate bases for judging literary merit.

With these findings Long articulated a central paradox for reception theorists in the nineties: how to incorporate the insights of the postmodernism which has revolutionized our conceptualization of reception, while studying those who consciously and demonstrably reject some of its main insights into their own makeup and constitution as individuals. How can we take account of both our academic insights into the "reader" as itself a cultural construction, and our ethnographic insight into the active and at times resistant nature of the reader's consciousness? Put another way, the challenge is for us to use Radway's (1988a) insightful research design for cultural reception (discussed in more detail in the section below), based as it is on inherently fluid subjectivities, while studying processes engaged in by those who actively resist the principles on which this design is based. Certainly this will be no mean task, as long as the rift remains this broad between our thinking in the academy about individuals in the postmodern world, and the thinking of those individuals themselves.

Despite the difficulties involved, Long's work moves us down this road, helping to build a new model for cultural reception which is theoretically sophisticated, true to the categories she derives from her subjects themselves, and also practical from the researcher's point of view. What is at stake in her new version of reception study are a series of questions quite different from those posed by researchers in earlier reception work. While her ethnographic method allows Long to retain the British Cultural Studies' focus on reception as an active process, capturing as it does readers' active and creative interpretations of the books they discuss, her analytic focus highlights the constraints the broader culture places on the ability of readers to receive literature creatively. Long does not want to argue that reading is a dominated process, entirely determined by cultural forces and authorities and the constraints these place on reader creativity, nor does she want to lose sight of the relationship between reader interpretations and the way the interpretations of particular groups articulate with social and cultural stratification in our society. In Long's model, reception is a site of struggle. As Delli Carpini and Williams (forthcoming) term it, reception is a process in which the subject, however conceived, is only relatively autonomous from broader social, economic and political structures. Long maintains that the fragmentation of the postmodern individual is not entirely complete, at least in the middle-class individuals she studies:[8] thus her focus on processes of creative reception or, in Radway's (1988a: 373) terms, "a world not yet surrendered."

Books, which span the gamut in common parlance from high culture to cultural "trash," are a particularly good medium for illustrating these connections. Whereas Radway's (1984) reception work had stressed the activity and creativity of women readers of popular romance novels, the "resistance" Long discusses in her work is more limited by a notion of cultural authority and the constraints it imposes. Perhaps the reception of, or at least subjects' selective exposure to, the classics and other "high-level" literature Long's subjects read is in fact more constrained by these notions than were Radway's original subjects, given their less "serious" fare. Ang's (1985, 1991) turn in studying the television audience, however, from creative processes of reception to a focus on the structuring of the audience "from above," suggests that insights must be incorporated into a model for purely popular cultural reception as well, which are in some ways similar to those in Radway and Long. Like their work, Ang's work suggests how important it is, when considering the actual activity and constitution of the audience itself, to consider the power of cultural judgments made by those in the industry which are then incorporated by those studying the industry and the audience.

While Radway had studied women particularly as a dominated group within patriarchal society, Long's informants are constituted rather differently. Her focus on the middle-class and upper-middle-class, the primary constituency of reading groups, constitutes a shift from Radway's (and the Birmingham School's) emphasis on less powerful groups. The latter emphasis led to a bipolar focus either on the question of the way groups "resist" hegemonic cultural practices and interpretations of cultural objects, or the way cultural practices and meanings contributed to the domination of groups. Long adds one more level of complexity: she looks at the way the primarily middle-class members of her groups help to reproduce and participate in hegemonic cultural ideas, patterns, and meanings. Her approach acknowledges explicitly that hegemonic cultural processes do not exist and reproduce in abstraction from those who carry them (albeit often unconsciously), even when cultural receivers themselves have a complicated and perhaps ambivalent relationship to institutions powerful in our society's cultural and other realms.

Long's conclusions are supported by more recent work by Lichterman (1992), who looked at the way readers of self-help books pick and choose, relatively freely, the recommendations and advice to which they attend from the large numbers of books they consult. Readers move in a relatively fluid way from one book to the next, or into and out of the "thin culture," as Lichterman terms it, which self-help books provide. Thin culture denotes the expectations readers share that they can adopt concepts in these books – "loving too much," for instance – tentatively, without exclusive or enduring commitment to them. They can use different discourses from these books interchangeably to articulate the same lived experience. Self-help reading is a thin culture for two, interrelated reasons, Lichterman argues. First, the readers understand these books as mass-produced commodities, any of which may be of only limited value. Second, they read self-help psychology in relation to other cultural points of reference. The self-help reading culture remains "thin" as readers juggle their popular psychology with religious teachings, feminist insights, and media images of contemporary personal life.

In Lichterman's model of self-help reception, readers take the concepts in their books seriously, even though they see the books themselves as belonging to a lower-status "pop" genre, because they understand "form" and "content" differently from cultural critics. He argues that while his readers thought of the books as written to appeal to a large audience, readers at the same time tended to think of the concepts offered by their self-help reading as scientifically legitimate and unaffected by production processes. By assigning status and authority to the self-help books in this ambivalent way, they could read the books "believingly yet loosely, defining and redefining aspects of lived experience with a variety of partly discountable terms" (Lichterman 1992: 443). They could move back and forth between the books and other sources of guidance, relating somewhat ambivalently to all such sources.

Lichterman introduces "thin culture" as a way of avoiding what he sees as some ambiguities in the notion of "interpretive community" (Lindlof 1987; Radway 1984), and to highlight what the latter

concept may not illuminate by itself. Lichterman notes that it is not
clear, for instance, whether interpretive community should designate only a local group of readers or whether one might use the
term to refer to interpretive conventions shared by readers
throughout one society. It appears that some individual readers in
Lichterman's study may have belonged to several interpretive communities. Rather than map out these interpretive communities,
Lichterman wants to focus on the qualities of readers' relations
with self-help – the ambivalence and the pulls that readers in his
study felt from other cultural reference points while making sense
of self-help books. He argues that "thin culture" highlights this
tentative quality of reception, in contrast with other possible qualities of reception culture. The concept also emphasizes the question
of how self-help reading relates to a broader, changing cultural
context that offers other points of reference for personal life. Thus,
Lichterman proposes that "thin culture" enables reception scholars
to join research on a specific audience with those broader questions about change in values and ideologies that have often been
asked with the assumption of passive mass media audiences.[9]

## Cultural industries and the "image" of the audience

Following her rethinking of ethnography, and perhaps in consequence of it, Radway's newest research project (1988a, 1990) no
longer falls into the category of "reception" study *per se*. In the
project, she continues Long's study of "middlebrow" culture by
examining the rationale used by editors and other officials in the
Book of the Month Club in reviewing the many books the Club
reads, and in deciding on their monthly featured selections and
alternates. The "image" of the audience, which editors and others
project in constructing rationales for their evaluations of books,
is often invoked in the discourses Radway analyzes; but direct
exploration of the audience itself, and of audience interpretation, is
no longer Radway's primary focus. Instead, her current research
focuses on the way those who make books available for large groups
of people themselves construct, and consequently respond to, their
own idea of the reader and his or her preferences. The very notion
of audience is problematized, complicated, and expanded in this
work. In effect, audience comes to be seen as itself a constructed

entity, with Radway's study elucidating a particular historical stage in its construction.

Invoked in the discourses Radway examines, in addition to a notion of audience preference and taste, are notions of standards for evaluating literature, of high and low culture, and of the "ideal" reader as positioned somewhere within a literary world marked by these distinctions. Inspired like Halle and Lamont by Bourdieu's (1984) work on the relationship between cultural judgments about cultural products and social stratification, these concepts, and concomitantly issues of power and reproduction, become the real subject of Radway's investigation. How do notions of the "typical reader" become part of discourse about culture in the USA? What relationship does this reader, as constructed by book clubs and book sellers, have to those with actual power, both cultural and otherwise, in American society? Are social elites particular "kinds" of readers, both in their own eyes, and according to the discourse about readers which takes place in the rhetoric of book sellers, book publicizers, and book clubs? Finally, what is the relationship between culture and power in modern, mass society? These are some of the questions which, inspired by Bourdieu's investigations of French culture, Radway seeks to answer in the American context.

Preliminary findings in this new study have been quite interesting (Radway 1988a, 1990). Radway (1988a) discusses the way various segments of the literary audience, in particular the audience for fiction, is constructed by the editors of the Book of the Month Club, in their critical evaluation of the works they consider for the Club. She finds that fiction is most often valued because it draws an editor into its story, making him or her "care" about its characters, rather than for some more distanced, colder, abstract type of aesthetic excellence. In a more general discussion, Radway (1990) notes the tension between the notion of art and its mass-produced quality in modern democratic societies, and the historical role of the mass book club as it played an important role in making literary art accessible to the mass audience. She finds that the extended debate over book clubs which took place during the period of their establishment was in fact a discussion of the role of culture in a modern democratic and mass society. Ultimately, by continually addressing its readers as individuals, who must make up their own, individual minds about literature, the Book of the Month

Club skillfully sidestepped the key issue it really faced in forging its identity, which was determining what forms of association and public debate might make democracy possible in a mass society. The notion of "middlebrow" culture which emerged from this debate was therefore a complicated concept, embodying both a complex, contested notion of cultural authority, while retaining the sense that the judgment of individuals – a judgment never freely executed in mass society – is our ultimate standard. The implication of Radway's argument is that, given the definition of the book club which emerged, its critical potential to serve as an important locus for cultural and political debate between different political groups and actors in democracy society was never realized.

Ang's most recent project (1991) parallels Radway's current work. While Radway focuses on cultural authority as it infuses the discourse of a book-selling organization, Ang, in her book *Desperately Seeking the Audience*, focuses on the commercial forces driving television as an industry which have led to the prominence of certain concepts of its audience in the industry and, as a consequence of industry discourse, in academic discourse and in society at large. Ang investigates how, in different parts of the television industry, executives and the studies they support construct a particular structured model of the audience, a model which has in turn informed much academic work on reception. Like Radway's, Ang's work seeks to problematize the very notion of audience itself as a fixed entity and, concomitantly, the possibility of reception study, which necessarily invokes a relatively fixed notion of audience. Similar to Radway's (1988b) suggested research design, Ang ends by recommending that ethnographic methods be employed in order to help construct a new, and vastly differentiated, notion of television "audiences" in their infinite diversity. Such a method of investigation will help begin the deconstruction of the monolithic view of the television audience which has emerged from decades of rationalized institutional discourse.

The importance Radway, Long, and Ang place on notions of cultural authority, and on discourses structuring the audience itself, serves to "muddy up" the concept of reception. As a result of this new perspective, the very notion of "reception" begins to seem inadequate, conjuring as it does in its naive sense an image of one or a group of readers or viewers receiving and interpreting cultural products in some unmediated fashion, in imaginary isolation from other interpretations and judgments of those products to which readers have already, either directly or indirectly, been exposed.

## The problem of the popular: viewer as cultural dupe or active subject

While in contrast to Radway's new work Long retains a focus on cultural reception indicative of the former's earlier study, she joins Radway in turning from mass or popular culture to "middlebrow" cultural forms. Indeed, incorporating the study of more popular, "low," or what is sometimes rather unfortunately termed "mass" culture into our evolving paradigm for reception study presents some significant difficulties. Most obviously, our concept of cultural authority itself requires modification if we are to open our discourse to include popular and/or mass forms. Mass culture – television, for example, or popular music – is rarely evaluated in the language of standards customarily used to discuss "high" or "middlebrow" cultural forms. While these traditions are changing slowly, the general absence of this discourse from the culture surrounding the reception of mass culture, in which most of its consumers have come of age, is significant. Television viewers, while they must consciously or unconsciously reconcile their viewing activity with the general cultural disdain in which entertainment television is bathed, are not continually preoccupied with the voice of the critics naming this show a "classic," and that one "popular trash." These distinctions simply are not customarily applied to television, an art with which more people are involved on a day-to-day basis, and for a greater period of time, over a greater period of years, than with any other within the spectrum of culture in America. It is interesting to note, however, that this situation is changing; the presence of current television reviews in the "Arts" section of the *New York Times,* and the recent inclusion of a television review column in the revised format of the *New Yorker,* indicate the development of a television aesthetic modelled after customary evaluations of high cultural forms.[10] The development of this aesthetic, similar to the developments which have occurred in the history of the novel and the history of film, is itself an interesting object of study in a field lacking adequate theorization of the differentiations made between high and low culture.[11]

Our theorization of the relationship between culture and power is also at issue as we rethink the problem of the popular. Some of the studies discussed here indicate that facility with "low" or mass cultural forms functions in important ways as markers of status, class, prestige, and even social mobility in our culture – that it is these cultural forms with which many are intensely involved in our culture. Yet academic prejudices against this possibility remain in pockets within our interdisciplinary field, bolstered by broader attitudes toward these distinctions still prevalent in certain literary and intellectual circles in our culture. Some still assume that there is only an inverse relationship between cultural power and importance, and the realm of the popular. An editor for an academic press voiced these sentiments recently when, commenting on a manuscript about television and culture, she recommended that it be rewritten without reference to television at all. How could such a manuscript have broad appeal when she herself, a member of its potential audience, "didn't even own a television set," a fact she proudly proclaimed. The academic audience's identification with such markers of distinction continues to position us outside not only the cultural mainstream, but increasingly outside political and social centers of power as well (even Bill Clinton is, iconically, a known addict of Hollywood films and "trash" novels). A revamped theoretical framework, one which rethinks the relationship between popular culture and societal power, is needed.

My own work is an attempt to bridge several dimensions of popular cultural meanings and audiences. In *Women Watching Television* (Press 1991) I engage both the model of cultural hegemony[12] and Birmingham School notions of the active, resistant subject. Conducting in-depth interviews with working-class and middle-class women of different generations about their interpretations of entertainment television, I found that middle-class women were more attentive to gender-specific dimensions of television portrayals, while working-class women were more likely to discuss television's class-related meanings. I conclude that television exerts a gender-specific hegemony over middle-class women, and a class-specific hegemony over working-class women.

In *Imagining our Lives* (Press and Cole forthcoming) we continue to study the female audience; but in this work we focus more specifically on the continuity between the political content of television and political culture more generally. Conducting ethnographic focus group interviews with pro-life and pro-choice women of different social classes, we investigate the areas of continuity, disjuncture, and outright resistance to entertainment television narratives of abortion decisions. We find different themes of affirmation and resistance to television's "classed" discourse of abortion among the different groups of women we studied. In all of my work, I find that television reception is a complicated process, and the relationship between television and culture complex. The study of these processes requires a model sophisticated enough to accommodate the many dimensions of these processes, yet simple enough in some respects to allow women to speak somewhat for themselves as cultural viewers, and as the creators of cultural meanings.

Liebes and Katz (1990) introduce yet another dimension to the model of viewer reception of popular television texts, and an important one: that of intercultural variation. In a unique and rigorous study, they analyze and compare the range of interpretations of the same episode of *Dallas* offered by distinct cultural groups around the globe. Conducting ethnographic interviews with viewers of the television show *Dallas*, they compare interpretations made by family and friend groups of different nationalities viewing in three countries: Israel, the United States, and Japan. Like Griswold, they find that different national groups construct the meaning of basic elements of the show – family, wealth, relationship – quite differently. Their study indicates the importance of including comparative work in our studies of cultural reception, particularly as cultural media like television are increasingly distributed worldwide.[13]

Cruz moves the analysis of popular cultural audiences back one level of abstraction. In his forthcoming work, he asks how particular interpretive publics with specific reception strategies come into being. Seeking to answer this question for the case of African American music in nineteenth-century America, Cruz (1993) – like Ang (1991) – questions the status of audiences as preformed social aggregates, already assembled as "receivers" and instead highlights the dialectical development of such bodies and the interpretations of culture they make. In his view, cultural analysis must consider the dynamics of historical change and intergroup conflict which bear on this process.

## Methodological Issues

Given the current centrality of ethnography in emerging models of reception study in our field, attention to the precepts of this method is a reasonable recommendation. The work of Halle, Lamont, Griswold, Radway, Lichterman and Ang all suggest that a focus on reception alone, narrowly defined, is incomplete. Their work suggests that the audience is influenced in its reception by the defining frames of culture industries and critics. Even more extreme, their work suggests that the audience itself is a construct resulting in part from these forces. Yet crucially, while such insights represent a departure from the ethnographic flavor of both Ang and Radway's earlier work, in their newer work each proceeds to recommend a return to ethnography, although it is a non-naive ethnography that they recommend, one that takes account of the constructed nature of audiences and readers.

### Toward a cultural model for reception study

The ethnographic work so popular in reception study is under attack from recent theoretical critiques questioning its epistemological power. Consequently, no sooner had she acknowledged herself an ethnographic reception researcher, Radway proceeded to reject this identity. In recent critical reflections, Radway began to reappraise the method of ethnography itself, concurrent with its close critical scrutiny in anthropology, its discipline of origin.[14] As she writes, "the activity of actually 'doing ethnography' produced many surprises, not the least of which was the realization that even ethnographic description of the 'native's' point of view must be an interpretation or, in words adapted from Clifford Geertz, my own construction of my informants' construction of what they were up to in reading romances" (Radway 1991: 5). Faulting her own former "preoccupation with the empiricist claims of social science" (1991: 5), Radway goes on to discuss possible revisions to the method of investigation, and the method of writing, in *Reading the Romance*, that she might make were she to be rewriting the book today.

Radway's (1988b) revised approach to ethnography is quite revealing of current tendencies in the emergent paradigm of reception study characterizing our field. It is perhaps fitting that Radway, her study of romance readers firmly establishing her as a pioneer in American reception study, has taken the lead in questioning earlier models and gone the furthest theoretically toward laying out a new and revised model for ethnography-based reception study. Neatly summed up in her article "Reception study: ethnography and the problems of dispersed audiences and nomadic subjects" (1988b), Radway's new model offers an ethnographic research design which attempts to map out, in the wake of reevaluations and criticisms of recent work, the appropriate direction for future reception studies in the cultural studies tradition. This piece clearly indicates the transformation in Radway's thinking about "reception" from its conceptualization as a more narrow research issue to a much more diffuse and ambitious series of questions about culture and action. In particular, Radway seeks to modify the ethnographic model of reception study she employed to enable it to capture a postmodernist notion of "subjectivity" as fluid, destabilized, and shifting rather than the unified, coherent self which the ethnographic method was developed to investigate (1988b: 368). As an antidote to her earlier assumption of a unified self as cultural receiver, Radway proposes that a team of ethnographers collaborate to study the many sites of cultural practice, and the reception incorporated into this practice – in particular, family, school, and leisure. Her assumption is that specific subjectivities cohere, impermanently and fluidly, around these sites. It is within this framework that the more narrow questions of the reception of specific cultural products can be studied in their proper cultural context.

With this plan, Radway illustrates just how far thinking about cultural reception has changed from the time of her earlier (1984) work. Beginning with the idea of investigating text interpretation alone, she moved quickly in that work to the consideration of the context of consumption and interpretation, and its determinative effects. The research design (Radway 1988b) indicates an entirely new stage in Radway's thinking, wherein the notion of context itself is broadened so as to include a sense of the culture as a whole. The ethnography of reception in this context more closely resembles ethnography in an anthropologically "holistic" sense: reception is seen to be complexly intertwined with the group's whole way of life, its understanding inseparable from a more holistic examination of cultural processes in this more extensive sense. In this research design, the turn from the sociology of culture's initial emphasis on cultural products, to a much broader focus on the cultural context within which products "high and low" are produced, received, and appropriated, is complete. The influence of postmodernist theories of individuality complicate the proposed study even further by challenging the unified individual as the locus of ethnographic work: subjectivities are fluid, continually reconstituted, appearing in different forms at different cultural sites (Lyotard 1984; Harvey 1989; Rosenau 1992). Teasing out these recombinant subjectivities – explaining not one subject but subjectivity in its infinite transmutability – will become one of the primary tasks of the postmodernist ethnographer of reception.

Radway is cognizant of the sense in which reception study so broadly conceived is impracticable, mentioning that the problems of coordinating such an extensive ethnographic team, the pressures on employed academics to publish quickly and regularly, and the diffuseness of the possible sites of "reception" so broadly conceived all combine to make implementation of this research design problematic. The ideas she expresses are, therefore, both powerful and paralyzing, particularly in the context of the single-authored projects most of us feel structurally tied to produce due to time constraints, coordination problems, and the academy's relative discrediting of joint publications. Also daunting is our need for clearly defined, and simply (or "elegantly") constructed, studies; a focus on the reception of "X," with "X" being defined as books, photographs, or even television, centers a study much more effectively than does a more diffuse focus on general cultural processes of reception. At least, one can expect that reviewers at National Endowment for the Humanities (NEH), National Science Foundation (NSF), and other granting agencies will see it that way.

Other studies discussed in this chapter suggest other modifications of ethnographic theory and practice for reception studies. In particular, new work combines ethnography with structural, historical, and institutional analysis (Radway 1988a, 1990; Halle 1991a, 1991b, 1994). Sociologists accomplish this through combining depth interviews with the sociological analysis of the relative position of different groups (Press 1991; Lamont 1992). Some use group interviews, often in semi-ethnographic settings, to accomplish this contextual analysis and comparison (Long 1986, 1987; Press and Cole 1994, forthcoming). Some eschew the former altogether, focusing on the discursive structuring of the audience through institutional practice (Ang 1991; Cruz 1994). The methods deemed appropriate for reception study are as broad as the definitions of reception mushrooming in our field.

## Conclusion

In this chapter, I have commented on the current state of the interdisciplinary endeavor of reception study. Inspired by a number of theoretical traditions, reception study at present takes many forms. Some researchers focus on the cultural activity of the relatively powerful, and emphasize the way their reception of culture helps solidify social inequality. Others focus on the relatively powerless and disadvantaged, examining their resistance to or compliance with their own social positioning. Others eschew a focus on those who receive culture, focusing instead on the discursive and social construction of audiences as groups, and as receivers, of culture and cultural products. Overall, the definition of reception, and of the concept of culture itself, is widely contested and debated in this varied, interdisciplinary body of work.

In conclusion, it is perhaps time for us all to reevaluate reception study in our field – to rethink its position, and its goals – as part of a general reevaluation of the concept of culture and its analytical uses in the academy. With disciplinary boundaries being questioned and changed throughout the American university, traditional standards of evaluation challenged, and traditional subjects replaced, the impact for the sociology of culture may be a new interdisciplinary identity, in which our traditional categories and topics are overturned by new ideas. One of them may be to broaden the notion of "reception" by divorcing cultural study almost completely from its focus on particular products to a preoccupation with culture in a much broader sense. The notion of reception and the relative autonomy of those individuals and/or groups receiving cultural products must also be theorized more precisely in our new model. All of the facets of reception as a site of struggle must be further conceptualized. Reception study in our field is in the kind of flux one might expect given the paradoxes of its theoretical and institutional supports.

## Notes

I am much indebted to Bruce A. Williams and to Paul Lichterman for frequent discussions of this topic, and for their comments on an earlier draft.

1 Allen mentions in particular the work of Eco (1990), Fish (1980), Holub (1984), Holland (1975), Iser (1978), and many others in this context.

2 See also Hall (1980) on the history of these debates at the Center for Contemporary Cultural Studies, University of Birmingham (home of the "Birmingham School"). See also Hebdige (1979), McRobbie (1990), and Willis (1977, 1978), among others.

3 By "mainstream mass communication research" I mean, of course, a wide variety of traditions in reception study, including the "two-step flow theory" (Katz and Lazarsfeld 1955), the "uses and gratifications" paradigm (Rosengren 1985), and a tradition of experimental research aimed at determining, in a highly controlled laboratory environment, the precise impact of media "exposure." See Klapper (1960) for an excellent summary of the field's early stages.

4 For an extended commentary on the work of Bourdieu, and an extensive bibliography of his work, see Lamont (1992).

5 Radway's use of "ethnography" in this work was partial at best. She investigated a small, middle-class midwestern group of women who were romance reading fans. She located them through her key informant, a woman (whom she called "Dot") who issued a romance newsletter for romance fans who patronized the bookstore in which she worked. Radway's sample, therefore, was small, and homogeneous in terms of social class, geographic location, and race. She also tended in her analysis toward an overreliance on the opinions of Dot.

6 Ang's study has been widely criticized for its methodological weaknesses. In confining her data to letters she received in response to a newspaper advertisement, she of course had a very partial, self-selected sample. In addition, letters lack the dialogic quality of the ethnographic interviews and observations Radway, for example, collected.

7 The theme of postmodernism is a continuing one in current works on cultural reception, and in many of those discussed here. While the literature on postmodernism is immense, the topic is well treated in works by Harvey (1989) and Rosenau (1992). See also Lyotard (1984).

8 I am indebted to conversations with Clay Steinman for insight into this point.

9 I am indebted to Paul Lichterman for extensive discussion about and explanation of his work.

10 I am indebted to Bruce A. Williams for pointing this out to me in discussion.

11 See Levine (1988) for a critique of the historical dimension of the distinctions we normally make between high and low culture.

12  As developed in Gramsci (1971) and Gitlin (1980, 1983).
13  See McLuhan (1989) on the "global village," and also Schiller (1992) and Wallis (1990) on the international nature of communication and culture.
14  On the debates about ethnography in anthropology, see the classic Clifford and Marcus (1986) and, more recently, Hammersley (1992).

# 10

# Methodological Dilemmas in the Sociology of Art

## Anne Bowler

To date, the important contribution of sociology to the study of culture and the arts has been to demonstrate the necessity of understanding the work of art and role of the artist in their social, political, and historical contexts. Empirical studies of the social and institutional matrices within which aesthetic objects are materially produced have pointed to the implicitly collective nature of artistic production (Becker 1974, 1982). Such studies have problematized traditional art-historical and literary-critical conceptions of the artist as isolated genius. Similarly, sociological research has shown the crucial role of economic and organizational factors in structuring the emergence of new artistic genres and styles (White and White 1965; Zolberg 1983; Crane 1987). Such work speaks directly to current debates on canon formation, posing a serious challenge to unreflexive classifications of timeless "great works" and demonstrating the ways in which the category of the "great work" is itself a socially and historically contested terrain. Investigations into the composition of audiences and forms of audience response have revealed the interdependence of access to culture with economic, political, and social position (Bourdieu 1984; Gans 1974, 1985). Finally, there now exists a wide body of work on the social uses of art in the reproduction of systems of stratification and class power (see, for example, Bourdieu 1984; DiMaggio 1982). In sum, long before concepts like hegemony and "the Other" became the fashionable rallying cry in literature departments across the country, sociologists had turned their attention to the analysis of the inextricable connection between art, ideology and power.

Too often, however, sociological analyses concerned solely with the organization of systems of cultural production, the social role of the artist as tastemaker or the class structure of audiences have resulted in mechanistic conceptions of the relationship between cultural forms and social processes. Describing the connecting links between art and society has been a largely one-sided project for sociologists, for whom cultural forms and practices continue to appear as the manifestation, measure or byproduct of some pre-sumably more basic social factor, e.g., institutional strain, group solidarity, stratification, etc.[1] As Goldfarb (n.d.: 15–16) has written, "the arts' place in society is situated, and their day-to-day func-tioning is explained, but their real distinctiveness, their broader cultural and political significance in the historical development of society is ignored."

In his now paradigmatic essay, "Art as collective action," Howard Becker (1974) noted, not without irony, the tendency of sociological studies of art to write of the organizations and institutions of artistic production without reference to the social actors or activities through which those very organizations and institutions came into being. Today, we might make a structurally similar observation, noting the number of studies grouped together under the heading "sociology of art" which confine themselves to the analysis of the social conditions of artistic production and reception without reference to the ostensible object of analysis: the work of art. The implications of this are significant. First, it undermines the subdiscipline's self-description as the sociology of *art*.[2] Second, it calls into question the sociological claim that the work of art is, in the final analysis, a *social* product. For if the work of art is both socially located and materially produced, why does it continue to be so systematically excluded from the domain of sociological inquiry? Third, the relationship between cultural forms and social processes remains obscure.[3] Specifically, sociology cannot account for the ways in which cultural forms and practices do not simply reflect an already given social world but, rather, play a constitutive role in the construction of that world (Wolff 1992: 707).

Taken together, these shortcomings underscore the need for new methodological strategies in the sociology of art capable of grasping the complex interplay of aesthetic, social, economic, and political factors. Toward this end, this chapter presents two arguments: first, for the autonomy of artistic works and practices as objects of inquiry in their own right; second, for the importance of attention to ques-tions of meaning. These arguments pose a direct challenge to both the traditional doctrine of aesthetic neutrality in sociology which mandates that not only questions of aesthetic judgment but the work of art itself remain outside social analysis and other sociological approaches to art which attempt to bracket questions of meaning in the attempt to place the subdiscipline on a presumably more objective footing. The last section of the chapter presents examples of the application of these arguments from some recent work in the sociology of art, highlighting specific methodological strategies and showing their fruitfulness for future research.

## The Autonomy of Art

Two of the more persistent problems in the sociology of art may be formulated by the following pair of questions: What is the relationship of art to society? And how should this relationship be studied? Implicit in each of these questions is a tacit assumption that art is not reducible to society in some simple, uncomplicated way, that the nature of the relationship of art to society requires clarification, and that art is a legitimate area of sociological study. In other words, each of these questions pivots around some concept of the *autonomy* of art, however relative, provisional or contingent one might want this concept to be and, further, points to the significance of the concept of autonomy for sociological analysis.[4]

Thus invoked, however, it is necessary to provide a cautionary note about a concept with a long and troubled past. Part of this derives from a confusion over multiple and competing definitions of the term, not unlike the concept of culture. More problematic, however, is its common association with the radical doctrine of aesthetic autonomy espoused most dramatically by various late-nineteenth century aestheticist movements and perpetuated today, in various forms, by art historians and literary critics who continue to bracket social and political questions in favor of the formal properties of the allegedly free-floating work.[5] As stated at the beginning of this chapter, it has been the very real and significant contribution of sociology precisely to demystify this concept of autonomy, what Eagleton (1990) has called the ideology of aesthetic autonomy.

For this reason, it may be argued that the term should be abandoned altogether. Nevertheless, the continued importance of the concept becomes clear when we consider two other definitions of autonomy advanced first in the aesthetic philosophy of the Frank-furt School (in particular, the work of Adorno and Marcuse) and, more recently, in the philosophical and sociological work of Bürger, Habermas, and Goldfarb: a historical/institutional definition which traces the historical development and structure of the autonomous institution of art in modern society and a methodological definition concerned with the autonomy of art as an object of inquiry in its own right.[6] What follows is a brief sketch of the first definition, which points out some of its strengths for how we might begin to conceptualize the institutional status of art in modern society. However, the bulk of my discussion is directed at the second definition, where I present an argument for its importance for the contemporary sociology of art.

The autonomous status of art in the historical/institutional sense refers to the institutional framework for the production and reception of aesthetic works in modern bourgeois society (Bürger 1984). It is widely acknowledged that the autonomous institution of art may be understood as part of a historical process of cultural differentiation which began during the Renaissance and reached definitive form by the late eighteenth century when it received its most systematic philosophical elucidation in the work of Kant. Historically, we find the origins of the autonomous institution of art first in the decline of the religious/cultic functions of art with the development of artistic production for court and patron. Nevertheless, it is only with the emergence of the modern capitalist market that, as Weber (1979: 342) observed, "art becomes a cosmos of more and more consciously grasped independent values which exist in their own right." The emergence of a differentiated sphere of art is thus coterminous with the processes of societal rational-ization and capitalist modernization from which the two modern systems of state and economy arise (Habermas 1984).

The contribution of this concept of autonomy is twofold. First, it allows for the distinction to be made between two interrelated but distinct dimensions of this historical development: (1) the institu-tional framework of art in modern society; that is, the development of systems of production and reception mediated by the mechanisms of a commercial, capitalist market; and (2) the doctrine or ideology of aesthetic autonomy as the necessary opposition of art and society. Second, it reveals the fundamentally contradictory character of the autonomous status of art in modern society. For the freedom of artistic production from its traditional religious and courtly functions is inextricably tied to the status of art as a commodity. Consequently, the "liberation" of art from traditional religious and courtly modes of power involves the reinscription of the aesthetic in the abstract modes of power of the modern market.

While the historical/institutional definition of autonomy does not solve the problem of the relation of art to society once and for all, it does, however, provide us with more solid historical grounds on which to understand the relation of art to other spheres in *modern* society. Specifically, it allows for a conceptualization of art as a sphere always connected with but not simply reducible to other social spheres. Similarly, it allows for the complex, historically changing structure of this relationship, something that neither traditional Marxist formulations of art-as-ideology or traditional art-historical conceptions of the free-floating, transcendent object have been able to grasp. Particularly important is the fact that it gives the question of the relationship of art and society itself an important place in the analysis. The methodological definition of autonomy addresses these issues in more detail.

If the concept of autonomy in the historical/institutional sense delineated above has been recognized as an important contribution to the analysis of art, the methodological definition of the autonomy of art, by which I mean the analysis of artistic works and practices as objects of inquiry in their own right, has had a more problematic history (Goldfarb 1985, 1989: 204–5). The primary source of resistance can be located in the doctrine of aesthetic neutrality which has dominated sociological approaches to art and culture (Bird 1979; Zolberg 1990: 44–5). As Bird (1979) has cogently noted, there are two interrelated but analytically distinct aspects of this doctrine: first, the insistence that sociologists resist questions of aesthetic judgment; and secondly, that the work of art itself remain outside the domain of sociological analysis. Bird (1979: 30) states, "The sociologist must confine himself or herself to the objective facts of production and consumption ... found in the social relations governing the production of art: 'the socialization and careers, the social positions and roles' of artists, 'the distribution and reward systems', [and] 'tastemakers and publics.'" Thus, we can see that the very subject matter of the subdiscipline carries with it an implicit problem. Engagement with the aesthetic object threatens to implicate the social scientist at any moment in matters involving questions of meaning and judgment (Goldfarb 1985: 3; Wolff 1989: 10). To do so places the scholar, particularly the young scholar not yet established in the field, at risk of the charge of not being properly "sociological."

The methodological argument for the autonomy of art poses a direct challenge to the principle of aesthetic neutrality. Artistic works and practices are neither a reflection of society nor a secondary byproduct of some presumably more basic or "objective" social mechanisms. At the core of this argument is the decisive rejection of a base/superstructure model of art and society which has plagued both successive developments in Marxist aesthetics and, in different forms, sociological approaches to the study of art within which the work of art continues to appear as the manifestation of some other social processes (Williams 1989: 165–6). Particularly influential in this regard has been Williams's thoroughgoing critique of the concepts of base and superstructure as well as poststructuralist theories of discourse and power which point to the active role of language and other sign systems in society (Barthes 1972a, b; Foucault 1980, 1984; Williams 1977). As Wolff (1992: 707) has more recently written, "far from reflecting the already-given world, . . . cultural forms participate in the production *of* that world."

While it is easy to assert, in theory, one's rejection of a base/ superstructure model of culture, the extent to which the work of art is absent from analysis means that the model is, in practice, implicitly upheld. Thus, central to the project outlined here is the development of a sociological approach which can account for what Williams, following Bakhtin, has called the "specificity" and Goldfarb has termed the "distinctiveness" of aesthetic forms and practices (Williams 1977, 1989; Goldfarb 1985, 1989). In this view, sociological approaches which continue to privilege generalizability as a methodological criterion for the study of art run the risk of smoothing over precisely those contradictions and differences between cultural objects (as well as between cultural and other social factors) from which significant sociological insight may be gleaned.[7] What this means, in practice, is coming to terms with questions of genre, form, content, narrative, representation, aesthetic convention and intertextuality – questions which can only be addressed by direct engagement with the work of art.

Two points need to be made clear at this juncture. First, the methodological argument for the autonomy of artistic works and practices is not an attempt to simply reverse the traditional causal framework of base and superstructure nor does it privilege aesthetic and cultural factors over other social forces.[8] To the contrary, the central thrust of Williams's critique of the base/superstructure model of society is to show their mutual *interdependence*. Second, the argument for the inclusion of artistic works and practices in sociological analysis is not based on the assumption that the meaning or significance of a particular work resides solely in the artist's intentions or is somehow "embedded" in the object and thus simply needs to be unearthed or revealed. Rather, the central contribution of what has come to be called the "cultural studies" approach following the work of Williams has been to demonstrate the ways in which the meaning or significance of cultural works and practices may be altered by changes in social location and historical context.[9] The task, as Williams (1989) has argued, lies in a focus on the elucidation of the specific and historically changing relations between cultural works and practices with social institutions and processes.

In sum, like the institutional/historical definition of aesthetic autonomy, the methodological definition is useful for the sociology of art. Specifically, it allows for the conceptualization of artistic production as a sphere always connected with but not reducible to other social processes. Similarly, it allows for the analysis of aesthetic works and practices without recourse to the myth of the transcendent object or artist-as-genius. Finally, this approach positions the relationship of artistic works and practices with social processes at the center of analysis. For the autonomy of art in both of these definitions does not imply that art and society are somehow "separate" in some absolute sense but that the autonomy of art as either a differentiated sphere or an object not reducible to some other social factor *itself* becomes an important focus of the analysis.

## The Problem of Meaning

From the foregoing, it might be easy to conclude that sociologists who continue to exclude the work of art from analysis simply suffer from an out-moded allegiance to a base/superstructure model of society. Arguably, in some instances, this may be the case. But the problem is not nearly so simple. Until recently, sociologists have paid relatively little attention to the study of art, designating it a subject matter more properly relegated to the fields of philosophy, art history and literature (Zolberg 1990: 29–52). While sociologists have begun to turn their attention to the study of culture and the arts, what distinguishes the sociological approach to art from that of the humanities is the sociologist's focus on the institutions in which aesthetic objects are produced and received, leaving questions of meaning to art historians and literary critics.

In part, this may be the result of a subdiscipline which has only recently begun to develop. As Crane (1987: 148) has observed, "systematic analysis of visual materials by social scientists has rarely been done and few guidelines exist for a sociological examination of aesthetic and expressive content in art objects." More is at stake here, however, than the growing pains of a relatively new field of inquiry. For many sociologists, explicit disavowal of questions of meaning appears as a necessary condition for remaining faithful to, if not the positivist tradition in sociology, a commitment to "rigorous" social science. Wuthnow (1987), for example, noting the strong association of interest in cultural issues with "the branch of sociology that emphasizes its humanistic elements rather than its scientific aspirations," states, "Culture remains, by many indications, vaguely conceptualized, vaguely approached methodologically, and vaguely associated with value judgments and other sorts of observer bias" (pp. 5–6). More recently, a statement of this position can be found in DiMaggio's (1991) call for "an analytic sociology of culture, distinct from criticism and textual interpretation" (p. 153).

It is not my intention here to inveigh against the evils of positivism. Moreover, I would like to explicitly state my own commitment to a rigorous sociology of art. The question is, what does "a rigorous sociology of art" mean? My own objective is to move beyond the notion of some simple dichotomy between the empirical and theoretical, including the presumed binary opposition between institutional and interpretive approaches to the study of culture.[10] Nevertheless, the impulse toward a simple refusal to engage questions of meaning and interpretation has to be acknowledged as problematic. First, it is nothing new to point out that the very act of choosing what *kind* of art to study entails an evaluative component which assigns significance to the objects selected for analysis, something few sociologists of culture today would deny. Beyond this initial step, however, the traditional strategy adopted by sociologists to eliminate an evaluative component from their research has been to work with existing systems of classification. But as Wolff (1992) and Bird (1979) have demonstrated, far from guaranteeing the objectivity of the analysis, such a strategy actually tends to confirm and reinforce existing aesthetic hierarchies. Finally, although sociologists have, for the most part, abandoned the crude notion that art simply reflects society, the refusal to engage questions of meaning nevertheless tacitly begs a form of residual reflectionism through the assumption that the "objective" facts lie in the organization of production and consumption rather than the meaning(s) of the artistic works and practices in question.

It will be noted that sociologists have not altogether ignored the problem of meaning in the pursuit of methodological strategies appropriate to the analysis of culture and the arts. One of the more serious attempts to address this problem may be found in Wuthnow's (1987) *Meaning and Moral Order*. According to Wuthnow, sociology has been hindered by a subjectivist approach to culture that privileges the problem of meaning in cultural analysis. But because meaning, presumed to reside in the psychological states of individuals, is ultimately inaccessible to the social scientist, sociologists should be advised to go "beyond the problem of meaning" and confine themselves to the observable aspects of culture that can be studied objectively (Wuthnow 1987: 60–5). As Wuthnow (1987: 335) states, "Even if cultural analysis is regarded as an interpretive science, the need remains to put its claims on as solid an empirical footing as possible."

Three underlying assumptions in Wuthnow's argument warrant brief examination. The first of these is Wuthnow's repeated association of the sociological interest in meaning with a "subjective" approach to the study of culture. As Griswold (1987a: 3) has observed, there is no reason why meaning has to be conceptualized solely at the level of the individual. Rather, meaning is constructed as an ongoing process in the complex and often changing intersection of a plurality of factors. Meaning is no more located in the psyche of a single individual than it is somehow eternally "embedded" in the work of art, as traditional art historians and literary critics would have it.

A second assumption in Wuthnow's argument is that abandoning the problem of meaning is the necessary prerequisite toward the establishment of an objective approach to culture. According to Wuthnow, sociology's "subjectivist" approach to the study of culture has its roots in the discipline's underlying adherence to the dualism of subject and object which associates culture with the subjective while society or social structure are viewed as objective realities (Wuthnow 1987: 23–8). Ostensibly, it is Wuthnow's intention to get beyond this subject/object dualism. The strategy Wuthnow proposes is to abandon the problem of meaning, the central concern of "subjectivist" approaches, and thus render the sociology of culture "objective" (1987: 60–5, 333). But as Calhoun (1992a) has incisively observed, this does not dispense with the subject/object dualism. Eliminating the dualism of subject and object would necessitate rejecting the definition of meaning as subjective. Instead, by relegating meaning to the subjective, Wuthnow merely reinscribes the dualism of subject and object on another level.

The third assumption in Wuthnow's argument, that a "poststructuralist" approach will provide sociologists with a methodological foundation for the objective analysis of culture, is particularly problematic.[11] According to Wuthnow (1987: 51–3, 60) poststructuralist approaches to cultural analysis are characterized by a "shift away from the problem of meaning" in favor of a focus on the formal relations between cultural symbols and sign systems. This is fundamentally misleading. The problem of meaning sits at the core of the poststructuralist project.[12] Arguably, the central contribution of the wide body of often quite disparate work done under the heading of poststructuralism has been to show that meaning neither emanates from the experience of a single knowing subject nor is fixed in some absolute, ahistorical sense. As historian Joan Scott (1988: 5), who has argued for the usefulness of poststructuralist theory for the analysis of gender, has written: "Instead of attributing a transparent and shared meaning to cultural concepts, poststructuralists insist that meanings are not fixed in a culture's lexicon but are rather dynamic, always potentially in flux. Their study therefore calls for attention to the conflictual processes that establish meanings, to the ways in which such concepts as gender acquire the appearance of fixity." In any case, the problem of meaning does not disappear simply by declaring it outside the purview of analysis. For it is precisely the insight of poststructuralist theory to show the crucial role discourses, language and representation play in the construction of social worlds (see, for example, Foucault 1979, 1980).

## Implications for Research

Thus far, I have argued for the autonomy of artistic works and practices as objects of inquiry in their own right and the importance of attention to questions of meaning. In presenting these arguments, I have drawn on insights from work within the field of sociology as well as other work outside the field properly defined; namely, cultural studies and poststructuralist theories of discourse and representation. Two important points need to be made clear here. First, neither argument represents an attempt to reverse the causal framework of base and superstructure, as previously noted, or assign culture the status of an independent variable. An important insight associated with early work in cultural studies, specifically with reference to the research that came out of the Birmingham Centre in the 1970s, explored the various ways in which audiences may make critical use of popular culture.[13] Such studies directly contributed to the increased awareness of the importance of cultural analysis that has taken place in the social sciences since the early 1980s. They also provided a useful and necessary corrective to the antipathy for popular culture held by traditional Critical Theory as well as the generally "high cultural" focus of earlier work in the sociology of art. Nevertheless, the utility of the contemporary cultural studies approach as it has developed since the late 1970s remains limited for the sociology of art for two reasons. The first has to do with the simple fact that, to date, work in cultural studies has been almost exclusively on popular culture. The value of a cultural studies approach to Abstract Expressionism, for example, is not yet clear. A second, potentially more serious problem derives from the unfortunate tendency which can be noted in the wide body of work that now calls itself "cultural studies" to automatically privilege cultural factors as sources of opposition to systems of stratification and social control. It has become something of a maxim in such work that culture (specifically, popular culture) equals resistance.[14]

Second, my argument for the analysis of aesthetic works should not be viewed as an attempt to privilege the analysis of aesthetic factors over other social processes. The contribution of poststructuralist theories of discourse and representation, as I have suggested, has been to demonstrate the ways in which systems of representation play a constitutive role in social relations. Poststructuralist approaches to gender, for example, have traced the ways in which historically shifting cultural definitions of femininity have informed both institutional barriers to women in public life as well as a succession of strategies in feminist practice (Parker and Pollock 1981; Riley 1988; Scott 1988). Similarly, studies in the area of race and ethnicity have examined the role of cultural images and stereotypes in the construction of specific social groups as subjects of systems of power and social control (Gates 1986; Pratt 1986). Power, as these analyses demonstrate, rests not just on the organization or control of certain material factors but also the social *meanings* given to these factors (Weedon 1987: 2). Nevertheless, the wholesale adoption of poststructuralist theory for the sociology of art remains deeply problematic. The formal emphasis of poststructuralist analyses of texts often operates to minimize the significance of social factors and thus simply turns the sociological tendency to ignore the aesthetic dimension on its head. In its most extreme forms, social and material factors disappear altogether. Society simply becomes another "text."[15]

What is needed, therefore, is the development of a sociology of art capable of surmounting the traditional impasse that has existed between institutional and interpretive approaches to the study of culture and the arts. In practice, this means an approach capable of simultaneous attention to aesthetic issues and social structure. One area of scholarly inquiry which has begun to develop such an integrative approach to the study of culture in recent years has been the feminist analysis of art.[16] The creation of a substantial body of work in this area since the early 1970s has articulated two central problems which provide concrete illustration of the methodological arguments advanced in this chapter: first, the problem of explaining the exclusion of women's artistic production from the modernist canon and theoretical literature on modernity; and second, the related problem of the representation of women in the modernist work of art. The last section of this chapter therefore turns to empirical examples of these problems demonstrating that they can only be adequately addressed in a framework which combines attention to institutional factors with the analysis of works of art and questions of meaning.

## Institutional Analysis and the Work of Art

Prior to the late nineteenth century, institutional barriers to women's participation in artistic production took the form of the exclusion of women from membership in the prestigious and influential academies. In practice, this meant the restriction of women from a system of academic training and privilege during a period significant for the professionalization of art and the rationalization of its methods of study (Parker and Pollock 1981: 27–8, 87). Most significant, by many accounts, was the exclusion of women from the life-class. For the study of the nude constituted not only the most privileged course within the academic curriculum but was considered to be the very cornerstone of the education and training of great artists (Chadwick 1988: 167; Parker and Pollock 1981: 33–5, 87).

By the late nineteenth century, however, academy membership was no longer the central issue. Alternatives to academic training and exhibition combined with the declining influence of the academies in the face of modernist challenges to tradition meant a shift in the complex relations among the institutions of artistic production and reception, the artistic career and the nature and definition of the work of art. How then may we account for the exclusion of the work of female artists from the modernist canon? The case of Mary Cassatt (1844–1926), the subject of an important study by feminist art historian Griselda Pollock (1980), illustrates the necessity of bringing the work of art into the analysis.

Despite the social and cultural norms that defined artistic work as an unsuitable career for the middle-class, respectable woman of the late nineteenth century, existing documentation strongly supports the conclusion that the professional success of Mary Cassatt was based on those institutional criteria that Lang and Lang (1990) have identified as necessary for the creation and survival of artistic reputation. In the late 1870s, she became an active member of the French Impressionists, the only American ever to exhibit with the group.[17] In addition to Degas, her work was admired by Pissaro, Gauguin and the writer and critic Huysmans (Harris and Nochlin

1976: 237, 239; Rubinstein 1982: 134). Critical acclaim for her work did not end with her association with the Impressionists, however. Cassatt went on to work and exhibit to critical praise in France up until the last decade of her life (Bullard 1972; Harris and Nochlin 1976: 237–41; Matthews 1984; Seldin 1987). The first biography of Cassatt, financed by the American collector James Stillman and written by Achille Segard, appeared in 1913.[18] Later in this century, preservation of Cassatt's artistic reputation became the project of art historian and curator Adelyn Breeskin, who compiled a complete record of Cassatt's oeuvre.[19]

In light of these factors, how can we explain the marginalization of Cassatt in the modernist canon? Until recently, references to Cassatt have been conspicuously absent from leading art history survey texts.[20] As late as 1973, Cassatt merited only brief discussion in a major history of Impressionism (see Rewald 1973). And it was not until 1970 that a retrospective of the artist's work at a major national museum took place.[21] As Pollock's study suggests, the answer to this puzzle lies in an analysis of the modernist work of art.

A central point of agreement in otherwise competing definitions of aesthetic modernism lies in the recognition of artists' increasing rejection of traditional narrative modes of representation in favor of the attempt to create a new, universal language of form. But this emphasis on form did not mean the absence of content. Rather, underlying the increased attention given to formal concerns was the idea that new techniques in art were needed to represent the new "contents" of a rapidly changing, specifically modern world: technology, the meaning of progress, and the changed consciousness of time and space. Two of the central themes of early modernist painting and literature, war and the public life of the city, illustrate this point. Particularly important, as Pollock notes, is the representation of public space: the fascination with the city streets, cafés, and arcades of Baudelaire's "painter of modern life" to which the "respectable" woman had limited access. In this context, the work of women artists, like Cassatt, whose canvases shared the stylistic orientation and formal characteristics of other innovative artists of the day but who consistently depicted interior, domestic spaces fell outside the definition of what "counted" as modernist (Pollock 1988: 50–90; Wolff 1990: 34–66).

It will be noted, of course, that Cassatt's work was not exclusively confined to the private spaces of the bourgeois home.[22] Moreover, male colleagues of Cassatt, such as Degas and Renoir, also painted domestic scenes.[23] But there is a notable asymmetry at work here, as Pollock (1988: 50–90) demonstrates. The public spaces painted by Cassatt are confined to the settings and subjects of polite society: elegant, bourgeois families in the park, debutantes at the theater, etc. The public spaces represented by Degas and Renoir are not so circumscribed. In addition to the scenes of bourgeois recreation in settings like parks, gardens, and the theater favored by the Impressionists, their canvases also included backstage scenes of dancers, courtesans, mistresses and kept women in settings like the cafe, cabarets, or brothels.[24] This asymmetry is particularly significant when we consider that it is as a painter of maternal scenes of mother and child that Cassatt is most often characterized despite the fact that such canvases constitute less than one-third of her total oeuvre (Breeskin 1981). Most importantly, it is as a painter of the maternal that Cassatt has been criticized and derided by modern art historians.[25]

## The Significance of Meaning in Content and Form

The marginalization of women artists in art history has not, of course, meant the absence of the representation of women in art. In fact, through the course of the nineteenth century, a period in which women continued to be largely excluded from academic training, women, in particular the female nude, became ever more present in painting as objects of representation (Parker and Pollock 1981: 115–16). This points to the importance of coming to terms with the meaning of women's increased presence in painting as objects of representation at the same time that women's artistic production continued to be excluded from the modernist canon.

Traditionally, sociologists concerned with the problem of meaning in art have focused on content. Content analysis, developed in the 1920s for the study of political propaganda and subsequently extended to the analysis of the mass media and popular culture, has provided valuable insight into the character and substance of cultural forms of communication in the modern world (McCormack 1982). And, as McCormack (1992) has recently argued, content analysis continues to be a useful tool for the study of culture.

Nevertheless, the limits of content analysis become clear when we consider the case of a series of exhibitions in late nineteenth-century Britain analyzed in a study by Wolff (1990: 12–33).

Two of the more prominent themes revealed by a content analysis of some of the more well-known works of British painting and literature in the mid to late nineteenth century center around the cult of domesticity and trope of the "fallen woman." Works depicting the sanctity of family life and the moral charge of women as mothers and wives received praise from the influential criticism of Ruskin (Wolff 1990: 13–14).[26] A series of exhibitions organized by social reformers for the poor of London's East End in the 1880s emphasized Old Master portraits of the Madonna and Child. Existing documentation records sizable numbers of viewers: from 10,000 in 1881 to 76,000 in 1892 (Wolff 1990: 21–2). At the same time, portraits of the "fallen woman" in painting, literature and the theater were neither uncommon nor unpopular. One canvas, *Past and Present* by Augustus Egg, depicting the fate of the unfaithful wife as a homeless prostitute, for example, drew both crowds of viewers and shocked reactions from the press when shown at the Royal Academy in 1858 (Wolff 1990: 26).

Confined to the analysis of content, it would be tempting to conclude that, taken together, the themes of domestic life and the fallen woman formed a seamless web of moral meaning in the cultural life of nineteenth-century Britain: the exaltation of the bourgeois family on the one hand and dire warnings of the consequences for sexual transgression on the other. This conclusion, however, is complicated by a formal convention characteristic of some of the more successful painters of the fallen woman and female sexuality more generally. As Wolff observes, an artist's adoption of a neoclassical mode of representation allowed for the portrayal of female sexuality in ways which open up the possibility of a different reading. Nude figures set in Ancient Greece or Rome rendered the female body an object of exoticism displaced from the moral dangers of modern life. Adopting the stylistic conventions of neoclassicism transformed the body into an expression of the classically derived formal values of harmony, balance and order. *Babylonian Marriage Market* (1875) by Edwin Long, for example, which sold at Christie's in 1882 for a sale-room record of over six thousand pounds, featured a number of scantily clad young women being sold off in order of beauty to potential husbands. Praised by

Ruskin for its "great merit," it received favorable critical responses in the same journals which had objected to Egg's *Past and Present* (Wolff 1990: 27). The representation of women constitutes the focus (or content) of each painting. But what in one context appears to have signified moral instruction in another context appears to have signified sensual pleasure removed from contemporary mores. In neither case is the ultimate "meaning" of the painting certain. We cannot know for sure how individual viewers responded to either canvas. Rather, the goal of the analysis is to map out a field of possible meanings available within the network of various factors, both social and aesthetic.[27]

## Conclusion

This chapter has presented two major arguments relevant to the development of methodological strategies adequate for a sociology of art: the importance of the autonomy of art as an object of analysis in its own right and the need for sociologists to take seriously the question of meaning. In practice, this does not imply the abandonment or rejection of a "scientific" approach to the study of art. It does, however, call for a "shift in the center" which no longer privileges the analysis of social over aesthetic factors or claims an objective status for itself by abdicating questions of meaning. What this entails is the legitimization within sociology of a number of diverse analytical and interpretive methods whose importance cannot be decided by reference to traditional scientific standards alone. The potential strength of the sociology of art lies not in attempting to make the subdiscipline adhere to a single theoretical framework or set of methodological principles. We can no longer be satisfied with the artificial separation that has existed between the study of society and the study of art. This is the challenge for the sociology of art.

## Notes

An earlier version of this paper was presented at the 87th Annual Meeting of the American Sociological Association, August 1992. For their helpful comments and suggestions, I would like to thank Vera Zolberg, Jeff Goldfarb and David Weisberg.

1   Griswold (1987a), Zolberg (1990), and Wolff (1992) have all made this
    observation.
2   Becker (1982) acknowledged this point in the preface to *Art Worlds* with
    the following statement: "it might be reasonable to say that what I have
    done here is not the sociology of art at all, but rather the sociology of
    occupations applied to artistic work" (p. xi).
3   An eloquent statement of this problem has been made in Raymond
    Williams (1989: 165): "What at last came through, theoretically, in the
    significant new keywords of 'culture' and 'society', was the now familiar
    model: of the arts on the one hand, the social structure on the other, with
    the assumption of significant relations between them."
4   Recent evidence of this can be seen in Alexander's (1990) introduction to
    a volume of essays on culture and society which positions the autonomy
    of culture at the center of analysis.
5   See Bürger (1984) for an analysis of the radical doctrine of aesthetic
    autonomy advanced by aestheticist movements of the nineteenth century.
    For a current example of the attempt by art historians and literary critics
    to bracket social and political questions, see my analysis (Bowler 1991) of
    Italian futurism and fascism.
6   There is another definition of autonomy central to both the early and later
    work of the Frankfurt School: the critical capacity of the autonomous
    work to resist domination (Adorno 1984, 1988; Goldfarb 1982) and the
    defense of the differentiation of art as an autonomous sphere as part of
    the "incomplete project of modernity" (Habermas 1981).
7   In addition to Williams, this is a point that is increasingly made in a
    number of different fields, including the social sciences. For an excellent
    example in anthropology, see Abu-Lughod (1993).
8   See Swidler (1986) on this issue.
9   See, for example, Williams's (1973) analysis of the changing significance
    of artistic-literary representations of urban and rural experience in Eng-
    land from the late sixteenth century to the mid-twentieth century. More
    generally, the construction of meaning in art and literature as a dynamic
    interaction between specific historical conditions of production and
    reception (audience, the individual reader, critical response, etc.) has been
    the center of work by Bakhtin (1981) and reception theory, most notably,
    Jauss (1982). More recently, this point has been taken up by American
    sociologists like Griswold (1987a) who combine institutional and inter-
    pretive approaches to culture.
10  Griswold (1987a, b) and Wolff (1982, 1990, 1992) are exemplary of this
    attempt to forge links between institutional and interpretive analyses.
11  It will be noted that Wuthnow's use of the term poststructuralist is an
    idiosyncratic one within which he groups together the work of Douglas,
    Foucault and Habermas (Wuthnow 1987: 50). Legitimate objections may
    be raised about this system of classification. What is at issue here, however,

is Wuthnow's definition of the salient characteristics of a poststructuralist approach to culture.

12   Wuthnow acknowledges that poststructuralist theory addresses the
problem of meaning in so far as it analyzes the ways in which systems of
meaning *work*. Nevertheless, Wuthnow (1987) repeatedly insists that
poststructuralist approaches involve the "de-emphasis" on the problem of
meaning (p. 53), and a "shift away from the problem of meaning" (p. 60).
More problematic perhaps is the fact that poststructuralism rejects the
distinction Wuthnow makes here between how meaning is constructed
and meaning *per se*.

13   The most enduring examples of this type of study are probably the early
analyses of British youth subcultures undertaken by Hall and Jefferson
(1976) and Hebdige (1979). For an overview of the theoretical and empirical issues central to the cultural studies approach which came out of the
Birmingham Centre, see the excellent discussion by Hall (1992).

14   A recent example of this tendency appears in a volume on women viewers'
responses to popular television (Brown 1990). Invoking Bakhtin's concept
of the carnivalesque to interpret women's responses to soap opera does
not, by itself, form a convincing foundation from which to conclude that
the "feminine discourse" of soap opera watchers constitutes the sub-
version of dominant, patriarchal social norms (Brown, 1990: 183–98).

15   Derrida and De Man are perhaps the most famous examples of this
tendency.

16   With respect to painting, see the important studies by Parker and Pollock
(1981), Pollock (1980, 1988), Nead (1988, 1992) and Wolff (1990). See also
the collections of essays on feminist art criticism edited by Betterton (1987)
and Raven et al. (1988).

17   It is likely that Cassatt's status as the only American member of the Impressionist group increased her visibility in French art circles. In the catalog
accompanying the second one-person exhibition of her work at the Paris
gallery of her dealer Durand-Ruel in 1893, the critic André Mellario wrote
"Cassatt is perhaps, along with Whistler, the only artist of eminent talent,
personal and distinguished, that America possesses" (quoted in Bullard
1972: 17).

18   On Stillman's role, see Bullard (1972: 19).

19   See the catalogs published by Breeskin in 1970 and 1979. Breeskin's work
is important in the context of Lang and Lang's (1990) findings on factors
relevant to the survival of artistic reputation. According to Lang and Lang's
study, survival of artisitic reputation is dependent, in part, on the existence of survivors willing and able to act as mediators to an artist's posterity
(p. 285). It is also important to note that through her relationship with
several important American collectors, Cassatt played an instrumental
role in the introduction of Impressionist painting to an American audience
(see Bullard 1972: 18; Petersen and Wilson 1976: 89; Seldin 1987).

20 The first inclusion of Cassatt (or any other female artist) in Janson's classic survey appeared in 1986. The fourteenth edition of Gombrich's survey text, published in 1984, contains no reference to Cassatt.

21 "Mary Cassatt: 1844–1926." Exhibition, National Gallery of Art, Washington, DC September 27, 1970 through November 8, 1970. An earlier retrospective of Cassatt, at the Baltimore Museum of Art, was held in 1941.

22 See, for example, *At the Opera* (1879), *The Loge* (1882) and *The Boating Party* (1893–94). According to art historian Chadwick (1988), the emergence of the domestic interior as a legitimate subject for painting in the nineteenth century was an important factor facilitating the careers of late nineteenth-century female painters like Cassatt (p. 182).

23 See, for example, *The Bellelli Family* (ca.1860–2) by Degas or Renoir's *Young Girls at Piano* (1892).

24 See, for example, *Absinthe* (1876), *Café-Concert: At Les Ambassadeurs* (1876–7), *Two Laundresses* (1884) or *The Rehearsal* (ca.1877) by Degas. Among Renoir's paintings, see *Portrait of Rapha* (1871), *Cabaret of Mother Antony* (1866), *At the Cafe* (ca.1877) or *Parisian Women in Algerian Dress* (1872). This schism becomes even more pronounced when we include Manet, whose work Cassatt particularly admired.

25 For a discussion of criticism of Cassatt on these grounds, see Harris and Nochlin (1976: 240), Vogel (1988: 49), Langer (1988: 123–4), and Pollock (1988: 83). Interestingly, a note of this criticism appears even in works devoted to a reappraisal of Cassatt. In the introduction to *Mary Cassatt: oils and pastels*, curator and art historian John Bullard (1972) contrasts Cassatt with Degas in the following manner: "While his range of interests were wider, encompassing more of the male pursuits of Victorian society, Cassatt *limited herself* to depicting an essentially domestic, feminine world" (p. 16, emphasis added).

26 In the production of literature, the cult of domesticity found support through the strong moral code enforced by prominent publishers of fiction like Mudie and W. H. Smith. See Wolff (1990: 18).

27 Mode of reception is also an important issue here. Wolff (1990: 27) notes that more "risqué" works deemed unacceptable for public exhibition could nevertheless be found in billiard rooms or in gentlemen's clubs. This is further indication that such works did not necessarily serve to "instruct" young women in the dangers of sexuality and underscores Wolff's point about the need to examine the relationship of aesthetic factors to production and reception.

# 11

# Cultural Conceptions of Human Motivation and Their Significance for Culture Theory

## Steve Derné

Despite its recent resurgence, culture theory has failed to develop a convincing model of culture's causal effects. In an influential article, Ann Swidler (1986: 273–4) argues that "the reigning model used to understand culture's effects on action" still focuses on "culture as values." Swidler notes that few sociologists "really believe" this "thoroughly criticized" Weberian-Parsonian model that sees culture as shaping "action by supplying ultimate ends or values." Indeed, most theorists now recognize that cultural values are socially contested (Clifford 1986: 19; Stromberg 1986; Swidler 1986; DiMaggio 1987), that culture users interpret cultural symbols in diverse ways (Stromberg 1981, 1986), and that even the shared acceptance of values may not generate similar actions (Swidler 1986; DiMaggio 1987: 448). But this realistic assessment of the limited constraining power of values leaves scholars with a theoretical dilemma. As anthropologist Peter Stromberg (1981: 545) points out, the rejection of the idea of shared cultural values has proved difficult to reconcile with the idea that culture "exert[s] some regular influence on the behavior of group members."

In this chapter, I shift the focus from prescriptive elements of culture like values to commonsense, but nonetheless cultural, descriptions people use to orient themselves in the world. I argue that informal, commonsense understandings of human motivation, which I call social frameworks for understanding action, are an important element of the cultural apparatus, which limit the "strategies of action" (Swidler 1986) people use to negotiate other elements of the cultural apparatus. Although these cultural understandings are not fully shared, they nonetheless constrain even active culture users who manipulate cultural symbols for their own purposes. I locate that constraining force of culture not in the directive, but in the descriptive; not in providing values, but in asserting how action will be understood; not in internalized ideas but in social practices (see also Schneider 1976; D'Andrade 1984: 93–7).

By focusing on how commonsense understandings of human motivation constrain even those who buck social norms or work to transform society, I reconcile the idea of cultural constraint with the recognition that individuals often contest cultural norms. By emphasizing how cultural constraint is driven not by internalized values, but by the consequences that arise from social practices in which people act on their commonsense understandings, this approach reconciles cultural constraint with the fact that cultural elements are often not shared.

I frame my argument by describing social constructionist theories that have highlighted commonsense understandings as culturally variable. While social constructionist approaches have described the interactions that shape commonsense thinking, they have not explored how a focus on commonsense understandings might improve our understanding of cultural constraint. I then argue that commonsense understandings of human motivation are an important constraining element of culture by comparing middle-class American men's understanding that action is chosen by the individual with upper-caste north Indian Hindu men's understanding that individual actions are motivated by group pressures. I bring the social constructionist argument that commonsense knowledge is culturally constructed to bear on questions of cultural constraint by asking the following sorts of questions: How do frameworks for understanding action constrain individuals? How do these frameworks shape collective strategies of change? How do these frameworks shape social institutions?

## Social Constructionist Traditions

A range of social constructionist theoretical traditions, including Berger's sociological phenomenology (Berger and Luckmann 1966), Blumer's (1969) symbolic interactionism, Garfinkel's (1967) ethnomethodology, and Shweder's (1991) cultural psychology hold that what actually goes on in the world does not dictate the terms by which the world is understood. Rather, as Shweder (1991: 156) puts it, "social constructionist theories ... argue that people categorize the world the way they do because they have participated in social practices, institutions and other forms of symbolic action ... that presuppose or in some way make salient those categories." Even such seemingly self-evident commonsense understandings as notions about what constitutes the self are shaped by the sociocultural environment (Geertz 1973; Douglas 1982).

Scholars are giving increasing attention to commonsense understandings as an important component of culture (Geertz 1973; Douglas 1982; Lutz 1988). As Mary Douglas (1982: 1) puts it, "anything whatsoever that is perceived at all must pass by perceptual controls," which are primarily "cultural." Berger and Luckmann's (1966: 15) project in the sociology of knowledge focuses on "what people 'know' as 'reality' in their everyday" lives. Ethnomethodology's project focuses on the commonsense knowledge people use to make sense of their social world (see Heritage 1984: 4). For anthropologist David Schneider (1976: 202–3), such understandings make up culture. "Culture," he says, "constitutes a body of definitions, premises, statements, postulates, presumptions, propositions, and perceptions about the nature of the universe and [the person's] place in it." Schneider's definition contrasts culture with norms: "Where norms tell the actor how to play the scene, culture tells the actor how the scene is set and what it all means" (see also D'Andrade 1984).

Partly because their main concern is an analysis of the processes that generate commonsense knowledge, social constructionists have often neglected the causal issues of greatest interest to sociologists. For instance, Berger's sociology of knowledge focuses on analyzing "the process in which" reality is socially constructed (Berger and Luckmann 1966: 1). Ethnomethodology's fundamental concern is similarly with understanding, as Heritage (1984: 76) puts it, how "social actors come to know, and know in common, what they are doing and the circumstances in which they are doing it." This developing understanding of how social practices, institutions and interactions generate commonsense knowledge has been proceeding without an appreciation of how the commonsense knowledge that is continually generated shapes and constrains individuals. How do commonsense cultural understandings constrain? How do they influence social life? In short, what are the social consequences of particular commonsense understandings?

## Social Frameworks for Understanding Action

This chapter answers these questions by focusing on commonsense understandings of human motivation. Every cultural apparatus must fulfill certain orientational requirements (Geertz 1973: 363). Among these is some understanding of what motivates people's actions. I argue that a focus on social frameworks for understanding action – the understanding of why people act the way they do, which is dominant among some social groups – provides one way of understanding culture's causal effects.

A growing body of anthropological studies of ethnopsychology – indigenous understandings of the psyche and mental processes – demonstrates the rich variety of cultural conceptions of human motivations (Heelas and Lock 1981; White and Kirkpatrick 1985; Lutz 1988). Actions can be understood, for instance, as driven by gods or spirits, by respect for elders, by spells cast by witches, by "substances" in the village soil (Daniel 1984), or by the self based on individual interests and desires. Nevertheless, two general types of understanding are fundamental (see Heelas 1981b). According to one understanding, actions are chosen by individuals themselves, while through the lens of a second understanding, actions seem to be driven by forces outside the individual.

### Two distinctive frameworks for understanding action

Bellah et al.'s (1985) discussion of "languages" – distinct vocabularies attached to discourse – points to the individualistic understanding of action that is dominant among white middle-class American men today. Bellah et al. (1985: 81) argue that most Americans are limited by a "language of radical individual autonomy" and "cannot think about themselves or others except as arbitrary centers of volition." The American understanding, they argue, focuses on "the autonomous individual, presumed able to choose the roles he [or she] will play and the commitments he [or she] will make, not on the basis of higher truths, but according to the criterion of life-effectiveness as the individual judges it" (Bellah et al. 1985: 47; Varenne 1977; Heelas 1981a: 4; see also Swidler 1986: 276; Shweder 1991).

By contrast, the commonsense understanding of the north Indian Hindu men I interviewed[1] holds that action is driven by social pressures from an individual's social group (Derné n.d., 1992a, b, c; see also Kakar 1981; Roland 1988; Shweder 1991). When describing their motivations, Hindu men focus on the importance of maintaining their honor by following the dictates of their caste and family (Derné n.d., 1992a, b, c; Kakar 1981; Roland 1988). While the American focus on individual autonomy leads them to valorize the act of leaving home (Bellah et al. 1985: 56ff; Varenne 1977), Hindu men want to live with their parents in joint families where they can be guided by elders (Derné 1992a, b, 1993; Kakar 1981; Roland 1988).

My exploration of how frameworks for understanding action constrain individuals follows a brief description of the distinctive features of these understandings. What are frameworks for understanding action?

## Commonsense *understandings*

First, social frameworks for understanding action are commonsense descriptions of the world. Common sense, as Swidler (1986: 279) puts it, is the set of cultural assumptions so unselfconsciously held that they seem a "natural, transparent, undeniable part of the structure of the world." As Berger and Luckmann (1966: 2) argue, people do not ordinarily trouble themselves about what is "real" to them and about what they "know" unless they are stopped by some sort of problem. They take their "reality" and "knowledge" for granted. Because the understanding is usually so informal, so much a matter of common sense that it is left unsaid, it remains unchallenged (Geertz 1975; see Douglas 1982: 5; Bourdieu 1984: 424; Heritage 1984: 31; Bellah et al. 1985: 27).

## *Merely ways of understanding action*

Second, these different cultural understandings of what drives action are not accurate descriptions of actual differences in what influences the actions of individuals. In all societies, people are motivated both by individual desires and by group pressures. It is only the cultural description of one influence as primary that varies from society to society.

Social frameworks for understanding action are not ways of acting, then, but ways of understanding or perceiving actions. Social groups have an important influence on actions of middle-class American men even though they are unlikely to recognize that influence. In their accounts of their own success, for instance, middle-class American men emphasize their own individual effort, ignoring the contributions of family and neighbors, which are often just as essential (Varenne 1977: 28–9; Bellah et al. 1985: 82). At a more general level, the imperative that Americans be self-reliant and make decisions on their own is itself not chosen by the individual but is imposed by society (Varenne 1977: 47–8; Dumont 1980: 9–10; Bellah et al. 1985). Similarly, individual interests play an important part in driving the actions of individual Hindu men even though they may see even their most self-interested actions as directed by the received authority of caste and family. An individualistic understanding of action, then, does not imply greater individual autonomy, just as a collectivist understanding does not imply stronger group control. Culture is not behavior, and indigenous ethnopsychologies are not a completely accurate description of psychological motivations (see Ewing 1991: 132–4).

I will show that while these understandings constrain, it is not by actually shaping motivations. Rather, understandings of motivation constrain individuals by driving social practices that attach real social consequences to the appearance of being motivated by one pole of human experience rather than another.

### The secondary understandings that are always present

Third, since fundamentally opposed understandings reflect universals of human experience (Heelas 1981b), even if one understanding of action tends to be dominant among some social group, other conflicting ways of understanding action always coexist in any society (Lutz 1988; Hewitt 1989; Derné 1992c, 1993). While middle-class American men's framework for understanding action focuses on individual volition, this focus is sometimes tempered by "second languages" (Bellah et al. 1985; Derné 1992c) which allow for a discourse based on shared commitments to communities. Similarly, because total passivity or powerlessness runs counter to the human experience of being able to act in the world (Heelas 1981b: 47), various second languages recognizing the importance of the individual complement the dominant Indian first language that sees action as driven by forces external to the individual (Mines 1988; Derné 1992c). One instance of the Hindu second language recognizing individual volition is the Indian constitution's provisions making individuals important bearers of rights and obligations (Béteille 1983; see also Mines and Gourishankar 1990). The spiritual realm is, as Alan Roland (1988: 228, 240) argues, another arena in which Indians can emphasize "particular proclivities of a person." My own work indicates that many Indian men experience refreshing individualism in their relationships with their brothers (Derné 1993), and that Indian men are often acutely aware of their individual sensual desires (Derné 1992c).

People may be less familiar with their culture's second languages. They may have less facility using the vocabulary of second languages, which may be less rich than the dominant first language. Thus, while Hindu men experience individual desires and inclinations, they may still use the first language of group control to talk about these desires. Bellah et al. (1985: 20–1) similarly argue that because of the American "first language of individualism," Americans "have difficulty articulating the richness of their commitments" to others.

While second languages allow people who share the dominant understanding of action to express aspects of human experience that are contrary to their first language, there are other groups in both the USA and India who do not embrace the dominant framework for understanding as their primary orientation. American women, for instance, think much more in terms of relationships to others than in terms of the isolated individual that dominates the thought of American men (Gilligan 1982; Bellah et al. 1985: 111). African-Americans, recognizing how their life-chances are limited by forces outside themselves, are more likely to emphasize collective strategies for advancement than are European-Americans who focus more on individual volition (Stack 1974; Weis 1985). While members of the American middle class focus on success through individual initiative, members of the American working class may focus more on advancement through adherence to external authority (Carnoy and Levine 1985). Similarly, lower-caste Indians may have an individualistic rather than collectivist understanding of the world (see Khare 1984; Appadurai 1986a: 751–2). They understand the social roles that constrain them as something imposed by the efforts of the powerful, rather than as a legitimate part of the social order (Berreman 1971; Mencher 1974). Similarly, while upper-caste Indian men try to advance their position by strengthening their families, Indian women, often isolated and subjugated in their husbands' households, may try to advance their own position by persuading their husbands or sons to separate from the joint family, breaking up the larger groups that upper-caste Hindu men prefer to hold together (Bennett 1983).

Social constructionists, Foucauldians and others have discussed the processes by which some understandings come to be "dominant" and privileged over others. This chapter sets aside this question.[2] My analysis proceeds from a recognition that in both India and the USA certain understandings are widespread among dominant groups. I argue that even individuals who are members of dominant groups are constrained by the understandings, which their own practices may have generated. For instance, Indian husbands who use the focus on being guided by elders to control their wives may also be constrained by this understanding should they want to separate from their parents or marry for love in the face of their parents' objections (Derné n.d., 1992b). The focus of this chapter is on how the dominant commonsense understanding of a powerful group constrains members of that group – even if they reject that understanding as their personal orientation.

## Strategies of Action and Cultural Constraint

Social frameworks for understanding action constrain individuals by limiting the strategies of action individuals can use to buck social pressures. Swidler (1986: 273) argues that a focus on "strategies of action" – "persistent ways of ordering action through time" – is vital for understanding "culture's causal effects." Swidler (1986: 276) rightly criticizes sociologists' "excessive emphasis on the 'unit act,' the notion that people choose their actions one at a time according to their interests or values." Rather, she argues, "action is necessarily integrated into larger assemblages." Routine patterns of action are one type of such larger assemblages of action. Most of the time, most individuals take for granted the propriety and meaningfulness of their actions. Hindu men take for granted the propriety of joint-family living, arranged marriages, restrictions on women's movements outside of the home, and limitations on the contacts between husband and wife. These routine patterns of action are so general in Hindu society that individuals need no strategies for accomplishing them. They simply act. The individual needs a strategy of action only when embarking on a novel path.

Strategies of action are general tactics that people use to pursue diverse, but particular goals. The particular aim of the strategy is usually novel, but often the strategy of action itself is not. Strategies of action are usually used to present or frame actions in ways that are comprehensible and unthreatening to others. As Goffman (1971: 85) argues, individuals are "constrained to sustain a viable image of [themselves] in the eyes of others." Because the social framework for understanding action is the shared, commonsense understanding of dominant groups, those whose actions do not appear to fit the dominant framework may be mistrusted as lacking normal human attributes (see Goffman 1974: 188).

## The collectivist framework and Hindu strategies of action

Social frameworks for understanding action limit the strategies of action available to individuals by determining the picture individuals need to present of themselves to avoid being distrusted as someone whose actions make no sense. As seen through Hindu men's collectivist framework for understanding action, individuals who follow their social group are trustworthy and those who act independently of it are anomalous, confusing, and worthy of suspicion. Because of the understanding that individual volition is threatening, Hindu men are constrained to present their actions as in accord with some social group, even as they act unconventionally and separately from their social group.

The commonsense understanding that actions should be driven by one's social group generates a vocabulary of legitimate action focusing on such concepts as honor and tradition. Most Hindu men who embrace the dominant framework for understanding action as their personal orientation spontaneously use this vocabulary because they believe action should be driven by considerations of honor. Because this vocabulary is rich and familiar, moreover, many use it to justify their actions even as they act based on an individual volition they sense only vaguely. Finally, because social practices – that themselves result from a shared understanding of action – assert that Hindu people acting on individual volition are not to be trusted, even those who do not embrace the dominant framework as their personal orientation are constrained to use a vocabulary of honor and tradition to justify their actions in order to avoid being discredited as dangerously individualistic. These people are "innovative mimetists" who deliberately mimic the honorable role to conceal their unacceptable agendas (see Derné 1992b; Jadwin 1992).

The men I interviewed use arguments that work within the dominant framework for understanding action to justify even unconventional acts. Another paper (Derné 1992b) describes how Ramesh Mishra[3] married a woman of his own choosing against the initial objections of his parents. Ramesh's personal orientation to action is an individualistic one (Derné 1992b: 213–14): He believes, for example, that his unconventional idea that close contact and "mutual understanding" between husband and wife are essential parts of the good life came "from inside myself." Yet, in order to justify a dishonoring love marriage, Ramesh does "culture work" (Derné 1992b) that makes sense within the dominant collectivist framework for understanding action.

Culture work is the combination and manipulation of cultural components such as stories, beliefs, and values to attribute meaning to particular actions. To make the argument that his marriage would not be dishonoring, Ramesh manipulates existing cultural stories to attribute meaning to his own actions, while using the assumptions of the dominant framework. Ramesh focuses on the fact that his beloved is of the same caste as himself to manipulate existing cultural stories that hold that love marriages fail. Accepting the dominant understanding that love marriages usually fail, Ramesh argues that this is because the man and woman are typically of different backgrounds. Ramesh conjectures that arranged marriages, like love marriages, might face difficulties if the man and the woman are of different backgrounds:

> If one is from a higher family and another is from a lower family, there will be difficulties whether the marriage is a love marriage or an arranged marriage. When marriages occur between families of the same status, no complications arise – whether it be an arranged marriage or a love marriage. This is because [the boy and the girl] understand each other's family's circumstances. But if the situation and circumstances of the boy's family and the girl's family are different then understanding is impossible and fighting and separation are born.

Ramesh focuses not on the personal characteristics of the woman he had chosen to be his bride, nor on his own personal, individual happiness that he hopes to gain by marrying her, but instead on the family of the woman he had chosen to marry. Appeals to his own happiness or appeals which focus on his beloved's personal characteristics, while making sense within the American framework which sees action as chosen by the individual in accord with his or her own interests and desires, would make little sense according to the Hindu framework which sees action instead as determined by the individual's social ties. Although Ramesh himself emphasizes individual volition, he is nonetheless constrained to use strategies of action that explain his unconventional acts in a way that makes sense according to the collectivist framework for understanding action.

Other Hindu men use the same strategy of making arguments that work within the dominant framework for understanding action to justify even unconventional acts. Men often refer to honor to justify actions that might appear unconventional. Sunil Gupta, a married 35-year-old, intends to give his son a chance to meet the woman he will choose to be his wife before marrying her. Sunil justifies this departure from tradition by basing it on his concern with protecting his family's honor: "Even if [my son] does not want to see the girl, I will show him. I have seen marriages in which the boy refused to marry the girl. In those cases, the [family's] honor [pratishtha] falls." Sunil's decision to show his son the girl he chooses for him, while unconventional, is still framed as based on a concern with the family's honor.

Men also sometimes use the vocabulary of tradition to justify unconventional actions. Many of the men interviewed live in families that are less than ideally joint. These men often comment that it is a tradition that when a family becomes large, brothers separate (see Derné 1993). Ramchandra Mishra, a married 32-year-old, comments, for instance, that when his children grow "there will be a division of the family. It is a tradition. We move according to the tradition that when a family becomes large, the brothers separate." Ramchandra, like many men, hides his individual interests by focusing on how joint-family splits are driven by social traditions.

Another way that men deemphasize how individual inclinations drive actions is to focus on the demands of changing times. Anil Gupta, 76 years old, talks of his sons' separations from his family as a response to changing times: "In our people's time, the joint family had importance. In the new age, the joint family has no importance . . . [because] the modern form of society has changed." Anil encouraged his sons to separate from the joint family once they had obtained white-collar jobs. By presenting the separation of the family as in accord with society, Anil claims the actions were not spurred by his own individual initiative but by social trends.[4] People use similar arguments to justify showing a son his bride before the wedding. Sunil Gupta says, for instance, that he will allow his son to meet the girl he has chosen for him "because the time is changing. Whatever my parents did was right, but now circumstances have changed." Vinod Gupta, 34 years old, used a similar argument to convince his father to show him the girl he had chosen for him. Vinod insisted on meeting the girl: "While my brothers married with money and dowry, I told my family that I would marry only after seeing the girl." Despite his insistence, Vinod deemphasizes his demand in explaining his father's actions, focusing instead on social trends: "I married with the changing times – I married after meeting my wife. My father knew to change with the times."

Another way of framing unconventional actions as in accord with the dominant understanding is to assert that the actions are in accord with some respected group in society (see also Derné 1994a). Thus, men say – not always disparagingly – that educated people can marry for love, or allow their wives to work outside the home. Shyam Gupta, a 50-year-old heading a small joint family that includes his sons and daughters-in-law, comments that educated people allow their wives to go outside the home:

Interviewer:   "But, here if a woman works outside the house, then the society does not understand this as good?"
Shyam:   "No, in the society there are two types of people – those who are educated and those who are not. Those who are educated regard it as very good that the woman is earning as well as the man. It is people from the lower classes [nimna shreni] that do not understand it as proper [ucit]."

Hindu strategies of action, then, use a vocabulary that focuses on honor, tradition, and moving in accordance with contemporary trends and respected social groups. Even as Hindu men act on their individual desires by breaking with social norms, they are constrained to use the rich, legitimate vocabulary that deemphasizes the individual volition most Hindu men find threatening. While the collectivist framework for understanding action does not keep men from innovating, it does constrain them by limiting the strategies they can use to do so.

### Limitations on the ability to use strategy of actions

By limiting the strategies men can use to present themselves in a way that others can understand, frameworks for understanding action also limit the actions that can be effectively pursued. In Hindu India, the dishonor that attaches to some actions is so great that no strategy of action can present them as occurring with the consent of some respected social group. Perhaps Ramesh Mishra's efforts at getting his parents to consent to a love marriage succeeded only because the woman he wanted to marry was of the same caste as Ramesh. By contrast, Vijay Mishra found it impossible to justify marrying a woman who was both a widow and from a different caste. Financially empowered by his stable teaching post (see also Mines 1988; Derné 1994a), Vijay became an "unapologetic rebel" (Derné n.d.) who simply braved the consequences of dishonor by marrying in court. Vijay describes how his brothers have boycotted him because of their concern that his dishonoring marriage will make it difficult for them to arrange their own marriages. Had Vijay tried to be an innovative mimetist, he would have had little success. His family was too firmly opposed to the wedding. While strategies of action which present actions as in accord with the framework for understanding action are effective in some circumstances, they are of limited use in others. Some actions are simply too discrediting. Vijay's description of being boycotted suggests, moreover, that it is often social consequences more than internalized understandings that constrain individuals' actions.

### Practices and cultural constraint

Why are men constrained to use certain strategies of action? Not all men are "true believers" (Derné n.d.; Jadwin 1992) who see themselves as automatically guided by social pressures. Many, like Ramesh Mishra, have an individualistic orientation. Yet, while Ramesh Mishra told me that it makes little difference "what people think," he nonetheless carefully presented his love marriage as an arranged one by marrying with the usual showy wedding procession and the usual rituals performed by Hindu *pandits* (Derné 1992b: 212–13). This suggests that the constraint of culture often comes not from internalized understandings, but from the power of society that is dramatized in social practices.

Hindu men's collectivist framework for understanding action is made compelling by social practices in which people act on the dominant understanding of action. In their day-to-day lives, Hindu men who distrust actions independent of one's social group act in ways that tell others that independent actions render a person untrustworthy. Because many Hindu men see individuals acting outside of social controls as dangerous, they believe such individuals must be dishonored. For the men interviewed, the main consequence of dishonor is being boycotted, which men consistently describe as the refusal to eat with, drink with, sit with, or talk with the dishonored individual. People boycott those who act dishonorably to bring the dishonored individual under the control of the society, and because they fear coming into contact with a dangerous person who is outside of his family's control (see Derné 1992b: 204). The social practice of dishonoring people who act separately from their social group reinforces the commonsense understanding that individuals acting outside their social group are dangerous, while graphically illustrating the social consequences of appearing to act based on one's own individual interests.[5]

A person who wants to maintain social support must sustain a viable image of himself or herself in the eyes of others. Knowing that they may be boycotted if they appear to be motivated by selfish reasons, Hindu men usually try to present themselves as acting with the guidance of society.

## Individualistic understandings and American strategies of action

In Hindu India, men's focus on how actions are guided by social pressures constrains them to present themselves as guided by family and society. But how does the American understanding that actions are chosen by the individual constrain? Even as Americans work to help others, they are often constrained to use a vocabulary of individuality to justify their actions. Even as Americans try to put social pressure on others, they are often constrained to use a vocabulary of individual volition to do so.

To illustrate this argument, we briefly consider Varenne's (1977: 166–87) description of an American couple, Sue and John, who marry in the face of parental opposition. While Ramesh Mishra broke sharply with Hindu cultural tradition by marrying for love, Sue and John play out a variation on what Varenne (p. 166) calls "the fundamental drama of [American] culture: the assertion of the individuality of a grown-up child through a break with one community and the creation of a new one" (see also Bellah et al. 1985; Hewitt 1989). Sue's effort to justify her decision to marry John and her parents' genuine attempt to prevent the marriage illustrate how American strategies of action are constrained by the American framework for understanding action.

Both Sue and her parents use a common vocabulary that makes sense according to the individualistic American framework for understanding action. First, both Sue and her parents take it for granted that Sue has the right as an autonomous individual to decide for herself whether she wants to marry John. To justify her marriage, Sue needed only remind her friends of the commonsense wisdom that "everybody is free to do whatever they like" (Varenne 1977: 172). While Sue's parents opposed Sue's marriage, "they could not argue that [Sue] belonged to them by right or duty." Instead, they tried to convince her that "she was more like them than she was like John, and thus, rationally speaking, ought to [herself choose to] continue participating in their community" (p. 174). Sue's mother continually tried to convince Sue that she did not "love John." Sue's mother tried to convince Varenne (p. 173), for instance, that the situation with John "is just like that other guy [Sue] thought she loved. Mitch. While they were going together, it was Mitch and only Mitch, the great love. When he left her, she forgot him right away. If she just waited, it would be the same thing with John. No, she does not love John."

Second, both Sue's and her parents' arguments reflect the commonsense understanding that the ultimate test of whether Sue should marry John is whether she, individually, would be happy with John (p. 180). Sue's parents argue, for instance, that because Sue likes "living in an intellectual atmosphere, with plenty of books and intelligent, substantive discussions" she would never be "happy" with John (p. 180). By contrast, neither Sue nor her parents debated whether Sue had a duty to obey her parents. Such a focus on duty makes little sense according to the American understanding that focuses on individual choices.

While their aims are opposed, both Sue and her parents work within the American framework for understanding action, according to which Sue has the right to make her own decisions based on what will bring her inner self the most happiness. Even as Sue's parents try to force Sue to bow to their pressure, they are nevertheless constrained to work within the dominant American framework for understanding action which holds that Sue has the right to make her own decisions based on what she thinks will make her most happy.[6]

How does this focus on the constraint of frameworks for understanding action avoid the difficulties of the "culture-as-values" paradigm? While the culture-as-values paradigm asserts that internalized values guide actions, I argue that culture constrains by driving social practices that individuals confront as external constraints. Because I focus on how social practices constrain by attaching consequences to appearing to be motivated in certain ways, my account of cultural constraint is consistent with a recognition that frameworks for understanding action are not fully shared. Rather than shaping individual behavior by providing actors with goals, frameworks for understanding action constrain by defining the social understandings that actors must contend with. Rather than emphasizing how culture shapes behavior by shaping the internal motives of actors, I locate the constraining force of culture in the power of society apparent in social practices.

## Shaping Collective Strategies for Change

While my own work focuses on understanding cultural constraint at the individual level, it is worth noting that frameworks for understanding action might also influence and constrain collective strategies for change, the programs used to combat social problems, and the way social institutions work.

For instance, frameworks for understanding action may limit not only the strategies individuals use to buck social pressures, but the strategies groups use to bring about social change. When people are faced with conditions they want to change, the best way of doing so is not self-evident (Snow et al. 1986; Derné 1991). People need to choose between competing paths.

Because American men tend to focus on how people choose actions on their own based on their own calculation of what will make them most happy, "when Americans try to get something done," as Swidler (1986: 281) argues, "they are likely to create voluntaristic social movements" like religious revivals, reform campaigns, and voluntary local initiatives that created much of American public schooling (Varenne 1977: 29–35; Bellah et al. 1985: 167; Swidler 1986: 281). These strategies, Swidler rightly notes, "rest on the cultural assumption that social groups . . . are constituted by the voluntary choices of individuals." By contrast, American social movements which focus on group justice are often seen as illegitimate (Thurow 1980), and meet with public disapproval. Even in accomplishing collective acts, then, Americans may be constrained by the individualistic framework for understanding action that focuses on individual choices.

Indian social movements appear to be similarly influenced by the Indian focus on the collectivity. Lower-caste groups, for instance, often focus on raising the status of the group (rather than the status of the individual) by adopting upper-caste customs, asserting an elevated group origin, embracing alternative religions like Buddhism or Islam, or creating new religious groups in which people can claim membership (Rudolph and Rudolph 1967; Srinivas 1969; Berreman 1976; Juergensmeyer 1982; Mujahid 1989). The focus on group pressure is apparent in women's groups' tactics of boycotting offenders to combat dowry extortions, wife-beating, and liquor sales (Kishwar and Vanita 1991: 126, 179, 226). The social movements and tactics people choose to improve their position, then, may be shaped by whether the dominant lens through which people understand human motivation focuses on the individual or on group membership, individual choices or social pressures.

By alerting people to some aspects of human experience rather than others, frameworks for understanding action may also influence the political vocabularies that are effective in a particular society, and hence the social programs used to combat social problems. Because American policymakers needed to present old-age insurance to a public that saw the world in terms of autonomous individuals, they needed to describe the social security system as an insurance program that everyone pays into, rather than as a need-based safety-net (see Zollars and Skocpol 1990). Because American policymakers understand individuals as choosing actions on their own, the American system of criminal justice focuses on altering the individual's cost-benefit calculations by punishing offenders (rather than, for instance, developing shaming mechanisms) (see Bayley 1976; Braithwaite 1989). Some American efforts at controlling pollution focus on manipulating the cost calculations of individuals and corporations, by, for instance, providing credit for meeting pollution-cutting standards to corporations that buy polluting cars from individuals. To note one final example, the US President Bush spoke comfortably of solving the problems of American education by providing parents with "school choice." American policymakers, in other words, confront social problems by manipulating the cost calculations individuals make. As Bellah et al. (1991: 61) have argued, this focus on the pursuit of individual advantages is often an impediment to Americans' ability to effectively understand and confront public problems.

In societies with a collectivist orientation, programs are more likely to emphasize duty to a social group. John Braithwaite (1989) has demonstrated, for instance, that the Japanese effectively control crime by emphasizing apology, compensation, and forgiveness, rather than punishment (see also Bayley 1976). Braithwaite (1989: 137) similarly argues that Japanese regulatory agencies are able to change business behavior in a relatively short time because of the Japanese focus on reminding corporations of their moral responsibility to society. Similarly, the Indian focus on the social group makes state intervention a legitimate way of solving problems. Corporation malfeasance, for instance, sometimes results in calls to nationalize corporations (see for instance Kishwar and Vanita 1991: 101). In contrast to the US Republican Party's focus on "school choice," Indian courts have strictly limited competition for students by ruling that private colleges cannot charge more than what is charged in government-run colleges (*India Abroad*, 21 August 1992, p. 29).

In short, I would suggest that an exploration of how frameworks for understanding action shape social institutions,[7] social movements, and programs designed to solve social problems might also be a fruitful path for future research.

## Conclusions

This chapter suggests that an important constraining power of culture lies not in values, but in commonsense but nonetheless cultural descriptions of the world. Commonsense understandings of what motivates people generate a vocabulary of legitimate action which constrains the strategies that individuals and social groups can use to pursue their own interests. The paper also tentatively suggests that the constraint of cultural constructions of human motivation may also influence social institutions and the tactics groups of people use to confront social problems.

The approach I have suggested also has the advantage of recognizing both human agency and cultural constraint (see Derné 1992b), a problem that social theorists have been struggling with for some time (Bourdieu 1984; Giddens 1984; Archer 1988). Although able to contest norms, individuals are still limited to performing culture work that makes sense within the dominant framework for understanding action if they hope to avoid the discredit of appearing to lack what are defined as normal human attributes.

Finally, by seeing cultural constraint as driven by the social practices of powerful groups, the approach described here reconciles cultural constraint with the fact that even commonsense understandings are not always shared. My shift in focus from values to cultural constructions of human motivation offers one way of solving some of culture theory's persistent dilemmas, while offering a useful way of understanding culture's causal significance.

This chapter is limited, however, by its focus on the dominant groups in society. One might ask how the framework for understanding action of the dominant group influences subordinate groups like women, lower-class or lower-caste people, or religious or ethnic minorities – even if these groups do not embrace that orientation as their own. How might subordinate groups' frameworks for understanding action affect them differently than the ways that the dominant group's framework constrains the dominant group? Might subordinate groups, who must be familiar with the dominant group's framework for understanding action as well as their own framework, have more cultural tools in their cultural repertoire? All of these are important questions to be answered by further research.

## Notes

Acknowledgments: The US Department of Education supported this research with Foreign Language and Area Studies fellowships which financed my study of Hindi, and with a Fulbright-Hays Doctoral Dissertation Research Abroad grant which funded the research itself. Awadesh Kumar Mishra, Nagendra Gandhi, Parvez Kahn, and Ramchandra Pandit assisted me in conducting and translating interviews. An earlier version of this paper was presented at the Annual meeting of the American Sociological Association in Washington, DC in 1990. Diana Crane, Elizabeth Long, and Cheryl Zollars made helpful comments on an earlier draft of this paper. Related discussions with Arlie Hochschild, Lisa Jadwin, John Palattella, Jean Pedersen, Peter Stromberg, Ann Swidler and Hervé Varenne were also helpful.

1   I conducted open-ended, in-depth interviews with 49 upper-middle-class, upper-caste Hindu men living in Banaras, north India. The interviews concerned men's actions and ideas surrounding joint-family living, arranged marriages, restrictions on women's movements outside the home, and limitations on husband–wife interactions within the home. For a discussion of my methodology and the representativeness of the people I interviewed see Derné 1992a, b, c.

2   Like Michel Foucault, my focus is on practice-based knowledge that has become such a matter of common sense that it is assumed to lack a history. While Foucault's main interest is the study of formal scientific thinking, my focus is on the thinking of common people. While Foucault focuses on the practices that generate forms of knowledge and the institutions that support them, my focus is on how commonsense notions constrain the actions of individuals. (For this discussion of Foucault I am indebted to Smart 1985.)

3   I have changed the names of the people I interviewed to protect their privacy.

4   While Anil's presentation of the causes of his action is in accord with the dominant framework for understanding action, it is not an accurate account of the trends in modern India (see Derné 1992c, 1993).

5   See Derné 1992b: 204–205 for examples of such boycotts. See Derné n.d. and 1994b for a discussion of the real difficulties men have arranging marriages for their sons and daughters or brothers and sisters should they act dishonorably.

6   In the American context, some actions are so self-evidently nonindividualistic that they are difficult to justify with an individualistic vocabulary. As Varenne (1977: 185–7) points out, it was "normal" for Sue to choose to form her own community. What would have been really rebellious (and difficult to justify) would have been for Sue to decide to never leave home and remain in her parents' home (see also Bellah et al. 1985: 58).

7   Frameworks for understanding action might, for instance, shape the way

that businesses are organized (Kakar 1981: 119; Roland 1988: 210; Haragopal and Prasad 1990). Because so many Indians like to be guided by superiors, many Indian businesses institutionalize the "active support, respect, and involvement of senior authority figures" in order to increase productivity (Roland 1988: 36).

# References

Abbott, Andrew 1988: Transcending general linear reality. *Sociological Theory*, 6, 169–86.

— 1990: Conceptions of time and events in social methods. *Historical Methods*, 23, 140–50.

Abu-Lughod, Lila 1993: *Writing Women's Worlds: Bedouin stories*. Berkeley: University of California Press.

Abzug, Rikki and Mezias, Stephen 1993: The fragmented state and due process protections in organizations: the case of comparable worth. *Organization Science*, 4, 433–53.

Adamson, Walter E. 1980: *Hegemony and Revolution: a study of Antonio Gramsci's political and cultural theory*. Berkeley: University of California Press.

Adler, Judith 1979: *Artists in Offices: the ethnography of an academic art scene*. New Brunswick, NJ: Transaction.

Adorno, Theodor 1984: *Aesthetic Theory*. Edited by Gretal Adorno and Rolf Tiedemann, translated by C. Lenhardt, London: Routledge.

— 1988: Commitment. In A. Arato and E. Gebhardt (eds), Francis McDonagh (trs), *The Essential Frankfurt School Reader*, New York: Continuum, 300–18.

Agnew, John A. 1989: The devaluation of place in social science. In John A. Agnew and James S. Duncan (eds), *The Power of Place*, Boston, MA: Unwin Hyman, 9–29.

Alexander, Jeffrey C. 1988a: Three models of culture and society relations: toward an analysis of Watergate. In Jeffrey C. Alexander (ed.), *Action and its Environments*, New York: Columbia University Press.

— 1988b: Culture and political crisis: 'Watergate' and Durkheimian sociology. In J. Alexander (ed.), *Durkheimian Sociology: cultural studies*. Cambridge, UK: Cambridge University Press, 187–224.

— 1988c: Introduction: Durkeimian sociology and cultural studies today. In J. Alexander (ed.), *Durkheimian Sociology: cultural studies*, Cambridge, UK: Cambridge University Press, 1–21.

— 1990: Analytic debates: understanding the relative autonomy of culture. In J. Alexander and S. Seidman (eds), *Culture and Society: contemporary debates*, Cambridge, UK/New York: Cambridge University Press, 1–29.

— 1992: General theory in the postpositivist mode: the 'Epistemological

Dilemma' and the search for present reason. In S. Seidman and D. G. Wagner (eds), *Postmodernism and Social Theory: the debate over general theory*, Cambridge, MA/Oxford: Blackwell, 322–68.

Alexander, Jeffrey C. and Seidman, Steve (eds) 1990: *Culture and Society: contemporary debates*. Cambridge, UK/New York: Cambridge University Press.

Alexander, Jeffrey C. and Smith, Philip 1993: The discourse of American civil society: a new proposal for cultural studies. *Theory and Society*, 22, 151–207.

Allen, Robert C. 1987: *Channels of Discourse: television and contemporary criticism*. Chapel Hill: University of North Carolina Press.

Almond, Gabriel and Verba, Sidney 1989 (1963): *The Civic Culture: political attitudes and democracy in five nations*. California: Sage.

Altheide, David L. and Johnson, John M. 1980: *Bureaucratic Propaganda*. Boston, MA: Allyn and Bacon.

Altheide, David L. and Snow, Robert P. 1991: *Media Worlds in the Postjournalism Era*. New York: Aldine.

Amburgey, Terry L. and Lippert, Paul G. 1989: Institutional determinants of strategy: the legitimation and diffusion of management buyouts. Manuscript, University of Wisconsin.

Aminzade, Ronald 1981: *Class, Politics, and Early Industrial Capitalism: a study of mid-nineteenth-century Toulouse, France*. Albany: SUNY Press.

— 1992: Time and historical sociology. *Sociological Methods and Research*, 20, 456–80.

Anderson, Benedict 1983: *Imagined Communities: the origin and spread of nationalism*. London: Verso.

Ang, Ien 1985: *Watching Dallas: soap opera and the melodramatic imagination*. Translated by Della Couling, London/New York: Methuen. (First published as *Het Geval Dallas* in 1982 by Uitgeverij SUA, Amsterdam.)

— 1991: *Desperately Seeking the Audience*. London/New York: Routledge.

Appadurai, Arjun 1986a: Is homo hierarchicus? *American Ethnologist*, 13, 745–61.

— 1986b: *The Social Life of Things*. New York: Cambridge University Press.

— 1988: How to make a national cuisine: cookbooks in contemporary India. *Comparative Studies in Society and History*, 30, 1–24.

Appleby, Joyce 1978: *Economic Thought and Ideology in Seventeenth-Century England*. Princeton: Princeton University Press.

Archer, Margaret S. 1985: The myth of cultural unity. *British Journal of Sociology*, 36, 333–53.

— 1988: *Culture and Agency: the place of culture in social theory*. New York: Cambridge University Press.

Argyris, Chris 1962: *Interpersonal Competence and Organizational Effectiveness*. Homewood, IL: Irwin.

Aronowitz, Stanley 1973: *False Promises*. New York: McGraw-Hill.

— 1988: *Science as Power*. Minneapolis: University of Minnesota Press.

— 1993: *Roll over Beethoven: the return of cultural strife*. Hanover, NH: Wesleyan University Press.

Ashcraft, Richard 1986: *Revolutionary Politics and Locke's Two Treatises of Government*. Princeton: Princeton University Press.

Baker, Jean 1983: *Affairs of Party*. Ithaca, NY: Cornell University Press.

Bakhtin, M. M. 1981: *The Dialogic Imagination*. Translated by Michael Holquist, Austin: University of Texas Press.

Balfe, Judith H. 1981: Social mobility and modern art: abstract expressionism and its generative audience. *Research in Social Movements, Conflict and Change*, 4, 235–51.

— (ed.) 1993: *Paying the Piper*. Urbana: University of Illinois Press.

Barley, Stephen R., Meyer, Gordon W. and Gash, Debra C. 1988: Cultures of culture: academics, practitioners and the pragmatics of normative control. *Administrative Science Quarterly*, 33, 24–57.

Barnes, Barry and Shapin, Steven 1979: *Natural Order*. Beverly Hills, CA: Sage.

Baron, James N., Jennings, P. Devereaux, and Dobbin, Frank R. 1988: Mission Control?: the development of personnel systems in US industry. *American Sociological Review*, 53, 497–514.

Baron, James N., Dobbin, Frank R. and Jennings, A. Deveraux 1986: War and peace: the evolution of modern personnel administration in US industry. *American Journal of Sociology*, 92, 350–83.

Barrett, Marvin 1978: *Rich News, Poor News*. New York: Crowell.

Barthes, Roland 1972a: *Critical essays*. Translated by Richard Howard, Evanston: Northwestern University Press.

— 1972b: *Mythologies*. Translated by Annette Lavers, New York: Hill and Wang.

— 1983: *The Fashion System*. New York: Hill and Wang.

Baudrillard, Jean 1988: *Jean Baudrillard: selected writings*. Edited by Mark Poster, Palo Alto: Stanford University Press.

Bauer, Catherine 1934: *Modern Housing*. Cambridge, MA: The Riverside Press.

Baughman, James L. 1992: *The Republic of Mass Culture*. Baltimore: Johns Hopkins University Press.

Baxandall, Michael 1985: *Patterns of Intention: on the historical explanation of pictures*. New Haven: Yale University Press.

Bayley, David H. 1976: *Forces of Order: policing modern Japan*. Berkeley: University of California Press.

Becker, Howard S. 1951: The professional dance musician and his audience. *American Journal of Sociology*, 57, 193–209.

— 1963: *The Outsiders: studies in the sociology of deviance*. London: Free Press.

— 1974: Art as collective action. *American Sociological Review*, 39, 767–76.

— 1982: *Art Worlds*. Berkeley: University of California Press.

Beisel, Nicola 1992: Constructing a shifting moral boundary: literature and obscenity in nineteenth century America. In Michèle Lamont and Marcel Fournier (eds), *Cultivating Differences: symbolic boundaries and the making of inequality*, Chicago: University of Chicago Press, 104–30.

— 1993: Censorship, the politics of interpretation, and the Victorian nude. *American Sociological Review*, 58, 145–62.

Bell, Daniel 1973: *The Coming of Post-Industrial Society*. New York: Basic Books.

— 1976: *The Cultural Contradictions of Capitalism*. New York: Basic Books.

Bellah, Robert N. 1970: *Beyond Belief*. New York: Harper and Row.

Bellah, Robert N., Madsen, Richard, Sullivan, William M., Swidler, Ann and Tipton, Steven M. 1985: *Habits of the Heart: individualism and commitment in American life*. Berkeley: University of California Press.

— 1991: *The Good Society*. New York: Knopf.

Benavot, Aaron, Cha, Yun-Kyung, Kamens, David, Meyer, John W. and Wong, Suk-Ying 1991: Knowledge for the masses: world models and national curricula, 1920–1986, *American Sociological Review*, 56, 85–100.

Bendix, Regina 1992: National sentiment in the enactment and discourse of Swiss political ritual. *American Ethnologist*, 19, 768–790.

Benedict, Ruth 1934: *Patterns of Culture*. New York: Houghton Mifflin.

Benevolo, Leonardo 1977: *History of Modern Architecture*. Cambridge, MA: MIT Press.

Bennett, H. Stith 1980: *On Becoming a Rock Musician*. Amherst: University of Massachusetts Press.

Bennett, Lynn 1983: *Dangerous Wives and Sacred Sisters: social and symbolic roles of high caste women in Nepal*. New York: Columbia University Press.

Bensman, Joseph and Lillienfeld, Robert 1991: *Craft and Consciousness*. New York: Wiley.

Berezin, Mabel 1991: The organization of political ideology: culture, state and theatre in fascist Italy. *American Sociological Review*, 56, 639–51.

— 1994a: Theatrical form and political meaning: state subsidized theater, ideology, and the language of style. *American Journal of Sociology*, 100, in press.

— 1994b: *Communities of Feeling: spectacle and politics in fascist Italy*. Manuscript, University of Pennsylvania, Department of Sociology.

Berger, Peter L. and Luckmann, Thomas 1966: *The Social Construction of Reality: a treatise in the sociology of knowledge*. New York: Doubleday.

Berreman, Gerald D. 1971: The Brahmannical view of caste. *Contributions to Indian Sociology* (n.s.), 5, 18–25.

— 1976: Social mobility and change in India's caste society. In George A. DeVos (ed.), *Responses to Change: society, culture and personality*, New York: D. Van Nostrand, 294–322.

Béteille, André 1983: *The Idea of Natural Inequality*. Delhi: Oxford University Press.

Betterton, Rosemary (ed.) 1987: *Looking On: images of femininity in the visual arts and media*. London/Westminster, MA: Pandora Press/Unwin Hyman.

Biggart, Nicole Woolsey 1989: *Charismatic Capitalism: direct selling organizations in America*. Chicago: University of Chicago Press.

Bijker, Wiebe E. and Pinch, Trevor 1987: The social construction of facts and artifacts: or how the sociology of science and the sociology of technology might benefit each other. In Wiebe E. Bijker, Thomas P. Hughes and Trevor Pinch (eds), *The Social Construction of Technological Systems*, Cambridge: MIT Press, 17–50.

Bijker, Wiebe E., Hughes, Thomas P. and Pinch, Trevor (eds) 1987: *The Social Construction of Technological Systems*. Cambridge, MA: MIT Press.

Bird, Elizabeth 1979: Aesthetic neutrality and the sociology of art. In Michèle Barrett, Philip Corrigan, Annette Kuhn, and Janet Wolff (eds), *Ideology and Cultural Production*. New York: St Martin's, 26–48.

Blau, Judith R. 1984: *Architects and Firms*. Cambridge, MA: MIT Press.

— 1988: Study of the arts: a reappraisal. *Annual Review of Sociology*, 14, 269–92.

Blau, Judith R., Land, Kenneth C., and Redding, Kent 1992: The expansion of religious affiliation: an explanation of the growth of church participation in the United States 1850–1930. *Social Science Research*, 21, 329–52.

Blau, Peter M. 1956: *Bureaucracy in Modern Society*. New York: Random House.

Blau, Peter M. and Schoenherr, Richard A. 1971: *The Structure of Organizations*. New York: Basic.

Bloor, David 1976: *Knowledge and Social Imagery*. New York: Routledge.

Blumer, Herbert 1969: *Symbolic Interactionism: perspective and method*. Berkeley: University of California Press.

Boden, Deirdre 1994: *The Business of Talk: organization in action*. Berkeley: University of California Press.

Bourdieu, Pierre 1977: *Outline of a Theory of Practice*. Cambridge, UK/New York: Cambridge University Press.

— 1984: *Distinction: a social critique of the judgement of taste*. Cambridge, MA: Harvard University Press.

— 1985: The social space and the genesis of groups. *Theory and Society*, 14, 723–44.

— 1988a: Flaubert's point of view. *Critical Inquiry*, 14, 539–62.

— 1988b (1984): *Homo Academicus*. Stanford, CA: Stanford University Press.

— 1989: *La noblesse d'état*. Paris: Les Editions de Minuit.

— 1990a (1965): *Photography: a middle-brow art*. Stanford, CA: Stanford University Press.

— 1990b: *In Other Words*. Stanford, CA: Stanford University Press.

— 1990c: *The Logic of Practice*. Stanford, CA: Stanford University Press.

— 1992a: *Les règles de l'art*. Paris: Seuil.

— 1992b: Commentary on the commentaries. *Contemporary Sociology*, 57, 158–61.

Bourdieu, Pierre and Wacquant, Loïc D. J. 1992: *An Invitation to Reflexive Sociology*. Chicago: University of Chicago Press.

Bowler, Anne 1991: Politics as art: Italian futurism and fascism. *Theory and Society*, 20, 763–94.

Brain, David 1989: Discipline and style: the Ecole des Beaux-Arts and the social production of an American architecture. *Theory and Society*, 18, 807–68.

— 1991: Practical knowledge and occupational control: the professionalization of architecture in the United States. *Sociological Forum*, 6, 239–68.

Braithwaite, John 1989: *Crime, Shame and Reintegration*. Cambridge, UK: Cambridge University Press.

Braudel, Fernand 1976: *Afterthoughts on Material Civilization and Capitalism*. Baltimore: Johns Hopkins University Press.

Braverman, Harry 1974: *Labour and Monopoly Capital: the degradation of work in the twentieth century*. New York: Monthly Review Press.

Breeskin, Adelyn 1970: *Mary Cassatt: a catalogue raissonné of the oils, pastels, watercolors, and drawings*. Washington, DC: Smithsonian Institution.

— 1979: *Mary Cassatt: a catalogue raissonné of the graphic work*. Washington, DC: Smithsonian Institution Press.

— 1981: Introduction. In *The Art of Mary Cassatt, 1844–1926*, exhibition catalog. Tokyo: Asahi Shimbun, unpaginated.

Brewer, John 1989: *The Sinews of Power*. Cambridge, UK: Cambridge University Press.

Brint, Steven 1992: Hidden meanings: cultural content and context in Harrison White's structural sociology. *Sociological Theory*, 10, 194–208.

Brown, Mary Ellen (ed.) 1990: *Television and Women's Culture: the politics of the popular*. London: Sage.

Brubaker, Rogers 1992: *Citizenship and Nationhood in France and Germany*. Cambridge, MA: Harvard University Press.

Buchmann, Marlis 1989: *The Script of Life in Modern Society: entry into adulthood in a changing world*. Chicago: University of Chicago Press.

Bullard, E. John 1972: *Mary Cassatt: oils and pastels*. Washington, DC/New York: National Gallery of Art and Watson-Guptill.

Burawoy, Michael 1979: *Manufacturing Consent: changes in the labour process under monopoly capitalism*. Chicago: University of Chicago Press.

Bürger, Peter 1984: *Theory of the Avant-Garde*. Translated by Michael Shaw, Minneapolis: University of Minnesota Press.

Burnett, Robert 1992: Concentration and diversity in the international phonogram industry. *Communication Research*, 19, 749–69.

Burnett, Robert and Weber, Robert Philip 1989: Concentration and diversity in the popular music industry 1948–1986. Paper presented at the annual meeting of the American Sociological Association, San Francisco.

Burns, Gene 1992: Commitments and non-commitments: the social radicalism of US Catholic bishops. *Theory and Society*, 21, 703–33.

Burstein, Paul 1985: *Discrimination, Jobs, and Politics: the struggle for equal employment opportunity in the United States since the New Deal*. Chicago: University of Chicago Press.

Calhoun, Craig 1982: *The Question of Class Struggle: social foundations of popular radicalism during the Industrial Revolution*. Chicago: University of Chicago Press.

— 1992a: Beyond the problem of meaning: Robert Wuthnow's historical sociology of culture. *Theory and Society*, 21, 419–44.

— 1992b: Culture, history, and the problem of specificity in social theory. In

S. Seidman and D. G. Wagner (eds), *Postmodernism and Social Theory: the debate over general theory*, Cambridge MA/Oxford: Blackwell, 244–88.

— 1993a: The rise and domestication of historical sociology. In Terrence McDonald (ed.), *The Historic Turn in the Human Sciences*, Ann Arbor: University of Michigan Press.

— 1993b: Civil society and the public sphere. *Public Culture*, 5, 267–80.

Callon, Michel 1986: Some elements of a sociology of translation: domestication of the scallops and the fishermen of St Brieuc Bay. In John Law (ed.), *Power, Action, and Belief. Sociological Review Monograph*, London: Routledge.

— 1987: Society in the making: the study of technology as a tool for sociological analysis. In Wiebe E. Bijker, Thomas P. Hughes and Trevor Pinch (eds), *The Social Construction of Technological Systems*. Cambridge, MA: MIT Press, 83–103.

Callon, Michel and Latour, Bruno 1992: Don't throw the baby out with the bath school! A reply to Collins and Yearley. In Andrew Pickering (ed.), *Science as Practice and Culture*, Chicago: University of Chicago Press, 343–68.

Campbell, Colin 1987: *The Romantic Ethnic and the Spirit of Modern Consumerism*. Oxford: Blackwell.

Cantor, Muriel G. 1987: Popular culture and the portrayal of women: content and control. In Beth B. Hess and Myra Ferree (eds), *Analyzing Gender: a handbook of social science research*, Beverly Hills, CA: Sage, 190–214.

Cantor, Muriel G. and Cantor, Joel 1992: *Prime-time Television: content and control*. Newbury Park, CA: Sage.

Cantor, Muriel G. and Pingree, Susanne 1983: *The Soap Opera*. Beverly Hills, CA: Sage.

Carnoy, Martin and Levine, Henry M. 1985: *Schooling and Work in the Democratic State*. Stanford, CA: Stanford University Press.

de Certeau, Michel 1984: *The Practice of Everyday Life*. Berkeley: University of California Press.

Chadwick, Whitney 1988: Women artists and the politics of representation. In A. Raven et al. (eds), *Feminist Art Criticism: an anthology*, New York: Icon Editions/HarperCollins, 167–85.

Chaffee, Steven H. and Yang, Seung-Mock 1990: Communication and political socialization. In Orit Ichilov (ed.), *Political Socialization, Citizen Education, and Democracy*, New York: Teachers College Press, 137–57.

Charle, Christophe 1990: *Naissance des 'intellectuels,' 1880–1900*. Paris: Les Editions de Minuit.

Chartier, Roger 1989: Texts, printing, readings. In L. Hunt (ed.), *The New Cultural History*, Berkeley: University of California Press, 154–75.

Clark, Burton. 1960: *The Open-Door Colleges: a case study*. New York: McGraw Hill.

Clifford, James 1986: Introduction: partial truths. In James Clifford and George Marcus (eds), *Writing Culture: the poetics and politics of ethnography*. Berkeley: University of California Press, 1–26.

— 1988: *The Predicament of Culture: twentieth-century ethnography, literature, and art.* Cambridge, MA: Harvard University Press.

Clifford, James and Marcus, George (eds) 1986: *Writing Culture: the poetics and politics of ethnography.* Berkeley: University of California Press.

Clignet, Remi 1985: *The Structure of Artistic Revolutions.* Philadelphia: University of Pennsylvania Press.

Cohen, Abner 1974: *Two Dimensional Man: an essay on the anthropology of power and symbolism in complex society.* Berkeley: University of California Press.

Cohen, Jean L. 1985: Strategy or identity: new theoretical paradigms and contemporary social movements. *Social Research,* 52, 663–716.

Cohen, Jean L. and Arato, Andrew 1992: *Civil Society and Political Theory.* Cambridge, MA: MIT Press.

Cole, Robert E. 1989: *Strategies for Learning: small-group activities in American, Japanese, and Swedish Industry.* Berkeley: University of California Press.

Coleman, James 1990: *Foundations of Social Theory.* Cambridge, MA: Belknap.

Collins, Harry M. 1982: Tacit knowledge and scientific networks. In Barry Barnes and David Edge (eds), *Science in Context,* Cambridge, MA: MIT Press.

Collins, Harry M. and Yearley, Steven 1992a: Epistemological chicken. In A. Pickering (ed.), *Science as Practice and Culture,* Chicago: University of Chicago Press.

— 1992b: Journey into space. In A. Pickering (ed.), *Science as Practice and Culture,* Chicago: University of Chicago Press.

Collins, Patricia C. 1992: Transforming the inner circle: Dorothy Smith's challenge to sociological theory. *Sociological Theory,* 10, 73–80.

Collins, Randall 1992: Women and the production of status cultures. In Michèle Lamont and Marcel Fournier (eds), *Cultivating Differences: symbolic boundaries and the making of inequality,* Chicago: University of Chicago Press, 213–31.

Comaroff, Jean and Comaroff, John 1991: *Of Revelation and Revolution: Christianity, colonialism, and consciousness in South Africa,* Vol. 1. Chicago: University of Chicago Press.

Comaroff, John and Comaroff, Jean 1992: *Ethnography and the Historical Imagination.* Boulder, CO: Westview Press.

Commons, John R. 1934: *Institutional Economics: its place in political economy.* New York: Macmillan.

Conzen, Kathleen Neils, Gerber, David A., Morawska, Ewa and Pozzetta, George 1992: The invention of ethnicity: A perspective from the USA. *Journal of American Ethnic History,* 12, 3–41.

Corrigan, Philip and Sayer, Derek 1985: *The Great Arch: English state formation as cultural revolution.* Oxford/New York: Blackwell.

Corsaro, William 1985: *Friendship and Peer Culture in the Early Years.* Norwood, NJ: Ablex Publishing.

Coser, Lewis A. 1978: Issue editor: the production of culture. *Social Research,* 45, 2.

— Kadushin, Charles and Powell, Walter W. 1981: *Books: the culture and commerce of publishing.* New York: Basic Books.

Cozzens, Susan 1993: SKAT and social theory. Address to the annual meetings of the American Sociological Association, Miami.

Crane, Diana 1972: *Invisible Colleges*. Chicago: University of Chicago Press.

— 1976: Reward systems in art, science, and religion. In Richard A. Peterson (ed.), *The Production of Culture*, Beverly Hills, CA: Sage, 57–72.

— 1987: *The Transformation of the Avant-Garde: the New York art world 1940–1985*. Chicago: University of Chicago Press.

— 1992a: *The Production of Culture: media and the urban arts*. Newbury Park, CA: Sage.

— 1992b: High culture versus popular culture revisited: a reconceptualization of recorded cultures. In Michèle Lamont and Marcel Fournier (eds), *Cultivating Differences: symbolic boundaries and the making of inequality*, Chicago: University of Chicago Press, 58–73.

Creighton, Andrew 1990: The Emergence of Incorporation: standardization and growth in the nineteenth century. PhD dissertation, Department of Sociology, Stanford University.

Cruz, Jon 1994: Testimonies and artifacts: elite appropriations of African-American music in the nineteenth century. In Jon Cruz and Justin Lewis (eds), *Viewing, Reading, Listening: audiences and cultural reception*, Boulder, Colorado: Westview Press.

Csikszentmihalyi, Mihalyi and Rochberg-Halton, Eugene 1981: *The Meaning of Things*. New York: Cambridge University Press.

Dalton, Melville 1950: Conflicts between staff and line managerial officers. *American Sociological Review*, 15, 342–51.

D'Andrade, Roy G. 1984: Cultural meaning systems. In Richard A. Shweder and Robert A. Levine (eds), *Culture Theory: essays on mind, self and emotion*, Cambridge, UK: Cambridge University Press, 89–119.

Daniel, E. Valentine 1984: *Fluid Signs: being a person the Tamil way*. Berkeley: University of California Press.

Davis, F. James 1991: *Who is Black?: one nation's definition*. University Park, PA: Pennsylvania State University Press.

Davis, Gerald F. and Powell, Walter W. 1992: Organization–environment relations. In *Handbook of Industrial and Organizational Psychology*. Vol. 3, (2nd edn), New York: Consulting Psychologists Press, 315–75.

Davis-Blake, Alison and Uzzi, Brian 1993: Determinants of employment externalization: a study of temporary workers and independent contractors. *Administrative Science Quarterly*, 38, 195–223.

Dayan, Daniel and Katz, Elihu 1992: *Media Events: the live broadcasting of history*. Cambridge, MA: Harvard University Press.

Deal, Terrence and Kennedy, Allan 1982: *Corporate Cultures*. Reading, MA: Addison-Wesley.

Delli Carpini, Michael X. and Williams, Bruce A. forthcoming: Methods, metaphors, and media messages: the uses of television in conversations about the environment. In Ann N. Crigler (ed.), *Political Communication and Public Understanding*, Cambridge, UK: Cambridge University Press.

Denisoff, R. S. 1975: *Solid Gold*. New Brunswick, NJ: Transaction.

Denzin, Norman K. 1990: Reading cultural texts: comment on Griswold. *American Journal of Sociology*, 95, 1,577–80.

— 1991: *Images of Postmodern Society: social theory and contemporary cinema*. Newbury Park, CA: Sage.

— 1992: *Symbolic Interactionism and Cultural Studies*. Cambridge, MA/Oxford: Blackwell, 1992.

Derné, Steve n.d.: Culture in action: family, gender and emotions in North India. Unpublished manuscript.

— 1991: Purifying movements and syncretic religious movements: religious changes and the 19th century Munda and Santal peasant revolts. *Man in India*, 71, 139–50.

— 1992a: Beyond institutional and impulsive conceptions of self: family structure and the socially anchored real self. *Ethos*, 20, 259–88.

— 1992b: Commonsense understandings as cultural constraint. *Contributions to Indian Sociology* (n.s.) 26, 195–221.

— 1992c: Hindu men's languages of social pressure and individualism: the diversity of South Asian ethnopsychologies. *International Journal of Indian Studies*, 2, 40–71.

— 1993: Equality and hierarchy between adult brothers: culture and sibling relations in North Indian joint families. In Charles Nuckolls (ed.), *Siblings in South Asia*, New York: Guilford, 165–89.

— 1994a: Violating the Hindu norm of husband–wife avoidance. *Journal of Comparative Family Studies*, 25.

— 1994b: Arranging marriages: how fathers' concerns limit women's educational achievements. In Susan Seymour and Carol Mukhopadhyay (eds), *Women, Education and Family Structure in India*, Boulder, CO: Westview.

Deyo, Frederic (ed.) 1987: *The Political Economy of the New Asian Industrialism*. Ithaca: Cornell University Press.

DiMaggio, Paul 1982: Cultural entrepreneurship in nineteenth century Boston, Parts I and II. *Media, Culture and Society*, 4, 33–50, 303–22.

— 1987: Classification in art. *American Sociological Review*, 52, 440–55.

— 1988: Interest and agency in institutional theory. In Lynne G. Zucker (ed.), *Institutional Patterns and Organizations: culture and environment*. Cambridge, MA: Ballinger, 3–22.

— 1991a: Social structure, institutions, and cultural goods: the case of the United States. In Pierre Bourdieu and James S. Coleman (eds), *Social Theory for a Changing Society*, Boulder, CO: Westview Press and Russell Sage Foundation, 133–55.

— 1991b: Constructing an organizational field as a professional project: US art museums, 1920–1940. In Walter W. Powell and Paul J. DiMaggio (eds), *The New Institutionalism in Organizational Analysis*, Chicago: University of Chicago Press, 267–92.

— 1992: Cultural boundaries and structural change: the extension of the high culture model to theater, opera, and the dance, 1900–1940. In Michèle Lamont and Marcel Fournier (eds), *Cultivating Differences: symbolic boundaries and the making of inequality*, Chicago: University of Chicago Press, 21–57.

DiMaggio, Paul and Powell, Walter W. 1983: The iron cage revisited: institutionalized isomorphism and collective rationality in organizational fields. *American Sociological Review*, 48, 147–60.

— 1991: Introduction. In Walter W. Powell and Paul J. DiMaggio (eds), *The New Institutionalism in Organizational Analysis*, Chicago: University of Chicago Press, 1–40.

DiMaggio, Paul and Stenberg, Kristen 1985: Conformity and diversity in the American resident stage. In Judith Balfe and Margaret Wyszomirski (eds), *Art, Ideology, and Politics*, New York: Praeger, 116–39.

Dobbin, Frank 1992: The origins of private social insurance: public policy and fringe benefits in America, 1920–1950. *American Journal of Sociology*, 97, 1416–50.

— 1994: *Forging Industrial Policy: the United States, France, and Britain in the railway age*. New York: Cambridge University Press.

Dobbin, Frank, Sutton, John, Meyer, John and Scott, W. Richard 1993: Formal promotion schemes and equal employment opportunity law: the institutional construction of internal labor markets. *American Journal of Sociology*, 99, 396–427.

Dobbin, Frank, Edelman, Lauren, Meyer, John W., Scott, W. Richard and Swidler, Ann 1988: The expansion of due process in organizations. In Lynne G. Zucker (ed.), *Institutional Patterns and Organizations: culture and environment*, Cambridge, MA: Ballinger, 71–100.

Douglas, Mary 1982: Introduction to grid/group analysis. In Mary Douglas (ed.), *Essays in the Sociology of Perception*, London: Routledge, 1–8.

— 1986: *How Institutions Think*. Syracuse, NY: Syracuse University Press.

— 1991: Jokes. In C. Mukerji and M. Schudson (eds), *Rethinking Popular Culture*, Berkeley: University of California Press.

Douglas, Mary and Isherwood, Baron 1979: *The World of Goods*. New York: Basic Books.

Dubin, Steven C. 1992: *Arresting Images: impolitic art and uncivil actions*. New York: Routledge.

Dumont, Louis 1980 (1966): *Homo Hierarchicus: the caste system and its implications*. Translated by Mark Sainsbury, Louis Dumont, and Basia Gulati, Chicago: University of Chicago Press.

Durbin, P. and Mitcham, C. (eds), 1978: *Research in Philosophy and Technology*. Greenwich CT: JAI Press.

Durkheim, Emile 1915: *The Elementary Forms of the Religious Life*. New York: Macmillan.

— 1933: *The Division of Labour in Society*. New York: Macmillan.

Dyson, Kenneth 1983: The cultural, ideological and structural context. In Kenneth Dyson and Stephen Wilks (eds), *Industrial Crisis: a comparative study of the state and industry*. Oxford: Martin Robinson, 26–66.

Eagleton, Terry 1990: *The Ideology of the Aesthetic*. Oxford/Cambridge, MA: Blackwell.

Eco, Umberto 1990: *The Limits of Interpretation*. Bloomington: Indiana University Press.

Edelman, Lauren 1990: Legal environments and organizational governance: the expansion of due process in the American workplace. *American Journal of Sociology*, 95, 1,401–40.

— 1992: Legal ambiguity and symbolic structures: organizational mediation of civil rights law. *American Journal of Sociology*, 97, 1,531–76.

Edelman, Lauren and Petterson, Stephen 1993: Symbols and substance in organizational response to civil rights law. Paper presented at annual meeting of the American Sociological Association, Miami.

Edwards, Richard 1979: *Contested Terrain*. New York: Basic.

Eisenstein, Elizabeth 1979: *The Printing Press as an Agent of Change*. New York: Cambridge University Press.

Elias, Norbert 1978–82 (English transl.; German orig. 1939): *The Civilizing Process*, two volumes: Vol. 1 *The History of Manners*. Oxford/New York: Blackwell; Vol. 2 *Power and Civility*. Oxford/New York: Blackwell.

Ennis, Philip H. 1992: *The Seventh Stream: the emergence of rock n' roll*. Hanover, NH: Wesleyan University Press.

Ericson, Richard V., Baranek, Patricia M. and Chan, Janet B. L. 1987: *Visualizing Deviance: a study of news organization*. Toronto: University of Toronto Press.

Esaisson, Peter 1992: Scandinavia. In David Butler and Austin Ranney (eds), *Electioneering: a comparative study of continuity and change*, Oxford: Clarendon Press, 202–21.

Esherick, Joseph W. and Wasserstrom, Jeffrey N. 1990: Acting out democracy: political theatre in modern China. *Journal of Asian Studies*, 49, 835–66.

Ewing, Katherine P. 1991: Can psychoanalytic theories explain the Pakistani woman?: intrapsychic autonomy and interpersonal engagement in the extended family. *Ethos*, 19, 131–60.

Faulkner, Robert R. 1983: *Music on Demand: composers and careers in the Hollywood film industry*. New Brunswick, NJ: Transaction.

Fayol, Henri 1949 (1919): *General and Industrial Management*. Translated by Constance Stours, London: Pitman.

Featherstone, Mike 1992: *Consumer Culture and Postmodernism*. Newbury Park, CA: Sage.

Feenberg, Andrew 1991: *Critical Theory of Technology*. New York: Oxford.

Fine, Gary Alan 1979: Small groups and culture creation: the ideoculture of Little League baseball teams. *American Sociological Review*, 44, 733–45.

— 1983: *Shared Fantasy: role-playing games as social worlds*. Chicago: University of Chicago Press.

— 1987: *With the Boys: little league baseball and pre-adolescent culture*. Chicago: University of Chicago Press.

— 1992: The culture of production: aesthetic choices and constraints in culinary work. *American Journal of Sociology*, 97, 1,268–94.

Finer, Samuel E. 1975: State- and nation-building in Europe: the role of the military. In Charles Tilly (ed.), *The Formation of National States in Western Europe*, Princeton: Princeton University Press.

Finke, Roger and Stark, Rodney 1992: *The Churching of America: winners and losers in our religious economy*. New Brunswick, NJ: Rutgers University Press.

Fischer, Claude 1992: *America Calling*. Berkeley: University of California Press.

Fish, Stanley 1980: *Is There a Text in This Class?: the authority of interpretive communities*. Cambridge, MA: Harvard University Press.

Fiske, John 1987: *Television Culture*. London: Methuen.

— 1989: British cultural studies and television. In R. C. Allen (ed.), *Channels of Discourse*, London: Routledge, 254–89.

Fligstein, Neil 1985: The spread of the multidivisional form among large organizations, 1919–1979. *American Sociological Review*, 50, 377–91.

— 1990: *The Transformation of Corporate Control*. Cambridge, MA: Harvard University Press.

Foucault, Michel 1970: *The Order of Things*. New York: Vintage.

— 1972: *The Archaeology of Knowledge*. New York: Harper.

— 1977: Two Lectures. In Leo Marshall, John Mepham, Kate Soper, Colin Gordon (eds), *Power/Knowledge: selected interviews and other writings 1972–1977*. New York: Pantheon Books, 78–108.

— 1978: *Human Sexuality*. New York: Pantheon.

— 1979: *Discipline and Punish*. New York: Vintage.

— 1980: *The History of Sexuality*, Vol. I. Translated by Robert Hurley, New York: Vintage.

— 1984: *The Foucault Reader*. Edited by P. Rabinow, New York: Pantheon.

Freedberg, David 1989: *The Power of Images*. Chicago: University of Chicago Press.

Freilich, Morris (ed.) 1989: *The Relevance of Culture*. New York: Bregen and Garvey.

Friedland, Roger and Alford, Robert 1991: Bringing society back in. In Walter W. Powell and Paul J. DiMaggio (eds), *The New Institutionalism in Organizational Analysis*, Chicago: University of Chicago Press, 232–66.

Friedlander, Saul (ed.) 1992: *Probing the Limits of Representation: Nazism and the 'final solution'*. Cambridge, MA: Harvard University Press.

Frith, Simon 1983: *Sound Effects: youth, leisure and the politics of rock'n' roll*. London: Constable.

— 1992: The industrialization of popular music. In James Lull (ed.), *Music and Communication*, Newbury Park, CA: Sage, 49–74.

Frith, Simon and Horne, Howard 1987: *Art into Pop*. London: Methuen.

Fulbrook, Mary 1983: *Piety and Politics: religion and the rise of absolutism in England, Würtemberg, and Prussia*. Cambridge/New York: Cambridge University Press.

Fuller, Bruce and Rubinson, Richard (eds), 1992: *The Political Construction of Education*. New York: Praeger.

Gamson, William A. *et al.* 1992: Media images and the social construction of reality. *Annual Review of Sociology*, 18, 373–93.

Gamson, William A. and Modigliani, A. 1989: Media discourse and public opinion: a constructionist approach. *American Journal of Sociology*, 95, 1–37.

Gans, Herbert J. 1974: *Popular Culture and High Culture*. New York: Basic Books.

— 1979: *Deciding What's News*. New York: Pantheon.

— 1985: American popular culture and high culture in a changing class structure. *Annual of American Cultural Studies*, 10, 17–37.

Garfinkel, Harold 1967: *Studies in Ethnomethodology*. Englewood Cliffs, NJ: Prentice-Hall.

Garfinkel, Harold, Lynch, M. and Livingston, E. 1981: The work of discovering science construed with materials from the optically discovered pulsar. *Philosophy of the Social Sciences*, 11, 131–58.

Garnham, Nicholas 1986: Contribution to a political economy of mass-communication. In Richard Collins (ed.), *Media, Culture and Society: a critical reader*, London: Sage, 9–32.

Gates, Henry Louis (ed.) 1986: *"Race," Writing and Difference*. Chicago: University of Chicago Press.

Geertz, Clifford 1968: *Islam Observed: religious development in Morocco and Indonesia*. New Haven: Yale University Press.

— 1973: *The Interpretation of Cultures*. New York: Basic.

— 1975: Common sense as a cultural system. *Antioch Review*, 33, 5–26.

— 1980: *Negara: the theatre-state in nineteenth century Bali*. Princeton: Princeton University Press.

— 1983 (1977): *Local knowledge: further essays in interpretive anthropology*. New York: Basic.

Gellner, Ernest 1983: *Nations and Nationalism*. Ithaca, NY: Cornell University Press.

George, Nelson 1988: *The Death of Rhythm and Blues*. New York: Pantheon.

Giddens, Anthony 1976: *New Rules of Sociological Method: a positive critique of interpretive sociologies*. New York: Basic Books.

— 1983: *A Contemporary Critique of Historical Materialism*. Berkeley: University of California Press.

— 1984: *The Constitution of Society: outline of a theory of structuration*. Berkeley: University of California Press.

— 1987: Structuralism, post-structuralism, and the production of culture. In Anthony Giddens and Ralph Turner (eds), *Social Theory Today*, Stanford, CA: University of Stanford Press, 195–223.

— 1990: *The Consequences of Modernity*. Stanford, CA: Stanford University Press.

Gilbert, Nigel and Mulkay, Michael 1984: *Opening Pandora's Box*. Cambridge/New York: Cambridge University Press.

Gilligan, Carol 1982: *In a Different Voice: psychological theory and women's development*. Cambridge, MA: Harvard University Press.

Gilmore, Samuel 1987: Coordination and convention: the organization of the concert art world. *Symbolic Interaction*, 10, 209–27.

— 1988: Schools of activity and innovation. *Sociological Quarterly*, 29, 202–19.

Gilmore, William J. 1989: *Reading Becomes a Necessity of Life*. Knoxville: University of Tennessee Press.

Ginsberg, Benjamin 1986: *The Captive Public*. New York: Basic Books.

Gitlin, Todd 1978: Media sociology: the dominant paradigm. *Theory and Society*, 6 (1), 205–54.

— 1980: *The Whole World is Watching*: mass media in the making and unmaking of the New Left. Berkeley: University of California Press.

— 1983: *Inside Prime Time*. New York: Pantheon.

Goffman, Erving 1971: *Relations in Public: microstudies of the public order*. New York: Harper and Row.

— 1974: *Frame Analysis: an essay on the organization of experience*. New York: Harper and Row.

Goldfarb, Jeffrey C. n.d.: Classical sociological theory and the sociology of the arts. Unpublished paper, Department of Sociology, The Graduate Faculty, New School for Social Research.

— 1982: *On Cultural Freedom: an exploration of public life in Poland and America*. Chicago: University of Chicago Press.

— 1985: Sociology, democracy and the arts: a critique of Herbert Gans's and Howard Becker's sociology of culture. Paper presented at the annual meeting of the Social Theory, Politics, and the Arts Conference.

— 1989: *Beyond Glasnost: the post-totalitarian mind*. Chicago: University of Chicago Press.

— 1991: *The Cynical Society: the culture of politics and the politics of culture in American life*. Chicago: University of Chicago Press.

— 1992: *After the Fall: the pursuit of democracy in Central Europe*. New York: Basic.

Goldstone, Jack 1991: *Revolution and Rebellion in the Early Modern World*. Berkeley: University of California Press.

Gombrich, E. H. 1984: *The Story of Art*, fourteenth edn. Englewood Cliffs, NJ: Prentice-Hall.

Goodwin, Andrew 1992: Rationalization and democratization in the new technologies of popular music. In James Lull (ed.), *Music and Communication*, Newbury Park, CA: Sage, 75–100.

Goody, Jack 1977: *The Domestication of the Savage Mind*. Cambridge, UK: Cambridge University Press.

Goudsblom, Johan 1967: *Dutch Society*. New York: Random House.

Gould, Stephen Jay 1989: *Wonderful Life: the Burgess shale and the nature of history*. New York: Norton.

Gouldner, Alvin W. 1954: *Wildcat Strike*. Yellow Springs, OH: Antioch Press.

— 1959: Organizational analysis. In Robert K. Merton, Leonard Broom, and Leonard S. Cottrell, Jr (eds), *Sociology Today*. New York: Basic, 400–28.

— 1976: *The Dialectic of Ideology and Technology*. New York: Seabury.

Gramsci, Antonio 1971: *Selections from the Prison Notebooks*. New York: International Press.

Granovetter, Mark 1985: Economic action and social structure: the problem of embeddedness. *American Journal of Sociology*, 91, 481–510.

Gray, Jack 1977: Conclusions. In Archie G. Brown and Jack Gray, (eds), *Political Culture and Political Change in Communist States*. New York: Holmes and Meier, 253–72.

Greenfeld, Liah 1989: *Different Worlds*. New York: Cambridge University Press.

— 1992: *Nationalism: five roads to modernity*. Cambridge, MA: Harvard University Press.

Griswold, Wendy 1981: American character and the American novel. *American Journal of Sociology*, 86, 740–65.

— 1986: *Renaissance Revivals: city comedy and revenge tragedy in the London theatre 1576–1980*. Chicago: University of Chicago Press.

— 1987a: The fabrication of meaning: literary interpretation in the United States, Great Britain, and the West Indies. *American Journal of Sociology*, 92: 1,077–117.

— 1987b: A methodological framework for the sociology of culture. *Sociological Methodology*, by Clifford Clogg (ed.). American Sociological Association, 14, 1–35.

— 1990: Provisional, provincial positivism: reply to Denzen. *American Journal of Sociology*, 95, 1,580–3.

— 1992a: Mushroom in the rain: the uses of culture in comparative and historical sociology, *Newsletter of the Sociology of Culture Section of the American Sociological Association*, 7, 9–12.

— 1992b: The writing on the mud wall: Nigerian novels and the imaginary village. *American Sociological Review*, 57, 709–24.

— 1993: Recent moves in the sociology of literature. *Annual Review of Sociology*, 19, 455–67.

Grossberg, Lawrence 1992: Rock and roll in search of an audience. In James Lull (ed.), *Music and Communication*. Newbury Park, CA: Sage, 152–75.

Gupta, Akhil 1992: The song of the nonaligned world: transnational identities and the reinscription of space in late capitalism. *Cultural Anthropology*, 7, 63–79.

Gupta, Akhil and Ferguson, James 1992: Beyond culture: space, identity, and the politics of difference. *Cultural Anthropology*, 7, 6–23.

Gusfield, Joseph R. 1963: *Symbolic Crusade: status politics and the American temperance movement*. Urbana, IL: University of Illinois Press.

Habermas, Jürgen 1970: *Toward a Rational Society*. Boston, MA: Beacon.

— 1975: *Legitimation Crisis*. Boston, MA: Beacon.

— 1981: Modernity versus postmodernity. *New German Critique*, 22, 3–14.

— 1984 (1981): *Theory of Communicative Action, Vol 1: reason and the rationalisation of society*. Translated by Thomas McCarthy, Boston: Beacon.

— 1989 (1962): *The Structural Transformation of the Public Sphere*. Cambridge, MA: MIT Press.

Hacking, Ian 1983: *Representing and Intervening*. Cambridge, UK: Cambridge University Press.

Hagstrom, Warren 1965: *The Scientific Community*. New York: Basic Books.

Halbwachs, Maurice 1992 (1941, 1952): *On Collective Memory*. Chicago: University of Chicago Press.

Hall, John A. 1988: States and societies: the miracle in comparative perspective. In J. Baechler, J. A. Hall and M. Mann (eds), *Europe and the Rise of Capitalism*, Oxford/New York: Blackwell, 20–38.

Hall, John R. 1987: *Gone from the Promised Land: Jonestown in American cultural history*. New Brunswick, NJ: Transaction.

— 1990a: Social interaction, culture, and historical studies. In H. Becker and M. McCall (eds), *Symbolic Interaction and Cultural Studies*. Chicago: University of Chicago Press, 16–45.

— 1990b: Epistemology and sociohistorical inquiry. *Annual Review of Sociology*, 16, 329–52.

Hall, John R. and Neitz, Mary Jo 1993: *Culture: sociological perspectives*. Englewood Cliffs, NJ: Prentice Hall.

Hall, Peter A. 1993: Policy paradigms, social learning and the state: the case of economic policy-making in Britain. *Comparative Politics*, 26, 275–96.

Hall, Stewart 1980: Cultural studies: two paradigms. In *Media, Culture and Society*, 2, 52–72.

— 1992: Cultural studies and its theoretical legacy. In L. Grossberg et al. (eds), *Cultural Studies*, New York/London: Routledge, 227–86.

Hall, Stewart and Jefferson, Tony (eds) 1976: *Resistance Through Rituals: youth subcultures in post-war Britain*. London: Hutchinson.

Hall, Stewart, Critcher, C., Jefferson, T., Clarke, J. and Roberts, B. 1978: *Policing the Crisis: the state and law and order*. London: MacMillan.

Halle, David 1984: *America's Working Man: work, home, and politics among blue-collar property owners*. Chicago/London: The University of Chicago Press.

— 1989: Class and culture in modern America: the vision of the landscape in the residences of contemporary Americans. In Jack Salzman (ed.), *Prospects: An annual of American cultural studies*, New York: Cambridge University Press, 373–406.

— 1991a: Bringing materialism back in: art in the houses of the working and middle classes. In Scott McNall, Rhonda F. Levine, and Rick Fantasia (eds), *Bringing Class Back In: contemporary and historical perspectives*, Boulder, CO: Westview Press, 241–59.

— 1991b: Displaying the dream: the visual presentation of family and self in the modern American household. *Journal of Comparative Family Studies*, 22 (2), 217–29.

— 1992: The audience for abstract art: class, culture, and power. In M. Lamont and M. Fournier (eds), *Cultivating Differences: symbolic boundaries and the making of inequality*, Chicago: University of Chicago Press, 131–51.

— 1994: *Inside Culture: class, culture, and everyday life in modern America*. Chicago: University of Chicago Press.

Hallin, Daniel C. 1986: *The Uncensored War: the media and Vietnam*. New York: Oxford University Press.

Hamilton, Gary G. and Biggart, Nicole Woolsey 1988: Market, culture, and authority: a comparative analysis of management and organization in the Far East. *American Journal of Sociology*, 94, 552–94.

Hammersley, Martyn 1992: *What's Wrong with Ethnography? methodological explorations*. New York/London: Routledge.

Hannan, Michael T. and Freeman, John 1977: The population ecology of organizations. *American Journal of Sociology*, 82, 929–64.

— 1989: *Organizational Ecology*. Cambridge, MA: Harvard University Press.

Hannerz, Ulf 1987: The world in creolisation. *Africa*, 57, 549–55.

Haragopal, G. and Prasad, V. S. 1990: Social bases of administrative culture in India. *Indian Journal of Public Administration*, 36, 384–97.

Haraway, Donna 1989: *Primate Visions*. New York: Routledge.

— 1991: *Simians, Cyborgs, and Women*. New York: Routledge.

Harris, Ann Sutherland and Nochlin, Linda 1976: *Women Artists: 1850–1950*. Los Angeles/New York: LA County Museum of Art/Alfred A. Knopf.

Harvey, David 1989: *The Condition of Postmodernity: an enquiry into the origins of cultural change*. Cambridge, MA: Blackwell.

Hauser, Arnold 1951: *Social History of Art*. New York: Vintage.

Hayles, N. Katherine 1991: *Chaos and Order: complex dynamics in literature and science*. Chicago: University of Chicago Press.

Hebdige, Dick 1979: *Subculture: the meaning of style*. London: Methuen.

Hechter, Michael 1975: *Internal Colonialism*. Berkeley: University of California Press.

— 1989: Rational choice foundations of social order. In Jonathan H. Turner (ed.), *Theory Building in Sociology: assessing theoretical cumulation*, Newbury Park: Sage, 60–81.

Heelas, Paul 1981a: Introduction: indigenous psychologies. In Paul Heelas and Andrew Lock (eds), *Indigenous Psychologies: the anthropology of the self*, New York: Academic Press, 3–18.

— 1981b: The model applied: anthropology and indigenous psychologies. In Paul Heelas and Andrew Lock (eds), *Indigenous Psychologies: the anthropology of the self*, New York: Academic Press, 39–64.

Heelas, Paul and Lock, Andrew (eds) 1981. *Indigenous Psychologies: the anthropology of the self*. New York: Academic Press.

Heirich, Max 1976: Cultural breakthroughs. In Richard A. Peterson (ed.), *The Production of Culture*, Beverly Hills, CA: Sage, 23–40.

Hempel, C. 1966: *Philosophy of Natural Science*. Englewood Cliffs: Prentice-Hall.

Henderson, Katherine 1991: On line and on paper. Dissertation, Sociology, University of California, San Diego.

Heritage, John 1984: *Garfinkel and Ethnomethodology*. Cambridge, UK: Polity Press.

Hewitt, John 1989: *Dilemmas of the American Self*. Philadelphia: Temple University Press.

Hirsch, Paul 1972: Processing fads and fashions: an organization set analysis of the cultural industry system. *American Journal of Sociology*, 77, 639–59.

— 1991: Undoing the managerial revolution? Needed research on the decline of middle management and internal labour markets. Paper presented at the annual meeting of the American Sociological Association, Cincinnati.

Hirschman, Albert O. 1977: *The Passions and the Interests: political arguments for capitalism before its triumph*. Princeton: Princeton University Press.

Hoare, Quintin and Nowell Smith, Geoffrey (eds), 1971: *Selections from the Prison Notebooks*. New York: International Publishers.

Hobsbawm, Eric J. 1968: *Industry and Empire*. New York: Pantheon.

— 1983: Introduction: inventing traditions; mass-producing traditions: Europe, 1870–1914. In Eric Hobsbawm and Terence Ranger (eds), *The Invention of Tradition*, Cambridge, UK: Cambridge University Press, 1–14.

— 1990: *Nations and Nationalism Since 1780*. Cambridge, UK: Cambridge University Press.

Hobsbawm, Eric J. and Ranger, Terence (eds) 1983: *The Invention of Tradition*. Cambridge, UK: Cambridge University Press.

Hoggart, Richard 1992 (1959): *The Uses of Literacy*. New Brunswick: Transaction.

Holland, Dorothy C. and Eisenhart, Margaret A. 1990: *Educated in Romance: women, achievement, and college culture*. Chicago: University of Chicago Press.

Holland, Norman N. 1975: *5 Readers Reading*. New Haven: Yale University Press.

Holub, Robert C. 1984: *Reception Theory: a critical introduction*. London and New York: Methuen.

Honneth, Alex, Kocyba, Hermann, and Schwibs, Bernard 1986: The struggle for symbolic order: an interview with Pierre Bourdieu. *Theory, Culture & Society*, 3, 35–51.

Hourani, Albert 1991: *A History of the Arab Peoples*. Cambridge: Harvard University Press.

Hughes, Michael and Peterson, Richard A. 1983: Isolating cultural choice patterns in the US population. *American Behavioral Scientist*, 26, 459–78.

Hunt, Lynn 1984: *Politics, Culture and Class in the French Revolution*. Berkeley: University of California Press.

— 1989a: Introduction: history, culture, and text. in L. Hunt (ed.), *The New Cultural History*. Berkeley: University of California Press, 1–24.

— (ed.) 1989b: *The New Cultural History*. Berkeley: University of California Press.

— 1992: *The Family Romance of the French Revolution*. Berkeley: University of California Press.

Hunter, James Davison 1991: *Culture Wars: the struggle to define America*. New York: Basic.

Iannaccone, Laurence R. 1991: The consequences of religious market structure. *Rationality and Society*, 3, 156–77.

Inglehart, Ronald 1990: *Culture Shift in Advanced Industrial Society*. Princeton: Princeton University Press.

Isaac, Larry and Griffin, Larry 1989: Ahistoricism in time-series analysis of historical process: critique, redirection, and illustrations from US labour history. *American Sociological Review*, 54, 873–90.

Iser, Wolfgang 1978: *The Act of Reading: a theory of aesthetic response.* Baltimore: Johns Hopkins University Press.

Jadwin, Lisa 1992: The seductiveness of female duplicity in *Vanity Fair. Studies in English Literature*, 32, 663–87.

Jameson, Fredric 1981: *The Political Unconscious: narrative as a socially symbolic act.* Ithaca, NY: Cornell University Press.

Janson, H. W. 1986: *The History of Art*, 3rd edn. New York and Englewood Cliffs, NJ: H. N. Abrams and Prentice-Hall.

Jasper, James and Nelkin, Dorothy 1992: *The Animal Rights Crusade: the growth of a moral protest.* New York: The Free Press.

Jauss, Hans Robert 1982: *Toward an Aesthetic of Reception.* Minneapolis: University of Minnesota Press.

Jepperson, Ronald 1991: Institutions, institutional effects, and institutionalism. In Walter W. Powell and Paul J. DiMaggio (eds), *The New Institutionalism in Organizational Analysis*, Chicago: University of Chicago Press, 143–63.

Jepperson, Ronald and Meyer, John W. 1991: The public order and the construction of formal organizations. In Walter W. Powell and Paul J. DiMaggio (eds), *The New Institutionalism in Organizational Analysis*, Chicago: University of Chicago Press, 204–31.

Johansson, Thomas and Miegel, Fredrick 1992: *Do the Right Thing: lifestyle and identity in contemporary youth culture.* Stockholm: Almquist and Wiksell.

Jordy, William 1963: The symbolic essence of modern European architecture of the twenties and its continuing influence. *Journal of the Society of Architectural Historians* XXII, 3, 177–87.

Juergensmeyer, Mark 1982: *Religion as Social Vision: the movement against untouchability in 20th Century Punjab.* Berkeley: University of California Press.

Kakar, Sudhir 1981: *The Inner World: a psycho-analytic study of childhood and society in India*, 2nd edn. Delhi: Oxford University Press.

Kanter, Rosabeth Moss 1979: *Men and Women of the Corporation.* New York: Basic Books.

Kastner, Alfred 1938: The architect's place in current housing. In *Housing Yearbook.* Chicago: National Association of Housing Officials, 225–36.

Katz, Elihu and Lazarsfeld, Paul 1955: *Personal Influence: the part played by people in the flow of mass communications.* Glencoe, IL: Free Press.

Kealy, Edward R. 1979: From craft to art: the case of sound mixers and popular music. *Work and Occupations*, 6, 3–29.

Keil, Charles 1966: *Urban Blues.* Chicago: University of Chicago Press.

Kellner, Douglas 1990a: The postmodern turn: positions, problems, and prospects. In G. Ritzer (ed.), *Frontiers of Social Theory: the new synthesis*, New York: Columbia University Press, 255–86.

— 1990b: *Television and the Crisis of Democracy.* Boulder, CO: Westview.

Kertzer, David 1988: *Ritual, Politics, and Power.* New Haven: Yale University Press.

Khare, Ravindra S. 1984: *The Untouchable as Himself: ideology, identity and pragmatism among the Lucknow Chamars.* New York: Cambridge University Press.

Khoury, Philip S. 1991: Continuity and change in Syrian political life: the nineteenth and twentieth centuries. *American Historical Review*, 96, 1,374–95.

Kishwar, Madhu and Vanita, Ruth (eds) 1991 (1984): *In Search of Answers: Indian women's voices from Manushi*. New Delhi: Horizon India Books.

Klapper, Joseph T. 1960: *The Effects of Mass Communication*. Glencoe, IL: Free Press.

Klatch, Rebecca E. 1987: *Women of the New Right*. Philadelphia: Temple University Press.

Knorr-Cetina, Karin 1981: *The Manufacture of Knowledge*. New York: Pergamon.

Krasner, Stephen D. 1988: Sovereignty: an institutional perspective. *Comparative Political Studies*, 21, 66–94.

— 1993: Westphalia. In J. Goldstein and R. Keohane (eds), *Ideas and Foreign Policy*, Ithaca: Cornell University Press.

Kuhn, Thomas 1970: *The Structure of Scientific Revolutions*, 2nd edn. Chicago: University of Chicago Press.

Kunda, Gideon 1991: *Engineering Culture: control and commitment in a high-tech corporation*. Philadelphia: Temple University Press.

Kurtz, Lester 1983: The politics of heresy. *American Journal of Sociology*, 88, 1,085–115.

Lachmann, Richard 1988: Graffiti as career and ideology. *American Journal of Sociology*, 94, 229–50.

Laclau, Ernesto and Mouffe, Chantal 1985: *Hegemony and Socialist Strategy*. Winston Moore and Paul Commack (trs.), London: Verso.

Laing, Dave 1985: *One Chord Wonders: power and meaning in punk rock*. Milton Keynes: Open University Press.

Laitin, David 1986: *Hegemony and Culture: politics and religious change among the Yoruba*. Chicago: University of Chicago Press.

Laitin, David and Lustick, Ian 1989: Hegemony and the state. *States and Social Structures Newsletter*, 9, 3–7.

Lamont, Michèle 1987: How to become a dominant French philosopher: the case of Jacques Derrida. *American Journal of Sociology*, 93, 584–622.

— 1989: The power-culture link in a comparative perspective. In C. Calhoun (ed.), Special Issue: *Culture*. *Comparative Social Research*, 11, 131–50.

— 1992: *Money, Morals, and Manners: the culture of the French and the American upper-middle class*. Chicago: University of Chicago Press.

Lamont, Michèle and Fournier, Marcel (eds) 1992: *Cultivating Differences: symbolic boundaries and the making of inequality*. Chicago: University of Chicago Press.

Lamont, Michèle and Wuthnow, Robert 1990: Betwixt and between: recent cultural sociology in Europe and the United States. In G. Ritzer (ed.), *Frontiers of Social Theory: the new syntheses*, New York: Columbia University Press, 287–315.

Lang, Gladys Engel and Lang, Kurt 1990: *Etched in Memory: the building and survival of artistic reputation*. Chapel Hill/London: University of North Carolina Press.

Langer, Cassandra L. 1988: Against the grain: a working gynergenic art criticism. In A. Raven et al. (eds), *Feminist Art Criticism: an anthology*, New York: Icon Editions/HarperCollins.

Lash, Scott 1990: *Sociology of Postmodernism*. New York: Routledge.

Latour, Bruno 1983: Give me a laboratory and I will raise the world. In Karen Knorr-Cetina and Michael Mulkay (eds), *Science Observed: perspectives on the social study of science*, London/Beverley Hills: Sage, 141–70.

— 1987: *Science in Action*. Cambridge, MA: Harvard University Press.

— 1988a: *The Pasteurization of France*. Cambridge, MA: Harvard University Press.

— 1988b: Mixing humans and nonhumans together: the sociology of a door-closer. *Social Problems*, 35, 298–310.

— 1990: Drawing things together. In Michael Lynch and Steve Woolgar (eds), *Representation in Scientific Practice*, Cambridge, MA: MIT Press.

— 1992: One more turn after the social turn. Mimeo, CSI-Ecole des Mines, Paris.

Latour, Bruno and de Noblet, Jocelyn (eds), 1985: Les vues de l'esprit. *Culture Technique* 14, 1–274.

Latour Bruno and Woolgar, Steve 1982: *Laboratory Life*. Beverly Hills, CA: Sage.

Laudan, L. 1977: *Progress and its Problems*. Berkeley: University of California Press.

Law, John 1987: Technology and heterogeneous engineering: the case of Portuguese expansion. In Wiebe E. Bijker, Thomas P. Hughes and Trevor Pinch (eds), *The Social Construction of Technological Systems*, Cambridge: MIT Press, 111–34.

Layton, Edwin Jr 1974: Technology as knowledge. *Technology and Culture*, 15, 31–41.

Leach, Edmund R. 1954: *Political Systems of Highland Burma*. Boston: Beacon Press.

Le Corbusier 1980 (1954) *The Modulor: a harmonious measure to the human scale universally applicable to architecture and mechanics*. Cambridge, MA: Harvard University Press.

Lefebvre, Henri 1974: *La production de l'espace*. Paris: Editions Anthropos.

Lehner, P. E. 1989: *Artificial Intelligence and National Defense*. Summit, PA: TAB Books.

Leiss, William 1972: *The Domination of Nature*. New York: George Braziller.

Levine, Lawrence 1988: *Highbrow/Lowbrow: the emergence of cultural hierarchy in America*. Cambridge, MA: Harvard University Press.

Lévi-Strauss, Claude 1966: *The Savage Mind*. Chicago: University of Chicago Press.

Lewis, Justin 1991: *The Ideological Octopus: an exploration of television and its audience*. New York: Routledge.

Lichterman, Paul 1992: Self-help reading as a thin culture. *Media, Culture and Society*, 14, 421–47.

Lieberson, Stanley 1992: Einstein, Renoir, and Greeley: some thoughts about evidence in sociology. *American Sociological Review*, 57, 1–15.

Liebes, Tamar and Katz, Elihu 1990: *The Export of Meaning: cross-cultural readings of Dallas*. New York: Oxford University Press.

Lindlof, Thomas 1987: Media audiences as interpretive communities. In James Anderson (ed.), *Communication Yearbook*, vol. 11, Newbury Park, CA: Sage, 81–107.

Lipset, Seymour Martin and Rokkan, Stein (eds) 1967: *Party Systems and Voter Alignments: cross-national perspectives*. New York: Free Press.

Lipsitz, George 1990: *Time Passages*. Minneapolis: University of Minnesota Press.

Long, Elizabeth 1986: Women, reading, and cultural authority: some implications of the audience perspective in cultural studies. *American Quarterly*, 38, 591–612.

— 1987: Reading groups and the postmodern crisis of cultural authority. *Cultural Studies*, 1, 306–27.

— 1993: From the chair. *Newsletter of the Sociology of Culture*, 7 (Spring/Summer), 1–3.

Long, J. Scott 1992: Measures of sex differences in scientific productivity. *Social Forces*, 71, 159–78.

Lopes, Paul D. 1992: Innovation and diversity in the popular music industry, 1969–1990. *American Sociological Review*, 57, 56–71.

Lowenthal, Leo 1950: Historical perspectives on popular culture. *American Journal of Sociology*, 55, 323–32.

Luker, Kristin 1984: *Abortion and the Politics of Motherhood*. Berkeley: University of California Press.

Lukes, Steven 1975: Political ritual and social integration. *Sociology*, 9, 289–308.

— 1985: *Durkheim: His Life and Work*. Stanford, CA: Stanford University Press.

Lull, James 1987: Thrashing in the pit: an ethnography of San Francisco punk subculture. In T. R. Lindlof (ed.), *Natural Audiences: qualitative research on media uses and effects*, Norwood, NJ: Ablex, 225–52.

Lurie, Allison 1983: *The Language of Clothes*. New York: Vintage.

Lustick, Ian 1993: Unsettled States, Disputed Lands: Britain and Ireland, France and Algeria, Israel and the West Bank–Gaza. Ithaca: Cornell University Press.

Lutz, Catherine A. 1988: *Unnatural Emotions: everyday sentiments on a Micronesian atoll and their challenge to Western theory*. Chicago: University of Chicago Press.

Lynch, Michael 1985: *Art and Artifact in Laboratory Science*. London: Routledge and Kegan Paul.

Lynd, Robert and Lynd, Helen 1929: *Middletown*. New York: Harcourt Brace.

Lyotard, Jean-François 1984: *The Postmodern Condition: a report on knowledge*. Translated by G. Bennington and B. Massouri, Minneapolis: University of Minnesota Press.

MacKenzie, Donald 1990: *Inventing Accuracy*. Cambridge, MA: MIT Press.

Malinowski, Bronislaw 1922: *Argonauts of the Western Pacific*. London: Routledge.

Mann, Michael 1986: *The Sources of Social Power*, Vol. 1: *A History of Power from the Beginning to A.D. 1760*. Cambridge/New York: Cambridge University Press.

— 1988: *States, War, and Capitalism*. Oxford: Blackwell.

March, James G. and Olsen, Johan P. 1984: The new institutionalism: organizational factors in political life. *American Political Science Review*, 78, 734–49.

Markert, John 1984: *Beyond Gatekeepers: romance publishing and the production of culture*. Unpublished PhD dissertation, Vanderbilt University, Nashville, TN.

Martin, Joanne 1992: *Cultures in Organizations: three perspectives*. New York: Oxford University Press.

Martin, Joanne, Sitkin, Sim and Boehm, Michael 1985: Founders and the elusiveness of a cultural legacy. In Peter Frost, L. Moore, M. Louis, C. Lundberg and J. Martin (eds), *Organizational Culture*, Beverly Hills: Sage, 93–108.

Martorella, Rosanne 1982: *The Sociology of Opera*. South Hadley, MA: Bergin.

Matthews, Nancy Mowll (ed.) 1984: *Cassatt and her Circle: selected letters*. New York: Abbeville Press.

Maurice, Marc A., Sellier, François and Silvestre, Jean-Jacques 1984: The search for a societal effect in the production of company hierarchy: a comparison of France and Germany. In Paul Osterman (ed.), *Internal Labour Markets*, Cambridge, MA: MIT Press, 231–70.

Maurice, Marc., Sorge, A. and Warner, M. 1980: Societal differences in organizing manufacturing units: a comparison of France, West Germany, and Great Britain. *Organizational Studies*, 1, 59–86.

Mazrui, Ali and Tidy, Michael 1984: *Nationalism and New States in Africa*. Nairobi: Heinemann.

McCall, M. M. 1977: Art without a market: creating artistic value in a provincial art world. *Symbolic Interaction*, 1, 32–43.

McCormack, Thelma 1982: Content analysis: the social history of method. *Studies in Communication*, 2, 143–78.

— 1992: From content analysis to cultural theory. *Culture: Newsletter of the Sociology of Culture Section*, 6, 16–17.

McDonald, Maryon 1989: *"We Are Not French!" Language, culture and identity in Brittany*. London: Routledge.

McGregor, Douglas 1960: *The Human Side of Enterprise*. New York: McGraw-Hill.

McLuhan, Marshall 1989: *The Global Village: transformations in world life and media in the 21st century*. New York: Oxford University Press.

McNeill, William 1982: *The Pursuit of Power*. Chicago: University of Chicago Press.

McRobbie, Angela 1990: *Feminism and Youth Culture: from "Jackie" to "Just Seventeen"*. London: Routledge.

Melucci, Alberto 1985: The symbolic challenge of contemporary movements. *Social Research*, 52, 789–816.

Mencher, Joan 1974: The caste system upside down or the not-so-mysterious east. *Current Anthropology*, 15, 469–93.

Mennell, Stephen 1985: *All Manners of Food: eating and taste in England and France from the Middle Ages to the present*. London/New York: Blackwell.

— 1989: *Norbert Elias: civilization and the human self-image*. London/New York: Blackwell.

Merelman, Richard M. 1984: *Making Something of Ourselves: on culture and politics in the United States*. Berkeley: University of California Press.

Merton, Robert 1970: *Science, Technology and Society in 17th Century England*. New York: Howard Fertig.

— 1973: *The Sociology of Science*. Chicago: University of Chicago Press.

Meyer, John W. 1977: The effects of education in an institution. *American Journal of Sociology*, 83, 53–77.

— 1978: The structure of educational organizations. In Marshall Meyer (ed.), *Environments and Organizations*, San Francisco: Jossey-Bass, 78–109.

Meyer, John W. 1994: Rationalized environments. In John Meyer and W. Richard Scott (eds), *Institutional Environments and Organizations: essays and studies*. Newbury Park, CA: Sage.

Meyer, John W. and Hannan, Michael (eds) 1979: *National Development and the World System*. Chicago: University of Chicago Press.

Meyer, John W. and Rowan, Brian 1977: Institutionalized oganizations: formal structure as myth and ceremony. *American Journal of Sociology*, 83, 340–63.

Meyer, John W. and Scott, W. R. 1983: *Organizational Environments: ritual and rationality*. Beverly Hills: Sage.

Meyer, John W., Boli, John, and Thomas, George 1987: Ontology and rationalization in the western cultural account. In George M. Thomas, John W. Meyer, Francisco O. Ramirez and John Boli (eds), *Institutional Structure: constituting state, society, and the individual*, Beverly Hills: Sage, 12–37.

Meyer, John W., Scott, W. Richard, Cole, Sally and Intili, Jo-Ann 1978: Instruction dissensus and institutional consensus in schools. In Marshall Meyer (ed.), *Environments and Organisations*, San Francisco: Jossey-Bass, 233–63.

Meyer, John W., Tyack, David, Nagel, Joane and Gordon, Audri 1979: Public education as nation-building in America: enrollments and bureaucratization, 1870–1930. *American Journal of Sociology*, 85, 591–613.

Meyrowitz, Joshua 1985: *No Sense of Place: the impact of electronic media on social behavior*. New York: Oxford University Press.

Mezias, Stephen 1990: An institutional model of organizational practice: financial reporting at the Fortune 200. *Administrative Science Quarterly*, 35, 431–57.

Mickiewicz, Ellen 1988: *Split Signals: television and politics in the Soviet Union*. New York: Oxford.

Mills, C. Wright 1963 (1959): The cultural apparatus. In *Power, Politics and People: the collected essays of C. Wright Mills*, New York: Ballantine, 405–22.

Mines, Mattison 1988: Conceptualizing the person: hierarchical society and individual autonomy in India. *American Anthropologist*, 90, 568–79.

Mines, Mattison and Gourishankar, Vijayalakshmi 1990: Leadership and individuality in South Asia: the case of the South Indian big-man. *Journal of Asian Studies*, 49, 761–86.

Mitchell, Timothy 1990: Everyday metaphors of power. *Theory and Society*, 19, 545–77.

— 1991a: The limits of the state: beyond statist approaches and their critics. *American Political Science Review*, 85, 77–96.

— 1991b (1988): *Colonising Egypt*. Berkeley: University of California Press.

Molotch, Harvey and Lester, Marilyn 1974: News as purposive behavior. *American Sociological Review*, 39, 101–12.

Montgomery, Roger 1989: Architecture invents new people. In Russell Ellis and Dana Cuff (eds), *Architects' People*, New York: Oxford University Press, 260–81.

Moorhouse, H. F. 1991: *Driving Ambitions: a social analysis of the American hot rod enthusiasm*. Manchester: University of Manchester Press.

Morawska, Ewa 1985: *For Bread With Butter: lifeworlds of the east central Europeans in Johnstown, Pennsylvania, 1890–1940*. London/New York: Cambridge University Press.

— 1991: Small town, slow pace: transformation of the religious life in a Jewish community of Johnstown, Pennsylvania (1920–1940). *Comparative Social Research*, 13, 127–78.

— 1994 *Insecure Prosperity: small-town Jews in industrial America, 1880–1940*. Princeton, NJ: Princeton University Press.

Morley, David 1980: *The Nationwide Audience: structure and decoding*. London: British Film Institute.

— 1986: *Family Television: cultural power and domestic leisure*. London: Comedia.

— 1989: Changing paradigms in audience studies. In Ellen Seiter, et al. (eds), *Remote Control*, London and New York: Routledge, 16–43.

Morrill, Calvin 1991: Conflict management, honor, and organizational change. *American Journal of Sociology*, 97, 585–622.

Mosse, George 1976: Mass politics and the political liturgy of nationalism. In Eugene Kamenka (ed.), *Nationalism*, New York: St Martin's Press. 38–54.

— 1990: *Fallen Soldiers: reshaping the memory of the World Wars*. New York: Oxford University Press.

Moulin, Raymonde 1987: *The French Art Market*. New Brunswick, NJ: Rutgers University Press.

Mujahid, Abdul Malik 1989: *Conversion to Islam: untouchables' strategy for protest in India*. Chambersburg, PA: Anima.

Mukerji, Chandra 1983: *From Graven Images*. New York: Colombia University Press.

— 1989: *A Fragile Power: scientists and the state*. Princeton: Princeton University Press.

— 1993: Territorial Gardens. In Thomas Haskell and Richard Teichgraeber (eds), *The Culture of the Market*, New York: Cambridge University Press.

Mukerji, Chandra and Schudson, Michael 1986: Popular culture. *Annual Review of Sociology*, 12, 44–61.

— (eds) 1991: *Rethinking Popular Culture*. Berkeley: University of California Press.

Münch, Richard 1992: Rational choice theory: a critical assessment of its explanatory power. In James S. Coleman and Thomas J. Fararo (eds), *Rational Choice Theory: advocacy and critique*. Newbury Park, CA: Sage, 137–60.

Nead, Lynda 1988: *Myths of Sexuality: representations of women in Victorian Britain*. Oxford/New York: Blackwell.

— 1992: *The Female Nude: art, obscenity, and sexuality*. London/New York: Routledge.

Neapolitan, J. 1986: Art, craft, and art/craft segments among craft media workers. *Work and Occupations*, 13, 203–16.

Nimmo, Dan and Combs, James E. 1983: *Mediated Political Realities*. New York: Longman.

Nooy, de W. 1991: Social networks and classification in literature. *Poetics*, 20, 507–37.

North, Douglass 1990: *Institutions, Institutional Change and Economic Performance*. New York: Cambridge University Press.

Orrù, Marco, Biggart, Nicole Woolsey and Hamilton, Gary G. 1991: Organizational isomorphism in East Asia. In Walter W. Powell and Paul J. DiMaggio (eds), *The New Institutionalism in Organizational Analysis*. Chicago: University of Chicago Press, 361–89.

Ortner, Sherry B. 1984: Theory in anthropology since the sixties. *Comparative Studies in History and Society*, 26, 126–66.

Ozouf, Mona 1988 (1976): *Festivals and the French Revolution*. Translated by Alan Sheridan, Cambridge: Harvard University Press.

Parenti, Michael 1993: *Inventing Reality: the politics of news media*. New York: St Martin's.

Parker, Rozsika and Pollock, Griselda 1981: *Old Mistresses: women, art and ideology*. New York: Pantheon.

Parsons, Talcott 1951: *The Social System*. Glencoe, IL: Free Press.

— 1961: Culture and the social system: introduction. In Talcott Parsons, Edward Shils, Kaspar D. Naegele and Jesse R. Pitts (eds), *The Origins of Society*, Volume 2. New York: Free Press, 971–93.

Peiss, Kathy 1986: *Cheap Amusements: working women and leisure in turn-of-the-century New York*. Philadelphia: Temple University Press.

Perez-Diaz, Victor M. 1993: *The Return of Civil Society*. Cambridge, MA: Harvard University Press.

Perrow, Charles 1987: *Complex Organizations: a critical essay*, 3rd edn. New York: Random House.

— 1991a: A society of organizations. *Theory and Society*, 20, 725–62.

— 1991b: Organizational theorists in a society of organizations. Address to the annual meeting of the American Sociological Association, Cincinnati.

Peters, Thomas and Waterman, Robert Jr 1982: *In Search of Excellence*. New York: Harper and Row.

Peterson, Karen and Wilson, J. J. 1976: *Women Artists: recognition and reappraisal from the early middle ages to the twentieth century*. New York: New York University Press.

Peterson, Richard A. 1972: A process model of the folk, pop, and fine art phrases of jazz. In Charles Nanry (ed.), *American Music: from Storyville to Woodstock*, New Brunswick, NJ: Transaction Books and EP Dutton, 135–51.

— 1976: The production of culture: a prolegomenon. In Richard A. Peterson (ed.), *The Production of Culture*, Beverly Hills, CA: Sage, 7–22.

— 1978: The production of cultural change: the case of contemporary country music. *Social Research*, 45, 292–314.

— 1979: Revitalizing the culture concept. *Annual Review of Sociology*, 5, 137–166.

— 1981: Entrepreneurship and organization. In Paul C. Nystrom and William H. Starbuck (eds), *Handbook of Organizational Design*, New York: Oxford University Press, 65–83.

— 1983a: Patterns of cultural choice: prolegomenon. *American Behavioral Scientist*, 26, 422–38.

— 1985: Six constraints on the production of literary works. *Poetics*, 14, 45–67.

— 1986: Stained glass television: a female evangelist joins the electronic church. *Journal of Popular Culture*, 19, 95–105.

— 1990: Why 1955? Explaining the advent of rock music. *Popular Music*, 9, 97–116.

— 1992a: Melding ethnographic and humanist definitions of culture. *Culture*, 6:3, 10–11.

— 1992b: Understanding audience segmentation: from elite and mass to omnivore and univore. *Poetics*, 21, 243–58.

— 1992c: Class unconsciousness in country music. In Melton A. McLaurin and Richard A. Peterson (eds), *You Wrote My Life: lyrical themes in country music*, Philadelphia: Gordon and Breach, 35–62.

— 1992d: La fabrication de l'authenticité: la country music. *Actes de la Recherche en Sciences Sociales*, 93, 3–20.

— 1993: The battle for classical music on the air. In Judith Balfe (ed.), *Paying the Piper*, Urbana: University of Illinois Press, 271–86.

Peterson, Richard A. and Berger, David G. 1975: Cycles in symbol production: the case of popular music. *American Sociological Review*, 40, 158–73.

Peterson, Richard A. and Ryan, John 1983: Success, failure, and anomie in arts and crafts work: breaking into commercial country music songwriting. *Research in the Sociology of Work*, 2, 301–23.

Peterson, Richard A. and Simkus, Albert J. 1992: How musical tastes mark occupational status groups. In Michèle Lamont and Marcel Fournier (eds), *Cultivating Differences: symbolic boundaries and the making of inequality*, Chicago: University of Chicago Press, 152–86.

Pevsner, Nikolous 1940: *Academies of Art*. New York: Macmillan.

Pfeffer, Jeffrey and Baron, James N. 1988: Taking the workers back out: recent trends in the structuring of employment. *Research in Organizational Behavior*, 10, 257–303.

Pfeffer, Jeffrey and Salancik, Gerald R. 1978: *The External Control of Organizations: a resource dependence perspective*. New York: Harper and Row.

Pickering, Andrew 1984: *Constructing Quarks: A sociological history of particle physics*. Chicago: University of Chicago Press.

— 1992: From science as knowledge to science as practice. In Andrew Pickering (ed.), *Science as Practice and Culture*, Chicago: University of Chicago Press.

Pizzorno, Alessandro 1987: Politics unbound. In C. Maier (ed.), *Changing Boundaries of the Political*, Cambridge/New York: Cambridge University Press, 27–62.

Polanyi, Karl 1944: *The Great Transformation: the political and economic origins of our time*. New York: Rinehart.

Pollock, Griselda 1980: *Mary Cassatt*. New York: Harper and Row.

— 1988: *Vision and Difference: femininity, feminism and histories of art*. London/ New York: Routledge.

Polsby, Nelson 1983: *Consequences of Party Reform*. New York: Oxford.

Powell, Walter W. 1978: Publishers' decision making: what criteria do they use in deciding which books to publish? *Social Research*, 45, 227–52.

Powell, Walter W. and Friedkin, Rebecca 1983: Political and organizational influences on public television programming. *Mass Communication Review Yearbook*, 4, 413–38.

— 1991: Expanding the scope of institutional analysis. In Walter W. Powell and Paul J. DiMaggio (eds), *The New Institutionalism in Organizational Analysis*, Chicago: University of Chicago Press, 183–203.

Pratt, Mary Louise 1986: Scratches on the face of the country; or what Mr Barrow saw in the land of the bushmen. In H. L. Gates (ed.), *"Race," Writing and Difference*, Chicago: University of Chicago Press, 138–63.

Press, Andrea L. 1991: *Women Watching Television: gender, class, and generation in the American television experience*. Philadelphia: University of Pennsylvania Press.

Press, Andrea L. and Cole, Liz 1994: Women like us: working-class women respond to television representations of abortion. In Jon Cruz and Justin Lewis (eds), *Reading, Viewing, Listening: audiences and cultural reception*, Boulder, CO: Westview Press.

— forthcoming: *Imagining Our Lives: television, women's talk, and the political culture of abortion*.

Putnam, Robert D. 1993: *Making Democracy Work*. Princeton: Princeton University Press.

Raboy, Marc 1985: Public television, the national question and the preservation of the Canadian state. In Phillip Drummond and Richard Paterson (eds), *Television in Transition*, London: BFI Publishing.

Radway, Janice 1984: *Reading the Romance: women, patriarchy, and popular literature*. Chapel Hill: University of North Carolina Press. (See also Radway 1991.)

— 1988a: The Book-of-the-Month Club and the general reader: on the uses of serious fiction. *Critical Inquiry*, 14, 517–38.

— 1988b: Reception study: ethnography and the problems of dispersed audiences and nomadic subjects. *Cultural Studies*, 2, 359–76.

— 1990: The scandal of the middlebrow: the Book of the Month Club, class fracture, and cultural authority. *The South Atlantic Quarterly*, 89(4), 703–36.

— 1991: Writing reading the romance. Introduction to the second edition of *Reading the Romance: Women, Patriarchy, and Popular Literature*. Chapel Hill: University of North Carolina.

Ragin, Charles 1987: *The Comparative Method: moving beyond qualitative and quantative strategies*. Berkeley: University of California Press.

Ramirez, Francisco O. and Rubinson, Richard 1979: Creating members: the political incorporation and expansion of public education. In John W. Meyer and Michael T. Hannan (eds), *National Development and the World System*, Chicago: University of Chicago Press, 72–82.

Raven, Arlene et al. (eds) 1988: *Feminist Art Criticism: am anthology*. New York: Icon Editions/HarperCollins.

Rewald, John 1973: *The History of Impressionism*. New York and Greenwich: Museum of Modern Art and New York Graphic Society.

Rieder, Jonathan 1985: *Canarsie: the Jews and Italians of Brooklyn against liberalism*. Cambridge, MA: Harvard University Press.

Riley, Denise 1988: *Am I that Name? Feminism and the category of "women" in history*. Minneapolis: University of Minnesota Press.

Robertson, Roland 1988: The sociological significance of culture: some general considerations. *Theory, Culture and Society*, 5, 3–23.

Robinson, Denna Campbell, Beck, Elizabeth B., and Cuthbert, Marlene 1991: *Music at the Margins: popular music and global cultural diversity*. Newbury Park, CA: Sage.

Roland, Alan 1988: *In Search of Self in India and Japan: toward a cross-cultural psychology*. Princeton: Princeton University Press.

Rose, Sonya 1992a: Text and context: A double vision historical method. Paper presented to the Social Science History Association, New Orleans.

— 1992b: *Limited Livelihoods: gender and class in 19th century England*. Berkeley: University of California Press.

Rose, Tricia 1989: Hit the road Sam: black women rappers and sexual difference. Paper delivered at the October, 1989 Meetings of the American Studies Association, Toronto.

Rosenau, Pauline Marie 1992: *Post-Modernism and the Social Sciences: insights, inroads, and intrusions*. Princeton: Princeton University Press.

Rosenblum, Barbara 1978: *Photographers at Work*. New York: Holmes and Meyers.

Rosengren, Karl Erik 1983: *The Climate of Literature: Sweden's literary frame of reference, 1953–1976*. Lund: Studentlitteratur.

— (ed.) 1985: *Media Gratifications Research: current perspectives*. Beverly Hills: Sage.

Ross, Andrew 1989: *No Respect*. New York: Routledge.

Rothenbuhler, Eric W. 1988: The liminal fight: mass strikes as ritual and interpretation. In J. Alexander (ed.), *Durkheimian Sociology and Cultural Studies*. Cambridge, UK: Cambridge University Press, 66–89.

Rothenbuhler, Eric W. and Dimmick, John W. 1982: Popular music: concentration and diversity in the industry, 1974–1980. *Journal of Communication*, 32, 143–49.

Rothenbuhler, Eric W. and McCourt, Tom 1992: Commercial radio and popular music. In James Lull (ed.), *Music and Communication*, Newbury Park, CA: Sage, 101–15.

Roy, Donald 1952: Quota restrictions and goldbricking in a machine shop. *American Journal of Sociology*, 57, 427–42.

Rubinstein, Charlotte Steiner 1982: *American Women Artists from Early Indian Times to the Present*. Boston, MA: Avon.

Rudolph, Lloyd I. and Rudolph, Susanne H. 1967: *The Modernity of Tradition: political development in India*. Chicago: University of Chicago Press.

Rudwick, Martin 1985: *The Great Devonian Controversy*. Chicago: University of Chicago Press.

Ruggie, John Gerard 1993: Territoriality and beyond: problematizing modernity in international relations. *International Organization*, 47, 139–74.

Russel, Colin 1983: *Science and Social Change 1700–1900*. London: Macmillan.

Ryan, John 1985: *The Production of Culture in the Music Industry*. New York: University Press of America.

Ryan, John and Peterson, Richard A. 1982: The product image: the fate of creativity in country music songwriting. *Annual Reviews of Communication Research*, 10, 11–32.

— 1993: Occupational and organizational consequences of the digital revolution in music making. *Current Research on Occupations and Professions*, 8.

Sahlins, Marshall 1976: *Culture and Practical Reason*. Chicago: University of Chicago Press.

Sarna, Jonathan 1978: From immigrants to ethnics: toward a new theory of "ethnicization". *Ethnicity*, 5, 370–8.

Sato, Ikuya 1991: *Kamikaze Biker: parody and anomy in affluent Japan*. Chicago: University of Chicago Press.

Scheppele, Kim L. 1988: *Legal Secrets: equality and efficiency in the common law*. Chicago: University of Chicago Press.

— 1993: "Just the facts, ma'am:" sexualised violence, evidentiary habits, and the revisions of truth. *New York Law School Review*, 109, 28–32.

Schiller, Herbert I. 1969: *Mass Communication and American Empire*. New York: Kelly.

— 1992: *Mass Communications and the American Empire*. Boulder: Westview Press.

Schneider, David 1976: Notes toward a theory of culture. In Keith Basso and Henry Selby (eds), *Meaning in Anthropology*, Albuquerque: University of New Mexico Press.

Schudson, Michael 1978: *Discovering the News: a social history of American newspapers*. New York: Basic Books.

— 1984: *Advertising, the Uneasy Persuasion*. New York: Basic Books.

— 1989: Toward a comparative history of political communication. *Comparative Social Research* 11, 151–63.

— 1992: *Watergate in American Memory: how we remember, forget and reconstruct the past*. New York: Basic Books.

Schwartz, Barry 1987: *George Washington: the making of an American symbol*. New York: The Free Press.

— 1991: Social change and collective memory: the democratization of George Washington. *American Sociological Review*, 56, 221–36.

Schwartz, Lawrence H. 1988: *Creating Faulkner's Reputation: the politics of modern literary criticism*. Knoxville: University of Tennessee Press.

Scott, James C. 1990: *Domination and the Arts of Resistance*. New Haven: Yale University Press.

Scott, Joan Wallach 1988 [1986]: Gender: a useful category of historical analysis. In *Gender and the Politics of History*, New York: Columbia University Press, 28–50.

Scott, W. Richard 1987a: The adolescence of institutional theory. *Administrative Science Quarterly*, 32, 493–511.

— 1987b: *Organizations: rational, natural, and open systems*, 2nd edn. Englewood Cliffs, NJ: Prentice-Hall.

— 1992: Institutions and organisations: toward a theoretical synthesis. Manuscript, Stanford University Department of Sociology.

— 1994: Conceptualizing organizational fields: linking organizations and societal systems. Manuscript, Stanford University, Department of Sociology.

Scott, W. Richard and Meyer, John W. 1983: The organization of societal sectors. In John W. Meyer and W. Richard Scott (eds), *Organizational Environments: rituals and rationality*, Beverly Hills: Sage, 129–54.

Segard, Achille 1913: *Mary Cassatt: un peintre des enfants et des mères*. Paris: Librairie Paul Ollendorf.

Seidman, Steven and Wagner, David G. (eds) 1992: *Postmodernism and Social Theory: the debate over general theory*. Cambridge, MA/Oxford: Blackwell.

Seiter, Ellen, Borchers, Hans, Kreutzner, Gabriele, and Warth, Eva-Maria (eds), 1989: *Remote Control: television, audiences and cultural power*, London/New York: Routledge.

Seldin, Donna 1987: *Mary Cassatt: an American observer*. New York: Universe Books.

Seligman, Adam B. 1992: *The Idea of Civil Society*. New York: The Free Press.

Selznick, Philip 1949: *TVA and the Grass Roots*. Berkeley: University of California Press.

Sewell, William H. 1980: *Work and Revolution in France: the language of labor from the old regime to 1848*. Cambridge/New York: Cambridge University Press.

— 1985: Ideologies and social revolutions: reflections on the French case. *The Journal of Modern History*, 57, 57–85.

— 1990: Review Essay of J. Scott's *Gender and the Politics of History*. *History and Theory*, 29, 71–88.

— 1992: A theory of structure: duality, agency, and transformation. *American Journal of Sociology*, 98, 1–29.

— 1993: Three temporalities: toward a sociology of the event. In Terrence McDonald (ed.), *The Historic Turn in the Human Sciences*, Ann Arbor: University of Michigan Press.

Shafir, Gershon 1980: *Intellectuals and the Popular Masses*. Dissertation, University of California, Berkeley.

Shapin, Steven 1989: The invisible technician. *American Scientist*, 77, 554–63.

Shapin, Steven and Shaffer, Simon 1985: *The Leviathan and the Air Pump*. Princeton: Princeton University Press.

Shils, Edward 1975: *Center and Periphery: essays in macrosociology*. Chicago: University of Chicago Press.

Shively, JoEllen 1992: Cowboys and Indians: perceptions of Western films among American Indians and Anglos. *American Sociological Review*, 57, 725–34.

Shklar, Judith N. 1984: *Ordinary Vices*. Cambridge: Harvard University Press.

Shue, Vivienne 1988: *The Reach of the State: sketches of the Chinese body politic*. Stanford, CA: Stanford University Press.

Shweder, Richard A. 1991: *Thinking Through Cultures: expeditions in cultural psychology*. Cambridge, MA: Harvard University Press.

Simpson, Charles R. 1981: *SoHo: the artist in the city*. Chicago: University of Chicago Press.

Siu, Helen F. 1989: Recycling rituals: politics and popular culture in contemporary rural China. In Perry Link, Richard Madsen and Paul G. Pickowicz (eds), *Unofficial China: popular culture and thought in the People's Republic*, Boulder, CO: Westview Press.

Skocpol, Theda 1979: *States and Social Revolutions: a comparative analysis of France, Russia, and China*. Cambridge: Cambridge University Press.

— 1984: Sociology's historical imagination. In Theda Skocpol (ed.), *Vision and Method in Historical Sociology*. Cambridge/New York: Cambridge University Press, 1–21.

— 1985: Cultural idioms and political ideologies in the revolutionary reconstruction of state power: a rejoinder to Sewell. *The Journal of Modern History*, 57, 86–96.

— 1992: *Protecting Soldiers and Mothers: the political origins of social policy in the United States*. Cambridge, MA: Harvard University Press.

Smart, Barry 1985: *Michel Foucault*. New York: Routledge.

Smelser, Neil J. 1992: Culture: coherent or incoherent. In R. Münch and N. J. Smelser (eds), *Theory of Culture*, Berkeley: University of California Press, 3–28.

Smith, Anthony 1986: *The Ethnic Origins of Nations*. London/New York: Blackwell.

— 1987: State-making and nation-building. In John A. Hall (ed.), *States in History*, London/New York: Blackwell, 228–63.

— 1991: *National Identity*. London: Penguin.

Smith, Dennis 1991: *The Rise of Historical Sociology*. Philadelphia: Temple University Press.

Snow, David A., Rochford, E. Burke Jr, Worden, Steven K. and Benford, Robert D. 1986: Frame alignment processes, micromobilization and movement participation. *American Sociological Review*, 51, 464–81.

Somers, Margaret 1992a: Narrativity, narrative identity, and social action: rethinking English working-class formation. *Social Science History*, 16, 591–630.

— 1992b: The political culture concept: the empirical power of conceptual transformations. CSST Working Paper No. 88, The University of Michigan, Ann Arbor.

— 1993: Where is sociology after the historic turn? Knowledge cultures and historical epistemologies. In Terrence McDonald (ed.), *The Historic Turn in the Human Sciences*, Ann Arbor: University of Michigan Press.

Soysal, Yasemin 1994: *Limits of Citizenship: guestworkers in the contemporary nation-state system*. Chicago: University of Chicago Press.

Spitulnik, Debra 1992: Radio time sharing and negotiation of linguistic pluralism in Zambia. *Pragmatics*, 2, 335–54.

Spohn, Willfried 1991: Religion and working-class formation in Imperial Germany, 1871–1914. *Politics and Society*, 19, 109–32.

— forthcoming: *Religion and Working-Class Formation in Germany, 1840–1914*.

Srinivas, M. N. 1969: *Social Change in Modern India*. Berkeley: University of California Press.

Stack, Carol B. 1974: *All Our Kin: strategies for survival in a black community*. New York: Harper and Row.

Steinmetz, George 1992: Reflections on the role of social narratives in working-class formation. *Social Science History*, 16, 489–516.

Steward, Margaret S. 1983: Women who chose a man's career: a study of women in ministry. *Psychology of Women Quarterly*, 19, 95–105.

Stinchcombe, Arthur L. 1965: Social structure and organizations. In James G. March (ed.), *Handbook of Organizations*, Chicago: Rand McNally, 142–93.

Strang, David and Bradburn, Ellen 1993: Institutions and interests in organizational regulation: HMO legislation in the States. Paper presented at the annual meeting of the American Sociological Association, Miami.

Strang, David and Meyer, John 1993: Institutional conditions for diffusion. *Theory and Society*, 22, 487–512.

Strang, David, Tuma, Nancy and Meyer, John 1992: Global diffusion of national policies. Manuscript, Cornell University Department of Sociology.

Stromberg, Peter G. 1981: Consensus and variation in the interpretation of religious symbolism: a Swedish example. *American Ethnologist*, 8, 544–99.

— 1986: *Symbols of Community: the cultural system of a Swedish church*. Tucson: University of Arizona Press.

Suleiman, Susan Rubin 1992: *Authoritarian Fictions: the ideological novel as literary genre*. Princeton: Princeton University Press.

Sutton, John R., Dobbin, Frank, Meyer, John W. and Scott, W. Richard, 1994: The legalization of the workplace. *American Journal of Sociology* (in press).

Swaan, Abram de 1990: Emotions in their social matrix. In A. de Swaan, *The Management of Normality*, London/New York: Routledge, 139–204.

Swidler, Ann 1986: Culture in action: symbols and strategies. *American Sociological Review*, 51, 273–86.

Szacki, Jerzy 1991: Znaniecki: Dylemat determinizmu i tworczosci, and Florian Znaniecki: Od Filozofii do socjologii. In J. Szacki, *Dylematy Historiografii Idei Oraz Inne Szkice i Studia*. Warsaw: Wydawnictwo Naukowe PWN, 132–66.

Sztompka, Piotr 1986: Some aspects of Florian Znaniecki's philosophy of the social sciences. In Z. Dulczewski (ed.), *A Commemorative Book in Honor of Florian Znaniecki on the Centenary of His Birth*, Poznan: Polska Akademia Nauk, 264–81.

Tarrow, Sidney 1977: *Between Center and Periphery: grassroots politicians in Italy and France*. New Haven: Yale University Press.

Tatarewicz, Joseph 1990: *Space Technology and Planetary Astronomy*. Bloomington: Indiana University Press.

Taylor, Frederick 1911: *Scientific Management*. New York: Harper.

Tetzlaff, David 1992: Popular culture and social control in late capitalism. In Paddy Scannell (ed.), *Culture and Power*, London: Sage, 48–72.

Thomas, George M. and Meyer, John W. 1984: The expansion of the state. *Annual Review of Sociology*, 10, 461–82.

Thomas, W. I. and Znaniecki, Florian 1918–20: *The Polish Peasant in Europe and America*, Vols I–IV. Chicago: University of Chicago Press.

Thompson, E. P. 1967: *The Making of the English Working Class*. New York: Pantheon Books.

— 1978: *The Poverty of Theory and Other Essays*. London: Merlin Press.

— 1991: *Customs in Common*. London: Merlin Press.

Thompson, James D. 1967: *Organizations in Action*. New York: McGraw-Hill.

Thurow, Lester 1980: *The Zero-Sum Society: distribution and the possibilities for economic change*. New York: Basic.

Thurston, Carol 1987: *The Romance Revolution: romantic novels for women and the quest for a new sexual identity*. Urbana: University of Illinois Press.

Tilly, Charles 1975: Reflections on the history of European statemaking. In C. Tilly (ed.), *The Formation of National States in Western Europe*. Princeton, NJ: Princeton University Press, 3–83.

— 1978: *From Mobilisation to Revolution*. Reading, MA: Addison-Wesley Publishing Company.

— 1986: *The Contentious French*. Cambridge, MA: The Belknap Press of Harvard University Press.

— 1991: Domination, resistance, compliance . . . discourse. *Sociological Forum*, 6, 593–602.

— 1992: *Coercion, Capital, and European States AD 990–1990*. London /New York: Blackwell.

Tiryakian, Edward A. 1988: From Durkheim to Managua: revolutions as religious revivals. In J. Alexander (ed.), *Durkheimian Sociology and Cultural Studies*, Cambridge: Cambridge University Press, 44–65.

Tiryakian, Edward A. and Nevitte, Neil 1985: Nationalism and modernity. In Edward A. Tiryakian and Ronald Rogowski (eds), *New Nationalisms of the Developed West*, Boston, MA: Allen and Unwin, 57–86.

Tolbert, Pamela and Stern, Robert N. 1989: Organizations and professions: governance structures in large law firms. Manuscript, Cornell University.

Tolbert, Pamela and Zucker, Lynne G. 1983: Institutional sources of change in the formal structure of organizations: the diffusion of civil service reforms, 1880–1935. *Administrative Science Quarterly*, 23, 22–39.

Tuchman, Gaye 1978: *Making News: a study in the construction of reality*. New York: Free Press.

— 1988: Mass media institutions. In Neil Smelser (ed.), *Handbook of Sociology*, Newbury Park: Sage, 601–26.

— 1989: *Edging Women Out: Victorian novelists, publishers, and social change*. New Haven: Yale University Press.

Tumarkin, Nina 1983: *Lenin Lives!* Cambridge, MA: Harvard University Press.

Turow, Joseph 1992: *Media Systems in Society*. New York: Longman.

Varenne, Hervé 1977: *Americans Together: structured diversity in a midwestern town*. New York: Teachers College Press.

Veblen, Thorstein 1904: *The Theory of Business Enterprise*. New York: Scribner's.

— 1953 (1899): *The Theory of The Leisure Class*. New York: Mentor.

Vogel, Lisa 1988: Fine arts and feminism: the awakening consciousness. In A. Raven et al. (eds), *Feminist Art Criticism: an anthology*, New York: Icon Editions/HarperCollins.

Vygotsky, L. S. 1978: *Mind in Society*. Translated by M. Cole. Cambridge, MA: Harvard University Press.

Wacquant, Loïc 1993: On the tracks of symbolic power. *Theory, Culture, and Society*, 10, 1–17.

Wagner-Pacifici, Robin and Schwartz, Barry 1991: The Vietnam Veterans Memorial: commemorating a difficult past. *American Journal of Sociology*, 97, 376–421.

Wallerstein, Immanuel 1974: *The Modern World-System I: capitalist agriculture and the origins of the European world-economy in the sixteenth century*. New York: Academic Press.

— 1979: *The Capitalist World-Economy*. Cambridge/New York: Cambridge University Press.

— 1980: *The Modern World-System II: mercantilism and the consolidation of the European world-economy, 1600–1750*. New York: Academic Press.

Wallis, Roger 1990: *The Known World of Broadcast News: international news and the electronic media*. London/New York: Routledge.

Walzer, Michael 1981: The distribution of membership. In Peter G. Brown and Henry Shue (eds), *Boundaries: national autonomy and its limits*, Totowa, NJ: Rowman and Littlefield, 1–35.

— 1988: The lonely politics of Michel Foucault. In *The Company of Critics: social criticism and political commitment in the twentieth century*, New York: Basic Books, 191–209.

Warner, R. Steven 1993: Work in progress toward a new paradigm for the sociological study of religion in the United States. *American Journal of Sociology*, 98, 1,044–95.

Waterman, Christopher A. 1990: *Juju: a social history and ethnography of an African popular music*. Chicago: University of Chicago Press.

Watkins, Susan Cotts 1991: *From Provinces into Nations: demographic integration in Western Europe, 1870–1960*. Princeton: Princeton University Press.

Weber, Eugen 1976: *Peasants into Frenchmen*. Stanford: Stanford University Press.

Weber, Max 1978: *Economy and Society*. Two Volumes. Edited by Guenther Roth and Claus Wittich, Berkeley: University of California Press.

— 1979: Religious rejections of the world and their directions. In H. H. Gerth and C. Wright Mills (eds and trans), *From Max Weber*, New York: Oxford University Press, 323–59.

Weedon, Chris 1987: *Feminist Practice and Poststructuralist Theory*. Cambridge, MA: Blackwell.

Weick, Karl 1976: Educational organizations as loosely coupled systems. *Administrative Science Quarterly*, 21, 1–19.

— 1979: *The Social Psychology of Organizing*, 2nd edn. Reading, MA: Addison-Wesley.

Weinstein, Deena 1991: *Heavy Metal: a cultural sociology*. New York: Lexington.

Weis, Lois 1985: *Between Two Worlds: black students in an urban community college*. Boston, MA: Routledge.

Weismantel, M. J. 1989: The children cry for bread: hegemony and the transformation of consumption. In Henry J. Ruiz and Benjamin S. Orlove (eds), *The Social Economy of Consumption*, Lanham, MD: University Press of America, 85–99.

White, Geoffrey and Kirkpatrick, John (eds) 1985: *Person, Self, and Experience: exploring Pacific ethnopsychologies*. Berkeley: University of California Press.

White, Harrison C. 1981: Where do markets come from? *American Journal of Sociology*, 87, 517–47.

White, Harrison C. and White, Cynthia A. 1965: *Canvases and Careers*. New York: Wiley.

Whyte, William Foote 1943: *Street Corner Society: the social structure of an Italian slum*. Chicago: University of Chicago Press.

Williams, Raymond 1958: *Culture and Society 1780–1950*. New York: Harper & Row.

— 1961: *The Long Revolution*. New York: Columbia University Press.

— 1966: *Communications*. London: Chatto and Windus.

— 1973: *The Country and the City*. New York: Oxford University Press.

— 1977: *Marxism and Literature*. Oxford: Oxford University Press.

— 1978: Base and superstructure in Marxist cultural theory. *New Left Review*, 82, 3–16.

— 1980: *Problems in Materialism and Culture: selected essays*. London: Verso.

— 1989: *The Politics of Modernism*. Tony Pinkney (ed.), London/New York: Verso.

Williamson, Oliver 1975: *Markets and Hierarchies: analysis and antitrust implications*. New York: Free Press.

Willis, Paul 1977: *Learning to Labour: how working-class kids get working-class jobs*. New York: Columbia University Press.

— 1978: *Profane Culture*. London: Routledge.

Wilson, William A. 1976: *Folklore and Nationalism in Modern Finland*. Bloomington: Indiana University Press.

Winner, Langdon 1986: *The Whale and the Reactor*. Chicago: University of Chicago Press.

Wolfe, Alan 1989: *Whose Keeper?: social science and moral obligation*. Berkeley: University of California Press.

Wolff, Janet 1981: *The Social Production of Art*. London: Macmillan.

— 1982: The problem of ideology in the sociology of art: a case study of Manchester in the nineteenth century. *Media, Culture and Society*, 4, 63–75.

— 1989: Against sociological imperialism: the limits of sociology in the aesthetic sphere. Presented at the annual meetings of the American Sociological Association, San Francisco.

— 1990: *Feminine Sentences: essays on women and culture*. Berkeley: University of California Press.

— 1992: Excess and inhibition: interdisciplinarity in the study of art. In L. Grossberg et al. (eds), *Cultural Studies*, New York/London: Routledge, 706–17.

Wolff, Janet and Sneed, John (eds) 1988: *The Culture of Capital: art, power, and the nineteenth-century middle class*. Manchester: Manchester University Press.

Woolwine, D. E. 1992: Reading science as text. In R. Wuthnow (ed.), *Vocabularies of Public Life: empirical essays in symbolic structure*, London: Routledge, 75–90.

Wright, Gwendolyn 1980: *Moralism and the Model Home*. Chicago: University of Chicago Press.

Wuthnow, Robert 1980: The world-economy and the institutionalization of science in seventeenth-century Europe. In Albert Bergesen (ed.), *Studies of the Modern World-System*, New York: Academic, 25–56.

— 1987: *Meaning and Moral Order: explorations in cultural analysis*. Berkeley: University of California Press.

Wuthnow, Robert and Witten, Marsha 1988: New directions in the study of culture. *Annual Review of Sociology*, 14, 49–67.

— 1989: *Communities of Discourse: ideology and social structure in the Reformation, the Enlightenment, and European Socialism*. Cambridge, MA: Harvard University Press.

Zald, Mayer N. 1994: Organization studies as a scientific and humanistic enterprise: toward a reconceptualization of the foundations of the field. *Organisation Science* (in press).

Zald, Mayer N. and Denton, Patricia 1963: From evangelism to general service: the transformation of the YMCA. *Administrative Science Quarterly*, 8, 214–34.

Zaret, David 1985: *The Heavenly Contract: ideology and organization in pre-Revolutionary puritanism*. Chicago: University of Chicago Press.
— 1991: Cultural analysis and sociology: recent trends and some desirable future directions. Paper presented to the Southern Sociological Society, Atlanta, Georgia.
Zelizer, Viviana 1979: *Morals and Markets: the development of life insurance in the United States*. New York: Columbia University Press.
— 1985: *Pricing the Priceless Child: the changing social value of children*. New York: Basic Books.
— 1988: Beyond the polemics on the market; establishing a theoretical and empirical agenda. *Sociological Forum*, 4, 614–34.
— 1993: Making multiple monies. In R. Swedberg (ed.), *Explorations in Economic Sociology*, New York: Russell Sage.
— 1994: *The Social Meaning of Money*. New York: Basic Books.
Zolberg, Vera L. 1980: Displayed art and performed music: selective innovation and the structure of artistic media. *The Sociological Quarterly*, 21, 219–31.
— 1983: Changing patterns of patronage in the arts. In J. Kamerman and R. Martorella (eds), *Performers and Performances: the sociology of artistic work*, New York: Praeger, 251–68.
— 1990: *Constructing a Sociology of the Arts*. New York: Cambridge University Press.
— 1992a: Barrier or leveler? the case of the art museum. In Michèle Lamont and Marcel Fournier (eds), *Cultivating Differences: symbolic boundaries and the making of inequality*. Chicago: University of Chicago Press, 187–211.
— (ed.) 1992b: Debating the social: a symposium on, and with, Pierre Bourdieu. *Contemporary Sociology*, 21, 151–61.
Zollars, Cheryl and Skocpol, Theda 1990: Cultural mythmaking as a policy tool: the Social Security Board's definition of individualism. Paper presented at the Annual Meetings of the American Sociological Association, Washington DC.
Znaniecki, Florian 1919: *Cultural Reality*. Chicago: Chicago University Press.
— 1934: *The Method of Sociology*. Chicago: University of Chicago Press.
— 1969: *On Humanistic Sociology*, edited by R. Bierstadt. Chicago: University of Chicago Press.
— 1987: *Approaches to Social Theory*, edited by S. Lindenberg et al. New York: Russell Sage.
Zucker, Lynne G. 1977: The role of institutionalization in cultural persistence. *American Sociological Review*, 42, 726–43.
— 1983: Organizations as institutions. In S. B. Bacharach (ed.), *Research in the Sociology of Organizations*, Volume II, Greenwich, CT: JAI Press, 1–47.
— 1987: Institutional theories of organization. *Annual Review of Sociology*, 13, 443–64.
— 1991: Postscript: microfoundations of institutional thought. In Walter W. Powell and Paul J. DiMaggio (eds), *The New Institutionalism in Organizational Analysis*, Chicago: University of Chicago Press, 103–7.

Zuckerman, Harriet 1988: The sociology of science. In Neil J. Smelser (ed.), *Handbook of Sociology*, Newbury Park, CA: Sage, 511–74.

Zuckerman, Harriet, Cole, Jonathan R. and Bruer, John T. (eds) 1991: *The Outer Circle: women in the scientific community*. New York: Norton.

Zunz, Oliver 1985: American history and the changing meaning of assimilation. *Journal of American Ethnic History*, 4, 53–73.

# Index